IMAGINING HUMAN RIGHTS
IN TWENTY-FIRST-CENTURY THEATER

Imagining Human Rights in Twenty-First-Century Theater

Global Perspectives

Edited by Florian N. Becker, Paola S. Hernández, and Brenda Werth

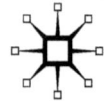

IMAGINING HUMAN RIGHTS IN TWENTY-FIRST-CENTURY THEATER
Copyright © Florian N. Becker, Paola S. Hernández, and Brenda Werth 2013

Softcover reprint of the hardcover 1st edition 2013 978-1-137-02709-2
All rights reserved.

First published in 2013 by
PALGRAVE MACMILLAN®
in the United States—a division of St. Martin's Press LLC,
175 Fifth Avenue, New York, NY 10010.

Where this book is distributed in the UK, Europe and the rest of the World, this is by Palgrave Macmillan, a division of Macmillan Publishers Limited, registered in England, company number 785998, of Houndmills, Basingstoke, Hampshire RG21 6XS.

Palgrave Macmillan is the global academic imprint of the above companies and has companies and representatives throughout the world.

Palgrave® and Macmillan® are registered trademarks in the United States, the United Kingdom, Europe and other countries.

ISBN 978-1-349-43950-8   ISBN 978-1-137-02710-8 (eBook)
DOI 10.1057/9781137027108

Library of Congress Cataloging-in-Publication Data is available from the Library of Congress.

A catalogue record of the book is available from the British Library.

Design by Integra Software Services

First Edition: January 2013

10 9 8 7 6 5 4 3 2 1

Transferred to Digital Printing in 2013

Contents

List of Illustrations — vii

Foreword: Postnational Theater Studies — ix
   Jill Lane

Acknowledgments — xiii

Introduction: Imagining Human Rights in Twenty-First-Century Theater — 1
   Florian N. Becker, Paola S. Hernández, and Brenda Werth

Section I Transitional Justice and Civil Society

1. Dead Body Politics: Grupo Cultural Yuyachkani at Peru's Truth Commission — 27
   Anne Lambright

2. Where "God Is Like a Longing": Theater and Social Vulnerability in Mozambique — 45
   Luís Madureira

3. The ESMA: From Torture Chambers into New Sites of Memory — 67
   Paola S. Hernández

4. Surpassing Metaphors of Violence in Postdictatorial Southern Cone Theater — 83
   Brenda Werth

Section II The "War on Terror" and the Global Economic Order

5. Place and Misplaced Rights in *Guantánamo: Honor Bound to Defend Freedom* — 101
   Lindsey Mantoan

6. Challenging the "Fetish of the Verbatim": New Aesthetics and Familiar Abuses in Christine Evans's *Slow Falling Bird* — 121
   Christina Wilson

7 Stages of Transit: Rascón Banda's *Hotel Juárez* and
   Peveroni's *Berlín*   137
   Sarah M. Misemer

8 Migrant Melodrama, Human Rights, and Elvira
   Arellano   155
   Ana Elena Puga

Section III Transnational Publics

9 "Get up, Stand up, Stand up for your Rights": Transnational
   Belonging and Rights of Citizenship in Dominican Theater   179
   Camilla Stevens

10 Theaters of Vigil and Vigilance: A Playwright's Notes on
   Theater and Human Rights in the Philippines   195
   Joi Barrios

11 "The Spectacle of Our Suffering": Staging the International
   Human Rights Imaginary in Tony Kushner's
   Homebody/Kabul   209
   Elizabeth S. Anker

12 Broadway without Borders: Eve Ensler, Lynn Nottage, and
   the Campaign to End Violence against Women in the
   Democratic Republic of Congo   227
   Kerry Bystrom

Bibliography   249

Notes on Contributors   271

Index   275

Illustrations

Cover Art by Carolina Soler

3.1	ESMA: Four Columns Building	75
3.2	ESMA: Iron Gates	77
5.1	*Honor Bound to Defend Freedom*	111
8.1	Sorrowful Mother: Elvira Arellano	171

Foreword: Postnational Theater Studies

Jill Lane

On May 17, 2012, at a quiet bank in Seville, Spain, customers were waiting in line to carry out their transactions—withdrawals, deposits, transfers—when they were interrupted by a long, low, earthy howl of a male flamenco singer standing in the doorway. As he deepened into his song, customers looked bewildered and bemused, while the manager quickly started making phone calls. But in no time a black-clad woman stepped onto the marble floor and began a fierce *taconeo*; she was promptly joined by three others, and then others still, who until then had appeared to be regular customers standing in line. Soon the bank was transformed into a temporary *tablao* and the customers into an audience. Some pulled out their phones to record the event. The song was the lament of a poor man in despair, having been thrown out on the street and left to fend for himself. Except that the culprit in this case was not an unrequited love but the bank itself, which had forced him out of his home and into poverty.[1]

This event is an evocative point of entry into the role that theater and performance can play in relation to human rights practice today. The action is the work of flo6x8, a collective that uses flamenco in a struggle against the abuses of the banking industry and the political interests that perpetrate and sustain those abuses. Their tagline is "y el verbo se vuelve carne" (and the verb turned to flesh), claiming the power of dance to realize a social desire or protest otherwise hemmed in by words alone—a dynamic that Naomi Jackson and Tania Phim might name "dignity in motion" (2008). This particular action was taken in the wake of the 19 billion euro government bailout of Bankia, Spain's largest mortgage lender, whose imminent collapse threatened the collapse of the Spanish economy and, with it, the future of the Euro. When and where can one establish meaningful engagement—dialogue, protest, or civic action—with such a complex and shifting conglomerate of finance and governance? Flo6x8, like an increasing number of creative dissident projects emerging in the context of the global economic crisis, opts for a practice of *situated freedom*: marking out a temporary space through embodied practice that both claims and enacts an alternative social economy. The bank, like all finance and retail operations, has no place—literally and figuratively—for individuals to act in any way other than as consumers. Surely inspired by the "occupy" tactics of Spain's 15M movement,[2] flo6x8 uses its own expressive presence to insist on another mode of engagement, temporarily taking over the space of the bank and suspending the norms of behavior otherwise in force. The aim is not to stop the daily business of the bank, even though it is inevitably slowed by the distraction of the dance; to do so would still engage the bank in terms of its ability to facilitate or restrict consumption by its customers.

What is a dancer to a bank? Flo6x8 describes their practice in terms close to the much celebrated notion of "temporary autonomous zones" (TAZ) proposed by the anarchist Hakim Bey: "We irrupt by surprise at bank branches and, for a brief lapse of time, we make them our own." In his much quoted gloss on the TAZ, Bey characterizes it as "an uprising which does not engage directly with the State, a guerilla operation which liberates an area (of land, of time, of imagination) and then dissolves itself to re-form elsewhere/elsewhen, *before* the State can crush it" (104). The TAZ resonates with the tactics of recent revolutionary practices, from the uprisings in North Africa and the Middle East to the student movements in Chile and Montreal, and to the *indignados* of Spain, Greece, or Israel, and the global Occupy movement. In contrast with the political landscape that Bey described in the 1980s, the new tactical insurgencies seek to "liberate" space, time, or imagination not only from the State but also from neoliberal markets. Dancing in a bank, momentarily "liberating" it of its own norms, is a way of both stating and enacting a wish for the world-as-it-is to be otherwise. The playfulness of flo6x8 does not diminish its serious human rights claim: "With the hope of a Nuremberg trial against the bank and governments under their corruption, our actions are a sample of what is to come."[3] While the dance in the bank may be untranslatable within the present terms of finance and banking, the dancer promises (maybe even threatens with) a future where another social logic will prevail.

That fundamental gesture—representing *and* materially enacting a desired social change—is especially available to performance as a genre, and characterizes almost all of the theater, drama, and performance analyzed in this volume. On stage, these plays act as a substitute, preview, and call for a process of justice that may sanction the abusers of power and change the conditions of abuse. The ontology of performance, which informs both theatrical production and courtroom trials, allows theater to evoke metaphorically the structural relations of a trial: the performers serve as the prosecution, the audience as potential jurors, while the absent abusers are called to the stand for cross-examination. Yet, like those dancers in the bank, the aim is not to mimic an actual trial, or to imagine that art can or should serve the function of a judicial process, but rather to use aesthetic practices to "liberate" a social and political imagination *in the very moment* of performance. If courtrooms are largely governed by performative speech ('I testify that...'; 'We find the defendant guilty'), then theater can instead proffer what Benjamin Arditi usefully calls "political performatives," actions that, in protesting a present injustice, both enact and enunciate a future political order. That future may be imminent only for the duration of the performance, but the performance nonetheless reorganizes our political imagination in that interim. Arditi writes, "political performatives anticipate something to come because participants already begin to experience—they begin to live—what they are fighting for while they fight for it" (2012).

The yet-to-come future signaled by the dancers—one in which leaders of corporations as well as governments might be held accountable for crimes against humanity—aspires to a changed relation among rights, citizenship, and the nation-state under the pressures of globalization. As is well known, we have witnessed a radical increase in the privatization of spaces, services, and functions once exclusive to the state. Sociologist Saskia Sassen argues that this type of "private authority" represents a new normative order, in which elements of that private authority are re-integrated as part of public policy and notions of the "public" good:

> Particular components of the national state begin to function as the institutional home for the operation of powerful dynamics constitutive or critical for "global capital." In so doing, these state institutions reorient their particular policy work or broader state agendas toward the requirements of the global economy even as they continue to be coded as national. (223)

Sassen analyzes this as a process of "privatized norm-making," among whose consequences is an increased distance between the state and the citizen (320). Sassen's research indicates that the "rights" of citizens are thus increasingly framed by privatized norms. Yasemin Nuhoğlu Soysal, in turn, signaled our entry into a period of *postnational* citizenship in which "what were previously defined as national rights become entitlements legitimized on the basis of personhood" (3). For both Sassen and Soysal, as for many others, the rise of a human rights regime in the postwar period represents a crucial framework for theorizing and legitimizing the status and rights of individuals in these larger postnational and transnational contexts (see also Camacho 2005).

The theatrical events analyzed here, like the dancer at the bank, step into that widening distance between the citizen and a semiprivatized state to claim a place in the new geographies of rights and citizenship. The volume answers an invitation offered earlier by performance scholar May Joseph in *Nomadic Identities* (1999) that asked us to understand citizenship as a continuous embodied performance whose analysis required a reconsideration of "the categories, assumptions, and practices of citizenship as a social agent in a transnationally interdependent world" (158). This anthology, then, does not simply share compelling stories in which theater stakes human rights claims, although its stories and those claims are certainly compelling. Rather the volume illuminates the relation between theater practice and this still emergent modality of human rights, in which rights to participatory citizenship adhere to personas rather than national territories. In so doing, it models a *postnational theater studies* in which this new conceptual and social geography underpins the most important questions in our field today. Like the dancer in the bank, it helps us to imagine the shape, complexity, and challenges of a citizenship yet to come.

Notes

1. See the action at: http://www.flo6x8.com/acciones/27-bankia-pulmones-y-branquias-bulerias, accessed June 8, 2012.
2. On 15M, see the official blog: http://tomalaplaza.net/ and see the "Spanish Revolution" section of the Internet Archive: http://archive.org/details/spanishrevolution.
3. In Spanish: "Irrumpimos por sorpresa en las sucursales bancarias y, por un breve lapso de tiempo, nos adueñamos de ellas. Con la esperanza de un juicio de Nuremberg contra la banca y los gobiernos bajo su corruptela, nuestras acciones son un botón de muestra de lo que está por venir." http://periodismohumano.com/economia/bankia-pulmones-y-branquias-por-bulerias.html, accessed June 8, 2012.

Acknowledgments

This book of essays has been inspired and informed by an ongoing dialogue sustained over the last five years through a variety of presentations, discussions, and workshops on the topic of human rights and theater. We are especially thankful to all participants of our work group, "The World and the Stage: Revisiting Paradigms, Envisioning Rights," first convened at the seventh *encuentro* of the Hemispheric Institute of Performance and Politics in Bogotá, Colombia, in 2009, and later reprised at the American Comparative Literature Association (ACLA) in New Orleans in 2010. We are also grateful to all participants of the work group, "Reassessing Theatrical Paradigms and Imagining Global Rights," held at the conference hosted by the American Society for Theatre Research (ASTR) that took place in Puerto Rico in 2009. At all three venues, participants shared innovative ideas and perspectives that helped lay the conceptual groundwork and formulate the central questions to this volume. We would also like to acknowledge the generosity of different institutions for funding our research on this collective endeavor over the years, including Bard College, American University, and the University of Wisconsin-Madison. We are indebted to Jill Lane for encouraging us to develop our ideas and present this project in other venues, such as ASTR, and beyond. Finally, we are especially grateful to Kerry Bystrom for her countless valuable contributions.

Introduction

Imagining Human Rights in Twenty-First-Century Theater

Florian N. Becker, Paola S. Hernández, and Brenda Werth

Human rights have emerged as a core concern of twenty-first-century theater and performance. As the present volume will document, the phenomenon is both pervasive and truly global. The chapters collected here examine a rich repertoire of plays and performance practices from or about countries across six continents, including Afghanistan, Argentina, Australia, the Democratic Republic of Congo, the Dominican Republic, Mozambique, Mexico, Peru, the Philippines, the United Kingdom, the United States, and Uruguay, as well as the extraterritorial detention center at Guantánamo Bay, Cuba. One of the two principal aims we pursue in this book is to chart the extraordinary diversity, depth, and complexity of the encounter between theater, performance, and human rights over the past two decades. The other aim is to open the way toward understanding the character and significance of this encounter: What have artists, audiences, and readers expected or desired from it? What should we—and what should we not—expect from it? What are the aesthetics, ethics, and effects of this encounter?

While exploring the intersection of theater and human rights is not the same as exploring whether or how theater *supports* human rights, one of the more specific questions that animates all of the following chapters and, indeed, the theatrical works and performance practices they examine is what we can or should expect theater or performance to do *for* human rights. We can make two important and related points about this question from the outset. First, although most of the artistic projects considered here are invested in some of the core ideas, political practices, and legal institutions that are generally designated today as the field of "human rights," this investment can and often does happily coexist with the critical questioning of some of these ideas, practices, and institutions. A commitment to the universal realization or fulfillment of human rights is consistent with a reflective attitude about how best to frame individual human rights or how to conceptualize human rights in general, and how to understand the relationship between human rights concerns and other problems of politics or social justice.

The second point about the question of what theater or performance might do *for* human rights is even more important for the purposes of this book. While most of the works and practices examined here do indeed express or presuppose some version of the expectation that theater or performance can do something for human rights, we have no naïve trust in the power of theater—or art more generally—to prevent human rights abuses. Most serious makers of theater in the twentieth and twenty-first-centuries are aware, often painfully, of the fact that theater and artistic performance are almost everywhere minority practices. In comparison to the electronic mass media of radio and television, film and newsprint, and especially internet-based platforms, even the most popular theatrical practices reach exceedingly small audiences. Furthermore, there is no predictable path leading from any artistic representation—theater included—to broad social mobilization or political action. With these caveats in mind, however, and as some of the contributions to this book will document, theater and performance can be and have been wielded strategically to achieve important effects in the case of some human rights abuses.

In view of these two points, it should not come as a surprise that this volume presents at least as many different versions of the thesis that theater is capable of doing something of significance for human rights as it discusses individual plays and performances. Each of the artistic projects our contributors analyze suggests distinctive answers to the questions of what it is that theater and performance might do for human rights; how they should go about doing it; and what pathways, networks, or mediations they may access or operate through to contribute to achieving their respective aims. What these diverse answers have in common is that they keep sight of the fact that these questions concern not only the nature of human rights and the relation between human rights and art or representation in general, but also, and crucially, the nature of *theater* as a distinctive representational practice.

A principal line of inquiry then becomes what theatrical performance can do for, about, or vis-à-vis human rights that other artistic practices or modes of representation cannot do—or cannot do as well. With regard to this question, too, the present volume does not offer one general answer. The otherwise diverse approaches of our contributors are, however, unified by the idea that attempts to answer the question must point to what distinguishes the *experience* of making or seeing theater—its distinctive quality and intensity. Their readings seek to understand individual theatrical texts or plays in their relation to human rights by tracing the kinds of perception and imagining that occur in or are generated by theatrical performances. Such perceiving and imagining, moreover, always has a cognitive aspect. As Diana

Taylor observes, "[e]mbodied practice, along with and bound up with other cultural practices, offers a way of knowing."[1] The way or ways of knowing offered by theater to its participants and audiences is linked inextricably to its capacity to generate a human connection through sensorial intensity, social intimacy, and the joint physical presence of bodies on and offstage.

In the remainder of this Introduction, we argue that the specific qualities of theatrical imagining—and particularly its intrinsically *public* character—are what connect theater most clearly and significantly to human rights. To do this, we explore the meaning of theatrical imagining and link it to the development of the bourgeois public sphere in eighteenth-century Europe, which also, and not coincidentally, served as the cradle for contemporary legal discourses and institutions of human rights.[2] With this background in place, we then turn to the question of how theatrical projects located well beyond the confines of Europe have approached the task of doing something for now-global understandings of human rights in the twentieth and twenty-first centuries, and delineate some of the challenges theater faces in this task and some of the unique resources it has to confront them. Finally, we give a more detailed overview of how our contributors engage with the theme of imagining human rights, diverse publics, and the notion of publicity in their globally diverse but locally specific readings of contemporary theater and performance.

Theater as Public Imagining

As we have suggested, theater essentially involves acts of imagination and is a practice of imagination. This simple fact points to the most fundamental link between theater and human rights. Human rights—both as a field of interrelated and often competing philosophical conceptions and as a network of actually existing social and legal practices and institutions—depend at every turn on acts of imagination. Human rights theorists of many disciplines and orientations have long paid attention to the vast range of cultural practices and products that together compose what we might call a "human rights imaginary."[3] This imaginary is not some extraneous illustration or embellishment. As we will see below, even the simplest among the countless interactions and institutional practices that together constitute and sustain the social reality called human rights centrally involve acts of imagination.

Although all representational arts involve such acts,[4] there is something quite distinctive about theatrical imagining: The kind of imagining that is intrinsic to theater as a practice of representation is essentially *public*. It is part of an essentially cooperative activity that takes place in a shared place and time.[5] Put briefly, the primary objects of theatrical imagination are the bodies of the performers, and its primary subjects are the members of the audience, in the following sense. For a theatrical representation to arise, the spectators must imagine the performers' bodies as different from what or how they actually are. They must imagine a twenty-first-century denizen of Brooklyn,

Buenos Aires, or Bamako they see before themselves as, for example, a Danish prince or a Scottish king; and if on some theatrical occasions they see or imagine a performer only as herself or himself, then they must imagine her or him to be in circumstances that are different, in some respect, from the ones in which they know her or him, in fact, to be.

Theatrical performances, then, are representational, and the representations they produce arise through shared acts of imagination about actually present human bodies. Theater thus brings the activity of imagining—often seen as quintessentially intrasubjective or private—into a public space, where it becomes a part of a necessarily interpersonal activity. Such imagining is an ongoing negotiation between different subjects, some of whom are spectators and others performers. All such negotiations are guided by the ground rules that constitute the practice of theater as such[6]—but aside from this they are flexible, fungible, and open-ended. Although the public and social spaces where theater takes place can be adversarial, politically contested, and fraught with conflict, they are of necessity shared and cooperative in this basic sense.

The notion of an audience or public that constitutes itself in and through such shared acts of imagination points to a fundamental conceptual and historical link between theater and the field of human rights. Each and every theatrical performance has its own "public." Indeed, most European languages use their version of the term as the most common word to designate theatrical audiences (*le public* in French, *el público* in Spanish, *il pubblico* in Italian, *das Publikum* in German and *ta publiczność* in Polish, etc.). A theatrical audience or public is an "interpretive community" in the strictest sense. Without the interpretive acts of its individual members, and without a great deal of concordance between these individual acts, the performance in question would not represent anything *theatrically*. For the performance to represent some specific person, thing, or feature theatrically, some set of spectators has to imagine that person, thing, or feature. The individuals who witness the performance *constitute* themselves as a theatrical audience or "public" not simply by watching or listening to the real actions of the performers before them, but rather by transforming these actions into a representation through their individual interpretive acts, and through the requisite consonance between these acts.

For similar reasons, one can speak of all the individual audiences that have seen a performance of a given specific theatrical text or written play as the public of that play, and of the spectators that have seen a specific production of a given play as the public of that production. And we can enquire into the makeup of these larger publics: Who has seen or tends to see a given play or production? What is the sociological composition of the play's or production's actual, probable, or intended public, along such dimensions as class, wealth or income, sex, level of education, or geographical, national, or ethnic origin? In what kinds of institutional setting is the play or production typically performed in a given local or national context, and what is the typical profile of the audiences who tend to assemble in that setting? As we will see, such questions can assume major interpretive significance, and become decisive in the case of the several plays discussed in this book that are performed (or designed to be performed) for a *transregional* or *transnational* public.

The Critical Public Sphere

Let us return to our claim that the fact that theater is essentially public links it to the concept and practice of human rights. What is the nature of this connection? The answer, we believe, is best elucidated through the broad notion of a *critical public sphere*, as introduced by Jürgen Habermas in 1962 and since developed and revised by many political theorists, sociologists, and historians.[7] Not every public constitutes or participates in a public *sphere* in this more specific sense. A public sphere, for Habermas, is defined by reference and in relation to a specific set of agents, agencies, institutions, or social structures—often, but not necessarily, a sovereign state—whose actions, measures, laws, or causal impacts are *criticized* within it. Perhaps the most direct way to show the relevance of the notion of the public sphere to human rights—and thus the best way to lay out the crucial point of contact between human rights and theater—is to give a brief sketch of the historical construction of west European "bourgeois" public spheres in the seventeenth and eighteenth centuries.

According to Habermas, the construction of critical public spheres in Europe was part and parcel of the ascendant bourgeoisie's effort to emancipate itself from the power of the individual territorial states and their political and administrative apparatus, whose composition and functioning was either straightforwardly absolutist (as in the case of France and many German principalities) or determined by aristocratic privilege (as in Great Britain). In various meeting places, clubs, coffee houses, cultural associations, and journals and other print media, members of the bourgeoisie began to present themselves—to themselves and to others—as a public of peers to whom the state and its government would have to justify the measures, policies, laws, and regulations that affected them. Importantly, the general claim articulated in and through the bourgeois public spheres was not directed against state interference *per se*; rather it was a demand to have any such interference *justified*. State measures, policies, laws, and regulations that adversely affected an individual would derive what legitimacy they had from the fact that they were—or at least that they could be—justified by appeal to reasons that were acceptable without irrationality by that individual and by his or her peers.

This emphasis on reason implies a certain principal parity between all members of the public sphere. If the justification offered to the adversely affected individual was to be rationally acceptable to him or her *as a member of the public sphere*, then it must be rationally acceptable to any other such member as well. What Habermas calls the bourgeois "idea" of a public sphere thus had built into it a version of the principle of universalizability. Factually speaking, of course, membership in any actually existing eighteenth-century bourgeois public sphere was far from universal. All such spheres excluded vast parts of the population of the societies in which they were situated: women; the propertyless; colonials; slaves; and various religious, linguistic, and ethnic minorities, to mention only the most evident groups.[8] Moreover, as the political theorist Nancy Fraser has recently reemphasized, all existing public spheres were geographically bounded, and each emerged within and in response to a specific sovereign territorial state and its administrative apparatus.[9] To the extent that it suppressed these facts and as Habermas also stresses, the bourgeois conception of the public sphere was indeed an "ideology." Nonetheless, the "idea" of the bourgeois public sphere was essentially universalistic. In this fact lies the persistent critical power and transformative potential of the notion, as well as its intimate link to the invention of human rights.

In constituting themselves as a public, European, white, male, non-aristocratic property owners viewed and presented their objections to the state and to aristocratic privilege—especially their objections to interference with their "private" or commercial affairs—not as objections to the infraction of the interests of European, white, male, non-aristocratic property owners, but as the violation of a fundamental interest of *human beings* in general in their freedom or autonomy. Abstracting from any of the qualities that differentiated them from each other, especially their respective social status, rank, and wealth, these individuals came to regard themselves and others first and foremost as "mere" or "pure" human beings. In their eyes, their "natural" humanity was the sole criterion qualifying them for and entitling them to membership in the public sphere. This criterion, as already noted, implied the parity or equality of all members of this sphere. The new, evaluative conception of humanity closely ties the capacity for autonomous action to the capacity to understand arguments and assess their rationality, and it construes the latter quite concretely as the capacity to participate in a sphere of discourse in which claims are raised and justifications assessed.[10] As a matter of normative principle if not actual fact, then, membership in the bourgeois public sphere was open not merely to white, male property owners but to anybody who had human standing or "dignity" in this evaluative sense, that is, to anyone with these capacities.

The Public Sphere and Human Rights

Given that a critical public sphere is a forum whose members raise claims to have the measures, policies, laws, or causal impacts of a specific set of agents, agencies, institutions, or social structures justified to them by that set of agents, agencies, institutions, or social structures, it can be no surprise that the emergence of bourgeois public spheres in eighteenth-century Europe was connected from the beginning to the proliferation of a discourse of *rights* and to the invention of the concept of *human* rights. These processes began with the Reformation and its consequences in seventeenth-century Britain and famously culminated in such founding documents as the American Declaration of Independence (1776) and the French Declaration of the Rights of Man and the Citizen (1789). The concept of individual rights fits well into the critical scheme we have outlined. As members of a discursive public sphere, individuals present themselves as holding a claim to having the effects of the power of other individuals or institutions *on* themselves justified *to* themselves. A claim made by such an individual is turned into a right, or a rights-claim, when the fact that he or she is impacted by the individual or institution in question is combined with the judgment that this causal impact affects him or her adversely, the truism that "might is not right" and, crucially, the substantive evaluative principle that adverse effects of power are just or *right* only if they are backed by reasons that are, or can be, accepted by the affected individual and all others who are relevantly similar to him or her.

The close link between the bourgeois idea of a public sphere and the concept of human rights should now be clear: The set of capacities that was recognized as the criterion for membership in the public sphere—the ability to act autonomously, to understand and assess arguments, and to participate in critical discourse—at the same time constitutes the evaluative conception of human standing or human "dignity" that grounds human rights: Whoever possesses these capacities is therefore a human rights holder.

Although the invention of human rights and the formation of critical public spheres in the eighteenth century were bound up with conceptions of a natural, objective, or (later) transcendental moral order, the notion and defense of human rights need not depend upon any such conception. The question of objectivity is not identical with the question of universality. The claim that human beings possess human rights implies the demand that everyone with human standing should have this status—the capacities constituting it—protected against the power of others. This demand is universal in content, but it need not be regarded as independent in principle from the human beings who actually make the demand or from the human beings for whom or on whose behalf the demand is made. The idea that human rights claims are not ultimately backed by any human-independent, natural, objective, or transcendental warrant may even highlight the responsibilities we take upon ourselves when raising human rights claims for or on behalf of others. Together with the critical awareness that the formulation of *specific* human rights, as they are enshrined in international and national law and as we know them from Western political discourse, have their roots in the historically and culturally specific conditions of eighteenth-century Europe, this idea should serve as an important reminder that genuine human rights claims must, in the last analysis, be understandable and acceptable to all those for whom or on whose behalf they are raised. This requirement does not negate the universality of human rights, but it should compel practitioners and theorists of human rights to continually question whether the philosophical conceptions and legal formulations of the specific human rights on which they rely or with which they are involved do in fact meet the standard of universality, or whether they carry with themselves any damagingly parochial or ethnocentric assumptions. If it is indeed possible "to have contextualization without relativization,"[11] as Richard Wilson hopes, many of these conceptions and formulations may have to undergo revisions in the light of previously unrepresented or under-represented cultural traditions that have different notions of humanity, autonomy, and participation in rational argument than the Western theoretical and legal discourses from which contemporary human rights policies and practices tend to be drawn.[12]

An openness to such revisions is especially urgent if, as Wilson also maintains, the language of human rights fills a discursive void left by the dissolution of Cold War master narratives.[13] Like any other discourse of legitimation, the language of human rights can be appropriated and mobilized to serve agendas of international power or economic domination. According to such critics as Rustom Bharucha, for instance, human rights discourse often operates to legitimize the control of the economies of the Global South in the guise of humanitarianism.[14] Human rights claims on behalf of others should be greeted with special vigilance when they are made by one political power or state against another. More generally, those practitioners and critics who take human rights seriously should not cease to inquire in what respects and to what extent the language of the international human rights regime might serve to reinforce, as opposed to challenge or alter, existing institutions and relationships of power and wealth. They should remain aware of the danger that the closures and limitations of human rights as a discourse, practice, and framework of political relations may sometimes make the pursuit of their realization complicit in the very patterns of domination it seeks to combat.

Human Rights and the Specificity of Theater

The historical connection we have traced between the emergence of bourgeois public spheres and the invention of human rights in eighteenth-century Europe highlights the crucial fact to which we referred at the outset: The establishment and operation of human rights has depended and continues to depend at every turn on efforts of imagination. The individuals who came together to form a public sphere to counter existing political institutions or social formations did so essentially through imagining themselves and each other as part of a community of peers. They had to imagine each other as sharing the same standing as human beings. Each of them had to imagine the others to possess the same fundamental capacities as oneself to act autonomously, to construct and understand arguments, and to assess their rationality.

Although these capacities for agency, reasoning, and discourse may be the only ones that are strictly necessary to ground the concept of human rights, they emerged as a part of a much fuller evaluative notion of human standing and human subjectivity. As scholars from Habermas to Lynn Hunt have emphasized, this new subjectivity came into being through the accretion of countless acts of imaginary identification across social lines that had previously seemed fixed and decisive.[15] This was a large-scale social-cultural process in which epistolary novels, private correspondence and diaries (often written with a view to publication), literary journals, and, as the art historian Michael Fried has shown, certain kinds of portrait painting all played a part.[16] The watchwords common to many of these practices—pity, sympathy, and, later, empathy—all imply a notion of identification. In writing, reading, or viewing images, the individual imagines other minds as essentially like his or her own: Placed in similar circumstances and with a similar biography, he or she would have experienced much the same emotions or "sentiments" as the other. Such acts of identification, moreover, are not a matter of unmediated feeling, although their decidedly intellectual aspects are sometimes overlooked. Most of the mental states imagined involve intentions, deliberations, thoughts, and attitudes, all of which comprise or imply propositional content and are structured by more or less tight and complex logical connections.

Theater and drama played a central yet often underrated role in the invention of human rights during the eighteenth century. While the acts of imagination through which the modern bourgeois subjectivity was constituted were frequently directed at and reflected upon in a public of print media and shared discussion, theater was unique in that these acts had to take place in a concretely shared public space. In their joint presence, the spectators of "serious comedies" and "bourgeois tragedies" were to identify not merely with the characters on stage but also with each other. In no forum was the construction of a public of "mere human beings" through the forces of imagination as concrete and tangible as in theater. While the earlier Enlightenment had regarded theater as just another instrument for the education of man's intellectual faculties, Denis Diderot and Gotthold Ephraim Lessing reinterpreted Aristotle's *Poetics* to construct dramatic forms and a theatrical aesthetic that would educate the character, attitudes, and emotional sensibility of the spectators. Through the mobilization of pity and fear, the theatrical imagination was to give rise to human fellow feeling, in a process that would amount to a kind of reorganization of moral psychology based upon "nature."

However—and as our contributors show in many ways—the role of the theatrical imagination in the construction and critique of the concept and social reality of human rights is by no means limited to processes of identification. Soon after Diderot and Lessing mobilized theater to establish a new ethic of mutual identification younger French and German writers like Louis-Sébastien Mercier and Jakob Michael Reinhold Lenz began to use the resources of the practice to unveil the blind spots and sometimes emptiness of the bourgeois rhetoric of natural humanity and human rights. For example, instead of portraying the bourgeois family as an expression of nature and as the realm in which human beings could encounter each other as "pure human beings," as Diderot had done in the 1750s, Lenz's plays revealed the family as a domain of inequality and oppression that systematically stunted the subjectivity of women, children, domestic servants, and other social inferiors. Some playwrights and practitioners did so by rediscovering the splendid isolation of the theatrical spectator from the goings-on on stage and stressing the fictionality of the represented happenings. Rather than aiming for a maximal degree of emotional identification, they relied upon and reinvigorated the distancing resources of such theatrical traditions as satire, farce, and tragi-comedy.

We mention these early examples from the European context to stress two facts about what we call the contemporary global theater of human rights: First, from the beginning, the theater of human rights participated not only in the construction and reinforcement of the discourse and social practice of human rights, but also, and in the same measure, in their immanent critique. Second, no single theatrical technique, style, or aesthetic stands in a privileged relation to the theater of human rights. Moreover, and as the individual chapters of this volume show in detail, there is no general way of correlating any specific theatrical technique, style, or aesthetic with any specific role, function, or attitude vis-à-vis human rights. Strategies aiming at identification or emotional effect can in principle serve to shore up the discourse of human rights or support aspects of human rights work, or they can serve to criticize them; the same is true of strategies aiming at generating a more detached spectatorial attitude. What both kinds of strategy have in common, however, is that they mobilize the theatrical imagination.

The many special possibilities of imagining human rights in and through theater and performance, we believe, will emerge in the following chapters. In presenting these possibilities, to reiterate, we do not seek to advocate any one general model of how theater relates to the actual practices, institutions, and legal structures of human rights today. We do not, for example, suggest that theater need only represent, "document," "bear witness," "memorialize," "raise awareness," or generate empathy—and that useful, relevant, or effective social initiatives or political actions will ensue. Some of these phrases can no doubt be filled with determinate content, but if they are intended to describe real social processes rather than mere aspirations, then the cultural critic or historian cannot avoid the work of elucidating the causal mediations and institutional pathways through which a particular play or performance practice achieves whatever real effect it may have.

More promising than any assertion of broad social or political efficacy is the thought that theater and performance, because of the joint presence of performers and audience and the intensity of the experience, have the potential to leave deeper traces in the spectator than other artistic practices, representations, or media. Through this joint presence in one place and time and its essential lack of reproducibility, theatrical performances can give rise to their own Benjaminian "aura."[17] There is also, in the Western tradition, a deep linkage between theater and pedagogy. Rarely seen as mere intellectual modeling, theatrical learning is more often conceived as essentially involving emotional, infraconscious, and physical processes. Learning, in this broad sense, is crucial to two of the most consequential theatrical projects of the twentieth century: Bertolt Brecht's aesthetic of critique, with its emphasis on the players' and spectators' distance from the represented events and characters, and Antonin Artaud's aesthetic of bodily shock, with its ambition to overcome rational mediation. These two diametrically opposed aesthetics arguably meet in the desire to reorganize the human sensory apparatus. Although neither Brecht nor Artaud would have had any patience for the concept of human rights, both remain crucial points of reference for the theater of human rights in the twenty-first-century. Much the same can be said of the plays of Samuel Beckett, whose apparent deconstruction of the idea of an integrated human subject position any theatrical project with a stake in defending the notion of human rights may have to contend with in one way or another.[18] The reduction of humanity by the catastrophic forces of modernity to which Beckett gave theatrical shape may be inimical to or corrosive of the concept and practice of human rights, as Giorgio Agamben's notion of "bare life" suggests,[19] or it may underscore their necessity, as Judith Butler's notion of "precarious life" indicates.[20]

It may sometimes be salutary to remind ourselves that some of the thorniest problems that arise in connection with theater and human rights in fact have little to do with the specificity of theater and are familiar from longstanding debates about various other modes of representation and art forms. Perhaps the most intractable among these problems is the question of whether, how, and to what avail human rights abuses should be represented artistically—a variant of the more general problem of representing violence or atrocity. In his work on the demands of Holocaust representation, Michael Rothberg discusses a version of "traumatic realism" in which "the claims of reference live on, but so does the traumatic extremity that disables realistic representation as usual."[21] Susan Sontag's well-known reflections on photographic images of atrocity, in the tradition of Benjamin's writings on photographic seeing and Adorno's question about the possibilities of art after the Holocaust, urge us to consider the ways in which any mode of representation may "reiterate" violence, "simplify," or "agitate" to "create the illusion of consensus."[22] In reference to human rights activism, James Dawes asserts that the "contradiction between our impulse to heed trauma's cry for representation and our instinct to protect it from representation—from invasive staring, simplification, dissection—is a split at the heart of human rights advocacy."[23]

Despite its general scope, the ethical question of representing violent human rights abuses arises with especial sharpness in connection with theater. Theater distinguishes itself from other modes of visual representation in that it is a practice of embodiment. The essential presence of the human body in theater explains why theatrical performances often address violations of bodily integrity and at the same time renders the problem of representing such violations especially acute. In their book *Violence Performed*, Patrick Anderson and Jisha Menon claim that violence "acquires its immense significance in a delicate pivot between the spectacular and the embodied; it is precisely this quality that demands consideration by scholars in performance studies."[24] In theater, the performer's body and its movement retain their actual characteristics and at the same time become the bearers of fictional, merely imagined attributes. This condition opens spaces of spectatorial indeterminacy that are essential for the dynamic relationship between performer and audience through which theatrical representations take shape. Which parts or aspects of the represented violent acts and their impact, spectators may wonder, are real, and which are merely represented? And in what relation do they, respectively, stand to the reality to which the theatrical fiction as a whole points? Many of the chapters that follow proceed from such questions to reflect on the epistemic value of representing violence or simulating pain and on its intended or actual ethical and political efficacy.

The questions of violence and spectatorship, central to avant-garde performance since the Futurists and Artaud, throw into relief what is perhaps the most thoroughgoing problem about human rights and artistic representations that is nonetheless specific to theatrical representation. Theatrical representing is done by individuals on stage, through individual actions and individual interactions. How, then, can theater represent anything but individuals, individual actions or individual interactions? Most human rights violations, it would seem, do not have the immediacy of torture. They come to pass through complex concatenations of countless interactions, mediated through large-scale institutional structures and their sometimes intended and sometimes unforeseen effects. How can theater go about portraying the social structures and processes that characterize modernity? How well can it portray realities such as "the bread price, unemployment, the declaration of war," to quote Bertolt Brecht?[25] Is theater condemned after all to oversimplify, personalize, or allegorize such realities and thus to mystify the social world?

Mapping Twenty-First-Century Theater and Performance

The chapters included in this volume do not, of course, capitulate in the face of these and many other challenges. Taking as their lead the specificity of theatrical imagining and the centrality of imagination to the theory and practice of human rights in a contemporary global context, they address three broad lines of inquiry about the intersection between theatrical and quasi-theatrical performance and human rights. These three lines of inquiry are united by the notion of a critical public sphere. Some of our contributors examine the manner in and extent to which a given play or performance project participates in an existing public sphere and how it might change it, while others focus on the manner in and extent to which a given play or project contributes to the emergence or construction of a new public sphere.

The chapters collected in the first section of this book, "Transitional Justice and Civil Society," ask whether and how theater and performance may work to help their audiences reimagine existing polities in the image of human rights. In the wake of large-scale social or national trauma, can theater and performance participate in constructing the kinds of interpretive communities through which forms of democratic citizenship can arise? The chapters that comprise the second section of the book, "The 'War on

Terror' and the Global Economic Order," turn to the challenges to human rights that have marked the first decade of our century and on which we may perhaps now begin to develop a historical perspective. Some of these challenges originate in the liberal democracies of the West. The chapters examine the ways in which theater and performance have sought to document the mechanisms and consequences of international economic flows and the waging of war, and to bring to public attention the points of contact or complicities between these two realities. The third section of the book, "Constructing Transnational Publics," addresses the fact that increasing numbers of innovative twenty-first-century theatrical projects are being produced for or seek to establish distinctively transnational publics for themselves. These projects respond to the fact that many human rights infractions today are not primarily or exclusively attributable to the actions or policies of individual states or intranational institutions but result from institutions, mechanisms, or human-made phenomena that have impacts across national boundaries. More importantly still, the institutions or structures that may be able to address or redress certain human rights infractions may also lie outside the ambit of any single nation state. Accordingly, then, the existing, emerging, or potential publics that are suited to exerting an influence on these structures would likewise have to cut across national and often linguistic boundaries. Our contributors ask whether and how theatrical projects that reach international audiences may contribute to the construction of transnational but truly critical public spheres.

1. Transitional Justice and Civil Society

What part can theater and performance play in the construction of the kinds of interpretive community that are a necessary condition of a functioning democratic polis? Can they help reconstruct such a polis after national trauma has ripped apart what political community may have existed before? Can they help establish such a polis where none existed in the first place, or where large parts of the population have been excluded from the political process and political discourse? Questions of this sort have often arisen in nations and societies undergoing what political scientists are wont to call "transitions to democracy" or, less ambitiously perhaps, "transitions to the rule of law." The chapters collected here examine whether and how theater and performance have worked to help their participants and audiences to reimagine existing polities in the image of human rights, or to imagine into existence new polities in the image of human rights. They investigate cases in which theatrical performances have created publics that span longstanding gender, economic, religious, racial, or ethnic divisions. They ask how new grassroots communities of activism and memory are formed and *per*formed, and what role theatrical and quasi-theatrical practices play in such processes. In particular, they elucidate how such practices relate to legal and quasi-legal proceedings, especially the trials and truth commissions that characterize transitions to democracy. Scholars including Hannah Arendt, Dwight Conquergood,

Shoshana Felman, Loren Kruger, and Paul Rae have commented on the inescapable theatricality of trials and other legal proceedings.[26] In her work on performance and the South African Truth and Reconciliation Commission (TRC), Catherine Cole argues that a shift of focus to performance studies can help us to approach critically the "public, embodied, and performed" dimension of the Commission's hearings.[27] The nature and consequences of the inevitable theatricality of such hearings and trials are deserving of special attention by all those who continue to take seriously the professed task of such proceedings, i.e. the unearthing of true or authentic expressions of actual, and often horrific, past experience.

Just as importantly, artistic performances may expand the human rights framework and move beyond the trial and other "legal, medical, media, and textual rationalities" that tend to dominate transitions from social trauma.[28] Shoshana Felman and Paul Rae have focused on the role of aesthetic production in both complementing the legal process and exposing its limits.[29] Hegemonic scripts of reconciliation and enactments of social catharsis can undermine the complexity of diagnosing and confronting human rights violations.[30] While theater and performance may assist and enable legally and institutionally driven responses to human rights violations, then, they may also have to resist these responses and articulate political and human rights claims that do not align unproblematically with the grander narratives of national reconciliation or international human rights regimes.

Anne Lambright's essay examines the relationship between the Peruvian Truth and Reconciliation Commission (CVR), and the activist theater collective Grupo Cultural Yuyachkani to provide insight into questions of public commemoration and mourning. Initially invited by the CVR to help bolster local participation in its hearings, Yuyachkani eventually saw its performances become part of the official program meant to promote social reconciliation in the wake of the violence of both national military forces and the Maoist guerilla group "The Shining Path." Lambright carefully examines the content of these performances and focuses especially on the use of ghostly figures and dead bodies, to argue that the embodiment of the dead enacted by the group did in fact turn it into a significant complement to the CVR. She concludes that the Yuyachkani performances gave their audiences "a dead to mourn," and in doing so, helped open a way for them to move beyond the trauma of the past. Supplementing the spectacle of reconciliation with spectacles of haunting, these performances spatialized the presence of the dead in national memory, and worked toward integrating rural populations, formerly the victims of both antistate and state violence, into a national critical public sphere.

The transformative potential of performance is central to Luís Madureira's essay on theater and citizenship in Mozambique. Madureira describes forms of theater and performance that have successfully bridged the country's entrenched urban-rural divide through forms and practices that attenuate the antinomy between urban elite art theater and rural popular theater, and that have absorbed or reworked numerous foreign texts and influences. Theater publics, Madureira shows, are playing a significant role in building a truly national public sphere that may eventually function as an essential part of a civil society capable of addressing the country's AIDS and refugee crises. During the last three decades, Mozambique's vibrant theatrical culture has fostered modes of political participation and active citizenship. Integrating dramatic works by foreigners and Mozambicans, collaborations between professional troupes and development projects have unsettled the longstanding divisions between national and colonial dramatic traditions, and urban and rural performative practices.

Paola Hernández examines the effort to appropriate a city space in Buenos Aires that was formerly controlled by Argentina's military dictatorship and to turn it into a functioning part of the country's critical public sphere. Since 2004, The Navy School of the Mechanics (ESMA), formerly a secret detention and torture center, has been transformed into a Museum of Memory. Drawing on studies of traumatic memory and performance, Hernández analyzes the museum as a stage to enact and perform some of the most grievous human rights violations that occurred during the dictatorship. Focusing on the potential that spatial and visual representations of grief may open up for agency, she explores the challenges posed by the effort to incorporate the multiple perspectives of debates on individual memory and public commemoration in the task of constructing a democratic polity consistent with the demands of human rights.

Brenda Werth's chapter develops a critical approach to examining the dramatic rendering of violence and its de- and recontextualized perception in two plays from Latin America's Southern Cone: Gabriel Peveroni's *Sarajevo esquina Montevideo* (Uruguay, 2003) and Griselda Gambaro's *La persistencia* (Argentina, 2007), works that reference the Bosnian War (1992–1995) and the Beslan schoolhouse massacre in Russia (2004), respectively. Both plays sought to inject new questions and concepts into Argentina and Uruguay's postdictatorial public spheres, whose ongoing debate about the dictatorships of the seventies and eighties has often been restricted to an exclusively national perspective. Counteracting the sometimes overly narrow terms of the discussion, Argentine and Uruguayan drama has frequently treated mass atrocity occurring in distant places and times, thereby providing a distancing and quasi-allegorical lens through which to view the mass violence in the two countries. As Werth argues, Peveroni's and Gambaro's plays do not simply adapt violence taking place elsewhere for the purpose of addressing national trauma. Rather, they link national and international events to acknowledge the distinct historical and geopolitical circumstances of violence and to reveal some of the wider forces and structures that may be at work in each case. By distancing the national past through the work of the theatrical imagination, the plays effectively supplement myopic perspectives on the "Dirty War" with a comparative framework for understanding and addressing state violence.

2. The "War on Terror" and the Global Economic Order

The chapters in this section ask how theater and performance practices have addressed the challenges to bodily integrity and cultural and economic survival set in motion by the triumph of neoliberal economic policies in the 1980s and 1990s and the "War on Terror" unleashed in the wake of the attacks on September 11, 2001. Authors in this section discuss plays in which cases of illegal detention, sanctuary, and international travel reflect the newfound experience of being in a world that the "War on Terror" transformed into "a suddenly reconfigured geography of conflict, without clear borders or visible actors."[31] Already in the wake of the First and Second World Wars, Hannah Arendt had written, "The fundamental deprivation of human rights is manifested first and above all in the deprivation of a place in the world."[32] This section reexamines the significance of this statement in a post–9-11 framework and asks what it means to be deemed an unlawful enemy combatant, an immigrant, or a refugee by a country that ostensibly works in consonance with the norms of international law yet still defines and upholds categories of individuals and groups whose basic rights and access to legal recourse continue to be denied.

The "War on Terror," described by President George W. Bush as a new kind of conflict never before faced by the United States, undermined democracy by pretending an exceptionalism that would allow the United States to justify actions undertaken outside of the body of domestic and international law.[33] Obtaining information from known and suspected terrorists became the key objective of this war, emphasized by Vice President Dick Cheney in his infamous remarks made just days after the September 11 attacks that the United States would "have to work sort of the dark side.... in the shadows of the intelligence world."[34] Cheney's statement foreshadowed the implementation of a host of unprecedented practices including torture disguised as "enhanced interrogation techniques" and the establishment of detention facilities outside of the United States known as "black sites."[35] The move away from previously accepted norms of warfare is apparent in a declaration made by Alberto Gonzales, then White House General Counsel, that the "War on Terror" had made the Third Geneva Convention and its rules governing the capture and detention of enemy fighters obsolete.[36] The effects of this exceptionalism, with its disregard for binding international agreements and the abandonment of the rule of law, have spilled into the Obama administration. President Obama has not yet fulfilled his vow to close the detention facility at Guantánamo within a year of taking office in 2008. Instead, he has continued the indefinite detentions without charge or trial and in March 2011, he reinstated the discredited military commissions.[37] According to the Center for Constitutional Rights, to date there remain 171 men imprisoned in Guantánamo, 89 have been cleared for release but remain in detention, and 47 are slated for indefinite detention without charge or trial.[38]

All of the chapters in this section present the emergence of twenty-first-century stateless zones that defy national territorial borders and require a reassessment of what it means to be beyond the law. The authors here illustrate the competing functions of sanctuary and illegal detention to affirm and to withhold basic human rights, respectively. Through their analyses of theatrical pieces and performances that address sanctuary and illegal detention, they participate in reimagining these socially, politically, and geographically exceptional zones and seek to reinsert them into a public discourse capable of challenging the prerogatives of the state through universal human rights claims. The authors here engage the works of playwrights and performance artists to focus on the human dimension of statelessness by shedding light on the experiences of the individuals who inhabit these exceptional zones. They further seek to expose the interconnectedness of these zones and their facilitation or denial of rights claims with a new global economic order structured in large part by the ideals of neoliberalism.

Lindsey Mantoan squarely addresses the impact of the United States' "War on Terror" and the 2003 invasion of Iraq on human rights and on long-established processes and institutions of international law. Her chapter examines how Victoria Brittain and Gillian Slovo's play, *Guantánamo: Honor Bound to Defend Freedom* (England, 2004), deploys the techniques of documentary theater to denounce the media spectacle of war and to provide an alternative access to the reality of war by presenting verbatim accounts of the daily existence of five individuals deemed "enemy combatants" and detained at Guantánamo. Raising the phenomenon of "stateless" persons, which stood at the center of Arendt's reflections on human rights and played a decisive part at the inception of the international human rights regime after the Second World War, Mantoan is thus concerned with an artistic project that addresses the public sphere of the English-speaking countries whose policies are co-responsible for the human rights abuses in Guantánamo. Implicit in her treatment is the question of whether documentary theater can help establish and keep alive a Western counterpublic that stands against the shrinking of the public sphere generated by the domination of corporate media and the uniform and often misinformed populations they create.

In dialogue with Mantoan's analysis is Christina Wilson's discussion of Christine Evans' *Slow Falling Bird* (Australia, 2003). An Australian play about an Australian detention center, premiered in the United States, *Slow Falling Bird* speaks to the global reach of the "War on Terror" and the gradual globalization of the artistic response to it. It frames the realities of counterinsurgency and statelessness through tropes and metaphors familiar to Australians from treatments of the "Stolen Generations" but new to US audiences. Evans' play discloses the racist attitudes and abuse often directed toward Iraqi and Afghan refugees awaiting asylum in the Australian refugee detention center Woomera. Like Mantoan, Wilson also investigates the use of documentary techniques, though her analysis questions the suitability of puristic documentary strategies of representation for approaching human rights violations in theater. Instead, she defends Evans' experimental aesthetic and her recourse to a variety of art forms and styles as a successful effort to open up the existing imaginary associated with the detention of "enemy combatants" and to help change the public debate.

Sarah Misemer's piece deals directly with the question of transnational flows in the contemporary international global order, and assesses the paradoxical role of national borders in global neoliberal capitalism. While the importance of national sovereignty has diminished in key respects and borders often no longer pose obstacles to the circulation of goods and services, they continue to restrict the free movement of human beings. The plays Misemer analyzes, Víctor Hugo Rascón Banda's *Hotel Juárez* (Mexico, 2008) and Gabriel Peveroni's *Berlín* (Uruguay, 2007), focus on the rise of two globalized cities of transit and commerce. Misemer's readings point to the fraught and contradictory relationship between actual global neoliberal policies and the supposed inviolability of bodily integrity that was so central to the classical liberal thought on which they draw for their legitimation. Misemer's interpretation questions the role of security as an increasingly prominent component of Western political discourse since the beginning of the "War on Terror" and traces the implications of the culture of fear it has brought with itself. Her questions concern essentially international social realities, focusing on such phenomena as migration, tax-exempt manufacturing zones, and the economic exploitation they allow. The enacted metaphor of an indefinite detention in the "stateless" zone of an international airport highlights the question of what would be an appropriate public sphere in which to address such phenomena: Where and how is such a sphere to be located or constructed?

Like Misemer, Ana Puga concerns herself with the nexus between global capitalism and migration. Puga's chapter on migrant melodrama considers the construction of the suffering of the other by those in a position of privilege, though her analysis narrows the geographical scope to focus on issues of human rights, perceptions of suffering, and questions of citizenship within US borders. Puga documents the plight of the undocumented migrant artist Elvira Arellano, who sought sanctuary in a Chicago church with her son in 2006 and 2007. Puga examines how journalistic accounts, social performances, and visual cultural productions of the case drew on melodramatic devices to portray Arellano variously as innocent victim, criminal, and martyr. The evocation of different melodramatic types in Arellano's depiction leads Puga to ask whether an equation between suffering and virtue is still a prerequisite for human rights claims to be recognized by existing audiences. As she reveals, the melodramatic construction of "good" and "bad" migrants underscores the tendency of media and other observers to fashion images of some individuals or groups as more virtuous than others, despite the definitionally evident fact that people are entitled to having their human rights protected quite irrespectively of their individual virtue or innocence. What, Puga asks, are artists to do when the existing imaginary of the populations from which they draw their audiences is not conducive to the formation of a critical public sphere? How might such audiences be changed to become part of a public capable of thinking through, defining, and helping to uphold human rights?

3. Constructing Transnational Publics

As Nancy Fraser notes, there has long been talk across different academic disciplines "of 'transnational public spheres,' 'diasporic public spheres,' 'Islamic public spheres' and even an emerging 'global public sphere.'"[39] As she also emphasizes, although certain media, news outlets, internet platforms, films, and even plays and performance practices no doubt have "transnational," "diasporic," "Islamic," or "global" publics, such audiences are not necessarily part of any *critical* public sphere.[40] At the same time, there is of course a long list of phenomena with respect to which "current mobilizations of public opinion seldom stop at the borders of territorial states." Fraser's examples are "global warming or immigration, women's rights or the terms of trade, unemployment or the 'war against terrorism,'" and one could add the international borrowing privilege, the arms trade, nuclear proliferation, the production and distribution of pharmaceuticals, water rights, and many others.[41] These are phenomena whose causes and consequences do not respect national boundaries. Some of them result in human rights violations. To qualify as a human rights violation, to be sure, an impact stemming from these phenomena has to be traceable to human agency or institutional design, or preventable through human agency or institutional reform. But when it is, it is unlikely that the institutions or agents in question will be contained within or tidily aligned with any particular nation or state. Nation states, as we have noted above, are by no means the only entities with respect to which critical public spheres can come (and have come) to be constituted. But how might theater, a small-scale and essentially localized practice, contribute to the construction or operation of the respective international public spheres that would correspond to and effectively criticize these international institutions or agencies? The chapters in this section investigate the ways in which theater and performance may be part of the frameworks of responsibility, communities of knowledge and debate, and cultures of reciprocal empathy that bring such public spheres into existence and sustain them. In what ways might theater work to build bridges of empathy, promote rational engagement, or construct understandings of responsibility between individuals and groups in different locales, and with what level of critical efficacy?

Camilla Stevens analyzes contemporary pieces by the Dominican playwrights Frank Disla, Claudio Mir, and María Isabel Bosch, to demonstrate the unique transnational identity of dramatists who travel back and forth between the United States and the Dominican Republic to create works whose production and reception spans a "common, yet multi-sited public sphere." This imagined public sphere, Stevens argues, corresponds to the expansion of a consciousness of shared human rights and a notion of artistic "citizenship" in a transnational political community.

In this collection's most personal piece, Joi Barrios reflects on her development as a transnational playwright and practitioner. She presents the rich trajectory of her work involving performance and human rights, beginning with her collaboration as an actor in the performance piece *The People's Oratorio*, inspired by the Universal Declaration of Human Rights and staged at University of the Philippines in December 1984. She then discusses her involvement in street theater performances aimed at protesting extrajudicial killings and providing a space for the visual representations of grief. This work used the streets as performance venues and church holidays as performance occasions, thus finding locales for keeping alive a resistant critical public sphere during times of martial law and for reconstructing such a sphere during times of transitional justice and continued extrajudicial violence. Last, Barrios discusses her own dramatic works, *Gabriela* and *Mrs. B*, for and with which she attempts to forge a transnational US-Filipino public that is nonetheless rooted in local specificity.

Elizabeth Anker lends a skeptical eye to the notion of transnational publics for human rights in her analysis of Tony Kushner's *Homebody/Kabul* (New York, 2001). Kushner portrays an English woman in London (Homebody) who, after discovering an outdated tourist guidebook for Afghanistan develops an exoticized fixation and sets off for Kabul. Anker argues that, although Kushner is successful in raising awareness of humanitarian issues pertinent to Afghanistan, on a deeper level the play reveals the limitations of the international human rights imaginary and the narcissism that is at the core of much of Western human rights activism. Through analysis of the Homebody's reflections, Anker critiques the Western tendency to commodify and aestheticize non-Western suffering and to frame humanitarian intervention as a form of self-reflection, redemption, or eroticized identification with an imagined other.

Kerry Bystrom focuses on Western human rights activism on behalf of the Global South. She contrasts a number of scripts, performances, and scenarios of political activism geared toward raising consciousness of the violence against women in the Democratic Republic of Congo (DRC). Bystrom's analysis focuses primarily on Eve Ensler's "V-DAY" campaigns and Lynn Nottage's *Ruined* (2009) to demonstrate the ways these theatrical pieces inform international audiences of the atrocities occurring in the DRC. Yet, she also argues that these works unintentionally reduce the complexity of the violence inflicted on these women to "a particular medicalized narrative of psychological and physical trauma." Bystrom's essay suggests that theater practitioners must balance a politics of accuracy with a politics of efficacy in their efforts to give aesthetic form to, and spread awareness of, the violence experienced by others. By expanding her discussion to include other modes of activism, such as Ensler's nongovernmental organization V-Day and a United States Congressional Hearing in which both Ensler and Nottage participated, Bystrom illustrates concretely the transnational convergences between performance, politics, and activism that inform much of contemporary human rights discourse.

* * *

Thirteen years into the twenty-first-century, there is no certainty that the world will show an increased recognition and fulfillment of human rights. Such a future appears to be belied by the persistence of debilitating world poverty, its attendant public health crises, the impact of anthropogenic climate change on the lives of millions, the impotence of smaller nations in the face of the intensifying competition between established and emerging economic powers over the natural resources of the Global South, the continuation of authoritarian rule in some of the planet's largest countries, the attenuation of recent hopes for democratization in some parts of the Arab world, and the brutal escalation of military oppression in others. However, this does not mean that the contemporary discourse and practices of human rights are inconsequential rejoinders to the realities of economic and military domination, or an expression of the triumphalist variant of liberalism that emerged shortly after the Cold War and regarded the actually existing representative democracies of the capitalist West as the final word of history. Instead, the discourse and practices of human rights have proven themselves to be the only remaining project of sustained social and political change with global acceptance, institutional traction, and some prospect of success.

We need not deplore this fact. The position of human rights in this respect can be celebrated in spite of the historical origins discussed above because the concept and institutions of human rights have come a long way since they were invented 300 years ago by a small and privileged minority at the Western extremity of the Eurasian continent. As the contributions to this volume make clear, they have shown themselves to be remarkably resilient to charges of relativism and ethnocentricity, and capable of gaining and maintaining the support of protesters, activists, and theorists throughout the world. We have suggested that the resilience and promise of human rights derive in part from their historical roots in and intimate conceptual relation to the notion and social reality of a *critical public*. These roots and this relation at the same time ground the role of theater and performance in the construction and critique of human rights. Human rights, we have argued, have their origin in the public critique of power. Socially consequential processes of critique like that of human rights are never limited to intellectual theorizing. They require not only careful deliberation on specific problems and general principles, but also experience and imagination—such as that generated in and by dramatic play.

The present volume shows that theater and performance continue to play an important part in such processes of imaginative construction and critique in many parts of the globe. They have contributed to building or rebuilding critical publics and more democratic polities in processes of "transitional justice." They have focused existing national publics on those individuals who have been displaced and deprived of effective citizenship rights by the "War on Terror" and the more brutal aspects of the global economic order. They have been at the forefront of imagining into existence the new transnational publics needed to redress abuses of human rights that cannot be attributed to individual nation states. In examining these manifold contributions, the following chapters attend closely to the individual theatrical event or performance—to its construction by the playwright and performers and its imaginative co-construction by the audience. But they also seek to analyze the institutionally mediated processes of reception, criticism, reconception, and reimagination in which individual theatrical events or performances are situated. We believe that the manifold roles of theater and performance with respect to human rights can only be assessed in relation to such larger processes of critique, and hope that readers will find the essays we present here worthwhile contributions to such a process.

Notes

1. Taylor, *The Archive and the Repertoire*, 13.
2. While the role of the novel in the formation of the public sphere has received much scholarly attention and resulted in a number of important studies, remarkably, this is not true with regard to the role of drama and theater in the same process—which, we believe, was of comparable import. See, for instance, Habermas, *The Structural Transformation of the Public Sphere*; Slaughter, *Human Rights, Inc.: The World Novel, Narrative Form, and International Law*; Dawes, *That the World May Know: Bearing Witness to Atrocity*; Hunt, *Inventing Human Rights: A History*; Bystrom, "The Novel and Human Rights."
3. This term has been used in different ways by a variety of human rights scholars, for instance Douzinas, "Human Rights and Postmodern Utopia," 238; Slaughter, *Human Rights, Inc*, 324; and Elizabeth Anker's contribution to this volume.
4. Walton, *Mimesis as Make-Belief*.
5. Compare Michael Bratman, "Shared Cooperative Activity."
6. The idea that theater is a "custom," "practice," or "institution" derives from Wittgenstein, *Philosophical Investigations*, 197, 199, 205. Compare J. L. Austin, *How to Do Things with Words* and "Performative Utterances." The concept of a practice has since been used in accounts of fictive narrative; see Peter Lamarque and Stein Haugom Olson, *Truth, Fiction, and Literature*, 29–52; and Amie Thomasson, "Fictional Characters and Literary Practices." On the distinction between constitutive and regulative rules, see John Searle, *Speech Acts*, 33–42; John Rawls "Two Concepts of Rules"; and H. L. A. Hart, *The Concept of Law*, Chapter V.
7. Habermas, *The Structural Transformation of the Public Sphere*; Oskar Negt and Alexander Kluge, *Public Sphere and Experience: Toward an Analysis of the Bourgeois and Proletarian Public Sphere*; Peter Uwe Hohendahl, "The Public Sphere: Models and Boundaries"; Seyla Benhabib, *The Claims of Culture*, especially 133–246; Nancy Fraser, "Rethinking the Public Sphere"; and "What's Critical about Critical Theory? The Case of Habermas and Gender."
8. Joseph Slaughter's treatment in *Human Rights, Inc.* and "Enabling Fictions and Novel Subjects" of the role of the *Bildungsroman* in the formation and elaboration of both the public sphere and the concomitant notion of human rights is particularly astute on these unacknowledged exclusions.
9. Fraser, "Transnationalizing the Public Sphere," 7.
10. Hannah Arendt's conception of "action" in *The Human Condition* is an influential elaboration of this broader tradition.
11. Wilson, *Human Rights, Culture, and Context*, 12.

12. An example of the kind of dialogic questioning and revision of Western and non-Western ideas of humanity and subjectivity to which we refer here, and which has deservedly received much philosophical attention, centers on the southern African notion of "ubuntu." See, for example, Mutua, "Human Rights and the African Fingerprint"; Metz, "Toward an African Moral Theory"; and, on a related notion, Wiredu, "An Akan Perspective on Human Rights."
13. Wilson, *Human Rights, Culture, and Context*, 1.
14. Bharucha, *The Politics of Cultural Practice*, 21.
15. Habermas, *The Structural Transformation of the Public Sphere*; Shaffer and Smith, *Human Rights and Narrated Lives*; Hunt, *Inventing Human Rights: A History*; Slaughter, *Human Rights, Inc.*; Dawes, *That the World May Know*.
16. Michael Fried, *Absorption and Theatricality*.
17. Benjamin, "The Work of Art in the Age of Its Mechanical Reproducibility."
18. See also Rae, *Theatre and Human Rights*.
19. Agamben, *Homo Sacer*.
20. Butler, *Precarious Lives*.
21. Rothberg, *Traumatic Realism*, 206.
22. Sontag, *Regarding the Pain of Others*, 6.
23. Dawes, *That the World May Know*, 9.
24. Anderson and Menon, *Violence Performed*, 5.
25. Brecht, "Der Messingkauf," 712.
26. Arendt, *Eichmann in Jerusalem*; Conquergood, "Lethal Theater," 343; Felman, *The Juridical Unconscious*; Cole, "Performance, Transitional Justice, and the Law," 167–187; Kruger, *Post-Imperial Brecht*, 337–375; Rae, *Theatre and Human Rights*, 45–48.
27. Cole, "Performance, Transitional Justice, and the Law," 167.
28. Felman, "The Juridical Unconscious," 164.
29. Felman, *The Juridical Unconscious*; Rae, *Theatre and Human Rights*, 45–48.
30. Boal, *Theater of the Oppressed*, 1–20.
31. Said, *From Oslo to Iraq*, 108.
32. Arendt, *The Origins of Totalitarianism*, 296.
33. Historian Arthur Schlesinger calls this exceptionalism, endorsed by President Bush, "the most dramatic, sustained, and radical challenge to the rule of law in American history" (qtd. in Fletcher and Stover, *The Guantánamo Effect*, 1–4).
34. *NBC News Transcripts*, September 16, 2001: 5, available at http://www.whitehouse.gov/vicepresident/ news-speeches/speeches/vp20010916.html. (Qtd. in Fletcher and stover, 1.)
35. Fletcher and Stover, *The Guantánamo Effect*, 3.
36. Ibid., 3–4.
37. "Obama's Record: Guantánamo Bay," The Center for Constitutional Rights, accessed July 15, 2011, http://ccrjustice.org/obamas-record-guantanamo.
38. "Guantánamo by the Numbers: What You Should Know and Do about Guantánamo," The Center for Constitutional Rights, http://ccrjustice.org/learn-more/faqs/guantanamo-numbers-what-you-should-know-and-do-about-guantanamo, last accessed on June 2, 2012.
39. Fraser, "Transnationalizing the Public Sphere," 7.
40. Fraser, "Transnationalizing the Public Sphere," 8.
41. Fraser, "Transnationalizing the Public Sphere," 14.

Section I

Transitional Justice and Civil Society

CHAPTER 1

DEAD BODY POLITICS: GRUPO CULTURAL YUYACHKANI AT PERU'S TRUTH COMMISSION

Anne Lambright

During the last two decades of the twentieth century, Peru was plagued by internal warfare, wrought by both the Maoist terrorist group Shining Path and by the state's severe military response to the guerrilla organization. In 2001, then President Alejandro Toledo authorized the Comisión de la Verdad y Reconciliación (Truth and Reconciliation Commission), or CVR, whose charge was to "investigate and make public the truth of the twenty years of political violence initiated in Peru in 1980."[1] A major truth uncovered by the Commission was the final count of the dead and disappeared—69,000, almost twice the original estimate. The activities, hearings, and final report of the CVR generated many cultural responses in the form of films, novels, art, and theater, most of which cite in some way the effects of terrorist violence on the human body—as it is tortured, torn apart, forced to migrate, or killed. Other works, such as the 20,000+ photos of the era archived by the CVR and displayed in an exhibit entitled *Yuyanapaq* (To remember), evoke a disembodied dead, through its images of the disappeared, assumed deceased, of whom there remains no corporeal evidence. Upon examining this collection of cultural artifacts one wonders, to what extent is the new allegory of the Peruvian national subject a mutilated, dismembered, displaced, or dead body?

Regarding the sociocultural role of the dead and their spirits, sociologist Gordon Avery asserts that "to study social life one must confront the ghostly aspects of it";[2] this statement rings particularly true in a social setting marked by acute, prolonged national violence. In pondering the ghostly aspects of Peru's reconciliation and recovery efforts, I was struck by the interventions of the country's most important theater group, Grupo Cultural Yuyachkani, during the public hearings of the CVR between 2002 and 2003. In three plays presented before and during the hearings—*Antígona*, *Adiós Ayacucho*, and *Rosa Cuchillo*—and other performative interventions by the group, the dead and their ghosts occupy a central role, especially in relation to the Andean peasant public called upon to bear witness at the investigations. A close examination of these works reveals that for Yuyachkani, dead bodies, and the ghosts they produce, become repositories of national memory, means of exploring collective and individual trauma, and, interestingly, active mediators between the people and the state. Indeed, by summoning the dead to speak to the living in the context of a transitional justice process, Yuyachkani relies on ghosts to help the country collectively confront its past and contemplate a future.

The Fujimori regime (1990–2000), which had been successful in capturing Shining Path's leaders and significantly shutting down its operations, was also silent on and unwilling to investigate the extent of the atrocities committed during the group's 12-year reign of terror, much less the brutality of its own counterterrorism efforts. It was not until 2001 that President Alejandro Toledo authorized the CVR, in an attempt to help the country process its recent past and make recommendations for the future. In 2002, Yuyachkani was invited by the CVR to assist with its public hearings in Huanta and Huamanga, Ayacucho—two of the towns that experienced the most direct and devastating state and guerrilla violence. The group first toured the area before the hearings, presenting works, and holding discussions and workshops to impress upon the local peasant population, mostly indigenous and mestizo, the importance of testifying. The following year, actors performed in public during the hearings themselves. This study asks, given a varied repertoire of works dealing with Peruvian cultural heterogeneity, ethnic and gendered violence in general, and the Shining Path era in particular, why did Yuyachkani resort to their two existing plays whose protagonists are deceased, and why did they summon more dead when creating original pieces to accompany the CVR's endeavor? It is as if Yuyachkani were suggesting that after years of sustained violence and real and symbolic terror, the dead are the most capable of embodying the national situation, of serving as the nation's memory, and of bridging individual and collective trauma—three central functions of the group's artistic interventions. Furthermore, after years of official silencing of the dead—of burying the facts of their existence by denying them the reality of a material burial—Yuyachkani's characters finally give Peru a dead to mourn, and serve to move the nation symbolically from a state of melancholia to one of mourning; a crucial step in the process of recovery from trauma.

It is not surprising that the Commission called upon Yuyachkani to contribute to the ritualistic and spectacular aspects of the public hearings. For over 40 years now, Yuyachkani has been creating and performing popular theater in Peru, and the collective is by far the longest continually running and most important popular theater group in Latin America. The group's name, which in Quechua means, "I am thinking, I am remembering," underscores its commitment both to Peru's indigenous cultures and to preserving and performing a collective national memory. Indeed, Yuyachkani's expressed mission is to "think Peru theatrically."[3] Throughout its existence, the group's political, intellectual, and aesthetic project has undergone many transformations, at times to the disappointment of those attached to its early emphasis on social revolution. Recently, excellent critical attention has been devoted to Yuyachkani's politics and its commitment to dramatizing the heterogeneity of the Peruvian nation, to giving voice to its marginalized groups, particularly the indigenous peoples, and to exposing the trauma of a country riven by domestic terrorism and state-sponsored violence.[4]

From the beginning of the Shining Path era, Yuyachkani was determined not to remain silent with regard to both the guerrilla and state violence that pummeled their country. In 1988, in coordination with Peru's Asociación Pro Derechos Humanos (Association for Human Rights, APRODEH), the group organized the first of three "Encuentros de Teatro por la Vida" (Encounters of Theater for Life) to explore dramatically the national situation. At the first event, the group manifested that

> este evento es nuestra modesta respuesta, desde el teatro, contra el peligroso avezamiento ante la muerte impune, contra la indolente costumbre que parece envolvernos inconteniblemente frente a la violación permanente de los derechos humanos...
>
> Nosotros nos negamos a que la vida del pueblo se consigne como un simple dato estadístico. Nos negamos a que los políticos y técnicos que manejan el país hagan pasar por verdad la inevitabilidad de la muerte de niños, mujeres y hombres del pueblo peruano.... Nosotros nos negamos rotundamente a ser cómplices de esta situación injusta.
>
> [this event is our modest response, through theater, to the (country's) dangerous acceptance of unpunished deaths, to the indolence that seems to entrap us when faced with the permanent violation of human rights...
>
> We refuse to accept that the life of the people be reduced to a simple statistic. We refuse to let the politicians and bureaucrats that run this country prove inevitable the death of Peruvian children, women, and men.... We absolutely refuse to be accomplices in this unjust situation.][5]

Along with the *Encuentros*, Yuyachkani created *Contraelviento* (1989), *Adiós Ayacucho* (1990), *Retorno* (1996), *Antígona* (2000), and *Santiago* (2001); these plays dealt directly with the issue of civil war and its victims, while others, such as *No me toquen ese valse* (1990), offered glimpses of the social consequences of years of sustained violence. Yet, when asked by the CVR to assist with the Public Hearings, among the various options, Yuyachkani chose *Adiós Ayacucho*, *Antígona*, and a new work, *Rosa Cuchillo*—created specifically for the CVR hearings. In these plays, the group charges specifically gendered and racialized (socially marginalized) dead bodies with the responsibility of speaking for the nation and with the burden of being the memory of events the nation endeavors to forget. With these selections, the group seems to find that, in the extreme violence of domestic terrorism and state-sponsored counterterrorism, the dead offer greater possibilities of remembering, resistance, and perhaps even recovery, than the living.

In this sense, it is worthwhile to reflect upon the role the dead and their bodies have come to play in nationbuilding. In her fascinating study of death and reburial in postsocialist eastern Europe, Katherine Verdery remarks that "a dead body is meaningful not in itself but through culturally established relations to death and through the way a specific dead person's importance is (variously) construed."[6] She studies how bodies, especially those of leaders and fallen heroes, become symbols of political order, as national meaning and symbolism are inscribed in the life, death, body, and burial situation of national figures. Verdery writes,

> Dead people come with a curriculum vitae or résumé—several possible résumés, depending on which aspect of their life is being considered. They lend themselves to analogy with *other people's* résumés. That is, they encourage identification with their life story, from several possible vantage points. Their complexity makes it fairly easy to discern different sets of emphasis, extract different stories, and thus rewrite history. Dead bodies have another great advantage as symbols: they don't talk much on their own (though they did once).[7]

In Latin America, certain dead people have acquired enormous symbolic value. Eva Perón, Ernesto "Che" Guevara, and Emiliano Zapata quickly come to mind as figures whose lives and images still inspire powerful creative and political acts. These are individuals whose deaths have been co-opted by the people, who have become popular heroes. Lyman Johnson notes that "since colonial times both governments and their political enemies in Latin America have struggled to control or direct the powerful symbolism associated with the bodies of the revered dead"[8] and that "the human remains of... heroes, and the locations associated with their sacrifices and martyrdoms, retain powerful emotional content that can be used to mobilize mass action on behalf of the nation, an ethnic group, or a class."[9] Johnson remarks on the profound symbolic power of the dead bodies of heroes and martyrs across times and cultures, and observes that in Latin America they have been particularly key in articulating national identity, but he also points out that fame and fortune during a lifetime does not guarantee a lasting significance in death. Furthermore, in Latin America, heroes may be dislodged from their lofty status, as heroes of the elite do not necessarily appeal to the lower classes, and political changes sometimes bring about a change in the recognition afforded to a specific dead person. What, then, asks Johnson, accounts for the staying power of certain figures? Upon examining the lives and deaths of the most iconic Latin Americans, Johnson determines several common attributes: the heroes have undergone humiliation, defeat, and political trials in their lifetimes; they have generally exhibited patience and courage in the face of calamity; they have undergone suffering and sacrifice; they endured a "good" death in the hands of their enemies; there is often a gory aspect to representations of their bodies; and their burial (or burials) and final resting place somehow correspond to the lives they lived.[10]

The dead bodies studied in Johnson's anthology are all famous, and mostly Creole male (Cuauhtémoc of Mexico and Túpac Amaru of Peru are the only indigenous examples; Eva Perón the only female). Yet, when the Yuyachkani decide to resurrect the dead, they turn to ordinary indigenous males and females, with the exception of the figure of Antígona, whose creation was nonetheless inspired by Andean peasant women. In his reflections on the group's participation in the events related to the hearings, artistic director Miguel Rubio notes that

> Será difícil aproximarse a la verdad de lo sucedido en estos 20 años no sólo por la complejidad del problema que implica lidiar con intereses opuestos de sectores contrarios a que se esclarezcan los hechos, responsabilidades y propuestas que de allí surjan para iniciar un camino de justicia y reconciliación; sino también por el difícil acceso a las comunidades andinas, los temores de la población por la latente amenaza de Sendero Luminoso en algunas zonas del país y por posibles represalias de violadores de los derechos humanos.
>
> [It will be difficult to arrive at the truth of the past 20 years, not only because of the complexity of the problem, which means dealing with opposing interests from competing sectors, to clarify the facts, responsibilities, and proposals that come from them in order to begin the path to justice and reconciliation, but also because of the difficult access to the Andean communities, the fears of the people regarding the latent threat of Shining Path in some areas of the country and the possible retributions by human rights violators.][11]

This "difficult access" refers not only to geography, but also to culture. Yuyachkani long ago realized the importance of appealing to Andean indigenous and mestizo peasantry through a form of theater that takes into account their culture, their language, and their performance traditions. The dead protagonists of the plays Yuyachkani took to the CVR hearings would not be the famous, iconic dead figures of the era, such as Shining Path leader Edith Lagos or resistance leader María Elena Moyano.[12] Rather, the dead that Yuyachkani resurrects seem to have a direct relationship with many of the photographed victims archived in *Yuyanapaq*—as if the theater group were pulling them out of the silence imposed by their static images and giving them a voice to tell the stories behind their stark representations.

In his readings of the activities of South Africa's Truth and Reconciliation Committee, Dominick LaCapra observes that the primary purpose of that commission was

> to combine truth seeking in an open forum with a collective ritual, requiring the acknowledgement of blameworthy and at times criminal activity, in the interest

of working through a past that had severely divided groups and caused damages to victims... This complicated past was now to be disclosed truthfully in order for a process of working it through to be historically informed and to have some chance of being effective ritually and politically in creating both a livable society and a national collectivity.[13]

Certainly in a heterogeneous society such as Peru (much like South Africa), the goal of creating a livable society and national collectivity is a weighty one. Centuries of symbolic and real violence against the indigenous peoples and their culture have created an ethnic divide within the nation that is difficult to overcome. Furthermore, of the 69,000 dead or disappeared (according to the final CVR report), the vast majority were indigenous or indigenous–mestizo *campesinos*. Working towards true reconciliation would mean involving indigenous peoples in the process of remembering, mourning, and recovery, by imbuing the ritual with indigenous culture.

Part of Yuyachkani's commission by the CVR was to tour the highland region before the hearings and use theater to communicate to the largely peasant population the importance of testifying in the public hearings. Yuyachkani took *Adiós Ayacucho* and *Antígona* to several highland towns for these events. *Antígona* is a one-woman version of Sophocles's classic tragedy, performed by one of Yuyachkani's founding members, Teresa Ralli, with script by Peruvian poet José Watanabe.[14] In this "free version" of the Greek drama, Ralli, an extraordinarily versatile actress, performs all the parts of the play: a female narrator; the newly crowned Creonte; Antígona herself; Creonte's son and Antígona's love, Hemón; a royal guard; and the blind prophet Tiresias. Role changes are indicated through the actress's voice and gestures, in how she drapes a long cape, and, at times, with changes in stage lighting and sound. The only props on stage are one wooden chair and a box containing the death mask of Polinices, Antígona's dead, unburied brother.

At first glance, the play seems a departure from Yuyachkani's previous work, which explores recognizably Peruvian issues: peasant uprisings in the highlands, internal migration from the highlands to the coast, terrorist violence, urban poverty, and cultural heterogeneity. In fact, there is nothing in the play that overtly references Peru; it takes place in ancient Thebes, and its plot and characters correspond directly to those of the original Greek tragedy. However, upon closer examination, it is clear that the work relates well to the Yuyachkani corpus, dealing with issues of the arbitrariness of power; the loss of social, cultural, and historical memory; the responsibility of the citizen; and, I argue elsewhere, the role of woman in the maintenance of a social conscience.[15] Yuyachkani's *Antígona*, Rubio and Ralli explain, is about women and the suffering that national violence has inflicted upon them. Specifically, in preparation for their version of the play, they spoke to many female relatives of the "disappeared" in Peru, and their testimonies of their searches for husbands, sons, and daughters directly inspired the writing of the play.

Yuyachkani's *Antígona* is, on the one hand, an act of memory, a direct challenge to the call of the female narrator, who at the end of the first scene demands, "empecemos a olvidar" [let's begin to forget].[16] But it is more than that; the fact that the play is centered on and expressed through the body of a single woman is significant. For Ralli, the desire to act alone stemmed from witnessing the extreme isolation of the female relatives as they searched for their family members, a solitude imposed by the fact that the women relatives of the disappeared in Peru have not organized on the same level as those of Argentina and Chile, for example. This aspect of the play is thus a reproduction of that loneliness (accentuated by the lack of props and scenery) and a reiteration of the corporeal boundaries imposed by a society traumatized by violence and corruption. But, it must also be seen in a sense as power—woman's body as a receptacle of national memory, yes, but also as (re-)creator of that memory and potentiator of resistance.

That the text is to a great extent about (re-)building a nation and a discussion of national values and the people's place in their determination, is evident in the various references to "patria" found throughout the play. While Creonte's opening lines affirm that, "Nuestra patria nuevamente es una tierra de sosiego" [Our country is once again a land of peace],[17] the *narradora* asks, "¿Qué ha sucedido en mi patria/para que los ojos tan jóvenes miren con tanta amargura?" [What has happened in my land/ such that young peoples' eyes regard with such bitterness?].[18] She later observes, "Un extranjero que cruzara Tebas de paso/ vería un pueblo de orden, un rey que gobierna/ y un pueblo que labora calmo./ No vería las turbulencias debajo del agua mansa" [A foreigner passing through Thebes/ would see an ordered country, a king who governs/ and a people calmly laboring./ He wouldn't see the turbulence below the still water].[19] This statement illustrates a constant oscillation between terms—calm/chaos; state/family; citizen/individual—that marks the work and through which we begin to glean an image of a nation in crisis. The question of state power versus individual conscience is made explicit in the struggle between Creonte and Antígona, who fight over the fate of Polinices's body. Creonte, as a representative of state power and symbol of that power abused, orders a "no tumba" [no tomb] for the traitor and an honor-filled burial for his brother, "el cuerpo de aquel cuya causa fue la patria" [the body of him for whom the fatherland was his cause].[20] Antígona's own first words highlight her role as judge and advocate: "Oh rey, no necesitabas mucho para hablar con voz de tirano" [Oh, king, you didn't need much to speak with the voice of a tyrant].[21] For Antígona, state power should manifest the opposite of tyranny, and she assumes a place of authority and power higher than that of the king himself, situating herself on the side of the divine: "Los dioses quieran, Creonte,/ que no te dure el privilegio de ordenar impunemente lo que te place,/ y quieran también acabar pronto con tu gozo de escuchar/ sólo el multitudinario/ e indigno/ silencio" [The gods want, Creonte/ for your privilege to freely order what you wish not to last,/ and they want to end quickly your pleasure at hearing/ only the multitudinous/ and indignant/ silence].[22] Antígona personifies the resistance to and transgression of boundaries necessary for the formation of a truly democratic society and her challenges will be severely punished; for in the opposing terms that sustain the fragile society—memory and forgetting, speaking and silence, the divine and the earthly—Antígona refuses to accept her designated place as a woman.

Indeed, the breakdown of order caused by power's arrogance implies a collapse in the symbolic order used to sustain power. In *Antígona*, the play, and Antígona, the character, the gendered symbolic system, which would associate the masculine with the divine, historical memory, and language, and the feminine with the profane, with the repressed and forgotten in history, and with silence, collapses, and it is woman's body that stands as the symbol of the nation, but no longer as an empty, passive receptacle of meaning, nor even as a reproducer of future citizens, but as an active challenge to the existing state and an agent of change. Indeed, comparisons between the male and female bodies in the text are pertinent: Polinices's dead body is exposed and omnipresent and motivates key actions, but it is without voice or agency. Eteocles, the masculine national hero, is buried. Hemón, who kills himself upon finding Antígona dead, is impotent before his father and, the text tells us, in its only reference to his body, becomes, along with Antígona, a shadow on the wall of the cave in which his love has been unjustly imprisoned. It is Antígona's body, however, that is the focus of this play. The *narradora* looks at her and remembers her adolescent body, her first period, and her budding curves—promise of a bright future irrevocably truncated by national trauma. But it is Antígona's imprisoned body and ultimately her dead body that receives the most attention. The *narradora* asks the dead woman, "Antígona,/ ¿ves este mundo de abajo?/ El palacio tiene ahora un profundo silencio de mausoleo/ Y desde ahí nos gobierna un cadáver que respira, un rey/ atormentado/ que velozmente se hace viejo." [Antígona,/do you see that world below?/ The palace now has a profound, mausoleum silence/ And from there we are governed by a cadaver that breathes, a king/ tormented/ who is quickly growing old].[23] Although she is dead, the woman's spirit retains the most vital role; it is masculine power that, while technically alive, is presented as a corpse.

The revelation at the end of the work that the narrator has been Antígona's sister, Ismene, points to one of Yuyachkani's central concerns when contemplating the Shining Path era. As Teresa Ralli suggests, "en Perú somos todos Ismenes" [in Peru, we are all Ismenes][24]—we are all the survivors whose silent complicity made the terror of the past years possible. But, rather than seeing Ismene as simply a living survivor, I would like to suggest that Yuyachkani also proposes her as a dead body—that of the living dead. Indeed, the actress's body incorporates not only the "surviving" narrator but also the dead Antígona and the dead Hemón, and in the end Ismene herself dons Polinices's death mask. Ismene is like the thousands of Peruvian women who go through life carrying their dead inside of them and their images on their faces. Ismene, like the rest of Peru, must carry the ghosts of the past into the future. By revealing Ismene as the physical porter of Antígona's voice and memory, Yuyachkani points to all Peruvians as "living dead," occupying what Giorgio Agamben describes as the "threshold" between life and death, "bare life" and "political life," as if it were the only possible subject position after such extended national trauma.[25]

In *Adiós Ayacucho* (based on a homonymous short story by Julio Ortega), Augusto Casafranco acts the part of Alonso Cánepa, a peasant leader disappeared by state authorities. Cánepa is unable to enter the next life because his murderer took some of his bones as souvenirs—in Andean culture the body must be intact for the spirit to rest. As Francine A'Ness points out in her reading of Yuyachkani's collaboration with the CVR, "The ignominious nature of Cánepa's death is as tragic as it is dehumanizing. Yet the play is neither macabre nor grotesque. Rather than attempting to compete with the media and approach the topic of violent death and disappearance through the explicit lens of documentary theater, the story is communicated through a simple monologue and a contemporary-dance-inspired aesthetic. In this way, there is little risk that the piece will further desensitize an audience accustomed to seeing and hearing about violence on a daily basis, or, conversely, retraumatize them by compounding the issue."[26] The play opens to reveal Cánepa's clothes laid out in a traditional Andean act of mourning. Q'olla, an Andean comparsa dancer,[27] also played by Casafranco, comes across the clothing and steals the shoes, giving Cánepa's spirit the opportunity to take over Q'olla's voice.[28] Cánepa's re-embodiment in Q'olla is culturally significant: the costume is that of a recognizable figure from the Virgen del Carmen Festival in Paurcartambo (Cuzco). The mostly indigenous and mestizo audiences to whom the play is directed, expect or assume that the man behind the mask—who speaks to them in Quechua—is indigenous. In this sense, the actor's body (Casafranco is white) is thrice masked—as the ghost of a peasant leader in the body of an indigenous man masked as a comparsa dancer.[29]

Cánepa tells the story of how his body was dismembered and parts thrown away or stolen by his murderers, and how he began his journey, with half a body, towards Lima to recover his remaining limbs, "a recuperar lo que es mío" [to recover what is mine].[30] He hides in the back of a truck on the way down from the highlands, finding one headed towards Lima: " 'El Peruanito.' Aunque ese nombre me produjo ciertos reparos" [The Little Peruvian. Although its name gave me pause], to which Q'olla responds, "Claro, no fuera que se desbarrancase y te mata dos veces por tu condición de doblemente paisano" [Sure, it could have fallen off a cliff and killed you twice for your doubly "country" man condition]. Cánepa believes that "llegando a Lima quizás tendría que descubrirme. La gente allá está acostumbrada a ver cadáveres en la televisión. En cuanto yo les contase mi historia no faltarían voluntarios para enterrarme" [Upon arriving at Lima I would have to show myself. The people there are used to seeing cadavers on television. Once I told my story, there would be no lack of volunteers to bury me]. On the way to the capital, Cánepa observes "la gente que cruzaba la carretera en determinados trechos. Otros iban sobre enormes piedras. La sospecha de que fueran como yo, desaparecidos, me sobrecogió. ¿No era yo el único que acaso iba a Lima a recobrar sus huesos?" [People crossed the highway at determined times. Others travelled on enormous stones. The suspicion that they were like me, disappeared, terrified me]. The voyage also leads him past trucks carrying indigenous prisoners to their death, cemeteries, and funeral processions, and finally, through Huanta, where "hacía poco fueron descubiertas tumbas secretas, enormes fosas comunes. Los cadáveres aún estaban en la plaza, irreconocibles" [Shortly before they had discovered secret tombs, enormous mass graves. The cadavers were still in the plaza, unrecognizable]. The image we receive of Peru is of a land of ghosts and corpses—a nation where death is the only truth. In a sense, Cánepa's bones are strewn all over the Peruvian landscape, as omnipresent as they are lost.

When narrating the portion in which Cánepa arrives in Lima, the actor removes the Qhapaq Q'olla mask, becoming again Cánepa's body. In the main square he finds the president, "el culpable de mi muerte" [the one responsible for my death], preparing to give a speech. There, Cánepa attempts to present the leader with a letter in which he demands the return of his missing bones. The missive, read aloud earlier through the voice of Q'olla, decries the desecration of dead bodies as a crime against the most basic of human values: "El elemental deber de respetar la vida humana supone otro más elemental aún que es un código de honor de guerra: los muertos, señor, no se mutilan. El cadáver es, como si dijéramos la unidad mínima de la muerte y dividirlo hoy como se hace en el Perú es quebrar la ley natural y la ley social" [The fundamental duty to respect human life presupposes another, even more fundamental one that is a code of honor in war: the dead, sir, may not be mutilated. The cadaver is, shall we say, the most basic unit of death and to divide it, as is done today in Peru, is to shatter both natural and social law]. The irony of the fact that Cánepa tries to present his letter to the president just before the leader is to speak on "the importance of Christian charity," is not lost on the audience.

As he approaches the president, Cánepa is stopped by guards, who torment him until a street child comes to his rescue, claiming Cánepa to be his father. With his letter unopened and trampled, Cánepa and the child are about to leave the main square when the peasant leader spots the Cathedral and enters with the child. What occurs there is rather remarkable; Cánepa makes his way to the tomb of Francisco Pizarro, the Spanish conqueror of Peru. There, he reconstructs his body using Pizarro's bones and lies down in the conquistador's tomb. He tells the child:

> Toma, la verdadera calavera de Pizarro puedes venderla. Y también éstos huesos. Salvo estos que me hacen falta. Este niño me miró los ojos y me dijo:
>
> —Oye, toda la gente creerá que eres Pizarro, está bien, te traeremos flores.
>
> Pero te juro que cuando sea presidente buscaré tus huesos,—juró pálido.
>
> Mi voz sonó como de otro en la amplia urna. Me escuché a mí mismo en el eco y entendí que mi hora era cercana. Ya me levantaría en esa tierra, como una columna de piedra y fuego.

["Take this, Pizarro's real skull. You can sell it. And these bones, too, except these, which I need." The boy looked me in the eyes and said, "Hey, everyone will think you are Pizarro. It's fine, we'll bring you flowers. But I promise that when I'm president I will find your bones," he swore, pale.

My voice sounded like another in the ample urn. I heard myself in the echo and understood that my hour was near. Soon I would rise from this earth, like a column of stone and fire.]

The ending clearly refers to the indigenous concept of Pachacutic, the idea that every 500 or 1,000 years the world, finding itself in an unsustainable situation, turns "upside down." It is a popular belief that the arrival of the Spaniards turned the Andean world upside down, for, as the great Inca Garcilaso de la Vega put it, "trocósenos el reinar en vasallaje" [we went from reigning to servitude],[31] the indigenous culture lost its dominance to the Europeans. Regional mythology tells of the last Inca, whose dismembered body is slowly regenerating from the head. Once complete, he will initiate a new Pachacutic, and the world will be turned right-side up again, with indigenous culture regaining its political and cultural hegemony.[32]

Furthermore, the subversion implied by the Andean peasant appropriating body parts and then occupying the final resting place of the man who conquered Peru is clear.[33] From this point on, the body revered as foundational of Peruvian culture will be a truly mestizo body—whose head and trunk (mind and soul) are Andean. The play is a sort of reverse conquest, the violence and desecration of the Andean body politic that began almost 500 years ago is now aimed at the icon of Spanish-ness.

The final play, *Rosa Cuchillo*, is a very brief, one-woman play based on Oscar Colchado Lucío's novel by the same name. The novel is narrated by three dead indigenous characters; in Yuyachkani's adaptation, Ana Correa portrays Rosa, the only female, who has died of sorrow and is traveling through the Andean afterlife, searching for her dead son as she makes her way to Hanaq Pacha, the Andean equivalent of heaven. There she is finally united with her son, Liborio, who like many young men in the highlands had been forcibly recruited by Shining Path and was eventually killed. Yuyachkani's *Rosa Cuchillo* touches on but a small portion of the cultural richness of the novel, which aims to create a truly Andean universe and presents a complex and thorough understanding of Andean mythology and world vision. For Yuyachkani, Rosa's primary attraction is her role as a mother searching for her dead child. Indeed, the audience learns that Rosa's quest in the afterlife is but an extension of her incessant searching while alive, when she and other mothers of disappeared children went out "turning over cadavers to see if they were our children." One can imagine the emotional appeal of this character at the CVR hearings, given that, as Ileana Diéguez notes in her study of the play, Rosa is a sonless mother acting in front of thousands of mothers who cannot recover their own sons.[34]

In the novel, Rosa remains in Hanaq Pacha and Liborio returns to earth, to lead a battle to initiate a Pachacutic. But in the play, after eight minutes of telling her story, it is Rosa's spirit that returns to earth, to be among those testifying at the public hearings:

> ahora estoy por aquí. Estoy recorriendo los pueblos, los mercados, los lugares donde se reúne la gente porque, ¿sabes qué?, todavía mi gente está enferma de miedo y de olvido y por eso estoy aquí y por eso te voy a limpiar y te voy a danzar y te voy a florecer para que florezca la memoria. Y por eso te voy a danzar y te voy a florecer para que florezca la memoria.
>
> [now I am here. I am remembering the towns, the markets, the place where people gather because, you know what?, my people are still sick with fear and forgetting, and for this reason I am here, and for this reason I am going to cleanse you and dance you and bloom you, so that memory may bloom. And for this reason I am going to dance you and bloom you so that memory may bloom.][35]

It is as if Rosa Cuchillo has become the mother of all of Peru, and she comes to ritually cleanse the country through a 17-minute dance that ends in her throwing rose petals over the audience, a traditional Andean gesture of adoration or purification.

Rosa is the first of the dead characters that appears to the audience as a spirit—Correa's body is painted a ghostly white and she dons a white *pollera*. Before the play, the character wanders among those gathering to watch, her slow, silent motion and piercing, eye-to-eye gazing add to her haunting appearance. The effect is uncanny, for as Derrida points out, we do not know if the ghost is alive or dead, spirit or body, and as such it oscillates between identity and presence: "The specter (says Derrida) is a paradoxical incorporation, the becoming-body, a certain phenomenal and carnal form of the spirit."[36] Rosa's embodiment in Ana Correa gives the indigenous woman a presence that resists identification—she is and isn't; she exists and she doesn't—and her movement among the audience powerfully suggests there must be other ghosts there as well, whose presence we can sense and whose identity we cannot fix.

Two other performances that accompanied the figures of Cánepa and Rosa Cuchillo in the streets of Huanta and Huancayo were the Mujer Ayarachi, silently danced by Teresa Ralli, and the installation piece *Tambobambino*, by group member and technician Fidel Melquiades. The Ayarachi is a dance from Puno, traditionally performed by men but often accompanied by women; the term "Ayarachi" refers to a crying soul or funeral music. Ralli plays a dead Ayarachi dancer—the dead mourning the dead. *Tambobambino* is an installation piece inspired by a Quechua song transcribed by writer and ethnographer José María Arguedas. It tells of a young musician, killed by the forces of a river—*yawar mayu*, a river of blood—and his floating instruments are all that remain. His beloved stands beside the river weeping, as a storm falls over the town and a condor watches. The piece consisted of three circles that evoked the three spheres of life in the Andean world. Ukuq Pacha, the underworld, is a circle with a Peruvian flag spread out and covered with the clothes of a dead peasant, laid out for mourning as in *Adiós Ayacucho*. The second circle, Kay Pacha, this world, has a masked man playing a lament, and the third, Hanaq Pacha, the afterlife above, shows a dancing dead woman with flags for wings. As its creator, Fidel Melquiades remarks, "Nunca pensé que esta imagen, que sólo conocía por un canto, iba a ser parte de una historia común. Nunca pensé que 'El Joven' se convertiría en cientos de jóvenes campesinos, quechuahablantes en su mayoría. Siempre pensé que el yawar mayu sólo era una metáfora..." [I never thought that this image, which I only knew through a song, was going to be part of our common history. I never thought that the "young man" would become hundreds of young peasant men, the majority Quechua speakers. I always thought the river of blood was just a metaphor...].[37] Inspired by a dead body and featuring images of death, again *Tambobambino* points to Yuyachkani's emphasis on the dead as witnesses and historians.

Alfonso Cánepa, Rosa Cuchillo, and the Ayarachi dancer performed outside the buildings in which the public hearings were held and spent days walking through the markets and the squares of Huanta and Huamanga. The short documentary "Alma Viva" records aspects of Yuyachkani's participation in the hearings at Huamanga. From that film and various testimonies by the actors themselves, it is clear that the mostly indigenous population felt a strong connection with the Yuyachkani characters. Indeed, Rubio tells of moments when indigenous people, likely feeling much more comfortable with the costumed actors than the suited Lima officials, would approach the characters and begin to give them their testimony. The question certainly is not why Yuyachkani turned to Andean characters but why they chose to present them in that particular vital status. Why does Yuyachkani turn to the dead to encourage the living to speak?

In many ways, dead bodies speak a truth that the living are unable to utter. Certainly in Peru dead bodies had begun to "speak," to bear witness to the atrocities committed upon them, long before official discourse even admitted the need for the country to collectively address the horrors. Also, by appearing as dead, Yuyachkani could maintain both a respectful distance from and an intimate closeness to the testifiers. That is, the actors did not presume to take the place of the living victims of the war; they did not appear as survivors, acting roles, and speaking about atrocities they did not witness and horrors they did not experience. Rather, by becoming dead, they were able to be everyone's son, daughter, brother, sister, mother, father; they were witnesses and victims, in collusion with but not the same as those whom they met on the streets of Huanta and Huamanga.[38] Furthermore, they were able to give voice to those forever silenced—as if all the 69,000 dead or disappeared had slipped on Cánepa's shoes.[39]

As well, through embodying the dead, the Yuyachkani provide these silenced victims with a form of agency—even if they can get no more real justice than the opportunity to tell their story. Derrida challenges us "to exorcise not in order to chase away the ghosts, but this time to grant them the right...to...a hospitable memory...out of a concern for justice."[40] In this regard, if former histories ("stories") of the nation have been inscribed in and through dead Creole bodies, the Yuyachkani propose that now the bodies upon which history is inscribed and the nation constructed be Andean, indigenous, feminine—marginalized bodies. In this sense, one is tempted to ask as to what extent the re-embodiment of the Andean dead is hinting at a political, social, and cultural Pachacutic.

Finally, by presenting the public with dead bodies, Yuyachkani dramatizes a function of the CVR of moving the country from a state of melancholia through an act of mourning. LaCapra, drawing on Freud, asserts that "mourning brings the possibility of engaging trauma and achieving a reinvestment in, or recathexis of, life that allows one to begin again... Through memory-work, especially the socially engaged memory-work involved in working-through, one is able to distinguish between past and present and to recognize something as having happened to one (or one's people) back then that is related to, but not identical with, here and now."[41] By providing dead, and their stories, to mourn, Yuyachkani helps the public work through their past in order understand the present and perhaps envision a future. Yuyachkani's dead do not attempt to close a chapter in Peru's history (as death brings closure to a life) nor to imagine impossible utopias of communal forgiveness and collective harmony. Rather, Yuyachkani's dead make present the ghosts Peru has refused to recognize, so that the nation may learn to live with—and care for and converse with—the specters of its history, acknowledging their inevitable place in the body politic as the nation moves into the future.

Acknowledgments

I am particularly grateful to the helpful comments of the "Cuerpos muertos" working group at the 2007 Encuentro of the Hemispheric Institute for Performance and Politics in Buenos Aires. Furthermore, this essay benefited greatly from the superb reading, insightful comments, and bibliographic suggestions of Priscilla Meléndez.

Notes

1. Comisión de la Verdad y Reconciliación, *Informe final*, "Prefacio," August 28, 2003, May 26, 2007. http://www.cverdad.org.pe/ifinal/index.php.
2. Avery, *Ghostly Matters*, 7.
3. Rubio, "Persistencia de la memoria," Spring 2003. June 12, 2007. http://hemi.nyu.edu/esp/newsletter/issue8/pages/rubio.shtml.
4. See, for example, A'Ness, Muguercia, Persino, Salazar de Alcazar, and Taylor.
5. Rubio, "Persistencia." All translations from Spanish are mine.
6. Verdery, *The Political Lives of Dead Bodies*, 28.
7. Ibid., 28–29.
8. Johnson, ed., "Why Dead Bodies Talk," 3.
9. Ibid., 4.

10. As will be seen below, the common, not famous, dead that the Yuyachkani adopt as icons and voices of the Shining Path period hold many of the traits Johnson lists.
11. Rubio, "Persistencia."
12. While they were not indigenous, it is important to note, nonetheless, that neither Lagos nor Moyano was a typical national hero. Both women, Lagos from a prosperous Andean family in Ayacucho and Moyano a poor black from the urban settlements in Lima, were multiply marginalized. Both became popular heroes to a great extent because of their marginality, and both were politically appropriated in various ways by the government and by Shining Path. Of Lagos, Victoria Guerrero writes,

    Edith Lagos es una de las figuras que persiste como mito de los inicios de la lucha armada de Sendero en el Perú. La masiva participación de pobladores en su entierro revela la existencia de un vacío y la urgente necesidad de encontrar referentes. Es decir, una nueva forma de narrar de los sujetos excluidos de un proyecto nacional fundado alrededor de una cultura occidental-criolla, minoritaria, y a espaldas de la gran mayoría de los miembros de la nación. Edith Lagos aparece como contraparte de aquellos primeros muertos anónimos del conflicto, cuya identificación fue anulada por el Estado, y cuyo cuerpo fue olvidado por una sociedad criolla altamente racista, hasta el punto de negar la injusticia y violencia que se ejercía sobre la población andina, sobre todo indígena, a quienes se les consideraba—se les considera—ciudadanos de segunda clase y menores de edad. Es decir, seres «feminizados» que no llegan a convertirse en sujetos sino en cuerpos, cuya materialidad es ignorada y cuyo silenciamiento debe aguardar por una significación desde la cultura dominante [Edith Lagos is one of the persistent mythologized figures of the Peruvian Shining Path armed conflict. The massive attendance at her funeral reveals the existence of an emptiness and an urgent need to find reference points, that is, a new way of narrating subjects excluded from a national project founded on a Westernized culture—Creole, minority, and on the backs of the great majority of the nation's members. Edith Lagos appears as a counterpoint to the conflict's early anonymous deaths, whose identification was annulled by the State, whose body was forgotten by a very racist Creole society, to the point of denying the injustice and violence exercised over an Andean, mostly indigenous, population, who were considered—who are considered—second-class, minor-age citizens. That is, "feminized" beings who are not subjects but rather bodies, whose materiality is ignored and whose silencing must await signification by the dominant culture] (Victoria Guerrero, «El cuerpo muerto y el fetiche en Sendero Luminoso: el caso de Edith Lagos», en Ciberayllu March 29, 2006. [on line], http://www.andes.missouri.edu/Andes/especiales/VG_CuerpoMuerto.html).

    Moyano was killed in a very public way, her body torn apart by a Shining Path bomb. Her life and death have been the subject of many forms of popular eulogy.
13. LaCapra, "Absence, Trauma, Loss," 696–697.
14. Yuyachkani's is not the only Latin American play to draw on Sophocles's *Antigone* to explore the trauma of rebel or state violence or conflicts between the individual and the state. Some other examples are Puerto Rican Luis Rafael

Sánchez's *La pasión según Antígona Pérez* and Argentine Griselda Gambaro's *Antígona furiosa*. The latter closely relates to Yuyachkani's work in that it was written in response to the atrocities committed by the state during Argentina's "Dirty War." It is not surprising that Antigone's story has captured the imaginations of Latin American playwrights. Commenting on Gambaro's piece, Taylor writes, "the Antigone plot specifically raises questions about political leadership and misrule, about the conflict between the so-called private and public spaces, about public fear and complicity, about a population's duty to act as a responsible witness to injustice, and about social practices and duties predicated on sexual difference that are as urgent today as they were in 441 B.C. The words in the Sophoclean text reverberate in the discourse of the dirty war." (Taylor, "Rewriting the Classics," 79).
15. Lambright, "A Nation Embodied," 133–152.
16. Watanabe, *Antígona*, 16.
17. Ibid., 19.
18. Ibid., 43.
19. Ibid., 49.
20. Ibid., 20.
21. Ibid., 22.
22. Ibid., 38.
23. Ibid., 64.
24. Persino, "Cuerpo y memoria," 97.
25. Curiously, in his study "Giorgio Agamben and the Politics of the Living Dead," Andrew Norris notes the affinity of Agamben's discussion of sovereignty and sacred life with the classic Greek play, *Antigone*. For Norris, Antigone's underground tomb "perfectly symbolizes Agamben's threshold between life and death. The result is a monstrous confusion of death and life.... If Antigone dares to insist that the dead are simply that, and as such beyond politics, Creon will prove her wrong by condemning her to the threshold in which politics and death find one another" (Norris, "Giorgio Agamben and the Politics of the Living Dead," 50.
26. A'Ness, "Resisting Amnesia," 403.
27. Q'olla is a dancer from the mestizo Qhapaq Qolla comparsas in Paucartambo, Cusco. As a Q'olla, this dancer represents a poor llama herder from the Qollao plateau. See Mendoza, *Shaping Society through Dance*.
28. Both A'Ness and Diana Taylor read this play as Cánepa's having recovered his bones and appearing before the audience as the now complete cadaver of the peasant leader. It is clear, however, that the body we see before us is of another, living, indigenous man (who speaks mostly Quechua) whose body is a vehicle through which Cánepa tells his story. Cánepa's bones, which were not stolen, lie now, according to the play, in Pizarro's tomb in the National Cathedral in Lima.
29. In this sense, I must respectfully disagree with A'ness's otherwise excellent reading of this and the other performances presented at the hearings. For A'ness the use of masks defamiliarizes the violence suffered by the victims. This may well be the case for audiences in Lima, but I propose that in taking on recognizably indigenous characters from popular or local culture, the Yuyachkani make the violence at once more immediate and identifiable for the indigenous audiences.

30. Grupo Cultural Yuyachkani, "Adios Ayacucho," Video and unpublished script. No Dates. All subsequent citations are from these sources.
31. Garcilaso de la Vega, *Comentarios reales de los incas*, 29.
32. For more on the concept of Pachacutic and the importance of the bodies of Túpac Amaru I and II, see Stavig, "Túpac Amaru, the Body Politic, and the Embodiment of Hope," 27–62.
33. Pizarro's body had its own interesting history. After dying a violent death at the hands of his enemies, Pizarro was first buried in a courtyard of the Cathedral and then in the Cathedral crypt itself, on orders of the King of Spain. Wishing to show the body to celebrate the 400th anniversary of Columbus's first voyage and 350th anniversary of Pizarro's death, in 1891 Peruvian officials placed a mummified body on display. This body remained the official body of Pizarro until in 1977, two boxes, one containing a head and the other the rest of the body, were found. Forensic evidence proved that these were truly the remains of Pizarro, and they replaced the mummy.
34. Diéguez, "Escenarios Liminales," 12.
35. Grupo Cultural Yuyachkani, "Rosa Cuchillo." All subsequent quotes are from this live performance.
36. Derrida, *Specters of Marx*, 6.
37. Rubio, "Persistencia."
38. LaCapra speaks of the "empathetic unsettlement" of the secondary witness (the historian, the writer): "Historical trauma is specific and not everyone is subject to it or entitled to the subject position associated with it. It is dubious to identify with the victim to the point of making oneself a surrogate victim who has a right to the victim's voice or subject position. The role of empathy and empathetic unsettlement in the attentive secondary witness does not entail this identity; it involves a kind of virtual experience through which one puts oneself in the other's position while recognizing the difference of that position and hence not taking the other's place" (LaCapra, "Absence, Trauma, Loss," 722).
39. Rubio hints at this aspect in a brief discussion of the group's thematic trajectory:

> Con la violencia que asoló y enlutó nuestro país, los supuestos básicos de nuestro trabajo afrontaron nuevos retos.... Los cuerpos de nosotros los peruanos, se degradaron a tal punto que comenzó a ser cosa corriente verlos masacrados, mutilados y expuestos a la intemperie, enterrados clandestinamente en fosas comunes o, peor, desaparecidos.... Si (antes) nuestros actores buscaban otro cuerpo dentro de su cuerpo, esta vez tuvieron que prestar el suyo porque en nuestra escena irrumpieron presencias que buscaban su propio cuerpo, concreto, material, desprovisto de toda metáfora.... así, nuestros actores, que habían tenido como centro la presencia, han debido trabajar la ausencia en sí mismos para evocar los cuerpos de los ausentes. [With the violence that devastated our country and threw it into a state of mourning, the basic assumptions of our labor found new challenges.... The bodies of us Peruvians were degraded to the point that it became commonplace to see them massacred, mutilated, and exposed to the elements, buried clandestinely in mass graves, or, worse, disappeared.... If (before) our actors searched for another body

inside their own, now they had to loan theirs out because of the sudden appearance on the scene of beings that were searching for their own body, concrete, material, void of all metaphor.... thus, our actors, who had had as their central presence, have had to work with the absence in themselves in order to evoke the bodies of the absent] (Rubio, El cuerpo ausente (performance política), 32–33.)

40. Derrida, *Specters of Marx*, 175.
41. LaCapra, "Absence, Trauma, Loss," 713.

CHAPTER 2

WHERE "GOD IS LIKE A LONGING":
THEATER AND SOCIAL VULNERABILITY
IN MOZAMBIQUE

Luís Madureira

*For Bela Madureira
in loving memory*

On the first two days of September 2010, after circulating intractably for days, rumor—"the poor man's bomb," as Achille Mbembe calls it—suddenly detonated in the sprawling, ramshackle periphery of Mozambique's capital.[1] During the preceding two weeks, anonymous text messages[2] had insistently called for widespread demonstrations against the steep and abrupt rise in the cost of living, arousing people to oppose the government-sanctioned increases in water and electricity rates and in the price of fuel, bread, and other basic food items. In the early morning of September 1, the shanty-towns erupted as announced. Thousands of people, for the most part youths, whom President Armando Guebuza's spokespeople would later brand "vandals and thugs," seized burning tires, boulders, pipes, variously sized tree trunks, and even torn-up bus stop equipment, to block the main roadways into the cities of Maputo and Matola.

The few cars and buses that ventured into the eerily empty streets were pelted with rocks. Some were set on fire. The demonstrators looted shops, especially those owned by Nigerians, vandalized fuel stations, and, most distressingly for the ruling party (Frelimo), after having unsuccessfully attempted to wreck a school carrying the president's name, they trampled on posters bearing his triumphantly beaming likeness: the ubiquitous and politically strategic remnants of the 2008 electoral campaign.³ For two seemingly interminable days, the inhabitants of Maputo's periphery kept the capital's privileged inner core in a veritable state of siege. By the time these civil disturbances had been ruthlessly quelled, 13 people reportedly lay dead and at least 300 wounded, mostly from the live ammunition fired indiscriminately by the police, despite public assurances by the Interior Minister that the police force would use only rubber bullets. In all, about two dozen shops had been ransacked,⁴ a handful of fuel stations and banking institutions vandalized, and several buses as well as other vehicles destroyed or set ablaze.

These events transpired around eight months into my eleven-month stay in Maputo, where I had been conducting research on theater. Since early February, I had pored through unpublished original and adapted play scripts;⁵ I had interviewed numerous theater practitioners (actors, current and former directors and set designers, playwrights, as well as drama students and teachers from the recently founded drama school at the national university); I had attended seminars, rehearsals, and workshops as well as multiple professional and amateur theater productions, including two theater festivals, and had seen several community and forum theater performances, a number of which had taken place precisely in the neighborhoods where the disturbances of early September occurred. I was trying to understand how the sustained and diverse performance culture, which has thrived in Mozambique since the early 1980s, entails a novel and effective mode of exercising citizenship. I wanted to gauge the extent to which, for both spectators and theater workers, drama constituted a powerful form of political participation. Ultimately, I wished to propose that Mozambican theater opened up spaces for the negotiation and rearticulation of ethnic, class, and gender identifications both against and alongside dominant nationalist discourses. Nevertheless, what happened on those two fateful days of September compelled me fundamentally to rethink my hypotheses.

The events of September made it imperative that I reconsider the theater–citizenship connection in the context of a widening social divide. I had glimpsed its early signs on the night I arrived in Maputo, as I drowsily watched an amalgam of tumbledown shanties unfurling like some peri-urban equivalent of Hegel's bad infinity from behind the window of the late-model, air-conditioned US Embassy van that drove me from the airport. By early September, I had become better acquainted with the meanders of those suburban precincts. Yet they remained, not just for me, but probably also for most of those who dwell in the urban zone of economic privilege, citizenship, and sociability, largely a foreign country. As Mozambican sociologist Carlos Serra queries in a recent interview: "What do we know of our compatriots' lives in the suburbs? What do we know of their dreams, their sorrows, their ambitions? We talk about them and make projects that involve them without ever contacting or listening to them"⁶ (Ricardo). To cite Mia Couto, Mozambique's best-known writer, "the inhabitants of the concrete nation woke up to the existence of another, greater nation" on the morning of September 1; on that day, Couto continues,

> the poor ceased to be the topics of workshops. The poor leaped from seminars held in luxurious hotels into day-to-day reality. The poor can bring the country of the others to a halt. Even if in the process they become poorer. For those who have little or no "tomorrow," this waste of the future is worth it... The perception which a certain Mozambique has of itself was turned upside down. The periphery became the center. Poverty found its own voice, with its poor resources, its impoverished hope.[7]

The inhabitants of this uncharted, peripheral world, as Serra notes in a study on social vulnerability, are in the main excluded from the benefits and privileges of Mozambique's dominant social order. They constitute a hybrid "counter-society," which produces new rules, new values, new identities, and new forms of social representation. While those who live inside the city's confines enjoy full citizenship rights, the shanty-town dwellers engage in a grueling and unremitting struggle for daily survival, forever poised "on a knife's edge," immured in a kind of "infra-citizenship."[8] In the despondent words of an old Maputo beggar, the periphery's residents have been dumped "in the trash can" of national history.[9] They flit "like ghosts" before the unseeing eyes of the privileged few, while barely subsisting in the social dead zones where "God is Like a Longing" ("Deus é como uma saudade"), to quote the hauntingly poetic phrase of a mental institution inmate.[10] Thus, if my aim was to develop a keener appreciation of contemporary Mozambican politics and culture as well as the intricate ways in which citizenship practices could evolve in relation to drama and performance, then the September riots surely demanded that I grasp the conditions of possibility of this putative link between theater and citizenship within the problematic social terrain unfolding just beyond the urban core where much of the theater in Maputo takes place. What the insurrection laid bare, to put it in starker terms, was the grievously deficient form of political participation as well as the flagrantly unequal access to public service afforded to the shanty-town inhabitants. And I began seriously to question whether theater could ever compensate for or supplement the quotidian denial of this fundamental human right. For it remains to be ascertained whether among the privileges denied to the "infra-citizens" of what Mia Couto calls Mozambique's "other, greater nation" are precisely performance and active and informed spectatorship.

In a narrow sense, the incidents of September 2010 only reaffirmed what many economists and social scientists had been asserting for some time. Despite the high-flying rhetoric issuing from the president's office about the "battle against poverty," for the past five years or so, both poverty and social inequality have been steadily rising in Mozambique. Thirty-five years after the country gained its independence, and notwithstanding the record economic growth it has been undergoing since the end of the civil war in

1993, the overwhelming majority of Mozambicans continue to have one of their basic human rights—"the right to a standard of living adequate for the health and well-being of himself and of his family"[11]—flagrantly violated. In the end, whether or not citizenship can ever emerge through performance and spectatorship in the badlands sprawling beyond the edges of "concrete city," the fact remains that during those first two days of September, the social actors from Maputo's periphery effectively reappropriated and resignified social space. As Couto suggests, and to paraphrase Georges Balandier slightly out of context, the September civil disturbances downgraded political power and its hierarchies. By disrupting, or upending, the social order, they ultimately lay bare the ruling class's vulnerability. They showed that power was not untouchable.[12] Ironically, the social drama the shanty-town dwellers enacted thoroughly fulfills the role that Pius Ngandu Nkashama ascribes to theater (in Africa): "through the power of its own law, theater confers upon itself the authority to attack hierarchies, challenge established rules, and contest political power" ("Theatricality" 243). Yet, precisely by dramatizing an extreme negation of a power and privilege that appear to have endured since the times when Maputo was still known as Xilinguine ("white people's city"), they also pointed to a troubling continuity between colony and nation.

In the face of this recognizably postcolonial persistence of colonial relations and conditions well into the national phase (a continuity that is all the more vexing in a country that, like Mozambique, declared itself a "people's republic" during the first decade of independence[13]), two crucial and related questions emerge. First, and perhaps most evident, is the question concerning the place and role theater and theatricality have historically played beyond the urban centers, not just in the outlying boroughs I have been discussing, but in the villages and countryside. A comprehensive treatment of this question certainly exceeds the scope of the present study. However, its significance requires that I advance at minimum some preliminary, and necessarily provisional arguments. This is, in fact, one of the main tasks of the present chapter. Second, if "theatricality has been a major dimension for upholding and contesting power structures and social (generic) differences"[14] and if theater remains, throughout Africa, "the most important expression of conflicts, contradictions, as well as fundamental social complexities,"[15] then it is essential to interrogate how (and indeed whether), in the course of Mozambique's tumultuous recent history, theater has ever succeeded in catalyzing, or at least symbolizing, social change and political participation in rural and peri-urban zones. In short, I need to consider the specific modes in which, and the extent to which, theater has grappled with and sought to address the suppression, by the national government, of the basic human right to enjoy equal access to public service and fully participate in national politics. In the following historical overview of theatrical activity in Mozambique, I attempt to broach these crucial issues, without drawing any definitive conclusions. In the main, I concentrate on the first two of what Carlos Serra designates the "three phases in the genealogy of Mozambican cities" (21): the colonial (1890–1974) and revolutionary periods (1975–1986).

I

During the colonial period, Maputo (known as Lourenço Marques) was sharply bisected into center and periphery. In the center resided the white settlers, along with a few assimilados (who inhabited mostly poor, working-class neighborhoods). In the periphery, where precariously built houses predominated, lived the "natives," or indígenas.[16] The colonial capital thus appears to have been mapped out in accordance with what Fanon famously defines as "the rules of a purely Aristotelian logic"; its topography was "divided in two [...;] the 'native' sector [was] not complimentary to the European sector. The two zones.... [followed] the dictates of mutual exclusion."[17] As Serra puts it, inside the city's geometrically arrayed center, the "native's" only function was to place his or her laborer's body at the settlers' service.[18] Not surprisingly, then, most of the theatrical activity in the colonial era was confined to white circles.

Around the turn of the century, references to several plays and musical comedies written and performed by white settlers began to appear in the local press. All the roles were performed by white actors, including those of black African characters. During the early decades of the twentieth century, a few metropolitan theater companies, usually bringing minor or "second-rate" actors, would tour the African colonies intermittently during the off-season in Europe. In the 1930s, most of the theater brought to the colonies consisted of recycled light comedies, musical comedies (*revistas*[19]) and vaudeville pieces that had been successful in Lisbon or Oporto in the preceding years. Up until the late 1950s, several local dramatists continued to produce light comedies, comic skits, and musical reviews focusing on local themes. Their subject matter overwhelmingly concerned the white population. Indeed, as a prolific Portuguese journalist asserts without irony in the early 1950s: "One could do colonial theater even without the intrusion [*intromissão*] of the native."[20]

As late as September 1967, while Portugal's prolific Teatro Alegre Company was touring colonial Mozambique, a local newspaper published a fairly typical background piece on the lesser-known, technical aspects of the company's production then on offer in the capital. More than 40 years later, the article's title, "A Gente invisível do teatro" (Theater's invisible people), brims with a trenchant, albeit unintended, irony. Ostensibly, it alluded to the electricians, sound engineers, prompters, and other technicians working behind the scenes, practitioners whose efforts were allegedly as essential as those of the actors "to make theater happen."[21] As if to underscore the irony, however, in the background of one of the photos illustrating the article, which depicts three of the technicians featured and interviewed for the piece, stands a black man holding a broom. The caption reads in part: "The theater people whom the audience never sees put their final touches on the set." To a white colonial readership, "theater people" referred presumptively to the three white technicians in the foreground, not the black man sweeping the stage wing. In an initial reading, the photo thus captures the "native's" insurmountable subordinate position not just on the colonial stage, but in the colonial order.

In effect, as Duarte Ivo Cruz notes, until the waning years of Portugal's colonial rule, black characters in metropolitan plays are, with few exceptions, generally treated condescendingly, regardless of the playwrights' political ideology;[22] their roles usually restricted to "naïve and devoted servants" who express themselves in some variety of a largely invented "Guinea Portuguese," harking back at least to Gil Vicente's early sixteenth-century farces.[23] The participation of the imperial center's cultural production in the task of defining and consolidating colonial practices by sustaining and naturalizing the unequal social and economic relations between the metropolis and the peoples and places subordinate to it is by no means a novel topic. It is nonetheless remarkable that the kind of "perfect closure" that binds culture inextricably to imperialism, the "circularity," or excision of any view that is outside the prevailing colonial outlook, which, according to Edward Said, renders any alternative to the imperial dispensation "unthinkable" in nineteenth-century England,[24] seems, in the Portuguese case, to have endured well into the twentieth.

Yet the intertwining between theatrical production and colonial ideology was by no means entirely seamless. For instance, in a 1952 response to Rodrigues Júnior, the journalist who claims that colonial theater could dispense with the natives' presence, the Portuguese historian Alexandro Lobato (a long-time resident of the colony) baldly asserts that "theatre in Mozambique [at least of the kind that leaves a lasting 'social influence'] does not exist."[25] Significantly, it is precisely in the late 1940s and early 1950s that a protonationalist Mozambican literary production, which turns to local cultures for its literary material and inspiration, begins to emerge. The most significant indigenous publication, and one of the rare venues for Mozambican as opposed to colonial literature, was the *Brado Africano* (African Call), published, with some suspensions and crucial editorial changes, between 1918 and 1974. The early work of several of those who are currently regarded as the nation's pioneering writers, José Craveirinha, Noémia de Sousa, and Rui Nogar, among others, initially appeared in *Brado Africano*.

II

Brado was the official journal of the Grémio Africano (African Guild) (later Associação Africana [African Association]), one of the two main organizations formed mostly by blacks and *mestiços* in the early twentieth century, which were among the first initiatives of local civil society to cooperate with, contest, and occasionally negotiate concessions from Portuguese colonial authorities. Ironically, although its role throughout the colonial period has usually been described as contestatory, Associação Africana put on a *revista* (musical comedy) entitled *Aqui é Portugal* (This is Portugal) as part of its African culture festival held on May 7, 1949. Encapsulating the surreal notion that Portugal, together with its far-flung colonial territories, constituted a single and indivisible national "body" (from the northern Portuguese province of Minho to the southeast Asian island of Timor[26]), *Aqui é Portugal* was one of the most emblematic catchphrases of Portuguese imperialism during Salazar's dictatorship (1928–1974). Since the only vestige of *Aqui é Portugal* (the *revista*) is a fleeting news item buried in the back pages of a dusty colonial daily, there is no way to ascertain whether its title was ironic; whether, despite the strict censorship the Salazar regime imposed on this popular genre from the late 1920s, this particular production succeeded in recovering the satirical mordancy that had defined it since its emergence in Portugal in the mid-nineteenth century; and indeed whether it was able simultaneously to reproduce and appropriate for its own ends, the coded, metaphoric language, the sly complicity with the audience, to which some of the metropolitan variants resorted in order surreptitiously to question power.[27] For, as the eminent theater scholar Luiz Francisco Rebello maintains, "the more or less scathing critique of power and of those who hold it, whether or not it strikes at its core, has always been . . . . a constant with the *revista*."[28]

Similar questions would pertain to the *revistas* presented by the theater troupe belonging to the other civic organization largely made up of blacks and *mestiços*, the Centro Associativo dos Negros de Moçambique (The Associative Center for the Negroes of Mozambique), allegedly the one that collaborated more closely with colonial authorities. According to the *Lourenço Marques Guardian*, the *revista Eu quero ser swingista* (I want to be a swing dancer), whose staging the paper commends as a requisite initial step toward building a "theater of greater depth and educational aims" represents the "first attempt at theater" by the blacks of Mozambique.[29] No less a personage than the colony's governor general "deigned" to attend one of its performances.[30] Noting that the piece has been stirring up "a lively interest" and was already enjoying a "great excess," the same paper reports that the *revista*, now "completely overhauled," would be brought to the stage again in May, 1949; the reporter anticipates a "sensational" opening night.[31] A comparable enthusiasm apparently surrounds the staging of the musical comedy *Xipamanine*[32] in September of the same year.[33] Aside from this "amusing revista," the program included several other skits and comic plays, whose titles—*Magaíça*,[34] *Sebastião, come tudo*[35] (Sebastian Eats It All), *Os engraxadores* (The Shoeshine Boys), *Moleque* (Houseboy), *Os bêbados* (The Drunkards), and *Chigubo*[36]—suggest a forthright and perhaps acerbic engagement with the quotidian experiences and concerns of the "native" population.[37] Without direct access to any of this fascinating material (assuming any of it survives), I can only speculate about its content and political outlook. The same goes for the audience, though one may conjecture that it included the indigenous literate, educated, and cultured minority (urban-based mestiços, black Africans, and even whites), from whose ranks were drawn many of the writers who had by then begun establishing the foundations for Mozambique's written culture. In this way, a small cultural elite assumes an aesthetic and political commitment to give voice to the interests and anxieties of the "native" majority. The main issue, in this respect, is whether the participation of this majority was as restricted in these performances as it remained, by and large, in the pages of *Brado Africano*; whether it was mainly absent from or uncharacteristically present in both the stage and the playhouse.

Another apposite question to consider in this context is therefore whether the political ambivalence Rebello identifies in the metropolitan variants of the *revista* registers on some level in its adaptation and transposition into a colonial setting. For Rebello, the *revista* represents a "class spectacle," in the sense that within it the privileged classes allow themselves to be (mildly) censured, while those in the underprivileged ranks attain a measure of vindication by cheering these bland rebukes.[38] In the last instance, then, the *revista* sustains, often unknowingly, the ideology of the ruling class. Because it never completely calls the latter into question, it ends up upholding the existing power structure, even when it mocks it. Thus, throughout the dictatorship, Rebello argues, *revista* producers kept up a sort of collusion with official censors, who permitted a restricted amount of coded and oblique broadsides of the regime so long as certain limits were observed. Notwithstanding the concessions and evasions such an arrangement demanded, Rebello concludes that the *revista* remained one of the few dramatic genres that succeeded in consistently, albeit covertly, challenging the regime.[39]

The question, again, is whether the Centro Associativo's adaptations of the genre reproduced the ambiguity that defined its relations with the colonial regime, a complex and occasionally fraught blend of collaboration with and contestation of colonial policies, which, for the most part, involved formally petitioning colonial authorities to address the obstacles faced by "native" professionals, mitigate the rise in the cost of living, lower the hut tax, or bring forced labor practices under control. At the same time, it was in the supposedly moderate Centro that Eduardo Mondlane, the future leader of the independence movement (Frelimo), founded, precisely in 1949, the student organization (Núcleo de Estudantes Secundários Africanos de Moçambique [The Nucleus of African Secondary School Students]—NESAM) that would play such a decisive role in Mozambique's political drive to nationhood.[40] Given the paucity of materials available, it can only be a matter of speculation how prominent a role theater might have played in this process.

In light of the highly successful revival of the comic and vaudeville forms by one of Maputo's most prolific and successful theater troupes (Gungu) in the 1990s, it would have been of inestimable value to examine these adaptations of the *revista* genre in an effort to gauge not only the parallels and variances between colonial and postindependence appropriations and resignifications of this form, but also to explore whether a similar ambivalence defines their politics. Despite their concessions and tergiversations, the Associação Africana and the Centro Associativo initiated the formation of a civil society during the colonial period. However circumscribed, their efforts on behalf of the indigenous population prefigure the struggle for independence in the 1960s. It is therefore licit to inquire whether the theatrical performances they produced for a brief period in the late 1940s may also have laid the foundations for the light comedies and vaudeville pieces currently enjoying a tumultuous popularity in Maputo.

To analyze their creative fusion of dialogue, music, mime, and dance (often traceable to indigenous performance practices), paying special heed to how "traditional" forms are simultaneously preserved and transformed, how they adapt new cultural and political content within the context of existing performance forms, would also be of particular relevance to more recent developments in Mozambican theater. Such creative adaptation is cogently exemplified by the innovative uses of wooden masks by performers of the Mapiko dance, from the northernmost province of Cabo Delgado, and of the Nyau dance, from Tete province in western Mozambique, both initiation dances. This creative transformation of traditional forms is also apparent in the reworked or "updated" versions of various songs, mimes, and oral narratives. Both the Nyau and Mapiko dances experienced extensive transformations during the armed struggle for independence (1964–1975). Dancers began to ridicule, satirize, and in effect resist colonial rule. They caricatured colonial types, fashioning masks that depicted European store-owners, the Virgin Mary, Catholic saints, and sipaios ("native" policemen). Alongside their erotic chants in the Nyau ceremony, women began to introduce songs lamenting colonial subjugation, or mocking the agents and representatives of colonial power. During the war of independence, Frelimo implemented both Mapiko and Nyau as tools for mobilizing for the struggle, as well as reflecting and criticizing aspects of traditional society itself.[41]

In their classic studies of national culture, Frantz Fanon and Amílcar Cabral have explored the complex ways in which "traditional" cultural forms reflect and in turn effect social and political transformation during nationalist struggles. There is as yet no body of sustained research into this process in Mozambique, and most of the evidence I have been able to gather is either patchy or anecdotal. As Fresu and Oliveira correctly suggest, however, many of these transformed traditional forms constitute a kind of incipient popular theater.[42] Indeed, a thorough investigation of these modes of popular expression and communication, combined with a comparative study of the diverse experiences that arise in association with them, could lay the groundwork for the development of a popular theater. As far as I know, this is not an area that is being researched by contemporary Mozambican theater studies in a consistent manner. This absence of sustained research into popular theater forms has not always been the norm, however.

Toward the end of the colonial period, in April 1971, four years before Mozambique's independence, Lindo Nhlongo, a young black writer, wrote what was probably the first Mozambican play with a strictly local theme, *Os Noivos ou Conferência Dramática sobre o Lobolo*[43] (The Bethrothed, Or, A Dramatic Conference on the Lobolo). Staged by Portuguese set designer Norberto Barroca, the play featured an all-black cast, dramatic dance expression, and benefited from the musical accompaniment of four African musical ensembles. According to Nhlongo, the play was the culmination of exhaustive research into the "traditional" customs and practices of southern Mozambique, which he carried out along with the painter-poet Malangatana Ngwenha in the 1960s.[44] The dramatic form the playwright selected for this cultural content was the Attic tragedy. In *Os Noivos*, the chorus plays a prominent and intrusive role, serving alternately as the mouthpiece for and moral arbiter of "tribal" or customary law. Occasionally, it also functions as a kind of distanced or "objective" ethnological informant. The action focuses on the hardships resulting from the continuing practice of lobolo (the "traditional" custom of bride-wealth) in a modern social and economic setting. Perhaps inevitably, given the strict censorship limiting most artistic expression in the colony at the time, *Os Noivos* presents its dramatic conflict almost as a metaphysical antinomy.

In the prologue, for example, the chorus defines the death of the protagonist (Dambana) as "the result of a clash between two civilizations. Dambana's roots lie in tribal life, but he lives in the city. Clinging to family traditions and living in contact with Western civilization, Dambana knows neither where he came from nor where he is going. The place he inhabits is a tribal society in transition. Since there is no law for a society in transition [...] Dambana sentenced himself to death, dying when he sought to live."[45] Notwithstanding the reduction (or expansion) of the play's central conflict into a conventional opposition between tradition and modernity, the chorus's initial lines already strongly imply that the inequities of the colonial dispensation not only inform but underlie this dilemma.

Addressing itself directly to the audience, the chorus announces in the prologue that the drama about to unfold will bring to life a social existence thoroughly unfamiliar to the mostly European audiences who watched it in a downtown Lourenço Marques theater: "I will sing to you of our men who leave/to work in the mines/in search of illusions/and money [...] I will sing to you of our women who initiate into sex so many [white] youths from the city./And I will sing to you of our *mufanas* [young children] who start working/When others are learning to play."[46] Toward the end of the piece, when Dambana returns from a second trip to the South African mines, which he was forced to make in order to repay the accumulating debt incurred from having had to produce an exorbitant *lobolo*, the chorus recites in its entirety one of Noémia de Sousa's best-known poems from 1950, *Magaíça*.[47] The poem depicts the "bewildered" migrant's wretched homecoming, as he carries suitcases "full of the false brilliance/of the scraps of the false civilization of the Rand compound"; he has depleted "his youth and health/his lost illusions/that will shine like stars/on the neckline of some lady/in the dazzling nights of some city."[48] As the chorus states in its opening lines, the play sets out to render visible those who had heretofore been unequivocally the invisible people of the theater: "I will sing this song to you so that when you see us pass by, you will see in us more than someone passing by, but someone who has feelings."[49] In the words of a colonial-era reviewer, *Os Noivos* obliged its white audiences to "take conscience of a different reality," to confront "another world," and gauge its immeasurable distance from their own, imbuing them with a sense of regret for knowing so little about the lives of "men who live right here, next to us."[50] Nearly two decades later, this review provides a compelling rejoinder to Rodrigues Júnior's claim that colonial theater could do without the natives' presence. Indeed, other contemporaneous reviews unanimously hailed Nhlongo's play as a "watershed," or a "new chapter" in the history of theater in Mozambique, understanding it as laying out the path toward the establishment of an authentic Mozambican theater.[51]

By all accounts, *Os Noivos* was a resounding "popular success," playing, for at least five months, to consistently packed audiences of primarily Europeans, in the downtown venue, and of mainly Africans, in an Indian-owned movie theater in the African suburb of Xipamanine. To cite another reviewer, it is indeed difficult to determine whether these two distinct audiences ever "complemented each other" as a result of Nhlongo's unprecedented collaboration with Barroca.[52] The production represented nevertheless a "major cultural breakthrough."[53] As Russell Hamilton asserts, it is of key historical significance as well that colonial authorities allowed the play to be staged at all.[54]

If, for most contemporaneous reviewers, the revelation of this previously concealed life-world was among the most valuable lessons *Os Noivos* had to impart, for one reviewer at least, the collaborative effort of the Portuguese set-designer Norberto Barroca (who had been in Mozambique for only a little over a year) represented the most exemplary aspect of the production. This exemplariness resided in the fact that Barroca had succeeded "in doing more for the culture, and theater of Mozambique" than most of the local (and predominantly white) theater people, who "dole out fine theories about popular theater," and yet had thus far shown themselves incapable of taking the "essential step of introducing to Mozambican theater all the wealth contained in the folklore, the songs and the problems of the people of Mozambique."[55] According to the same reviewer, Barroca's crucial contribution was to coordinate all these existing cultural elements in order to transform Nhlongo's "African-themed" drama into a spectacle whose unity highlighted "the beauty of the art and cultural practices of our people."[56]

While one might detect a hint of paternalism in this model of collaboration, whereby Europe lends its expertise and organizational skill to govern Africa's raw artistic talent, Barroca's partnership with Nhlongo adumbrates the collaborative work between Mozambican and European theater practitioners that was to prevail in Mozambique after independence. Perhaps what lay behind the reviewer's not-so-veiled rebuke of existing theater groups in the colonial capital was precisely a sense of disappointment over the critical opportunities for theatrical (and cultural) cooperation and exchange they had missed. Indeed, the close associations (dating back at least to the late 1940s) between the handful of white writers, living or born in Mozambique and ideologically as well as philosophically opposed to the social and political status quo in the colony, and black and mestiço artists, now widely recognized as the forerunners of national literature, never fully materialized in theater.

III

This kind of racial solidarity is exemplified in the friendship and political collaboration between Noémia de Sousa and João Mendes, a white activist who was arrested in 1947, imprisoned, and later exiled to Angola for his clandestine political activities. Sousa dedicates a group of five poems, later published as a separate, biblically named cycle, to Mendes: "The Book of John [*João*]." One of these poems, "Descobrimento" ("Discovery") (1949), in which, according to Hilary Owen, "the demands of creating Marxist solidarity across the nations require a rewriting of the Portuguese discoveries,"[57] opens with the following lines: "When your smooth, calm, white man's hand/reached out as a brother to me/and across Indian Oceans of prejudice/clasped with tenderness my intertwined mulatto fingers [...] when your voice..../brought me the white flag of the word 'SISTER'/then I felt..../the sole and terrible power of our brotherly embrace."[58] Four decades later, Sousa provided the following explanation for her poetic tribute to Mendes: "He was a white man who managed to build a bridge between the ethnic groups. People think I have paid a bit too much homage to this one person. But if they had lived through the times we did, they would have a better understanding of how important it was for us to have a white man among us, fighting for our ideals."[59] Such political and artistic allegiances (which, in some cases, assumed the form of protection and patronage, with all their attendant contradictions and limitations) were often determined by the political authoritarianism prevailing for most of the colonial period. As Portuguese sociologist Boaventura de Sousa Santos has observed, the "independence of African colonies occurred concomitantly with profound, progressive transformations in Portuguese society," signifying that with decolonization came "a shared sense of liberation, both for the colonizer and the colonized."[60]

At the same time, as Mia Couto notes, the term "decolonization" itself (which rarely, if ever, appears in postindependence Mozambican histories of the period) masks a crucial differend around its very definition. "Who decolonizes whom?"; were the independences of the former colonies "the result" of the metropolitan revolution that brought down the dictatorship in April 1974, or was it the wars of liberation that, along with the political struggle of the Portuguese people, brought about the "April Revolution"?[61] As I argue elsewhere,[62] it is critically important that we remain attentive to the "distance" [*distanciamento*] separating metropolitan and Mozambican conceptions of "liberation,"[63] particularly when assessing postindependence collaborative projects. Writing just on the eve of independence (and only a few months after the April 1974 Revolution), Hamilton gives a shrewd assessment of the double-bind that sometimes accompanied these relationships: "Certainly, in the practical sense, the good offices of a white elite have afforded some blacks and mestiços an opportunity that the general racist structure of Mozambican society would ordinarily deny them. But the lack of a certain self-determination has the disadvantage of a kind of vassalage which means that when the non-white becomes more than just a clever black lad he represents a threat to the white fief."⁶⁴ As the controversy that unfolded in the wake of a theater festival organized by Cena Lusófona⁶⁵ (the Portuguese Association for Theater Exchange) illustrates, this dynamics was not necessarily confined to the colonial period.

Since its foundation in 1995, with the backing of Portugal's Ministry of Culture, Cena Lusófona's main purpose has been to foster communication through theater among Portuguese-speaking countries. In the very year of its founding, the association organized a theater festival in Maputo. According to the inaugural issue of its journal, *Setepalcos* (Seven Stages), the festival would "naturally privilege Portuguese-language authors," placing a special emphasis on Gil Vicente, "a constitutive reference point for the language spoken in the seven [Portuguese-speaking or "Lusophone"] countries."⁶⁶ For Cena Lusófona's director, the primary focus was thus "language, of course," in particular, the "unceasing possibility of renovating what was bequeathed to us."⁶⁷ António Reis, another influential Portuguese theater director, interviewed in *Setepalcos*' first issue, considers likewise vital "the reinforcement of the ties with the Portuguese language," especially in a country like Mozambique, where the pressure exerted by the surrounding English-speaking countries is "worrisome."⁶⁸ The then president of a Luso-Brazilian cultural foundation, interviewed in the same issue, regards the Festival as an "unequivocal affirmation," on the part of the Mozambican people, that they "wish to remain within the Portuguese language family."⁶⁹ These pronouncements in favor of the promotion of the language of Camões (or Gil Vicente) suggest an uncritical embrace of the politics of *lusofonia*,⁷⁰ which the Portuguese government was actively pursuing at the time.

Although a thorough critique of this complex and contradictory notion is well beyond the scope of this chapter, it is fairly evident that to regard the advancement of the Portuguese language as central in a theater exchange ostensibly bereft of "paternalism and preconceived ideas"⁷¹ was to do precisely what Mia Couto had hoped the festival would refrain from doing: "not to create a center that conceives [ideas] and a periphery that executes [them]."⁷² Manuela Soeiro, the director of Mozambique's first professional troupe (Mutumbela Gogo), founded in 1986, which, since its founding, has collaborated closely and extensively with the best-selling Swedish author Henning Mankell, seems to address more trenchantly this call for the promotion of a common "mother tongue": "We want to expand into other geographies. It doesn't matter what languages are spoken there.... In Portugal, we're treated with a certain paternalism.... It's best to let each country create its own theater according to its own culture. We think Mozambican. Our theater will develop in keeping with that condition."⁷³

In an open letter on the state of Mozambican theater, published almost three years after the Festival, the members of Mutumbela and its sister troupe M'beu contend that no one from Cena Lusófona ever consulted Mozambican artists when they conceived and designed the Festival. The letter goes on to say that many Mozambican artists and intellectuals regarded the way the association went about organizing the festival as an "infringement" of their artistic and cultural autonomy. They criticized the "arrogant behavior" of those who conducted the process from Portugal, and deemed the selection of plays as "unilateral" and completely unmindful of the criteria proposed by their Mozambican counterparts.[74] Obviously, the contradictions and constraints that often define North–South collaborative projects subsist in the postindependence period. Even on this minor scale, what Aníbal Quijano has defined as the "coloniality of power" (*colonialidad del poder*) appears to endure well beyond the colonial era.[75]

IV

Whatever the specific character of the collaboration between Barroca and Nhlongo, *Os Noivos* was a fairly isolated cultural event. As Hamilton points out, it never quite signaled "the start, during colonial times, of a socially conscious theater" ("Portuguese-language Literature" 270). More to the point, none of the local companies ever took up the challenge that Fernando Gusmão (1919–2002), another Portuguese actor and set designer who spent nearly a year collaborating with the local university troupe in 1970–1971, would make in a later recollection of his experiences in Mozambique. What should really arouse the professional interest of any "man of the theater" working in Mozambique, according to Gusmão, is "the study of black theater which [...] has its own forms, and a mostly oral tradition of hundreds of years."[76] It would be nonetheless fundamentally inaccurate to characterize all of the theater produced by white Europeans as mainly supportive of the prevailing colonial dispensation. In effect, the extent of the involvement of the small group of politically liberal (or radical) Europeans, who dominated literary and cultural production in the waning years of colonial rule, in the agitprop theater that predominated immediately after independence has yet to be thoroughly explored.[77]

V

During the first phase of Mozambique's Afro-Marxist republic (1975–1989), several neighborhood amateur troupes, ardently committed to the principles of the "revolution," cropped up in major cities and townships. The most prolific and influential of these groups by far was the Grupo Cénico das Forças Populares de Libertação Nacional (The Theater Troupe of the Popular Army of National Liberation). Founded in 1973, in Nachingweya, Frelimo's military training camp, by liberation front combatants who are now prominent members of the country's political and financial elite, the group put on various plays criticizing both the colonial order and, in rarer instances, the abuses and excesses of postindependence society. Some of their most famous productions in the 1970s include *Monomopata, Resistência e Vitória Popular, A Sagrada Família*, and *Javali-Javalismo* [Wild Boar-Wild Boarism]; the first play was reportedly banned by the Frelimo régime for presenting too frank a critique of the "new society."

The group dissolved when many of its members left the armed forces and assumed a variety of prominent posts in government and later in the private sector. Most of these plays, only a few of which survive, fell into the category of agitprop style of drama and served to propagate the same nationalist and socialist messages that the state vigorously promoted.[78] At a time that, according to one of Mozambique's chief economists, Mozambique's emerging capitalist class is exercising its control over natural resources (obtained through its stranglehold on the state apparatus) in order to facilitate the largely unregulated penetration of foreign capital and thereby ensure their own unrestrained "primitive accumulation";[79] when most of the country's professed "liberators" have aggressively embraced neoliberalism, while the overwhelming majority of their fellow citizens can hardly eke out a living, in these "strange times"; these texts seem dolefully out of place.

Sagrada Família (Holy Family[80]), for example, a play staged by the Grupo Cénico das Forças Populares in the late 1970s, denounces the efforts by the colonial bourgeoisie and its local "lackeys" to reverse "the achievements of the revolution" in the wake of the nationalization of private housing, schools, hospitals, and farmland.[81] As the following "stage directions" illustrate, the play is especially ruthless with the "puppet managers," whom it portrays as outworn, "black-skinned" replicas of colonial bosses: "Ambrósio has no managing experience and the attitude he assumes had been surpassed long ago by his [white] predecessor. In reality [he] is no more than a puppet manager. And, as with all puppets, his ambition is boundless."[82] The "simple life in which...everyone works to support himself and on behalf of the People...in which nobody exploits our sweat."[83] upheld as the main aspiration of the political leadership by one of the play's young cadres, contrasts starkly with the unproductive capitalism, brazen corruption, and conspicuous consumerism that characterize the "lifestyle" of much of the current elite. The "new era," whose dawn prompts the collapse of "the old Society" and the end of "the bosses' reign," forecast in the epilogue,[84] would ring particularly hollow to a contemporary audience from Mozambique's urban peripheries. It is enough to wonder, in fact, how many of the Grupo Cénico's members now belong to the ranks of the "predatory" elite.[85]

A similar incongruity underpins a play about the Paris Commune (*A Comuna*) that dates from the same period. The script, purportedly the result of a collective effort, evolved out of a series of workshops that joined together national university students and railroad workers. Their principal objective was "to reaffirm international proletarianism," and guide the "people" toward the recognition that their own struggle was structurally linked to revolutionary processes occurring in other countries.[86] The play blends scenes from France's insurrectionary past and Mozambique's revolutionary "present." A Narrator intervenes frequently to establish relevant parallels between the two historical trajectories. At pivotal moments, and in a manner that vaguely recalls Brecht's technique in his own adaptation of the Commune episode (*The Days of the Commune*, 1948–1949), the Narrator draws the audience's attention to the fatal strategic errors committed by the

Communards (and, relatedly, to the fact that Mozambique's liberation fighters shrewdly averted similar mistakes). At the end of the play, following the brutal suppression of the Commune ("In Paris, everything went back to the way it was!"),[87] the Narrator turns to the Audience[88] and asks: "Comrades, will we allow the bourgeoisie and imperialism to do the same with our Revolution?" To the rousing strains of the Internationale,[89] originally the anthem of the Commune, the Audience roars: "No! Never again!"[90]

Needless to say, not only has "the bourgeoisie" returned in full force, but so has a particularly overreaching form of financial "imperialism." As Castel-Branco notes, dependency on foreign aid and investment constitutes a "fundamental characteristic" of Mozambique's economy at the turn of the millennium.[91] In 2007, for instance, 22% of the country's gross national product stemmed directly from development aid, a figure that is five times greater than the average for sub-Saharan nation-states, making Mozambique the 11th most foreign-aid dependent country in the world.[92] As it happens, foreign "donors wield immense and detailed power, and are at the very heart of decision-making and policy formulation, from the conception of issues and options through to writing the final policy. There is a real sovereignty question here: 'to what extent should non-Mozambicans be playing such a central role?' "[93] In this sense, the Commune's tragic flaws turn out to have been peculiarly prophetic. Like Aristotle's *hamartia*, the fatal error appears to have been already inscribed in the text itself. For, as its Introduction elucidates, *A Comuna* was as much the successful culmination of a collective project exemplarily joining proletarians and students as the chronicle of a failure.

However, due to a series of disagreements among the worker and student members of the collective concerning the supposed need to research in depth not only the historical figure of Napoleon III, but concepts such as bureaucracy and dictatorship of the proletariat before the play could be produced, *A Comuna* was never staged. Although the Introduction does not specify it, in the main it appears that the students advocated a stricter adherence to historical accuracy and ideological exactitude, while the workers, if one is to go by one of their testimonials quoted in the text, believed their life experiences provided them with sufficient knowledge to put on the play: "I also had never heard of Napoleon III before I came in here, just today. But that doesn't matter. I got to know very well what oppression was, and that experience will be of help."[94] Yet, the students' "error," which the Introduction's authors acknowledge in hindsight,[95] may in fact have already resided in the very conception of the project.

What precluded the Mozambican representation of the Paris Commune was, in essence, a consequence of the "the paradox of the spectator," as Jacques Rancière defines it, the notion that viewing is the opposite of knowing. From this perspective, the spectator is thought to remain in "a state of ignorance" both about the process of production of the performance or spectacle she or he views and about the reality which that performance or production arguably masks.[96] The students' task, then, was to transform the railroad workers from passive spectators into active participants: "Our first attitude, as [railroad workers], was to present ourselves as being completely ignorant about the Commune and, for that reason, wish to be suitably enlightened in order to begin working. Our first attitude, as [university students], was to assume the role of History teachers, explaining and providing texts about the Commune."[97] In keeping with the Brechtian paradigm that appears to have informed their endeavor, the students sought to compel the railroad workers "to exchange the position of passive spectators for that of scientific investigator or experimenter."[98] Nevertheless, as the dilemma that finally thwarted the staging of the play demonstrates, the logic underpinning their pedagogics essentially remained that of "straight uniform transmission: there is something—a form of knowledge... on one side, and it must pass to the other side. What the pupil must learn is what the schoolmaster must teach her."[99]

The plot of the drama of emancipation, which the student–worker collective set out to produce, had already been etched in graven letters before the first lines of the text were even committed to paper. The emancipatory promise of the Revolution that the group wished to perform had therefore already been foreclosed, subsumed in advance into a preexisting "international" story of liberation. By subscribing to the view that the path to social transformation was reducible to an enforceable program or "line," the students ended up reproducing the logic of radical state power. They thus became, paradoxically and much like the nation-state itself, "the true inheritors of the colonial tradition of rule by decree and rule by proclamation, of subordinating the rule of law to administrative justice so as to transform society from above."[100] By a supreme irony, the legacy of colonial power was reasserting itself at the very moment that the Audience thunderously interdicted its return. The watchword "never again" (*nunca mais*) is consequently turned inside out, signifying, in the last instance, a tragic recurrence of the same. If the perplexity and contradictoriness of Mozambique's recent history could be reduced to the elegant economy of an Attic tragedy, then the September riots would be the peripety induced by the "fatal error" that precluded *A Comuna* from ever being staged.

Acknowledgments

I am grateful to the Fulbright Program for awarding me a grant to conduct research on theater in Mozambique in 2010, and to the Graduate School at the University of Wisconsin, which also provided generous support for my research both in Portugal and Mozambique through a Vilas Associate Award in 2009 and 2010.

Notes

1. Mbembe, "La 'chose' et ses doubles dans la caricature camerounaise," 158.
2. For example, "Mozambicans, get ready to chill [curtir] on the great day of the general strike, September 1, 2010" (qtd in Miguel 64).
3. Lima, "Até à próxima crise em Moçambique," 72.

4. Two railroad freight cars loaded with cement and wheat were also looted.
5. Mostly in private collections, since only two of these texts had been deposited at the national archive. In this regard, I owe an enormous debt of gratitude to Dinis Chembene, Tela Chicane, Dadivo José Combane, Paulo Guambe, João Machado da Graça, Nelson Mabuie, Rogério Manjate, Joaquim Matavel, Gilberto Mendes, Lucrécia Paco, Manuela Soeiro, and António Sopa for their incredible generosity in availing their private collections and materials to me.
6. Unless otherwise noted, all translations from Portuguese and Rhonga are my own.
7. Couto, "As outras nações," 4.
8. Serra, *Em cima duma lâmina*, 19
9. Ibid., 47.
10. Ibid., 56.
11. Article 25 of the Universal Declaration of Human Rights states: "Everyone has the right to a standard of living adequate for the health and well-being of himself and of his family, including food, clothing, housing and medical care and necessary social services, and the right to security in the event of unemployment, sickness, disability, widowhood, old age or other lack of livelihood in circumstances beyond his control."
12. Balandier, *Le pouvoir sur scènes*, 53.
13. Ironically, the social inequality against which the protesters were revolting was the very same one that the Frelimo anthem (which was the national anthem until 1992) promised to overturn: "Unida ao mundo inteiro,/Lutando contra a burguesia,/Nossa Pátria será túmulo/Do capitalismo e exploração." (United with the whole world,/Struggling against the bourgeoisie/Our Fatherland will be the graveyard/Of capitalism and exploitation).
14. Fiebach, "Dimensions of Theatricality in Africa," 25.
15. Nkashama, *Théâtres et scènes de spectacle*, 11.
16. Between 1926 and 1933, the Portuguese regime enacted legislations defining Africans as a separate element of the colonial population, branding them as *indígenas* (natives). Those who learned to speak Portuguese, took commercial or industrial jobs, and conducted themselves as Portuguese citizens, were labeled *assimilados*. The colonial administration stringently applied the conditions for assimilation. According to a 1950 official census, for instance, assimilados represented less than 0.01% of the total population in the colonies. Male indígenas were required to carry identification cards and pay a head tax. If they were unable to raise the tax money, they were compelled to work for the colonial government for up to six months out of each year without wages. This compulsory labor system (*xibalo* in Rhonga) remained in force until 1962. Although the 1951 constitutional amendments officially abolished the distinction between indígenas and assimilados, reclassifying Angola, Mozambique, and Guinea as provinces with the same status as those in metropolitan Portugal and attributing Portuguese citizenship to all their inhabitants, regardless of status, most of its degrading and discriminatory aspects remained firmly in place until independence. In official colonial discourse, the term autóctone (autochthon or aborigine) gradually replaces indígena and becomes the most commonly used term until the end of the colonial period (1974).

17. Fanon, *The Wretched of the Earth*, 3–4.
18. Serra, *Em cima duma lâmina*, 21.
19. According to Luiz Francisco Rebello, the *revista* has its roots in the parodies staged by Italian comic actors in the Paris market theaters of the early eighteenth century (17). Its central aim was the satirical "review" (i.e. "revista") of the past year's most notable events. Its structure usually consists of a series of tableaux combining song, dance, and declamation, linked together by a figure peculiar to the genre, a sort of commentator or narrator called the *compére*.
20. Júnior, Rodrigues. *Para uma cultura moçambicana.* (Ensaio), 222.
21. *Notícias de Lourenço Marques*, September 14, 1967.
22. Cruz, "O Teatro em português," 18.
23. Ibid., 41.
24. Said, *Culture and Imperialism*, 25.
25. Lobato, *Sobre "Cultura Moçambicana,"* 75.
26. The present-day Republic of East Timor.
27. One of the subterfuges commonly utilized by 1930s Portuguese *revistas*, for example, was to press into service the figure Saint Anthony, Lisbon's patron saint, as a sly reference to the dictator, whose first name was António (Oliveira Salazar), and whose supposed abstemious nature was almost proverbial (Santos *A revista* 47).
28. Rebello, *História do Teatro*, 27.
29. Sunday supplement, *Lourenço Marques Guardian*, November 14, 1948.
30. Ibid., December 15, 1948, 1–2.
31. Ibid., April 25, 1949, 5.
32. The name of one of the capital's largest "native" boroughs at the time, where the Centro's headquarters were located. It is still one of the peripheral neighborhoods of Maputo.
33. Sunday supplement, *Lourenço Marques Guardian*, September 9, 1949, 5.
34. The term designates Mozambican migrant workers in South Africa's gold and diamond mines. It is also the title of one of Noémia de Sousa's best-known and more or less contemporaneous poems.
35. The refrain of a Portuguese popular song.
36. The name of a traditional war dance of Zulu origin from the South of Mozambique. It is also the title of one of José Craveirinha's poetic collections.
37. Sunday supplement, *Lourenço Marques Guardian*, September 15, 1949, 5.
38. Rebello, *História do Teatro*, 28.
39. Ibid.
40. Some of Mozambique's most prominent writers during the colonial period (the poet José Craveirinha and short story writer Luís Bernardo Honwana) were active in the Nucleus, which generally opposed the conservative policies of the Centro's leadership. Subsequently, several of the Nucleus's members were arrested and charged with alleged subversive activities, and in 1965, the Centro was ordered closed by colonial authorities. Coincidentally, it is also in the late 1940s (1948) that Mozambique's current president begins attending the primary school located at the Centro. In 2008, President Guebuza inaugurated Maputo's Municipal Cultural Center (N'tsyndza) in the Centro's former site.
41. Fresu and Oliveira, *Pesquisas para um teatro popular em Moçambique*, 22–40.

42. Ibid., 11–49.
43. Nhlongo would go on to write another play, *As 30 Mulheres de Muzeleni*, which deals (similarly) with the dilemmas and contradictions arising both from the traditional practice of polygamy and its displacement by prostitution in a modern context. The play opened to generally favorable reviews in the colonial capital barely a month before the April 25, 1974 Revolution that toppled Portugal's authoritarian regime. After independence, he directed a theater group for a while, producing at least one play, O xibalo acabou (Forced Labor Is Over) in 1980. As the title indicates, O xibalo portrayed the oppression and humiliation of the peasantry during the colonial period, and sought to trace the peasants' gradual attainment of a national consciousness.
44. Nhlongo, *Duas Peças de Teatro*, Back cover.
45. Ibid., 10, 35.
46. Ibid., 10.
47. At the time Sousa had been living in exile in Paris with her husband, a political dissident, since 1964.
48. Nhlongo, *Duas Peças*, 36.
49. Ibid., 7.
50. Ibid., iii–iv.
51. Ibid., v.
52. Ibid., iv.
53. Hamilton, "Portuguese-Language Literature," 269.
54. Ibid.
55. Nhlongo, *Duas Peças*, vii.
56. Ibid.
57. Owen, *Mother Africa, Father Marx*, 61.
58. Ibid., 88.
59. Ibid., 60.
60. Santos, "Between Prospero and Caliban," 34.
61. Couto, *Pensatempos*, 57.
62. Madureira, "Nation, Identity and Loss of Footing," 200–229.
63. Couto, "As outras nações," 58.
64. Hamilton, *Voices from an Empire*, 176–177.
65. Lusophone Scene, or Stage.
66. "O Projecto e a sua concretização," 12. The seven Portuguese-speaking (or "Lusophone") countries, besides Portugal, are: Brazil, Angola, Cape Verde, Guinea-Bissau, São Tomé e Príncipe, and Mozambique. (East Timor, the eighth Portuguese-speaking country, would attain its independence only in May, 2002.)
67. Barros, "Editorial," 3.
68. Reis, "Painel de Opinião." *Setepalcos: Revista do Programa Cena Lusófona*, 20. In 1995, following its first democratic elections of 1994, Mozambique had been admitted into the Commonwealth of Nations. It was the first member without any constitutional links with the British Empire or another Commonwealth nation to join the organization.
69. Sousa. "Painel de Opinião." *Setepalcos: Revista do Programa Cena Lusófona*, 31.
70. As Fernando Cristovão defines it, *lusofonia* functions on three interrelated levels. The more restricted definition refers to the eight nation-states that

gained their independence in the wake of the collapse of the Portuguese Empire, the so-called CPLP, Comunidade de Países de Língua Portuguesa (Community of Portuguese-speaking Countries). This level also encompasses other nations or regions located within other countries and cultures "with whom [Portugal] shares its Language and History," and territories where Portuguese-based creole languages have been or are currently spoken. The second level pertains to the other languages and cultures of Portuguese-speaking nations and regions that "remain in contact through a common language, which, through dialogue and exchanges, promotes and enriches each one of these languages and cultures." To the third and broader level belong individuals and institutions who are not from Portuguese-speaking countries or regions but "maintain a learned and friendly dialogue based on affinity ties and various other interests with the common [Portuguese] language and the cultures of the eight Portuguese-speaking countries and regions" (654–655).

71. Lucas, "Painel de Opinião," *Setepalcos: Revista do Programa Cena Lusófona*, 22.
72. Sousa, "Painel de Opinião," *Setepalcos: Revista do Programa Cena Lusófona*, 30–31.
73. Soeiro, "Painel de Opinião," *Setepalcos: Revista do Programa Cena Lusófona*, 29.
74. Fresu and Oliveira, *Um teatro*, 11.
75. In brief, Quijano's notion establishes colonial difference as the condition of possibility for sustaining and legitimating specific modes of political, economic, and epistemological hegemony. According to Walter Mignolo's iteration of the concept, coloniality of power resides in the capacity to project "European local knowledge and histories" as global designs (from Christocentrism to Hegel's "universal history" and recent ideologies of development) (17).
76. Gusmão, *A Fala da memória*, 185–186.
77. António Quadros (1933–1994), a white painter-poet who worked with Mário Barradas on the scenography of some of TALM's productions, was the protagonist of an episode that sheds a curious light on this continued participation of white artists and intellectuals in the cultural production of the early postindependence years. Under the pseudonym João Pedro Grabato Dias, Quadros cofounded (with the poet Rui Knopfli) the short-lived yet influential literary journal Caliban in 1971, and lived in Mozambique until 1983. In 1975, soon after independence, the Frelimo government published Eu, o Povo: Poemas da Revolução (I, the People: Poems of the Revolution). The collection's author was purportedly a Frelimo guerrilla fighter called Mutimati Barnabé João, who had been killed in action. It turned out, however, that the soldier poet was another of Quadros' pseudonyms.
78. A former playwright and theater director, currently a Ministry of Education official (Luís Savel) assured me that the Frelimo government never imposed any kind of censorship, and that the playwrights composed their proregime messages of their own free will, without any sort of official pressure or coercion.
79. Castel-Branco, "Economia extractiva," 77–78.
80. The allusion to Marx and Engels' famous text is of course intended.
81. Grupo, *Cénico, Sagrada Família*, 4.

82. Ibid., 38.
83. Ibid., 20.
84. Ibid., 51.
85. Rumor has it that President Armando Guebuza was once an actor in the troupe. The term "predatory state" was coined by Peter Evans to define a political and economic dispensation in which "those who control the state apparatus seem to plunder without any more regard for the welfare of the citizenry" (qtd. in Hanlon and Smart 107).
86. Colectivo de Trabalho Trabalhadores dos Caminhos de Ferro de Moçambique e Estudantes da Universidade Eduado Mondlane, *A Comuna*, 8.
87. Brecht, *Os Dias da Comuna*, 90.
88. The Audience (Plateia) is one of the play's dramatis personae and appears as the Narrator's recurrent interlocutor in the play.
89. This was a common, perhaps obligatory, finale to dramatic performances in the period.
90. Brecht, *Os Dias da Comuna*, 90.
91. Castel-Branco, "Economia extractiva," 64.
92. Ibid., 69.
93. Hanlon and Smart, *Do Bicycles Equal Development in Mozambique?*, 131.
94. Colectivo de Trabalho, *A Comuna*, 12.
95. Ibid., 13.
96. Rancière, *The Emancipated Spectator*, 2.
97. Colectivo de Trabalho, *A Comuna*, 10.
98. Rancière, *The Emancipated Spectator*, 4.
99. Ibid., 14.
100. Mandani, *Citizens and Subjects*, 135.

Chapter 3

The ESMA: From Torture Chambers into New Sites of Memory

Paola S. Hernández

> *I can take an empty space and call it a bare stage. A man walks across this empty space whilst someone else is watching him, and this is all that is needed for an act of theatre to be engaged.*[1]
>
> Peter Brook

The twenty-first-century has brought a new era of commemoration to Latin America, where totalitarian governments maneuvered numerous disappearances, violent acts, tortures, and denial of basic human rights, during the latter half of the twentieth century.[2] Within traumatic memory studies, historical narratives are part of the search for answers to these actions in the past perceived from the present. The expression of these narrative memories takes place through commemorations and museums of memory as well as through embodiment, in both the performative and the architectural sense. For Pierre Nora, the era of commemoration reflects the prevalence of *lieux de mémoire:* "hybrid places, mutants, compounded of life and death, of the temporal and the eternal,"[3] a lieu in which commemorations and museums are "part of the every day experience."[4] For him, these *lieux de mémoire* become part of an archive "if imagination invests it with a symbolic aura."[5] For Nora, "*lieux de mémoire* thrive only because of their capacity for change, their ability to resurrect old meanings and generate new ones."[6] While his argument is compelling, I suggest, following Diana Taylor, that Nora expands a binary between history and memory, or *lieux de mémoire* and *mileux de mémoire*, which are "the real environments of memory." This opposition can become problematic since it reproduces the hierarchy between the archival hegemonic place (*lieux*) and the non-archival, antihegemonic practices (*mileux*).[7] My interest in Nora stems from the intent to remember, the search to make memory the center of what a place can signify, but instead of emphasizing the need for an archival existence, my focus takes a more performative lens, and thus expands the idea of what a place can represent through commemorative acts.

This chapter analyzes the reconstruction of the Escuela Superior de Mecánica de la Armada (ESMA), the Navy School of Mechanics, a past torture chamber turned into a new "Museum of Memory" in Buenos Aires, Argentina. Following Mieke Bal's assertion that "reenactments of traumatic experience take the form of drama, not narrative, and are dependent on the time frame of the 'parts' scripted in the drama,"[8] I see the ESMA as a space that embodies memory in order to deal with the recent traumatic past of the last dictatorship (1976–1983). Within museum studies, Carol Duncan has also taken a fresh look at how art museums can be read as a "script" and a "dramatic field" where they become a "stage setting that prompts visitors to enact a performance of some kind."[9] Museums of memory rely on a dramatic approach in order to help interpret the past. However, I would like to suggest that the ESMA, now known as the ex-ESMA, reconfigures the notion of "museum" to create a more dynamic relationship between space, history, and memory under the word "site" or "spaces for memory." As Susana Draper argues, in order to understand the new topology of memory created by these new commemorative spaces, such as the ESMA, we need to think about these new "places as topos."[10] Thus, I see memory museums not just as a static form of representation, but also as interactive memory sites enabling the visitor to participate and collaborate in the vast undertaking of collective remembrance, inviting creative contributions; in other words, as a space that performs memory. According to Guillermina Walas, this new site invites a variety of practices, some based on testimonies, and others on embodied practices that invite visitors to walk less through a morbid past, and more into a new site of understanding the past.[11] I would also argue that this site blurs the boundaries between place and practice, between archive and repertoire, since scant wall texts require live guides to perform as actors in an empty, or mostly empty space.

This new site of memory, though on the outskirts of the urban center, has a close relationship with the city of Buenos Aires. Specifically, the center of Buenos Aires has led the way in creating spaces in which to perform cultural memory, and, on key occasions, denouncing human rights violations. For instance, consider the ritualistic walk of the Mothers of Plaza de Mayo whose search for their missing children began in 1977, as they quietly carried pictures of their children with questions such as "¿dónde están?" (where are they?). Today they are still demanding answers. Contemporary groups such as H.I.J.O.S. (Hijos por la Identidad y la Justicia contra el Olvido y el Silencio—Children for Identity and Justice against Forgetting and Silence) have also been able to bring to the public eye performances called "escraches" in which they publicize incriminating information about former torturers and other repressors, and expose their present whereabouts by revealing current home addresses and places of employment in a theatrical way. Another creative performance can be seen in the work of the GAC (Grupo de Arte Callejero), a street art performance group, which has appropriated public space as their own stage, constructing their own props of silhouettes of the disappeared around many different buildings in the city.[12] Elizabeth Jelin has aptly commented that personal memories of torture and imprisonment bring the body to the foreground and make it the center of attention.[13] From a performance point of view, these groups together with the Mothers of Plaza de Mayo have embodied memories through their walks, silhouettes, or escraches, and have created a moveable, visible, and political public stage to deal with a silenced and, many times, forgotten, past.

Since 1977, the Mothers of Plaza de Mayo have carried large photographs demanding to know the whereabouts of their loved ones. Their weekly marches around the plaza publicized the message of disappearance, turning it into an embodied practice of memory at a time when any public action was under intense scrutiny. Besides putting their lives at risk, their involvement turned the public's attention to the main square in order to make visible what had been kept a secret, turning the plaza into a central stage to denounce human rights violations. At a time when an estimated 520 clandestine detention centers around Argentina were used as torture chambers and extermination camps during the "Dirty War," the Mothers' walk was a public ritual structured so as to demand the right to know the fate of their children. Among these infamous centers, the ESMA requires special and critical attention for a number of reasons. Most importantly, this center facilitated the highest number of tortures, assassinations, and disappearances between 1976 and 1983.[14] This information became public in 1995 when retired Navy Captain Adolfo Scilingo, who had been an officer at the ESMA, publicly confessed to participating in the weekly "death flights," during which at least 2,000 of the prisoners from the ESMA were thrown alive from an airplane into the Río de la Plata.[15] Similarly, this place has a haunting and ubiquitous presence since it had a double function: a school for future generations of Marines and the largest clandestine center in Argentina. Lastly, the physical location of the ESMA and its beautiful architecture are impressive for its grandeur—about 42 acres in a very prestigious part of Buenos Aires—and for the fact that even though the ESMA is a large campus and is surrounded by two major and heavily transited streets, few residents could have ever imagined that the most extensive apparatus of disappearance and torture existed in such a visible area.

At the intersection between memory and museums lies the question of how history is retold to present and future generations. Andreas Huyssen asks, "What good is the memory archive? How can it deliver what history alone no longer seems to be able to offer?"[16] This memory framework has made it possible for old clandestine concentration camps to become public and specific spaces for archival information. But how does a museum of memory deal with personal and collective memories of a traumatic past? If we consider, as Susan Crane writes that "the museum stores memories" just like an "archive" and thus, becomes a "metaphor" for how collective memory operates,[17] the new site of memory at the ex-ESMA can be seen as a new approach to dealing with memories that have been silenced and obscured for many years.[18] The ex-ESMA generates, in Stanley Cohen's words, a "memory war" where there are those who want to suppress the past while there are others trying to renounce and break through silence and amnesia.[19] But it is more complicated than simply a conflict between suppression and disclosure; there is also a conflict about how to go about disclosing and remembering the past. Researching the ESMA and its future status as a memory site reveals the presence of different human rights groups that have opposing ideas on how to archive memory and history, and how to perform these many different memories to a broad range of audiences who might already have a predetermined idea.[20] Maurice Halbwachs claims that all individual memories "keep contact with the collective memory"[21] and that "the mind reconstructs its memories under the pressure of society."[22] How, then, can an ex-torture center serve as a space for the performance of traumatic personal and collective memories to the Argentine society that lived through this era? How can a society use a site of memory to convey a torturous past and portray different stories of trauma? How will the ex-ESMA perform history and traumatic memories and who are the individuals that will comprise its audience?

I would like to address these issues by analyzing distinct yet connected themes. Since the ESMA's *raison d'etre* was a school for the Navy, its use as a torture center, and its present-day function call for a reconsideration of its original design. Thus, I intend to look at the specific case of the reconstruction of the ESMA as a new space that encompasses many levels of history from its inception to the new memory site. This will entail understanding how memory, trauma, and history interconnect and how these memories can evoke new meanings for younger generations. Since the ESMA was an actual torture chamber, this site of memory will have a tremendous impact on how to relate to its audience the narratives of the victims. The site serves as an archival space since it houses different human rights organizations; yet, in this case, it is a space where there is still a need to understand traumatic memories and national history. Important to notice is that for the first time in Buenos Aires an archive of cultural memory will be housed in a place where atrocities were committed. In this sense, the ex-ESMA will have to perform as a highly regarded archival space, as well as an ex-torture chamber that unveils its most treacherous past where testimonial evidence will take center stage. Considering the significance of the new status of the ex-ESMA as a memory site, artists and activists have already started to use the space, where new modes of expression about the *desaparecidos*, their absence, and their lives will be portrayed. For instance, there are now a variety of buildings within the perimeter of the ex-ESMA that have been assigned to different organizations directed by human rights activists including the Mothers of Plaza de Mayo. One such building has been reconstructed as the ECuNHi (Espacio Cultural "Nuestros Hijos" Cultural Space "Our Children") run by Teresa Parodi and overseen by the Mothers as an artistic and cultural space for workshops, music recitals, and theater, all with the goal of keeping memory alive.[23] However, within the campus, two buildings stand out. The main building named "Cuatro columnas" (Four columns) for its Greek-like façade carries the emblem on its façade as the symbol of what ESMA once was and for what the new museum will be. The other one, the Casino de oficiales (Officers' Center) is an empty space that exposes where victims were kept, tortured, and finally taken to their final destination. In this building, testimony of survivors has become the connecting thread, the memory that helped build the informational signs that fill in the empty space that it is today. Survivors' testimony has been a fundamental part of the reconstruction of the memory site, while simultaneously giving the ex-ESMA the role of educator for future generations of past atrocities.[24] Throughout these two buildings and other parts of the campus, signs with fragments of victims' testimonies help fill in the empty space, giving visitors a chance to read and understand how different spaces functioned at the ESMA. Some are very concrete and explain how detainees were drugged and taken to the "final destination" by truck. Others are more personal and explain what it was like to live here. [25]

Historical Background of the ESMA

In 1924, the government of the city of Buenos Aires granted 42 acres to the Marines with the sole purpose of establishing a military school. Within this contract, a clause stipulated that in the event that the space was to be used for something else besides education, everything—the space and whatever was constructed on it—would be returned to its owner: the city of Buenos Aires. During the dictatorship, the ESMA was a school on the outside and a killing machine on the inside, yet it also functioned as a clandestine maternity ward for imprisoned women, and as one of the central administrative points for the Army, using its inmates as slave laborers. It is estimated that 5,000 people went through the ESMA: most of them remain disappeared and over 200 children were born in ESMA's clandestine maternity wards and illegally adopted. Many of these children still live without knowing their true identity.[26] The ESMA is a compound campus with an array of buildings that were used for different aims, such as classrooms, labs, exercise rooms, bedrooms, and the usual central space for official gatherings, parties, and more exclusive living dormitories called the casino for the higher-end officials. Even though the majority of the imprisoned were taken to the casino, a building that kept torture hidden, it is easy to imagine that the whole campus, teachers and students, inevitably got to know about it and even had to take part in this arrangement. Inside the ESMA, the prisoners were constantly moved from the upstairs attic to the basement where the tortures occurred. In order to be transferred from one side to the other, prisoners walked the same stairs the officers used to go up and down to their bedrooms, chapel, and the casino. Sharing a common space—one that served both the victim and the victimizer—has made the ESMA a unique and disturbing clandestine center. Of special interest is the casino, where in the lower levels of the building, the officers of the Army would live—some with their own family—while two floors above in the two attics, called the Capucha (hood) and the Capuchita (little hood), thousands of people were imprisoned over the years. A makeshift chapel built on the second floor close to the staircase also shared this common space. Since much of the Catholic Church viewed the military operations as a "just war," a number of priests relied on ritualistic confessions as a way to gather information from victims and pass it on to the military.[27] Cloaked as a Catholic ritual, this chapel served as yet another stage to perform an ambiguous act of being saved and getting tortured and/or killed, proof again of yet another juxtaposition to torture in the ESMA.

In the morning of March 24, 2004, the anniversary of the *coup d'etat*, President Néstor Kirchner, in a highly contested political role, theatrically and ritualistically removed the portraits of ex-dictators Reynaldo Bignone and Jorge Rafael Videla from the walls of the Patio de Honor, Colegio Militar (Military school). This symbolic transition was later celebrated with live music, commemorative speeches from survivors, Mothers of Plaza de Mayo, and even children born in the ESMA. This highly publicized event inaugurated the transition of the ESMA into the new Site of Memory. The official act ended with the signing of the official documents that turned the ex-torture center into a Site of Memory. For William Acree, "the performances of the day highlighted the nation at large as a victim of military rule and a group of citizens facing the opportunity to engage in a critical dialogue with the past to uncover the truth."[28] But while this was a new beginning for human rights, this theatrical act created controversy, and other human rights activists saw Kirchner's act of naming himself and his government the sole bearers of human rights while neglecting to mention any of the work done by President Raúl Alfonsín or by any others as "political egotism."[29] From its inception, the political debates made the ESMA a contested site exposing the fragile nature of memory, trauma, history, and the role that politics plays in commemoration. Almost four years later, on January 31, 2008, the Mothers and Grandmothers of Plaza de Mayo moved into the ex-ESMA, and quickly started to rename some of the streets of the campus, and a few buildings, such as the ECuNHi.[30]

Memory Discourses

The ex-ESMA solidly exemplifies how representations of traumatic memories have taken public center stage in Argentina. However, in today's reshaping of urban spaces and archival museums, it is impossible to avoid the "constitutive tension between past and present" that can create confrontations regarding how and what to "represent."[31] The term "traumatic memory," coined by Pierre Janet, a contemporary of Freud, states that trauma is induced by the disintegration of a person's capacity to synthesize information of the past turning these persons into fragmented beings.³² In their introduction to *Tense Past: Cultural Essays in Trauma and Memory*, Paul Antze and Michael Lambek astutely remark, "Personal memory is always connected to social narrative as is social memory to the personal. The self and the community are the imagined products of a continuous process."³³ In the specific case of a country's traumatic past, both the personal and the collective come together to intertwine their histories, their memories, and their traumas. It is through this "working through" together that a community can attest to the restoration and renovation of an ex-torture center and convert it into an interactive memory space. Andreas Huyssen has stated that in order to shape our collective imaginaries, we have to "read cities and buildings as palimpsests of space."³⁴ While the tension between who and what can be expressed in a collective "working through" of trauma, it is in Huyssen's layering of memory that the idea of space comes to light. If we consider Peter Brook's theatrical eye where a space turns itself into a theatrical stage, we can also see how this memory site calls for spectatorship. Museums, and particularly, museums of memory, call for active participants where we are asked to "change from spectator/bystander to witness, where we are asked to make our specific memory into historical memory."³⁵ In other words, the "working through" of trauma becomes a collective, live action in a site-specific space such as the ex-ESMA.

When speaking of traumatic memories, there is a need to understand that both the act of embodying the search for the disappeared and the actual political space where it is performed offer ways of working through trauma and addressing absence. Following Huyssen's idea that trauma needs to be articulated in order to become memory, S. J. Brison contends that all traumatic memories go beyond the need to be represented; they need a connection to the body, "blurring the Cartesian mind-body distinction."³⁶ However, she also points out that in order to make traumatic memories emerge, or work through trauma, there is a need for narrative to "reexternalize the traumatic events."³⁷ Thus, the idea of this working through traumatic events calls for a performative lens. Dori Laub has stated, "bearing witness to trauma is, in fact, a process that includes the listener."³⁸ He also observes how "testimonies are not monologues"³⁹ and require an audience who will listen. The need for an audience also resonates with Brison's own idea that "saying something about a traumatic memory does something to it."⁴⁰ Understanding traumatic memory this way calls attention not just to the survivor, but also to an audience that will hear or see its various representations.

Paul Ricoeur has declared that societies live with "the duty of memory."⁴¹ There is a duty to remember and "memory functions like an attempted exorcism in a historical situation."⁴² In other words, to archive memory demands a space to gather historical facts and to keep them from vanishing from private and collective memories. However, memory studies, especially those of traumatic times, are complex and ambiguous. They are regulated by memory and forgetting simultaneously, creating a difficult field of study. In her expansive studies, Elizabeth Jelin has stated that in order to understand the complexities of how a society remembers, there are "layers of memory" that encompass traumatic pasts both at the private and at the public level.⁴³ While Jelin thinks of the perception of memory as layers, Hirsch focuses on postmemory and underscores the relationship between past trauma and newer generations who have not experienced the same traumatic events but feel deeply influenced by them.⁴⁴ Postmemory, then, articulates itself through the photographs, which are the "enduring umbilical connection to life...connecting first- and second-generation remembrance."⁴⁵ Her approach to memory studies through the lens of a second generation emphasizes the need to "re-member, to re-build, to re-incarnate, to replace, and to repair."⁴⁶ In other words, the connecting thread between presence-memory and absence/forgetfulness brings to the foreground the actual gap of postmemory and the crucial role photography represents.

The ex-ESMA has many layers of memory to represent. In part it is a building that haunts society with a torturous past, but it is also the museum of "live representations" and public manifestations, while on the legal level it is the center of attention of the latest trials brought against 19 of the ex-repressors of the ESMA. While photographs and testimony will undoubtedly serve as the "umbilical cord of second-generation remembrance," traumatic memories will have to deal with the obscure past while still unveiling the present through the ongoing justice system. After the many years of silence and the so-called "reconciliation," the secrets of this place may not all have come to light. Thirty years after the dictatorship, some ex-repressors are admitting the crimes they committed against human rights, while many others will never speak.⁴⁷

Performative Space

On a cold, June day in 2007, a workgroup of the VI Hemispheric Institute for Performance and Politics at the "Encuentro," directed by Diana Taylor and Marianne Hirsch with the assistance of Brigitte Sion, took a tour of the ex-ESMA. At the time, the place had not officially opened, and only a few groups of people were allowed to take walks inside. Moreover, at the time of our visit, the campus was still housing part of the military and there were many restricted areas where we could not enter. During this walk, it became evident that the ex-ESMA is a complicated and hybrid space. With its monstrous past and its new façade as a memory museum, the space itself becomes, in Richard Schechner's words; a space that encompasses performativity.⁴⁸ The ESMA is liminal and performative since it breaks the defining lines between an old Army school, a space of torture, and now a new site that needs to perform a palimpsest of memories: individual, collective, national, historical, archival, and live performances through centers, such as the ECuNHi and the Cultural Center Haroldo Conti. The objective behind this new space of memory can be found in what Diana Taylor has identified as the "relationship between embodied performance and the production of knowledge"⁴⁹ or, in other words, the differentiation between written and oral histories and archives. For instance, the National Memory Archives will be housed in the building in which the old "Naval War School" stood, and the UNESCO will also be part of the ESMA campus, where they will create an international institute for human rights. However, it is also through the "repertoire," of embodied practices (dances, singing, theater) that the participants and the visitors of the ex-ESMA will be able to produce knowledge and be part of the transmission.[50] Consequently, this site becomes a center stage where both the discursive and the performative systems will unite in creating a space for the archival as well as the creative side of the repertoire. These can be seen through the different cultural centers that the ex-ESMA will house. Indeed, the last Cultural Center Haroldo Conti, named in commemoration to the Argentine writer who disappeared, opened in March 2010 (see figure 3.1).

The ex-ESMA becomes a place where this interdependence of power and knowledge will be exposed, negotiated, and criticized. Unlike some other museums of genocide such as the Holocaust Museum in Washington DC, Buenos Aires is faced with a space that does not need to re-create the stage, since the space itself is still there: it was the center stage for torturing and disappearing. For Vivian Patraka, the Holocaust museum "is also a performance site in the sense that its architect, designers, and management produce representations through objects and so produce a space, a subjectivity for the spectator."[51] The museum needs to *represent* the past, the memories, and the voices of those who are still disappeared in a theatrical sense. As Patraka notes, the Holocaust Museum in DC produces an artificial setting to recreate in its architecture and design a site-specific approach to history. Designers

Figure 3.1 "ESMA: Four Columns Building." Photo by Paola S. Hernández

went even as far as to create a smell of decay throughout the space, in order to "overwhelm the visitor, creating a heady awareness of the magnitude of the terror."[52] In contrast, the ex-ESMA embodies and represents the actual space of terror through real stimuli in a site-specific place, striking dissonance with the emptiness in the building. When walking around the campus, it is easy to perceive that even though the space represents the actual site of memory, the lack of furniture, except some windows, light, and water fixtures, represents the absence and the erosion of the events that happened there. The military ransacked the place before it departed, leaving gaping holes in the walls and emptying it of any connection to objects used during tortures. Despite these strategies to perpetrate forgetfulness, the ex-ESMA still embodies the hybridity of presence and absence by making of this place a site of memory, and a place for different human rights organizations to come together.

Representing the ex-ESMA as a memory site also entails the need for performance in a more theatrical sense. As Vivian Patraka underscores the theatricality and performativity involved in a museum of memory, stating that "in a museum of the dead, the critical actors are gone, and it is up to us to perform acts of reinterpretation to make meaning and memory."[53] When walking around the casino, now an empty space, we were faced with the cold frame of the building. For the most part, walls are peeling and stained, there are substantial water leaks from the roof, and a strong smell of dampness permeates the space and surrounds the visitor. In order to *represent* this space as the stage of what it once was, signs portraying fragments of testimony from survivors have been placed around different parts of the campus. However, there is still the need for guides to help connect the signs to the space and eventually to recent history. In order to fill in the gaps left by this narrative vacuum and give visitors a performative narrative of what we could not have otherwise known or understood, the guides tried their best to answer questions, thus the blurring of the archive and the repertoire.[54] For example, the guides pointed out a simple indentation on one of the inner campus streets. An otherwise overlooked mark, this indentation came to life when we were told that in that place there used to be a security chain that controlled cars that were coming in and out of the Casino carrying prisoners. Together with the sign next to the indentation the guides' testimony helped construct an understanding about the trafficking of prisoners in and out of the ESMA.

The performativity of the ex-ESMA lies within a theatrical structure involving stage, text, actors, and audience, while at the same time creating a hybridity between the real stimuli (smells, testimonies, architecture), their interpretation between the past and the present. For the ESMA today, the stage begins outside, in front of the iron gates that protect the campus. Attached to these gates are different silhouettes that represent the disappeared. All of these images are sculpted in cast-iron with copper-brown color accompanied by violent or sad expressions, such as yelling or crying. The most poignant is that of a pregnant woman looking lost while holding on to her belly. Similar to those silhouettes done by GAC and others, these figures haunt us with the dichotomy absence/presence of those who disappeared.

Figure 3.2 "ESMA: Iron Gates." Photo by Paola S. Hernández

From the beginning, the ESMA unsettles the audience with repeated images that represent absence through presence and presence through absence. If the silhouette serves as a metaphor for disappearance by highlighting its empty center, then perhaps the imposing architecture of the ESMA serves as an outline of the empty spaces at its center that conjures up the presence of those who are now absent (see figure 3.2).

While this image is powerful and does serve the purpose of making the audience aware of what this new Site of Memory will entail, it is through the signs and banners that the audience first actively participates in transforming the ESMA into a theatrical stage. Walking through this space instructs visitors not just to walk and understand but also to participate in this museum with questions about what actually happened. The main building with its four Greek-like columns that support the ESMA emblem on the front of its façade, illustrates this point. Besides having an impact on those who visit the ESMA or even those who just see this building from the outside of the iron gates, the emblem alters the meaning of ESMA from "Escuela Mecánica de la Armada—The Navy School of Mechanics" to "Espacio para la Memoria y para la Promoción y Defensa de los Derechos Humanos—Space for Memory and the Promotion and Defense of Human Rights." In turn, this transformative and suggestive emblem represents the new ESMA: while confronting the traumatic memory of a national past, it suggests that a new linguistic configuration as well as a new place where human rights will be promoted.[55]

As a site-specific Site of Memory, the ex-ESMA does not need to recreate a stage by injecting artificial sounds, smells, or images. However, an interesting theatrical event in the ESMA took place during its worst years under dictatorship. In 1979, due to the testimonies of some survivors exiled in Europe, the place was denounced as a torture concentration camp. Guided by their statements, the Inter-American Commission on Human Rights visited the building to find out if indeed the ESMA was a concentration camp. However, before the Commission ever reached it, information about the visit was leaked. The ESMA, then, was given a face-lift and many changes were added, doors were shut off, walls were built, and elevators were taken out. The goal was to contradict the survivors' narratives and prove to the Commission that the ESMA was, after all, a school for the Navy. Since it continued to operate both as a torture center and as a school, the remodeling directed the members of the Inter-American Commission on Human Rights to see only the types of performances that the armed forces wanted them to see and hid the less palatable performances operated as a school for the Navy. The carefully crafted reconstruction gave Human Rights Commission visitors the visual deception that the ESMA was indeed a school for the Navy. Ultimately, the military's new props and stage succeeded in fooling the Commission and the unsavory performance of reconstructing and hiding spaces went on until the end. It might be incomprehensible to think that the Human Rights Commission did not see that the ESMA was a theatrical stage; however, according to Stanley Cohen, "literal denial is more credible to foreign audiences: the sources of information are unknown; patron states are willing to look the other way; things are too complicated to understand."[56] This reconstruction is another example of a successful use of the "double message" that the junta patented to deny that Argentina had any political prisoners. Further, he writes, the "phenomenon of disappearances takes its very definition from the government's ability to deny that it happened. The victim has no legal corpus or physical body."[57] In this case, the lack of visual architectural evidence made this recreated stage a successful narrative in the hands of the military that had the power to change the mimetic space in order to represent their own political theater.

Conclusion

The highly performative day of March 24, 2004, when President Kirchner presented the ESMA as a new Site of Memory, prompted the drafting of a new legal document in which the old Navy School of Mechanics was repossessed by the city in order to have a new direction. Human rights organizations and ESMA survivors were named for the main committees (IEM—Instituto Espacio para la Memoria—Institute Space for Memory) whose voices, opinions, and testimonies would be the foundational beginning of the new design of the museum. The new life of the site emphasizes the value of memory and justice as well as the promotion of human rights. The main objective of the committees is to transmit knowledge to newer generations while preserving memory and searching for the truth. Representing the ESMA calls for a collective endeavor, one that searches for many different voices that will be willing to participate in order to activate human rights and invite society to take part in their political and cultural rights.

While the Mothers of Plaza de Mayo, the ECuNHI, and the Cultural Center Haroldo Conti have integrated new workshops geared toward education, artistic expression, and conferences on memory, the casino still stands as the sole and empty representative of the past. This space will remain empty, only inhabited by a few signs bearing survivors' testimony. The few signs that open up the space for testimony enforce memory, while at the same time their short fragments encompass the horror of what once occurred within those walls. The "Four columns" building will house a permanent exhibit with historical narrative and chronological facts. This place, as Guillermo Parodi suggested, "has an unforgettable history marked on its walls."[58] And even though the ESMA sits at the periphery of the downtown of Buenos Aires, it is the "place" that will call people to the outskirts of the city to commemorate the past. Indeed, this site has been a center for political speeches, activism, and artistic outlets since the transition in March 2004.[59] Following a tradition that started in 2004, the ex-ESMA has become a center stage similar to the Plaza de Mayo where issues of memory, truth, and justice call for collective encounters. However, as a central symbolic stage of memory, the ex-ESMA has also been highly politicized and criticized. Some critics fairly argue that this new Museum of Memory has given the current government an opportunity to promote their own agenda, while appropriating human rights as their own political slogan. They see the current government as "actors" who play the role of human rights advocates and this new Site of Memory as their new stage. While critics contest their viewpoints on ownership and the rights of those groups in charge of reconfiguring the ex-ESMA, the question of audience still remains unclear. It seems that as a political stage this site has become the current government's symbolic success, but as a Site of Memory and as an advocate for human rights, it is still uncertain how the different layers of memory will reach a wide variety of audiences at the local, national, and international level.

Notes

1. Brook, *The Empty Space*, 9.
2. I would like to thank Guillermina Wallas, Ana Elena Puga, and Brenda Werth for their insightful comments on this chapter.
3. Nora, *Realms of Memory*, 15.
4. Ibid., 20.
5. Ibid., 14.
6. Ibid., 15.
7. Taylor, *The Archive and the Repertoire*, 21–22.
8. Bal, *Acts of Memory*, ix.
9. Duncan, *Civilizing Rituals*, 1–2.
10. Draper, "The Business of Memory," 146.
11. Walas, "Alternativas testimoniales," 899.

12. For an in-depth analysis of H.I.J.O.S. and their work with escraches, read Diana Taylor's "YOU ARE HERE: H.I.J.O.S. and the DNA of Performance" in *The Archive and the Repetoire*.
13. Jelin, *Los trabajos de la memoria*, 113.
14. The ESMA was one of the largest clandestine detention centers: an estimated 5,000 detainees were tortured and were kept captive until their final destination was decided, which meant either death or freedom under strict surveillance. For more information on these centers, read the report *Nunca más* by CONADEP in 1984 (the Argentine National Commission on the Disappeared).
15. For more information on Adolfo Scilingo and the "Scilingo effect," see Marguerite Feitlowitz, *A Lexicon of Terror*, Chapter 6 "The Scilingo Effect."
16. Huyssen, *Present Pasts*, 6.
17. Crane, *Museums and Memory*, 5.
18. Subsequent democratic laws designed first by President Raúl Alfonsín, such as the Law of Due Obedience (1986), exonerated the majority of the military involved in human rights violations because they were under military law to follow orders. The General Pardons given by President Carlos Saúl Menem in 1989 and 1990 to all military personnel involved in the "Dirty War" and presented as "a definitive closure of past wounds" also created silence and memory gaps for the victims and their families, who were searching for answers about what had happened (Guglielmucci, "La objetivación de las memorias públicas sobre la última dictadura militar argentina (1976–1983): El 24 de marzo en el ex centro clandestino de detención ESMA," 248).
19. Cohen, *States of Denial*, 241.
20. A good source for the various points of view on the ESMA as a museum debate can be found in Marcelo Brodsky's *Memoria en construcción: el debate sobre la ESMA*. Excerpts from this book can be found on its website: http://www.lamarcaeditora.com/memoriaenconstruccion/pensamientoymemoria.htm.
21. Halbwachs, *The Collective Memory*, 43.
22. Ibid., 51.
23. For more information on the educational goals of ECuNHi and the Mothers of Plaza de Mayo, visit (http://www.nuestroshijos.org.ar).
24. Another example of creating a site of memory is the Parque de la Memoria, which opened in 2007 as a memorial to the disappeared. The park is located not far from the ESMA on the banks of the River Plate, into which many suspected "subversives" were thrown during the notorious "death flights." According to its website, the park "does not pretend to heal wounds or to act as a replacement for truth and justice, but aims to serve as testimony of and homage to those lives eradicated by a State that violated the most elemental rights." (http://www.parquedelamemoria.org.ar).
25. There are various testimonies by different survivors. I summarized those of Sara Osatinsky, Ana María Martí, and María Alicia Pirles, who were detained at the ESMA in 1979. For more detailed information on testimonies, see Munú Actis et al. *Ese infierno*.
26. Especially interesting work on this subject has been produced by teatroxlaidentidad ("theater for identity"), a collective of artists and members of the Grandmothers of Plaza de Mayo who, since 2000, have created and performed plays in order to ask the younger generation "¿y, vos, sabés quién sos?" ("And you, do you know who you are?"). The collective uses theater as a tool to

find the missing children of disappeared parents. For more information, visit http://www.teatroxlaidentidad.net.
27. Osiel, "The Mental State of Torturers," 132.
28. Acree, "The Trial of Theatre," 55.
29. Prominent cultural and lilterary critic Beatriz Sarlo has been very critical of the weight of political gains with human rights activism, especially the close involvement of Estela de Carlotto, one of the main Mothers of Plaza de Mayo in the current government. She sees this peculiar relationship as a dangerous liaison since she believes that the Mothers defend human rights that surpass any government and should be a public domain, not a political one. For more information, read "La pesadilla circular" or "¿Son los Kirchner los dueños de los derechos humanos?" by Luis Majul, both in lanacion.com.
30. Aizpeolea, "Las Madres de Plaza de Mayo." *Clarín* Feb 1, 2008.
31. Huyssen, *Present Pasts*, 10.
32. Kenny, "Trauma, Time, Illness and Culture," 153.
33. Antze and Lambek, "Introduction," xx.
34. Huyssen, *Present Pasts*, 7.
35. Patraka, *Spectacular Suffering*, 122.
36. Brison, *Aftermath*, 42.
37. Ibid., 46.
38. Laub, *Testimony: Crises of Witnessing in Literature, Psychoanalysis, and History*, 70.
39. Ibid., 70.
40. Brison, *Aftermath*, 48.
41. Ricoeur, *Memory, History, Forgetting*, 90. For a study of Ricoeur's concept of duty as applied to Southern Cone theater under dictatorship, see Puga, *Memory, Allegory, and Testsimony in South American Theatre*.
42. Ibid.
43. Jelin, "The Minefields of Memory," 24.
44. Hirsch, *Family Frames*, 22.
45. Ibid., 23.
46. Ibid., 243.
47. On December 11, 2009, the trial against human rights violators of the ESMA began. Some of the most notorious ESMA repressors are now on trial, such as Jorge Acosta (known as the "Tiger") and Alfredo Astiz (the "Actor" who infiltrated the Mothers of Plaza de Mayo in order to get information and later kidnap their founders). For more information, see "Tenso inicio del juicio por la ESMA," in lanacion.com.
48. Schechner, *Performance Studies: An Introduction*, 110.
49. Taylor, *The Archive and the Repertoire*, xix.
50. Ibid., 20.
51. Patraka, *Spectacular Suffering*, 122.
52. Casey, "Staging Memory," 84.
53. Patraka, *Spectacular Suffering*, 122.
54. I am borrowing the term "narrative vacuum" from Ernest van Alphen's essay "Symptoms of Discursivity: Experience, Memory, and Trauma," in Bal, *Acts of Memory*.
55. It is worth noting that in 1998, President Menem had signed a Presidential Decree to demolish the ESMA, in order to turn the place "into a symbol of national unity." In point of fact, the valuable land was to be sold to

new construction companies for the creation of a condominium complex (Guglielmucci, "La objetivación de las memorias públicas," 246). Human Rights groups quickly blocked the legislation to preserve the space for a future museum of memory.
56. Cohen, *States of Denial*, 105.
57. Ibid.
58. "Un espacio que conmociona," lanacion.com, November 4, 2009. http://www.lanacion.com.ar/nota.asp?nota_id=1193995.html.
59. For instance, on March 24, 2010, then president Cristina Kirchner, commemorated 34 years of the *coup d'etat* by giving a speech at the ESMA in front of the recently finished Haroldo Conti Cultural Center.

CHAPTER 4

SURPASSING METAPHORS OF VIOLENCE
IN POSTDICTATORIAL SOUTHERN CONE
THEATER

Brenda Werth

In postdictatorial Argentine and Uruguayan theater, atrocity occurring in distant places and eras has frequently provided a metaphorical lens through which to approach and reflect upon the local violence unleashed by the dictatorships of the seventies and eighties. This chapter is concerned with the metaphor of violence in two recent plays: *Sarajevo esquina Montevideo* (Sarajevo, at the Corner of Montevideo, 2003) by Uruguayan playwright Gabriel Peveroni, and *La persistencia* (Persistence, 2007) by Argentina's Griselda Gambaro. Both works introduce violent events happening outside of the Southern Cone region, specifically in Sarajevo during the Bosnian War (1992–1996) and in Beslan, Russia, during the schoolhouse massacre of 2004, respectively. Instead of adapting violent events occurring elsewhere with the central objective of addressing national trauma, these playwrights unsettle national frameworks of reception and gesture toward reconfiguring audience communities to perceive the representation of violence and human rights abuses from a transnational perspective. The following analysis examines the extent to which these twenty-first-century plays initiate a departure in their use of metaphor to establish, instead, a comparative framework for the perception of violence occurring both locally and across the globe.

Censorship and the constant threat of persecution during the dictatorships in Argentina (1976–1983) and Uruguay (1973–1985) trained theater audiences of those countries to be adept interpreters of metaphor. Theater scholar

Jean Graham-Jones writes, "Argentinean theatrical texts, especially during the early and most repressive Proceso years, were encoded so as to escape the censor's gaze, primarily through the countercensorial use of rhetorical figures as metaphor, allegory, and analogy."[1] The transition to democracy in these two countries prompted the question of how playwrights would represent state-orchestrated violence without being restricted to expressing themselves through metaphor. Not surprisingly, however, the national metaphor retained its staying power and can be seen to structure many prominent post-dictatorship works. Three years after the fall of the dictatorship, Gambaro resurrected her furious Antigone (*Antígona furiosa*, 1986) from ancient Greece to denounce authoritarianism and seek justice on behalf of those disappeared during the dictatorship. The dramatists Mauricio Rosencof (Uruguay), and Patricia Suárez and Leonel Giacometto (Argentina) used the historical events of WWII and the Holocaust as historical referents for portraying the violence of Southern Cone dictatorships in their plays *Las cartas que no llegaron* (The Letters that Never Came, 2003) and *La trilogía del nazismo* (The Nazi Trilogy, 2007).

Sarajevo esquina Montevideo and *La Persistencia* resist and undermine this specific legacy of metaphor use in the Southern Cone postdictatorial context. Of course, plays often reference events happening elsewhere, so what I pose as the novelty in Peveroni and Gambaro's works does not lie here. Rather, this analysis examines the broad question of how referencing distant suffering in twenty-first-century Argentine and Uruguayan theater may be perceived differently than in the past. Specifically, this chapter suggests that metaphors of place may generate novel meanings in an era in which transnational news media have revolutionized the perception of events occurring in faraway places.

The presence of characters such as the war photographer in *Sarajevo esquina Montevideo*, and the silent, onstage observer in *La persistencia*, suggest that the role of spectatorship was central to the vision of the playwrights. The ethical implications of witnessing violence from a distance have long concerned researchers across disciplines. In her book, *The Spectatorship of Suffering*, Lilie Chouliaraki asks, "Is it enough to witness the scene of distant suffering, in all its intensity and drama, in order to engage with suffering? What forms can our engagement with distant suffering take?"[2] Drawing on Chouliaraki's work, in addition to Luc Boltanski's analysis of the role of spectators in their responses to distant scenes of suffering and atrocity, I examine the specific engagement of theatrical spectatorship with representations of distant suffering, the concrete ways theater differs as a genre for mediating distance in the representation of suffering, and the potential of theater to help shape a new ethics of audience reception.

Imagining a new ethics of audience reception in Argentina and Uruguay requires consideration of the interplay between national and transnational frameworks. Both countries have developed complex memory politics during the postdictatorial period. New forms of perceiving and recollecting human rights abuses in other parts of the world must necessarily engage with these well-established, nationally framed memory networks. Drawing on Michael Rothberg's theory of multidirectional memory, Alison Landsberg's theory of prosthetic memory, and Hans Lehmann's theory on the politics of perception and the notion of "response-ability," I propose that, though these works may continue to employ metaphor to refract the perception of external events through a national optic, on another level, these plays establish the conditions for what Rothberg describes as "a form of comparative thinking that [...] is not afraid to traverse sacrosanct borders of ethnicity and era."[3] The comparative model, which I believe animates Peveroni and Gambaro's recent works, rejects the notion that the aesthetic rendering of events happening elsewhere must serve to inform or deepen the understanding of events happening in one's own national context.

Beyond examining how Peveroni and Gambaro seek to establish a comparative framework that surpasses the function of metaphor, this chapter also considers how their works may reassess the empathic and geographical boundaries that delimit spectator identification with events happening elsewhere. Chouliaraki states that spectator identification is often narcissistic and "cannot move the spectator beyond the reflex of caring only for those like 'us.' "[4] According to Chouliaraki, this leaves the " 'other' outside our horizon of care and responsibility."[5] In expanding the theatrical horizon of expectations to include representation of violent events and human suffering beyond national borders, Gambaro and Peveroni make a significant contribution by adding a theatrical perspective to the dialogue surrounding the ethics of spectatorship and the ways this transformative ethics engages contemporary human rights discourse.

PEVERONI'S *SARAJEVO ESQUINA MONTEVIDEO*

Sarajevo esquina Montevideo (2003) is the first of five plays written by Peveroni staged between 2003 and 2007 in Montevideo, including *El hueco (una tribu urbana)* [The Gap (An Urban Tribe) 2004]; *Groenlandia* (Greenland, 2005); *Luna roja* (Red Moon, 2006); and *Berlín*, 2007. Peveroni offers a poetic examination of universal themes of time, space, and history in his dramatic work, but he situates these themes in a contemporary twenty-first-century context in which new forms of globalized violence and a sense of aftermath permeate everyday experience. Like Peveroni, who came of age during the Malvinas/Falklands War and the Balkans Conflict, the young characters in his plays are accustomed to violence as a quotidian force in their lives. In Peveroni's work, however, the threat of violence transcends national boundaries and becomes as uprooted as his characters, who move about the world as if unhindered by spatial and temporal coordinates. As Sarah Misemer argues, the suspension of the time/space continuum is one of Peveroni's most evocative dramatic constructions.[6] Though Peveroni's works reference real places such as Berlin, Sarajevo, Montevideo, and Greenland, his characters negotiate between specific sites and the imaginaries they construct of these sites through memories, historical accounts, and utopian fantasies. It is the sudden interruption of violence in these plays that has the power to collapse a state of mind into a tangible, concrete place.[7]

Peveroni has collaborated with the stage director María Dodera on most of his dramas, including *Sarajevo esquina Montevideo*, *El hueco*, *Groenlandia*, and *Berlín*. A bold innovator of the use of unconventional performance spaces, Dodera seeks to create unique, adventurous experiences for spectators.[8] Her directorial vision influenced the decision to stage *Groenlandia* on the 25th floor of the tallest building in Uruguay, the futuristic Telecomunicaciones Tower in Montevideo.[9] Peveroni relates that *Sarajevo esquina Montevideo* began to take shape during conversations with Dodera and Iván Solarich, the lead actor of the play, both of whom are of Croatian descent and had a personal connection to the subject matter.[10] Dodera comments on the complex layering that this identification introduces in the creative process: "*Sarajevo esquina Montevideo* es ficción dentro de otra ficción y así sucesivamente. Donde las historias se confunden, se entrelazan, y la propia ficción no permite tomar el distanciamiento, atrapa al actor cuando éste como creador pretende cambiarla" [*Sarajevo esquina Montevideo* is fiction within fiction, and so on. Where (hi)stories are confused and interwoven and fiction itself does not allow for distance, it traps the actor when he tries to change it].[11] Ironically, then, in what first appears to be a documentary play about the Balkans War, is more accurately a documentation of an actor negotiating between autobiographical identification and fictional portrayal.

Subtitled *El Puente* (The Bridge), *Sarajevo esquina Montevideo* tells the story of the fictional Bora Parzic, a Croatian mathematician who spends his last days in a psychiatric hospital in Sarajevo before it is bombed during the four-year siege of the city between 1992 and 1996. The actor who plays the Bora/Actor character, Iván Solarich, is a Uruguayan of Croatian descent, though according to Solarich, the events depicted in the play are not autobiographical. Throughout the performance, Solarich plays both the role of Bora and the role of the *actor* playing the part of Bora. Each side of this split identity corresponds to a separate place of action: Sarajevo on the one hand, and El Cerro, a traditional neighborhood in Montevideo and once a haven for immigrants, on the other. The play premiered in Montevideo in April 2003 at the Teatro Puerto Luna, a theater located in El Cerro, the neighborhood in which half of the action of the play takes place.

In establishing identification between actor and character, and place and setting, the play creates an illusion of authenticity and seduces audiences into a contract of intimacy through contact with "the real." Coterminous with this intimacy is the "anxiety about truth," which, according to theater scholar Carol Martin, is "inherent in the very idea of documentary."[12] As Martin writes, "Much of today's dramaturgy of the real uses the frame of the stage not as a separation, but a communion of the real and simulated; not as a distancing fiction from nonfiction, but as a melding of the two."[13] This communion of fiction and nonfiction through the frame of theater, exemplary in *Sarajevo esquina Montevideo*, likewise implies an exploration of the claims of history.[14] As Alison Forsyth and Chris Megson note, "The once trenchant requirement that the documentary form should necessarily be equivalent to an unimpeachable and objective witness to public events has been challenged in order to situate historical truth as an embattled site of contestation."[15] *Sarajevo esquina Montevideo* employs strategies and rhetorical devices to construct verisimilitude through the well-researched historical backdrop, the detailed account of Bora Parzic's life, and the actor's confessional tone and direct speech with the audience. Indeed, Iván Solarich's Croatian heritage might appear to make his role as hyperhistorian, to use Freddie Rokem's term, even more compelling. To Rokem, actors function as "hyperhistorians" by serving "as a connecting link between the historical past and the 'fictional' performed here and now of the theatrical event." These hyperhistorians, writes Rokem, allow us "to recognize that the actor is 'redoing' or 'reappearing' as something/somebody that has actually existed in the past."[16] Iván Solarich, in interpreting the Actor/Bora, resurrects his own ancestral identity in his role as hyperhistorian, even though the characters Bora and the Actor remain fictional constructions. The contextual overlap between the site of the theater performance and the site of the action of the play also resurrects the identity of the Cerro neighborhood as it existed during the seventies in the minds of performers and spectators, thereby "haunting" the performance space with the past. As Marvin Carlson notes, "This process of using the memory of previous encounters to understand and interpret encounters with new and somewhat different but apparently similar phenomena is fundamental to human cognition in general, and it plays a major role in the theatre."[17] In *Sarajevo esquina Montevideo*, theater enables this reencounter with "authentic" identity, whether pertaining to person or place, while it simultaneously undermines claims of authenticity through a blurring of the divisions between the real and the fictional.

Sarajevo esquina Montevideo is structured into five vignettes: Entrada (Introduction), La construcción (Construction), Espejos (Mirrors), El baile (The Dance), and La destrucción (Destruction). Throughout the play, the main characters are paired together in a series of dialogues: the Actor and his mother (set in Montevideo); Lejla and Glig (a Muslim girl and Christian boy in love who succumb to the violence of the war, set in Sarajevo); the doctor and Bora (in the psychiatric hospital where Bora is, set in Sarajevo), and Bora and the Actor (a dialogue between characters interpreted by the same actor, set both in Montevideo and in Sarajevo).

In "La Entrada," Bora pronounces, "Hay una sola forma de cruzar este río" [There is only one way to cross this river], a phrase that Bora repeats four times in the first vignette and serves as refrain throughout the play. The character, El Camarógrafo (the cameraman), films spectators as they file into the dimly lit theater while television monitors around the stage emit white noise and the sounds of gunshots can be heard in the background. The introductory stage directions to this section also foreshadow the important role the camera will play in documenting historical events and the audience's response to the performance throughout the play.

"La Construcción" opens with Bora/The Actor alone onstage encircled by barbed wire, offering a detailed historical account of the origins of the bridge. In dialogue with the Nobel Prize winning author Ivo Andric's book, *The Bridge on the Drina* (1959), this section chronicles the violent foundation of the bridge amidst the wars and ethnic conflict between the Muslims and Christians during the sixteenth century under the expanding Ottoman Empire. In the first monologue, Bora expresses the need to construct a bridge over the Drina River, which separates Bosnia and Herzegovina from Serbia. Without cue, Bora then transitions into the Actor character, situated in Montevideo, who announces in metatheatrical fashion, "Yo soy actor, y ahora debería estar representando a Bora Parzic, un yugoslavo que vivió toda su vida con idéntica obsesión a la mía, la de construir puentes..." [I am an actor, and now I should be representing Bora Parzic, a Yugoslav who lived his life with an identical obsession as my own: to build bridges].[18] Bora is the primary narrator of this section, though he expresses difficulty in staying in character, "Otra vez me salí del personaje" [Once again I slipped out of character].[19] Several times his narration is interrupted by the Actor, who relates the story of his grandfather's escape from Yugoslavia after WWII and subsequent emigration to Uruguay. Their competing narratives reflect a tension between past and present that unsettles the Actor's identity: "Toda esta mierda de la guerra. Ya les dije de las historias de mi abuelo, de sus aventuras; todo muy heroico, es verdad, pero yo nací acá, en el Cerro, en Montevideo" [All of this crap about the war. I told you the stories about my grandfather and his adventures; all very heroic, it's true, but I was born here, in the Cerro, in Montevideo]. Toward the end of this section, the Actor confesses that he may not be able to play the role of Bora after all.

The third section, "Espejos," begins with the cameraman filming audience members while their images flash simultaneously on the television monitors. The cameraman develops several monologues in which he rationalizes the exploitative elements of his profession as war photographer: "A mí sí me pagan para ver lo que los demás quieren ver... en sus casas" [I am paid to see what others want to see... in their homes].[20] In this section audiences learn from interactions between the Actor and his Mother that the renewed violence in the Balkans in the nineties has triggered traumatic memories of the forced exile and immigration of her family to Uruguay during WWII. Tension arises between the Mother, who insists on revisiting the past and identifies strongly with her ancestors, and the Actor, a second-generation Uruguayan, who resists this attachment to past trauma and seeks to establish an identity that is not overshadowed by his mother's overpowering family narrative. Though the Actor expresses resistance to this retrospective identification with the stories of his ancestors, his interpretation of Bora nonetheless in many ways invokes the lost genealogy his mother longs to restore.

The fifth section, "El baile," marks the climax of the play with a violent, carnivalesque celebration fusing temporal and geographical registers. Before the festivities begin (held in honor of the doomed newlyweds Lejla and Glig), the Actor predicts the collapse of the bridge, the end of the play, and the demise of Bora and his grandfather. Against pronouncements of rupture and collapse, the Actor announces a symbiosis between his and Bora's character.[21] The wedding celebration gradually transforms into a battlefield and the cameraman films the deaths of Bora and Lejla. In the aftermath of this scene, the Mother explains her own connection to the war that forced her parents to emigrate to Uruguay: "No vi la guerra. La sentí por mis padres. Y por las cartas de los parientes desde allá, desde Yugoslavia. Sentía la tristeza de mi padre cuando leía silenciosamente estas cartas" [I didn't see the war. I felt it through my parents. And through the letters my relatives sent from there, from Yugoslavia. I felt my father's sadness when he read those letters silently].[22] The mother's articulation of her relationship to her parents and her inheritance of these memories introduces the possibility of resolution with her own son, who tells her at the end of this section, "quería decirte que te entiendo, que te entendí siempre" [I wanted to tell you that I understand you, that I always understood you].[23]

It is only at the very end of the play, in the section "La Destrucción," when the Actor, after embodying Bora's story over the course of the play, realizes that he understands the character profoundly, and this moment of identification compels him to revisit a traumatic scene from his own childhood, when, during the seventies under Uruguay's last military dictatorship, he witnessed firsthand the abduction and murder of his grandfather, a member of the socialist party. The Actor's last lines in the monologue describing the scene allude to another bridge, this one connecting the Cerro (the immigrant neighborhood) to the center of Montevideo: "Me fui caminando por Agraciada, el Viaducto, caminé todo el Paso Molino... el mismo camino que hacíamos con el abuelito... todo Carlos María Ramírez, el Puente... el puente... el puente de siempre... estaba ahí... separando el dolor de mi familia... debía cruzar el puente para decirle a mi madre lo que había pasado... pero me quedé allí llorando. Yo nunca le dije nada" [I went walking down Agraciada, the Viaduct, I walked down Paso de Molino... the same way I used to go with Grandpa... all the way down Carlos María Ramírez, the bridge... the bridge... the same bridge as always... was there... separating the pain from my family... I knew I had to cross the bridge to tell my mother what happened... but I stayed there crying. I never told her anything].

The end of the last section concludes with the bombardment of the bridge over the Drina and the cameraman's confirmation that he was able to photograph its destruction. The "embedded" presence of the cameraman throughout the dramatic text and his final remarks draw attention to his position as observer, the role of media and journalism in documenting war, and the relationships between this documentation and the reception of violence.[24] In her observations on the photography of war, Susan Sontag is critical of the assumption of a consensual, homogenized "we" that images of atrocity produce among viewers. Sontag notes that images that show the "arbitrariness of the relentless slaughter" produce repudiation that gives the appearance of being uniform and devoid of historical context or political nuance.[25] Transferring these concerns to the realm of theater raises the question of how the implied "we" generated by the congregation of an audience in a shared space might either strengthen or break down the assumption of a consensual "we" in the collective reception of representations of violence. In *Sarajevo esquina Montevideo*, the decision to have the cameraman film each spectator's entrance individually suggests an attempt at questioning the presumption of collective consensus among audience members.

Hans Lehmann writes that theater's "political engagement does not consist in the topics but in the forms of perception."[26] Related to Lehmann's interest in the forms of perception is a concern with the real and imagined communities of perception created by theater audiences. In her observations on spectatorship of televised suffering, Chouliaraki writes that "transnational news flows construe a 'beyond the nation' community by establishing a sense of a broader 'we.' This 'we,' I assume, is the 'imagined' community of the West, which inhabits the transnational zone of safety and construes human life in the zone of suffering as the West's 'other.' "[27] Chouliaraki's conceptualization of a broader "we" as an imagined community resonates well with the broad, transnational horizon of expectations imagined by Peveroni and Gambaro, though their works, by addressing violence occurring in Russia, the former Yugoslavia, Uruguay, and Argentina, do not represent or reinforce the imagined community of the West, and, in fact, they effectively blur distinctions between zones of safety and zones of suffering.

The motifs that run through Peveroni's work function metaphorically to accentuate the ways different kinds of boundaries define human interaction. In *Berlín*, a game of tennis organizes the 15 scenes of the play and divides characters into two linked but competing spheres. In *Sarajevo esquina Montevideo*, bridges connect geographical contexts to provide routes of escape, or alternatively, to facilitate persecution. Figuratively, they link individual and collective pasts and presents; they connect emotional states to geographical contexts. The bridge that is of most interest to this chapter is the one that constructs dialogue between perceptions of contemporary violence occurring in Montevideo and Sarajevo.

In establishing less common transnational connections—between Uruguay and ex-Yugoslavia in *Sarajevo esquina Montevideo*, and Argentina and Russia in *La persistencia*—Peveroni and Gambaro avoid reiterating binaries and hierarchies between North and South, West and East, that have historically constructed the Global South and the East as "the other." Françoise Lionnet and Shu-mei Shih write that "Globalization increasingly favors lateral and nonhierarchical network structures."[28] Peveroni and Gambaro's works reflect this assertion in their vision of transnational networks whose identities are not defined primarily by their relation to a dominant "West" or "North." In creating this bridge, Peveroni and Gambaro participate in reconfiguring a framework for understanding violence from a critical, comparative perspective that not only employs but in many ways also surpasses the metaphor of foreign atrocity for the purpose of analyzing national violence.

Griselda Gambaro's *La persistencia*

Griselda Gambaro addresses mass violence occurring outside of Argentina's national borders in her recent play, *La persistencia*, a disturbing piece based loosely on the schoolhouse massacre carried out largely by Chechen militants that took place in Beslan, Russia, in September of 2004 and killed over 350 people, over half of whom were children. Though unaccustomed to writing about current events, Gambaro relates that she was so profoundly affected by reading press accounts of the massacre that she began to write the play immediately, and *La persistencia* premiered in 2007 at the National San Martín Theater in Buenos Aires.[29] In interviews, Gambaro refers to herself as an observer of reality capable of synchronizing the signs around her and using theater as a tool to respond to reality.[30] Previous works such as *Antígona furiosa* (1986) and *Del sol naciente* (From the Rising Sun, 1984) appropriate the remote contexts of Ancient Greece and medieval Japan to address the Argentine dictatorship and the Malvinas/Falklands War.[31] *La persistencia* marks a departure in Gambaro's dramatic corpus precisely because establishing meaning of the play does not depend heavily on a metaphorical translation to the national context, as in the above-mentioned works. As in Peveroni's *Sarajevo esquina Montevideo*, Gambaro expands the theatrical horizon of expectations to create a new, transnational framework for the perception and interpretation of violent events.

Consisting of three scenes, the play opens to reveal a makeshift shack set against a barren landscape dotted with leather bags, assorted kitchen items, water jugs, and a wooden chest strewn about haphazardly. The first scene introduces the characters Zaida and Boris (sister and brother), and the silent figure (El Silencioso), peripheral to the action, who does not speak and remains a distant observer throughout the play. Enzo, the last character and mastermind of the schoolhouse massacre, enters shortly thereafter, wearing a bitter expression, and cursing the wind. The play proceeds to document the planning of the massacre and the characters' personal investment in carrying out the act of extreme violence. While Enzo seems to be motivated by hate and a quest for power veiled by vaguely defined ideological beliefs, his lover, Zaida, seeks to avenge the death of their young son. Enzo cultivates Zaida's anger, while Boris, who has become disillusioned by Enzo's hate campaign, begs Zaida to cry for her lost son and begin the process of mourning: "Llorá por tu hijo muerto, llorá por esos que asesinaste!" [Cry for your lost son, cry for those you killed].[32] Driven by what she views as her brother's betrayal of their mission, Zaida stabs Boris in the back, literally. Toward the end of the play, Zaida reveals she is pregnant and will groom her unborn child to carry on the legacy of hate and violence, "¡Sí! Apenas asome la barba en su rostro, antes aún, suprimirá a un enemigo. Apenas tenga fuerza en los brazos para sostener un fusil" [Yes! As soon as his beard begins to grow he will suppress the enemy. As soon as his arms are strong enough to hold a gun].[33]

Elsewhere I have argued that *La persistencia* represents a radical transformation of the Antigone motif and a "complete disengagement between maternity and mourning, roles strongly linked in Gambaro's postdictatorial memory plays *Antígona furiosa* (1986) and *Atando cabos* (Tying Loose Ends, 1991)."[34] Specific demands for justice and state accountability in these earlier plays are overpowered in *La persistencia* by a more abstractly constructed desire for vengeance against a nondescript other. Though the massacre alludes explicitly to Beslan, the representation of violence remains offstage, and this absence of a visual spectacle onstage allows audiences to conceptualize violence as part of a global or universal discourse in addition to a site-specific one.

While Peveroni narrates stories of immigration, exile, and war that transcend national borders, in *La persistencia*, Gambaro poses ironically the notion that childhood innocence is a universalizing, transnational discourse. To Boris it is unfathomable that Zaida could have carried out the massacre. He asks her, "¿Cómo pudiste, Zaida? Si todos los niños de la aldea eran tus niños..." [How could you, Zaida? If all of the town's children were your children], "¿No se parecían a tu hijo?" [Didn't they resemble your son?]. To which Zaida responds, "Oh sí. Eran iguales... En algún sentido" [Oh yes, they were all the same.... In a sense].[35] Further on Zaida states, "Ya no me engaño. Por eso pude. Que no me mientan más con el candor de los niños, con sus sonrisas encantadoras, sus dientes de leche, sus balbuceos conmovedores. Ni siquiera amo a los nuestros, pero lo disimulo" [I no longer deceive myself. That is how I could do it. No more lies about children's' candor, with their enchanting smiles, their baby teeth, their moving sounds. I don't even love our own, but I pretend].[36] Meanwhile Enzo proclaims darkly, "En este mundo no hay inocentes" [In this world, there are no innocents].[37]

Theater scholar Olga Cosentino observes that many of Gambaro's works address the experiences of children, such as *Conversaciones con chicos* (Conversations with Children, 1977), *El mar que nos trajo* (The Sea That Brought Us Here, 2001), *Dios no nos quiere contentos* (God Does Not Want Us Content, 2003) and *La persistencia* (2007). In an interview she asks Gambaro why she introduces perspectives in the majority of these works that go against the accepted social imaginary of childhood.[38] Gambaro responds, "Yo me alegro de poder romper esas convenciones. Si mi trabajo tiene una finalidad es remover lo estructurado, lo acomodaticio, la costumbre. La gente ve la foto de un desnutrido del Chaco y la indignación dura segundos. Creo que todo el arte tiene que sacudirnos de la anestesia en que vivimos" [I am happy to be able to break with those conventions. If my work has one aim, it is to unsettle that which is structured, easy-going, and customary. People see a picture of a malnourished child from Chaco and the indignation lasts a few seconds. I think all art should snap us out of the anesthesia we live in].[39] In another interview in which Gambaro discusses *La persistencia*, she expresses a general advocacy of children's rights, "Pareciera que en este siglo no se considera para nada, absolutamente, la vida de los chicos" [It would seem that in this century no one has consideration for the lives of children].[40] Gambaro's comments in interviews as well as her play reveal the tension between advocacy for children in a broad sense and the attempt to deconstruct the universal ideal of childhood innocence as defined by Western convention.[41]

The desacralization of the idea of universal childhood innocence expressed by Zaida and Enzo unsettles audiences to the point that when a performance I attended in June 2007 ended, spectators barely applauded, not knowing how to respond to such a disturbing portrayal. Gambaro's play could not be accused of exploiting the spectacle of distant suffering in order to nurture a sense of compassionate solidarity among audience members. On the contrary, Zaida and Enzo's hate-filled convictions produced an atomizing effect on the audience. Instead of providing audience members with representations of suffering and victimhood, Gambaro produces characters motivated by a desire for vengeance and victory, thus making it impossible for spectators to engage in the narcissistic identification that Chouliaraki links to a "politics of pity."[42] For the purposes of this study, what Gambaro does very productively is to show that it is possible to expand the frame of reference, but her ironic deconstruction of the discourse of universal childhood innocence points to the limits of a transnational imaginary, and that an expanded horizon of expectations does not equate to a general homogenization of cultural, social, and political beliefs.

As in *Sarajevo esquina Montevideo*, in *La persistencia*, Gambaro includes an outside observer, El Silencioso, a character whose constant presence on the periphery of the stage distracts the audience and prompts onstage characters to occasionally address him in the hope of winning his approval. Donning a long cloak, with a long white beard and a walking stick, El Silencioso appears as a stereotype of one who possesses knowledge, vaguely resembling a philosopher or a prophet, and yet throughout the play he never responds and he remains expressionless throughout the play. The presence of El Silencioso holds more significance for the audience than for the other onstage characters. Like the war photographer in Peveroni's *Sarajevo esquina Montevideo*, El Silencioso adds an additional dimension to spectatorship of Gambaro's play. He is a spectator of events occurring onstage, but he is also a spectator of the spectators seated in the audience, and in this way he resembles what Luc Boltanski in his book *Distant Suffering* describes as an impartial spectator, "the spectator of the spectator, who is posited in order to take into account the spectator's judgments on himself."[43] Though the presence of El Silencioso is unnerving, the only demand he can pretend to make on spectators is to make them more aware of the act and identity of being a spectator. Chouliaraki shifts attention away from the demands that scenes of suffering can make on the spectator and suggests, "We might wish to assume, instead, that the spectacle of suffering puts under pressure not the spectator, per se, but the norms that dominate the ethics of public life today."[44] Gambaro's play on one level makes audience members self-conscious in their role as spectators, but on another level, Gambaro's play shows the way theatrical performance can participate in the constant reassessment of the norms and ethics of public life.

Conclusion

Through introducing contemporary events occurring outside of the Southern Cone region, the staging of Peveroni and Gambaro's twenty-first-century works reflects what Andreas Huyssen calls "the compression of time and space brought by Modernity," which, "in the register of imaginaries [...] has also expanded our horizons of time and space beyond the local, the national, and the international."[45] The theatrical stage provides an ideal forum for an exploration of this simultaneous compression and expansion of time and space in concrete and figurative terms. Theater scholars Elinor Fuchs and Una Chaudhuri have drawn attention to "the idea of space and place conscious performance."[46] They write, "In recent decades, a vigorous inquiry into the role of spatial experience in constructing cultural meaning has been underway in many fields, resulting in renewed interest in topography, geography, and mapping, as well as new attention to the specificity of place."[47] Gestures toward more global interpretations of performance provide a productive complement—and sometimes contradiction—to this heightened scrutiny of place. Theater scholar Marvin Carlson remarks, "We are now at least equally likely to look at the theater experience in a more global way, as a sociocultural event whose meanings and interpretations are not to be sought exclusively in the text being performed but in the experience of the audience assembled to share in the creation of the total event."[48] Carlson's shift in focus to the "experience of the audience assembled" emphasizes that the perception of these events portrayed onstage by a group of theater goers, whether in the San Martín Theater in Buenos Aires or the Teatro Puerto Luna in Montevideo, remains largely a localized activity.

The perception of events happening elsewhere has been a central concern for memory theorists such as Andreas Huyssen, Michael Rothberg, and Alison Landsberg, whose respective theories of memory politics, multidirectional memory, and prosthetic memory all engage the ways events are mediated, circulated, and perceived across contexts. The events portrayed in Peveroni and Gambaro's works invite audiences to make a connection between national and international events without forcing the conversion of distant events into a metaphor for interpreting national events. In this sense, their treatment of the perception and remembrance of national and extranational events reflects more closely Michael Rothberg's concept of multidirectional memory. According to Rothberg, this concept stresses that memory is "subject to ongoing negotiation, cross-referencing, and borrowing: as productive and not private."[49] It is "meant to draw attention to the dynamic transfers that take place between diverse places and times during the act of remembrance."[50] Rothberg's multidirectional memory attempts to provide an alternative approach to memory theory that does not invoke a competitive or hierarchical relationship between memories. Yet, as Rothberg affirms, multidirectionality does not imply a neutralization of difference: "This project takes dissimilarity for granted, since no two events are ever alike, and then focuses its intellectual energy on investigating what it means to invoke connections nonetheless."[51] This chapter is motivated by a similar desire to identify the kinds of connections Gambaro and Peveroni establish through invoking distant events in their works, and to explore what these connections between historically dissimilar, geographically distinct events can reveal about the frameworks for perceiving these events.

Alison Landsberg's theory of prosthetic memory also concerns the transportability of memories and the ways they can be perceived and assimilated by different groups. What she describes as prosthetic memory "emerges at the interface between a person and a historical narrative about the past, at an experiential site such as a movie theater or museum. In this moment of contact, an experience occurs through which the person sutures himself or herself to a larger history."[52] I would argue that Peveroni and Gambaro create such an interface between audiences and narratives of distant events at the experiential site of the theater and thus help establish the conditions for this "suturing" to a broader framework. Like Rothberg, Landsberg envisions a comingling of distinct memories: "prosthetic memories do not erase differences or construct common origins. People who acquire these memories are led to feel a connection to the past but, all the while, to remember their position in the contemporary moment... ."[53] Similarly, theater goers establish connections to other places and events while being conscious of their localized positions as spectators in a specific theater, neighborhood, city, region, country, etc.

Huyssen, Rothberg, and Landsberg are interested in the human potential for agency or empathy at these memory interfaces. Landsberg writes, "A practice of empathy is an essential part of taking on prosthetic memories, of finding ways to inhabit other people's memories *as* other people's memories and thereby respecting and recognizing difference."[54] What is significant for our analysis of theater in this discussion of collective memory formation is the implied emphasis on the role of perception in facilitating recognition of difference, identification with other narratives, and the practice of empathy. This focus on perception generates productive dialogue between theories of memory and spectatorship. Hans Lehmann, in his book *Postdramatic Theatre*, writes, "the separation of the event from the perception of the event, precisely through the mediation of the news about it, leads to an erosion of the act of communication. The consciousness of being connected to others and thus being answerable and bound to them 'in the language,' in the medium of communication itself recedes in favour of communication as (an exchange of) information."[55] Here Lehmann addresses the larger question of how the contemporary dislocation between event and its perception breaks down more traditional notions of community and accountability. Lehmann suggests that "Theatre can respond to this only with a politics of perception, which could at the same time be called an aesthetic of responsibility (or response-ability)."[56] Indeed, it must be emphasized that the strength of these plays does not lie in their capacity to serve as alternative news venues. They do transmit information of the violent acts in Sarajevo and Beslan, but Peveroni and Gambaro adapt the information from these events selectively and abstractly.

The importance of their staging this dislocation between event and its perception lies in the possibility of overcoming geographical and emotional distance by gesturing toward frames of reference for generating new communities of spectatorship and forms of identification.

Citing the work of political philosopher Nancy Fraser, Rothberg suggests that "A theory of multidirectional memory can help us in the task of 'reframing justice in a globalizing world.'"[57] The works of Peveroni and Gambaro participate directly in this reconfiguration of the frame to show the ways in which the perception of violence is no longer restricted by geographical boundaries. They evoke "a global sense of place" that has radically altered historical notions of the jurisdiction of justice, the constitution of subjectivity, and processes of spectator identification[58] The agency in their work lies in the productive unsettling of traditional use of metaphors of atrocity that positions violence from distant lands in such a way as to talk about local violence, and the concomitant constructive reimagination of a horizon of expectations no longer in synch with territorial boundaries.

Notes

1. Graham-Jones, *Exorcising History*, 21.
2. Chouliaraki, *The Spectatorship of Suffering*, 2.
3. Rothberg, *Multidirectional Memory*, 17.
4. Chouliaraki, *The Spectatorship of Suffering*, 13. Although Chouliaraki refers specifically to television, her remarks address key issues regarding spectator identification that are central to theater as well.
5. Ibid., 14.
6. Misemer, "Juegos de apertura," 5.
7. Borkenztain, "En tránsito," 3.
8. Peveroni refers to María Dodera as his stage interpreter. Peveroni, *Sarajevo esquina Montevideo*, 4.
9. Barrios, "Entrevista a María Dodera: Las múltiples caras de la dramaturgia," *Entretablas*, http://entretablas.blogspot.com/2009/07/entrevista-los-macbeths-las-*multiples.html*., July 4, 2009 (July 1, 2011).
10. Peveroni, "De los Balcanes a la Villa del Cerro," Interview with Gabriel Peveroni, *El país*, April 25, 2003 (July 1, 2011).
11. Dodera, "Introduction," 4.
12. Martin, "Bodies of Evidence," 1.
13. Ibid., 2.
14. Trastoy, *El teatro autobiográfico*, 333.
15. Forsyth and Megson, *Get Real*, 3.
16. Rokem, *Performing History*, 13.
17. Carlson, *The Haunted Stage*, 6.
18. Peveroni, *Sarajevo esquina Montevideo*, 6.
19. Ibid., 7.
20. Ibid., 9.
21. Ibid., 14.
22. Ibid.
23. Ibid.

24. Misemer, "Bridging the Gaps in Cultural Memory," 40.
25. Sontag, *Regarding the Pain of Others*, 7–9.
26. Lehmann, *Postdramatic Theatre*, 184.
27. Chouliaraki, *The Spectatorship of Suffering*, 10.
28. Lionnet and Shih, *Minor Transnationalisms*, 2.
29. Pagés, "El horror detrás del horror," *La Nación*, June 17, 2007, http://www.lanacion.com.ar/918078-el-horror-detras-del-horror.
30. Cosentino, "Desconfío de tanta aprobación," Interview with Griselda Gambaro, June 28, 2008, http://edant.revistaenie.clarin.com/notas/2008/06/28/01703461.html.
31. Graham-Jones, *Exorcising History*, 132.
32. Gambaro, *La persistencia*, 51.
33. Ibid., 66.
34. Werth, *Theatre, Performance, and Memory Politics in Argentina*, 58.
35. Gambaro, *La persistencia*, 48, 44.
36. Ibid., 49.
37. Ibid., 35.
38. Cosentino, "Desconfío de tanta aprobación," Interview with Griselda Gambaro, June 28, 2008, http://edant.revistaenie.clarin.com/notas/2008/06/28/01703461.html.
39. Ibid.
40. Pagés, "El horror detrás del horror," *La Nación*, June 17, 2007, http://www.lanacion.com.ar/918078-el-horror-detras-del-horror.
41. See David Archard, *Children*.
42. Chouliaraki, *The Spectatorship of Suffering*, 13.
43. Boltanski, *Distant Suffering*, 49.
44. Chouliaraki, *The Spectatorship of Suffering*, 2.
45. Huyssen, *Present Pasts*, 4.
46. Fuchs and Chaudhuri, *Land/Scape/Theatre*, 4.
47. Ibid., 6.
48. Carlson, *Places of Performance*, 2.
49. Rothberg, *Multidirectional Memory*, 3.
50. Ibid., 11.
51. Ibid., 18.
52. Landsberg, *Prosthetic Memory*, 2.
53. Ibid., 9.
54. Ibid., 24.
55. Lehmann, *Postdramatic Theatre*, 184.
56. Ibid., 185.
57. Rothberg, *Multidirectional Memory*, 19.
58. Massey, *World City*, 15.

Section II

The "War on Terror" and the Global Economic Order

Chapter 5

Place and Misplaced Rights in *Guantánamo: Honor Bound to Defend Freedom*

Lindsey Mantoan

> *Contemporary documentary theatre represents a struggle to shape and remember the most transitory history—the complex ways in which men and women think about the events that shape the landscapes of their lives.*
>
> —Carol Martin[1]

"The purpose of holding the prisoners at Guantánamo Bay was and is to put them beyond the rule of law, beyond the protection of any courts."[2] These words, part of a speech Britain's Lord Justice Johan Steyn delivered in 2003 exhorting the British judiciary to condemn publicly the detention center at Guantánamo, indicate that the suspension of *habeas corpus* constitutes one of the fundamental problems with the facility and the policies the United States uses to authorize it.[3] In 2004 London's Tricycle Theatre Company included this quotation in its documentary play *Guantánamo: Honor Bound to Defend Freedom*. The explicitly political play, critiques the unlawful policies of the "war on terror" and in particular the US government's practice of detaining "enemy combatants" at Guantánamo Bay and Britain's complicity in these detentions. The detention center at Guantánamo stands as one of the most

---

Early drafts of this essay appeared in my master's thesis, "Telling Stories: Documentary Theatre as Trauma Historiogrpahy," and in a paper I presented at the American Society for Theatre Research's 2009 Conference. I am indebted to Charlotte Canning, Ann Cvetkovich, Kathryn and Barbara Mantoan, and Jisha Menon for their insights on this work.

striking examples of US abandonment of its own rule of law as a consequence of committing the country to an indefinite and extralegal war on terror. This impoverished war establishes what Giorgio Agamben would call a "state of exception" where sovereign authority exceeds the rule of law for a period of unspecified duration under the guise of protection. The US government's commitment to hide from public view the most vital policies of this new state, defined by the creation of new vocabulary that is not bounded by any clear endpoint, leaves us in "a permanent state of emergency."[4]

Although the debate about Guantánamo has shifted over time, from accusations about racial profiling as the primary method for detaining Arab men, to reports detailing torture, to the current dispute about what to do with the prisoners who have been granted release but have no state willing to take them in, the existence of a US military detention center located outside US civil jurisdiction and off US soil, profoundly changes the image and ideology of the United States. As Agamben explains, the "transformation of a provisional and exceptional measure into a technique of government threatens to radically alter—in fact has already palpably altered—the structure and meaning of the traditional distinction between constitutional forms."[5] The significance of Guantánamo implicates not only multiple democratic administrations but also the effectiveness of international law and perhaps even the future of constitutional democracy as a sustainable form of government. When prosecutors for the upcoming *USS Cole* and 9/11 trials continue to allege that the US Constitution does not apply to the detention facility at Guantánamo, they attempt to propagate a notion that some people's lives don't count and aren't worthy of protection or humanitarian treatment. The existence of Guantánamo depends on the assertion that some individuals can be denied basic human rights—*habeas corpus*, the protections established by the Geneva Conventions—under the state of exception. The premise of universal human rights, however, is that they are undeniable, precede government recognition, and hold regardless of an individual's associations, citizenship, or actions.

Although the play was written eight years ago, the problem of indefinite detentions continues. In April 2012, years after a federal US judge granted their release, two Chinese Muslim detainees were transferred out of the facility and relocated to El Salvador. These 2 transfers mark the first movement out of the prison in over 15 months, leaving 169 prisoners in the facility, 81 of whom have been granted release through the US judiciary.[6] Negotiations to repatriate or relocate detainees classified as ready for release regularly fail, and a number of those detainees who have been granted freedom refuse to return to their country of origin for fear that they will be murdered immediately. Efforts by the Obama administration to resettle some detainees in the United States were met with political uproar and were quickly abandoned. Although the Obama administration announced in 2009 the creation of a new facility in Thomson, Illinois, and its intention to relocate detainees to US soil, Congress blocked funds for both construction on the Thomson Correctional Center and the transfer of any detainee out of Guantánamo.[7] In December,

2011, Obama signed into law H.R. 1540, the "National Defense Authorization Act for Fiscal Year 2012," a bill that, in addition to allocating funds for defense and the military, requires the United States to hold in military custody any non-US citizen captured by the US armed forces and renews the ban on funds to relocate Guantánamo detainees. Although in his press release regarding the bill Obama asserted that he continues to oppose this restriction, the restriction nonetheless continues, and so the prisoners at Guantánamo continue to be in indefinite detention in military custody.[8]

Guantánamo has to be dealt with. In the material sense, the US government must decide what to do with the prisoners still languishing in their metal cells. In the broader sense, Americans have an ethical responsibility to confront Guantánamo as a situation that has inflicted grievous injury to real people and as an institution that has altered the fabric of the country's constitution. But it is not easy to address Guantánamo on these terms. For one, much about the detention center remains unknown; journalists and media outlets are systematically denied access to basic information about the facility; the rules that reporters must sign every time they enter the facility forbid them from speaking with detainees regardless of a prisoner's status; and the military, the Pentagon, and the Defense Department censor photographs and reports.[9] But more difficult and arguably more profound than this, Americans must deal with Guantánamo on a collective emotional level, considering it as a tragic event in the country's history, in order to be able to forcefully advocate for due process and other basic human rights that the detainees have been denied so far.

As a documentary play, *Guantánamo* offers a compelling methodology for examining the detention center both as a policy that has blighted the rule of law and as a personal experience in the state of exception that is the war on terror. Written by journalist Victoria Brittain and novelist Gillian Slovo, the piece belongs to the Tricycle Theatre's Tribunal Plays, theater about controversial historical events in which every character represents a real person and every word comes verbatim from interviews, letters, and public records. Since its first performance by Tricycle actors in London in 2004, various theater companies, non-profit human rights organizations, and communities of concerned citizens have produced *Guantánamo* as full-scale productions or staged readings in many major US cities and around the world.[10] Tricycle gave a special performance to congressional staffers on Capitol Hill during the US tour of their production.[11] Through critiquing both their own government and the US government, the playwrights of *Guantánamo* offer rich material for evaluating how performance can engage with international and extranational events such as the war on terror in order to complicate the representations offered through mainstream media and inspire action and advocacy.

Guantánamo remains a remote space, shrouded in mystery, revealed only sporadically and partially by the hazy reports of journalists, which makes the institution easy to ignore or forget; *Guantánamo* demonstrates that however distant and unimaginable it may be for many of us, the experience of Guantánamo remains very real for those who survived detention there. The play presents haunting, personal accounts of five British residents held at Guantánamo after they were captured, interrogated, and extradited while the US government ignored their universal human rights. These narratives demonstrate the trauma of losing home, family, and the sense of self. By presenting these lives on stage, in detail, embodied by actors and witnessed by audiences trying to imagine being stripped of their humanity, performances of *Guantánamo* offer the live encounter as a method for recognizing fundamental human rights.

The play does have a few shortcomings, including its singular focus on innocent people sent to Guantánamo at the exclusion of any debate about the capture and detention of actual terrorists, and its failure to address torture. Nevertheless, through its form; its juxtaposition of place, citizenship, and rights; and its critique of the othering produced by indefinite detentions, *Guantánamo* stands as a powerful example of the influence performance can have on our understanding of human rights.

Place and Misplaced Rights

Guantánamo foregrounds place as a vital weapon in and against the war on terror. The characters in the play critique the connections between place, citizenship, and rights in sophisticated ways that demonstrate that universal rights do not depend on a person's nationality or geographical location. Further, performances of the play, like all live performances, draw attention to the importance of place; by bringing together a group of people in a particular location to participate in a live event, *Guantánamo* reminds audiences that places create community and proximity enables new connections to be forged. Productions of the play contrast the vitality of the performance space with the vast emptiness of Guantánamo.

Guantánamo relates in painful detail the nightmare five British men lived through immediately before, during, and after their detention. Gambian Secret Service captured Wahab and Bisher Al-Rawi, two brothers who had planned to set up a mobile peanut oil processing plant in Gambia, and subjected them to British, US, and Gambian interrogation. They released Wahab within a month, but transferred Bisher first to Bagram Air Base and later to Guantánamo. Moazzam Begg had been in Afghanistan installing water pipes in villages and trying to start a school when the US air raids began and he moved his family to Pakistan. He was arrested shortly thereafter and taken to Kandahar, then Bagram, then Guantánamo. Jamal Al-Harith was captured in Pakistan where he had been on Tabligh, which he has described as a trip to learn more about a religion and the people who practice it. Ruhel Ahmed's story in the play begins with him already detained at Guantánamo, writing letters to his family requesting contact lenses and solution so that he can see properly. If his family sends these items, he never receives them.

Some of these men are British subjects, and some are immigrants already displaced from their native country by violence and political upheaval. These men, then, already challenge the facile connections among citizenship, rights, and geography. Guantánamo represents a place more elusive than a borderland, an in-between space where guards and government officials force identity positions on detainees who struggle to maintain a complex sense of self. According to anthropologists Akhil Gupta and James Ferguson, "even in more completely deterritorialized times and settings—settings not only where 'home' is distant but also where the very notion of 'home' as a durably fixed place is in doubt—aspects of our lives remain highly 'localized' in a social sense."[12] These men who languished at Guantánamo were denied not only their homeland, but also a sense of community in their new location, where guards often kept them in isolation. Jamal tells audiences about detainees who attempted to organize the other prisoners under a leader to fight for their rights: "when we tried to organize Emirs, they kept putting them [in isolation] so people were afraid to become Emirs now."[13] Thus, the localized aspects of prisoners' lives at Guantánamo were ruled by seclusion, denying them access to any form of diaspora wherein they could talk with others about the homeland—shared or not—that they had lost. Performances of *Guantánamo* bring together stories of detainees who were isolated at Guantánamo, creating a community of individuals who are no longer isolated from one another or from the larger world.

Gupta and Ferguson posit that "the representation of the world as a collection of 'countries,' as on most world maps, sees it as an inherently fragmented space."[14] Culture, however, bleeds over these arbitrary boundaries, or fails to stretch to the edges of these borders; conflating culture with nationality is a problematic endeavor. Political and military actors in the war on terror wield the construct of the nation, naturalized through rhetoric and policy, as a weapon against those whose citizenship could be called into question. *Guantánamo* interrogates the use of the nation-state as a tool for oppression by positioning the men represented in the text as living, breathing people with universal rights, regardless of their location or a particular government's recognition of those rights.

In the war on terror, the rhetoric of fervent patriotism casts the other as not only unknown, but unknowable, a dangerous individual who operates outside the jurisdiction of a nation-state, and therefore a figure unworthy of the protections of international law. In the wake of the 9/11 attacks, the US government focused counterterrorism efforts on individuals whose identities were hybrid and thus confusing and volatile. All of the detainees whose stories are detailed in *Guantánamo* unsettle the notion of citizenship as related to a single country. Jamal al-Harith, a British subject, had recently traveled through Iran to Turkey, then to Pakistan, where he was detained.[15] His capture was as much the result of his unsettled geographic location as his identity as a Muslim. Wahab and Bisher were Iraqis who had been living in England but relocated to Gambia where they were arrested. The script explains that "[t]he only difference between [the two brothers] is that Wahab al-Rawi has British citizenship and Bisher doesn't."[16] Bisher had retained his Iraqi citizenship in the hopes of reclaiming his ancestral house should Saddam

Hussein ever lose power. Although their geographic migration was identical, their citizenship status was not, which explains their different treatment at the hands of US agents. In this way, the detentions deny universal rights for those whose claims to citizenship can be cast as dubious.

Performances of *Guantánamo* place these personal stories on stage in countries around the world, and by so doing subvert the US government's agenda, which places these men outside the realm of recognized rights. Judith Butler reminds us that "[i]t is crucial to ask under what conditions some human lives cease to become eligible for basic, if not universal, human rights. How does the US government construe these conditions?"[17] By presenting Guantánamo as a very human experience, endured by these five men and those closest to them, the piece attacks the premise of the detentions: that some individuals' lives are less than human, outside the realm of shared humanity, not worthy of acknowledgement. Through claiming that these lives, their losses, and their pain are worthy of representation and witnessing, performances of *Guantánamo* demand recognition for the human rights ignored during their detentions. The act of putting these lives in front of audiences in multiple countries undermines not only the secrecy that the US government strives to maintain about Guantánamo, but also the notion that these lives can be forgotten or erased through Guantánamo.

The play further lays bare the links among citizenship, rights, and place when Clive Stafford Smith, an attorney in the script advocating for the rights of the detainees, tells audiences "none of [the people that they think are] the real bad dudes are in Guantánamo Bay, because the American Government would never put them there while there is a possibility that we'll get jurisdiction to litigate to get them out of there. So all of them are in Bagram air force base [*sic*] and places like that."[18] Herein rests a central paradox of Guantánamo: while the US government targets those with ambiguous citizenship, the government creates its own confusion about the connection between place and jurisdiction when it establishes legal black holes like Guantánamo and Bagram. The play underscores the hypocrisy of this thinking through comments like those of lawyer Gareth Pierce: "there is a process of shipping people for instance to Egypt, where you know they'll be tortured. [You] torture something out of them, then get them back to Guantánamo."[19] Although the policies surrounding Guantánamo condemn those who operate extranationally, the facility's operations rely on foreign entities to conduct its counterterrorism activities outside of the US government's jurisdiction.

Guantánamo begins with Steyn's speech, wherein he argues forcefully that the US government is circumventing international law in detaining those held at Guantánamo Bay without due process. Steyn tells audiences: "It is a recurring theme in history that in times of... perceived national danger, even liberal democracies adopt measures infringing human rights... which compromise the rights and liberties of individuals beyond the exigencies of the situation. Often the loss of liberty is permanent."[20] This speech reminds audiences that this is not the first time a government has resorted to unlawful measures in times of national crisis, and also implies that similar situations may arise in the future. The stakes here, Steyn pronounces, are dangerously high. The audience members must immediately confront their responsibility not only to demand an end to unlawful detentions at Guantánamo, but also to prevent future governments from disregarding human rights. This speech also highlights one of the fundamental problems with the concept of nations: because they are a construction that requires continual maintenance, nations must respond to every perceived threat (and they often do so using dangerous or disproportionate tactics). The play elucidates what exactly a nation tends to preserve when its government betrays the fundamental principles of its constitution in the name of national security.

The play immediately erases the symbolic barrier between the audience and the performers when the script calls for the actor playing Steyn to enter through the back of the auditorium and walk down the aisle to the stage, with the houselights remaining on during his opening monologue. By removing audiences from the security of a darkened auditorium, the play eliminates the possibility of passive spectatorship and calls on audiences to become active witnesses to the traumatic events about to be described, to imagine themselves enduring this trauma, and to recognize the far-reaching implications of the situation at Guantánamo. This moment of the performance does not allow individual spectators the anonymity that a darkened theater space provides, thereby drawing them into the public debate about this situation and heightening the vulnerability and rawness of the performance experience. Audience members encounter one another and can hold each other accountable for witnessing these testimonies.

The playwrights conclude the play with Steyn quoting John Donne, "who preached... more than four centuries ago: 'No man is an Island, entire to itself; every man is a piece of the Continent, a part of the main;... any man's death diminishes me, because I am involved in Mankind.' "[21] This metaphor, grounded in space and place, speaks to the concepts of core and periphery; islands represent the marginal and outside, whereas the mainland stands as the ideal. While the metaphor is problematic in its hierarchical treatment of geography, its sentiment indicates that all people exist as part of a global nation where each person bears responsibility to every other person, where everyone is entitled to fundamental rights regardless of citizenship or ethnicity, and where we have a duty to one another. This quotation calls on audiences to recognize unlawful detention of anybody as unlawful detention of everybody. The final words of the play come from a voiceover, stating that many detainees are still held at Guantánamo, and that they are being held indefinitely. At the time of this writing, this quotation remains true for many men held there, despite courts granting a number of them release or transfer. Although the meaning and force of this ending may change if Guantánamo closes and the detainees are brought to trial or sent to countries willing to take custody of them, this ending denies the audience a sense of closure about the situation. Notwithstanding this uncertainty, Steyn's speeches highlight that the situation at Guantánamo, while specific to a particular historic moment, has far-reaching implications.

Guantánamo as a place and an instrument in the war on terror is difficult to stage for a variety of reasons. We know so little about the facility—what it looks like and what goes on there—that we are left to speculate. Further, performances or visual images of Guantánamo risk aestheticizing these detentions and the various levels of violence they entail. Productions of *Guantánamo* refuse to represent torture onstage and make no effort to re-create the physical spaces of the detention center. Minimizing the representations of Guantánamo also emphasizes the emptiness of the detention facility: the place is a cultural vacuum. The audience is left to imagine the spaces and many of the events happening at Guantánamo, and, in the act of creating these images for themselves, audiences participate as active witnesses to the trauma narratives presented on stage, which in turn positions them as citizens actively involved in the discourse on the facility and the policies the US government claims authorize it.

By bringing together people from various countries, united by this single global event, the play enacts the challenging project of confronting the questions of cultural exchange and differences. The testimony, especially in the form of narratives of almost unimaginable pain delivered by figures removed from the mainstream discourse, challenges witnesses on both a personal and an interpersonal level. Shoshana Felman thus describes the work that testimony can do: "Texts that testify do not simply report facts but, in different ways, encounter—and make us encounter—strangeness."[22] The testimonies presented during performances of *Guantánamo* demonstrate the strangeness the institution of Guantánamo creates: multiple governments worked in concert to remove each of these prisoners from his home, with its familiar surroundings and customs and routines, and confine him to a foreign climate, a different set of rules, and a community of people with dissimilar values. Each of these testimonies offers personal experiences of trauma to audiences around the world, challenging them to acknowledge what is hard to hear, and recognize that differences never ought to deprive an individual of basic human rights. These testimonies reveal the hidden consequences of the war on terror, and by exposing the audience to what is strange to them—the experiences of those who survived detention at Guantánamo—lay bare that which the US government has sought to obscure.

Rights, Writing, and Documentary

The documentary form constitutes a methodology for generating grassroots, oppositional history, one that transmits cultural memory through both oral and written forms. *Guantánamo* as a historiography of the detention center creates an affective memory of five men captured, detained, and released by the United States, personalizing the distant, unimaginable institution and the experience of Guantánamo. Through this documentary play, these men present the history of their extradition and captivity in their own words, sharing with people around the world how they came to be detained and their treatment once at Guantánamo. The play is indeed an opportunity to express themselves, an opportunity they didn't have while they were held captive. The difficulty of talking about and understanding trauma, its primarily emotional rather than material remains, and the limitations and opportunities inherent in the process of creating histories complicate the process of remembering traumatic events. Michel de Certeau posits that "all historiographical research is articulated over a socioeconomic, political, and cultural place of production...It is therefore ruled by constraints, bound to privileges, and rooted in a particular situation."[23] Different methodologies of capturing history—such as historical writing, the news media, and performance—face diverse constraints and privileges, and are crafted in various places of production. By combining public record with interviews they directly conducted, the *Guantánamo* playwrights construct compelling personal narratives set in opposition to the more policy-focused stories generated elsewhere.

The nature of a traumatic event or experience, which defies easy representation, demands that a variety of historiographical methodologies be used to archive and remember it. The privileging of the written word and material archives in Western culture, and the resulting marginalization of oral histories, can limit nuanced understandings of particular events and feelings, especially those related to trauma. Similarly, representations in the news media of national and international events often focus more on facts than on lived experiences or the emotional aftermath of trauma. The traditional methodologies used to capture historical events have class and status implications, and socially and politically marginalized groups are often further underrepresented in historical writing or media coverage or are not allowed to tell their stories in their own voice. Oral histories such as the ones passed on through interviews and performed through documentary theater offer different privileges than do other forms of history, and often focus on people and events not represented through historical writing.

Guantánamo is wrapped in the mystery of disappearance; those sent there disappear from the world physically and symbolically, and although journalists such as Carol Rosenberg of the *Miami Herald* issue numerous reports about the state of the detention facility, it continually slips, under the radar, out of public consciousness. Similarly, the men held there stand as wholly classified individuals, with their actions, the government's actions toward them, their charges (if there are any), and often even their names are classified, sealed, and obliterated from public record. Keeping in mind Peggy Phelan's assertion that "theatre continually marks the perpetual disappearance of its own enactment,"[24] *Guantánamo*, by drawing attention to the fading nature of performance, dramatically underscores the importance of remembering; of continually acting, enacting, and re-acting; of finding ways to hold onto performance and Guantánamo. The live encounter, something that both disappears and provides public testimony, mirrors the ephemerality of human rights under the state of exception—they disappear but still exist in the public consciousness. Trauma scholar Ann Cvetkovich asserts:

> Trauma puts pressure on conventional forms of documentation, representation and commemoration, giving rise to new genres of expression, such as testimony,

and new forms of monuments, rituals, and performances that can call into being collective witnesses and publics. It thus demands an unusual archive.[25]

Documentary theater creates such an unusual archive, and is thus uniquely positioned as a valuable methodology for creating and recording histories of traumatic experiences and memories. Only by looking at trauma through a range of viewpoints and methodologies can survivors and witnesses begin to understand, historicize, and memorialize it.

Recovery from state-inflicted wounds requires public acknowledgement of the pain as well as an effort to restore the recognition of rights. In the case of Guantánamo, Americans must confront the tale of physical and emotional violence the government has inflicted by capturing, detaining without trial, and torturing detainees, in order to stop the cycle of trauma, to mend personal and constitutional wounds, and to renew a universal commitment to one another.[26] The play focuses on the particular traumatic experiences of five men who were found to be innocent of any terrorist activity. For the country to effectively contend with Guantánamo, however, the trauma inflicted on even the most high profile terrorists must be acknowledged and incorporated into our understanding of the detention center. While more must be done, the play provides an important step toward generating this understanding.

Documentary theater, through its focus on personal narratives and its consideration of a range of viewpoints, provides a form that productively juxtaposes prevailing histories of traumatic events. In her article "Feminist Performance as Feminist Historiography," Charlotte Canning proposes re/writing the history of feminism through "performance that foregrounds historiographical operations, making physical, gestural, emotional, and agonistic the processes that construct history out of the past."[27] *Guantánamo* performs a similar function for the public record of the detention facility by consciously striving to capture affect, emotion, and personal narrative, putting bodies on stage that rehearse working through trauma, and enabling actors and audiences to learn about these survivors through language, verbal patterns, gestures, and stories. Through emphasizing the value of multiple and alternative perspectives, documentary theater opens up new ways of performing historical analyses of traumatic events, ways that implicitly call attention to the performative nature of all efforts to historicize events (see figure 5.1).

The playwrights structure the narratives in *Guantánamo* as disjointed, interrupting each other, out of chronological order. By breaking up and interspersing the storylines of the figures represented, the pacing of the play parallels the fragmented nature of trauma narratives. Through witnessing these narratives, the audience enacts a vital step in the process of understanding trauma. Philosopher Susan Brison explains that the "communicative act of bearing witness to traumatic events not only transforms traumatic memories into narratives that can then be integrated into the survivor's sense of self and view of the world, but it also reintegrates the survivor into a community, reestablishing bonds of trust and faith in others."[28] Creating that trust requires witnesses to take ownership of these tragedies, both as

Figure 5.1 *Honor Bound to Defend Freedom.* Photo by David M. Allen

people whose impulses are understandably to ignore the pain, and as citizens whose governments are perpetrating these violations. No doubt these five men detained at Guantánamo never suspected that they might one day be apprehended and confined by a foreign government without due process. Citizens have an ethical responsibility to assimilate these detainees' stories into public consciousness and this process begins when audience members bearing witness to these testimonies contend with the very human belief that these experiences could never be their own, and the realization that those very thoughts had been shared by the people whose traumas are played out on stage. Through focusing on personal stories of lost autonomy, the play challenges audiences to consider what constitutes security—both national and personal—and what can and cannot be sacrificed to achieve it.

Understanding and historicizing trauma requires both analytical and affective responses, in part because the impact of trauma manifests itself not only in the brain but also in the body. Psychiatry professor Judith Lewis Herman finds that "traumatic events are extraordinary, not because they occur rarely, but rather because they overwhelm the ordinary human adaptations to life."[29] She offers examples of the physiological reactions to trauma that survivors experience, such as a low startle threshold, hyperalertness, and nightmares. Trauma survivors, according to Herman, "do not have a normal 'baseline' level of alert but relaxed attention. Instead, they have an elevated baseline of arousal: their bodies are always on the alert for danger."[30] The bodily reaction to traumatic events challenges the limits of the written word to fully comprehend and record trauma. *Guantánamo* foregrounds emotional responses to trauma and, by inviting actors to try on the experiences of trauma survivors, highlights the ways in which both the mind and the body absorb trauma.

Performances of *Guantánamo* allow trauma narratives to be passed on to an array of audiences through the visceral experiences of embodiment and affective witnessing. Actors performing these trauma testimonies model for audiences the act of putting traumatic experiences into the body and working through the emotional memories of lost freedom, torture, and being stripped of rights. Although *Guantánamo* depicts real people and events, productions of the play typically eschew realism, favoring instead a presentational acting style and minimal scenery, often representing through props or lighting the prison cells to which the captives have been confined and collapsing the physical and temporal distance between the detainees, their lawyers, government representatives, and the audience. According to Julia Brothers, an actress in the San Francisco Brava Theatre Center production, "we stood and spoke to the audience. There were no scenes. There was no dramatization. There were no beatings, no torture. Only the actual words of the men who were wrongly imprisoned."[31] This Brechtian style of acting, where the performer embodies a real person without "being wholly transformed into the character played," allows the audience to see both the figure represented, and the labor whereby the actor tries on that person's experiences.[32] Productions, then, balance on a fine line between seeking to achieve an affective history of these personal narratives while simultaneously establishing enough emotional distance to leave room for active, critical responses from the audience. The ethical issues wrapped up in portraying someone else's tragedy without claiming it as your own leave little room for error when it comes to performing trauma, and this tension imbues documentary theater with its ethical force and moral authority.

Some productions of *Guantánamo* project on an upstage screen images of the real people represented in the play, which serves as constant reminders that these stories are nonfiction, that they happened to living breathing people.[33] These projections allow audiences to see both the performer and the figure behind the performance. By subverting the audience's impulse to conflate actor and character, these projections achieve the alienation effect Brecht deemed necessary for performances seeking to motivate their audiences to action, rather than enabling passive catharsis. This alienation, where the actor simultaneously plays both the character and herself or himself, invites audience members to imagine what it might be like to put themselves in the place of someone captured and detained by a foreign government. The layering of real people with the substitution of actors portraying them creates a heightened sense of identification wherein witnesses relate to both the actor and the real person. To the extent that one might question the efficacy of documentary theater and its ability to inspire action and create meaningful change in policy and attitude, the historical and political strength of the genre resides in this curious blend of emotional and intellectual responses inspired by audience identification with both the actors and the figures they portray.

The historiographical operations of *Guantánamo* are foregrounded not only by its form, but also by the selection and ordering of material. Between the various narratives of the detainees the playwrights insert a segment from a press conference with Donald Rumsfeld in which he answers questions about the British attitude toward extradition, the transparency of facility policies, and the indefinite nature of the war and the detentions. Through including the obvious falsehoods and misrepresentations Rumsfeld perpetuated in this press conference, the play distinguishes the official story constructed by the US government and propagated by its representatives from the personal accounts presented through the script. Rumsfeld's resistance to answering some of the questions put forth by reporters draws further attention to the gaps in the public knowledge about Guantánamo detainees that this play attempts to fill. By juxtaposing Rumsfeld's public press conference with the personal interviews that form the backbone of the script, the playwrights highlight the view that the history of this event is being manipulated by those in power, people who are erasing the stories of those who lack power. Press conferences that suppress the truth about these detentions can inflict further trauma on the victims of Guantánamo; this play seeks to recuperate some of the detainees' lost agency by enabling them to tell their own stories.

Nevertheless, the survivors' voices are absent from performances of the text; instead the performers speak for them. Elaine Scarry examines the phenomenon whereby one person's pain is represented by another:

> Because the person in pain is ordinarily so bereft of the resources of speech, it is not surprising that the language for pain should sometimes be brought into being by those who are not themselves in pain but who speak *on behalf of* those who are. Though there are very great impediments to expressing another's sentient distress, so are there also very great reasons why one might want to do so, and thus there come to be avenues by which this most radically private of experiences begins to enter the realm of public discourse.[34]

Because the act of narrating and renarrating one's own trauma runs the risk of inflicting further trauma on the survivor, performance presents a powerful platform for trauma narratives to be witnessed again and again without the survivor continually representing, and possibly reliving, his trauma.

THE OTHER GUANTÁNAMO

The policies that created the Guantánamo detention center rely on the notion that some people are "other"—not American, not even human, without rights. The play examines the ways in which this othering supports the fallacy that rights could be denied to anyone and through performance enacts what Jill Dolan calls "finding one's feet in the shoes of another."[35] It is this effort, this trying to understand, this trying to create change that imbues *Guantánamo* with utopian performatives and hope.[36] Those who gather in the theater enact collective witnessing and begin the necessary process of envisioning change, a different world where rights are maintained and law aligns with justice.

Still, an often ignored yet nevertheless important other side to the debate about Guantánamo deserves our attention. To provide a voice in the play for those audience members who may have reservations about critiquing the detention center, the script includes Tom Clarke. Clarke's sister died in the World Trade Center and his grief over her death pervades his monologues. He continues to hope that those who perpetrated the attacks of 9/11 will be brought to justice. English professor Wendy S. Hesford finds that "Tom Clarke represents someone *working through* trauma at the interpersonal, intercultural and international level."[37] Indeed, Clarke's ambivalence about Guantánamo represents the internal conflict that marks the aftermath of trauma. In his second monologue, he says of the Guantánamo detainees, "[l]ock 'em up, throw away the key."[38] Yet in his third monologue, he expresses his anguish at the indefinite duration of these detentions: "Those who are innocent have lost three years of their life, much as I have lost, as I've been living in a sort of private hell since my sister was murdered, and although at least I . . . still sort of have my life, they've had theirs taken away."[39] Clarke's profound grief conveys the complex nature of Guantánamo as a facility and an institution to critique. Evidently the playwrights sought to include in the script more people conflicted about the detentions at Guantánamo, but none came forward to be interviewed.[40] Although the script presents a more robust argument against Guantánamo than for it, Clarke's inclusion in the play nevertheless demonstrates that there exists another perspective on Guantánamo, one similarly rooted in personal experience. Clarke's mixed views reflect an understandable anger about his sister, coupled with his assertion that the unlawfulness of the Guantánamo detentions taints the justice he seeks on behalf of the World Trade Center, Pentagon, and Flight 93 victims. The trauma Clarke works through cannot be resolved through his government's detention of enemy combatants at Guantánamo; resolution must come from public trials of those who perpetuated the attacks that caused Clarke's suffering.

Guantánamo relays the emotional and physical trauma of the detainees through letters they wrote to their parents, or through surrogates such as their families or their lawyers. Garth Pierce, a lawyer for some of the detainees, thus describes the experience of bearing witness to the atrocities:

> We read, we watch, we hear about atrocities—we know what man's inhumanity to man consists of, we know all that, but . . . we don't have the capacity to . . . react the way we should as human beings. But when you have [in front of you] men you're getting to know . . . it's tumbling out and they're reminding each other, they're telling things that they haven't told anyone . . . How do ordinary words tell it? But yet they do, if you are realizing the people who are telling it to you are the people who've survived it.[41]

The second-person voice of this passage becomes a direct address to the audience as Pierce exhorts witnesses to these narratives to remember that these stories are true personal experiences. His experience of witnessing this testimony becomes the audience's experience as he invites audiences to recognize their common humanity with the men whose stories are represented on stage.

Although *Guantánamo* hints at or briefly mentions the physical and emotional violence against detainees, the script never calls for it to be enacted on stage. Jamal describes his first interrogation thus: "And then that's when I, you know, the kicking and all that," but he refrains from detailing his torture.[42] In this way, the play avoids sensationalism and invites active participation on the part of the audience. The performative power of *Guantánamo* resides in audiences filling in these gaps in the story themselves, and turning to their own imaginations to create images and sounds that accompany the stories they hear narrated on stage. In this way, the play refuses to give more attention to the guards of Guantánamo than those whose stories the government is suppressing, unlike the much publicized photographic images of the abuse of Abu Ghraib, which clearly showed the guards' faces hovering over hooded prisoners who were denied subjectivity. Peggy Phelan claims that the Abu Ghraib photographs "are operations of war. In this sense, [they] function not only as documentary or aesthetic texts but also as weapons."[43] The play, on the other hand, wields testimony rather than imagery as a weapon against the US and British governments. Phelan further posits that the Abu Ghraib photographs position Western audiences as witnesses who express passive guilt over the situation. Phelan, quoting Susan Sontag, writes: "'The photographs are us'... thus the act of looking at these photographs repeats the original failure-to-see-the-other that the photographs frame so dramatically."[44] Performances of *Guantánamo* subvert this failure-to-see-the-other that Phelan links with the Abu Ghraib images by bringing audiences face to face with people embodying the other and requiring that audiences conjure the other, summoning him to the space through the imaginative power of their active spectatorship. *Guantánamo* makes apparent the othering that the detention center relies on, then subverts this othering through the act of performance, where the self and the other meet in one body. The strangeness that dangerously distances the other breaks down with every performative encounter.

Stuart Hall, in "The Spectacle of the Other," maintains that those whose identity markers situate them as minorities are often represented through "sharply opposed, polarized, binary extremes—good/bad, civilized/primitive, ugly/excessively attractive, repelling-because-different/compelling-because-strange-and-exotic."[45] The play presents people typically grouped together as a single entity, and shatters the often monolithic treatment of marginalized individuals by sharing their personal stories, each of which is varied and multifaceted. The colloquial speech of Ruhel Ahmed distinguishes him from Wahab, who speaks in formal, proper language. The play gives them, then, not just a voice, but *their own* voice. Audiences learn through the play that each of these men has a different family situation, a different relationship to his religion, and a different response to his detention.

Nevertheless, the play falls short of presenting a thoroughly compelling argument against Guantánamo as an institution and a policy by failing to address the full complexity of the men detained there. By only narrating the stories of people clearly innocent of terrorist activity, the play avoids getting into the ethics of denying a trial to anyone—innocent or guilty—whom a state holds captive. Although considered an anti-Guantánamo play, the piece could more accurately be considered a criticism of the capture and detention without warrant of random individuals who look a certain way or practice a certain religion. The power of the play resides in its representations of the individual suffering endured by its five subjects and their families, its creation of new understandings of the history and personal experience of this event, and its critique of citizenship and human rights. It does not begin to suggest answers to the other tough questions associated with Guantánamo, such as what the US government should do with those there who participated in acts of terrorism. In this way, the play provides a profound though narrow critique of Guantánamo.

Additionally, the play avoids wading into the controversy over torture. Although the piece critiques the abduction, relocation, detention, and isolation of Wahab, Bisher, Jamal, Moazzam, and Ruhel, it offers no real examination of torture, and four of the five men never mention physical abuse at all. One of the most damaging legacies of "black sites," or US military detention centers located off US soil and away from the US legal jurisdiction, is the preponderance of reports detailing US torture of detainees. As Elaine Scarry has astutely pointed out, because governments are only inclined to torture in exceptional circumstances, torture must be defined as an act for which not even "exceptional circumstances" provide permission.[46] Nevertheless, many now call for exceptions to the prohibition on torture, including law professor Alan Derschowitz, who advocates the use of torture warrants.[47] Mark Danner observed that torture has become in the United States something the president has the power to prohibit, rather than that which is always already prohibited.[48] Guantánamo routinely inspires impassioned arguments about detainee treatment, actionable intelligence, and ticking-bomb scenarios. By failing to address torture, *Guantánamo* sidesteps one of the fundamental issues related to its subject matter. The piece cannot be viewed as presenting a thorough case supporting universal human rights when it fails to advance an argument about the rights of every individual, regardless of citizenship, not to be tortured.

For those opposed to Guantánamo for any reason, it is important to ask what might be the most effective and ethical vehicle for advancing an argument against the detention center. How can this argument find and persuade an oppositional audience? Has *Guantánamo* succeeded in influencing the situation at the detention center, or national politics? Actor Julia Brothers answered this question thus: "I don't know that I can say that our production of the play was instrumental in changing government policies, but we did stir up some activism and once that happens, you never know how far reaching one person's actions will be."⁴⁹ The political influence of the play resides in the way it creates a sense of "we" among audiences as a community of people engaged in this issue, and between people with the means and opportunity to create or attend a production and those who are deprived of the liberty to do so. This collective "we" that performances of *Guantánamo* creates begins to reestablish the notion of shared humanity and universal human rights. Judith Butler articulates the power of this collective feeling: "Despite our differences in location and history, my guess is that it is possible to appeal to a 'we,' for all of us have some notion of what it is to have lost somebody. Loss has made a tenuous 'we' of us all."⁵⁰ The pain Guantánamo inflicts radiates outward from those detained there, to their loved ones, to those who directly caused this pain, to all the countries implicated in the institution. Elaine Scarry contends that "the act of verbally expressing pain is a necessary prelude to the collective task of diminishing pain."⁵¹ Because Guantánamo can be understood as a collective trauma, it must be processed, represented, and spoken about collectively. This sense of "we" thus becomes a vital step toward preventing governments from denying fundamental rights to any person.

While witnessing trauma testimony is an invaluable and important step in dismantling the mentality that created Guantánamo and the current state of exception, the compassion and sympathy performances of *Guantánamo* evoke can be problematic. Witnessing has the potential to generate feelings of complacency in audiences, who may believe that simply by *feeling* for the people whose stories they have just heard, they have done their part to make the world better. Lauren Berlant describes this phenomenon thus: "In operation, compassion is a term denoting privilege: the sufferer is *over there* ... But if the obligation to recognize and alleviate suffering is more than a demand on the consciousness ... then it is crucial to appreciate the multitude of conventions around the relation of feeling to practice where compassion is concerned."⁵² Performances of *Guantánamo* call on audiences to do more than remember the stories of trauma they hear.

The extent of atrocity of Guantánamo stretches beyond our imagination. Performances of *Guantánamo* allow us as audience members to *begin* to imagine specific elements of the detentions by providing us with personal narratives of horror and pain. These stories are too terrible to be conjured, yet they unfold on the stage and provide details audiences can use to anchor their imaginations in so they may begin to fathom Guantánamo as a lived experience. The live-ness of a performance, which brings spectators face to face with actors embodying suffering and survival, has the potential to disrupt compassionate complacency. Nevertheless, it remains for individual audience members to take real action to urge governments to not deny universal human rights and to not disregard domestic and international legal procedures. Performance, to borrow from Augusto Boal, can be a "rehearsal for the revolution,"⁵³ but it cannot enact a revolution itself. Each individual witness determines whether this rehearsal will be realized after he or she leaves the performance site.

Notes

1. Carol Martin, "Bodies in Evidence," *The Drama Review* 50.2 (Fall 2006), 9.
2. Victoria Brittain and Gillian Slovo, *Guantánamo: Honor Bound to Defend Freedom* (London: Oberon Books, 2008), 7.
3. Johan Steyn, "Guantánamo: A Monstrous Failure of Justice," *Common Dreams*, November 27, 2003. http://www.commondreams.org/views03/1127-08.htm.
4. Giorgio Agamben, *State of Exception*, trans. Kevin Attell (Chicago: University of Chicago Press, 2005), 2.
5. Agamben 3.
6. Charlie Savage, "Two Guantánamo Detainees Freed, the First in Fifteen Months," *New York Times*, April 19, 2012. http://www.nytimes.com/2012/04/20/world/americas/2-guantanamo-bay-detainees-freed-in-el-salvador.html?_r=1.
7. Barack Obama, "Presidential Memorandum—Closure of Detention Facilities at Guantánamo Naval Base," *Office of the Press Secretary*, December 15, 2009. http://www.whitehouse.gov/the-press-office/presidential-memorandum-closure-dentention-facilities-guantanamo-bay-naval-base.
8. Barack Obama, "Statement by the President on H.R. 1540," *Office of the Press Secretary*, December 31, 2011. http://www.whitehouse.gov/the-press-office/2011/12/31/statement-president-hr-1540.
9. For a detailed description of what reporters are allowed to photograph and write about when they tour the detention facility, see Jeremy W. Peter's "In Two Guantánamo Tours, Many Questions, Few Answers," *The New York Times*, August 11, 2010. http://www.nytimes.com/2010/08/12/us/12gitmo.html?_r=1&scp=2&sq=guantanamo&st=cse. Also, Carol Rosenberg, a reporter for the *Miami Herald*, spoke at length about the restrictions placed on journalists as part of Stanford's *Ethics and War* series, "Reporting Guantánamo: America's Experiment in Extraterritorial Detention," November 16, 2011.
10. For example, see The Bill of Rights Defense Committee, "Guantánamo Reading Project," for a list of US cities participating in staged readings of the play. http://www.bordc.org/grp/readings/hostcities.php.
11. William Hoyland, class discussion, University of Texas at Austin, October 2, 2008.
12. Akhil Gupta and James Ferguson, "Beyond 'Culture': Space, Identity and the Politics of Difference," *Culture, Power, Place: Explorations in Critical Anthropology*, eds. Gupta and Ferguson (Durham: Duke University Press, 1991), 39.
13. Brittain and Slovo 43.
14. Gupta and Ferguson 34.
15. Brittain and Slovo 13–14.
16. Ibid., 22.
17. Judith Butler, *Precarious Life: The Power of Mourning and Violence* (New York: New Left Books, 2004), 57.
18. Brittain and Slovo 33.
19. Ibid., 33.
20. Ibid., 7.
21. Ibid., 59.

22. Neil Campbell, *The Rhizomatic West: Representing the American West in a Transnational, Global, Media Age* (Lincoln, University of Nebraska Press, 2008), 90.
23. Michel de Certeau, *The Writing of History* (New York: Columbia University Press, 1988), 58.
24. Peggy Phelan, *Unmarked: The Politics of Performance* (New York: Routledge, 1993), 118.
25. Ann Cvetkovich, *An Archive of Feelings: Trauma, Sexuality and Lesbian Public Cultures* (Durham: Duke University Press 2003), 7.
26. For an account of torture at Guantánamo, see, for example, Delegates of the International Committee of the Red Cross, *ICRC report on the Treatment of Fourteen "High Value Detainees" in CIA Custody*, February 2007.
27. Charlotte Canning, "Feminist Performance as Feminist Historiography," *Theatre Survey* 45 (2004): 227.
28. Susan Brison, *Aftermath: Violence and the Remaking of a Self* (Princeton: Princeton University Press, 2002), x–xi.
29. Judith Lewis Herman, *Trauma and Recovery* (USA: Basic Books, 1992), 33.
30. Herman, *Trauma and Recovery*, 35–36.
31. Julia Brothers, email correspondence, June 17, 2010.
32. Bertolt Brecht, *Brecht on Theatre*, trans. John Willett (Great Britain: Methuen and Co., 1964), 193.
33. See for example TimeLine Theatre's production. http://www.talkinbroadway.com/regional/chicago/ch87.html.
34. Elaine Scarry, *The Body in Pain: The Making and Unmaking of the World* (New York: Oxford University Press, 1985), 6.
35. Jill Dolan, *Utopia in Performance: Finding Hope at the Theatre* (Ann Arbor: University of Michigan Press, 2005), 114.
36. See Dolan, especially the introduction, for an explanation of the utopian performative.
37. Wendy S. Hesford, "Staging Terror," *The Drama Review* 50 (2006): 38.
38. Brittain and Slovo 42.
39. Ibid., 44.
40. Hoyland discussion. See also Brittain and Slovo 5.
41. Brittain and Slovo 49–50.
42. Ibid., 40.
43. Peggy Phelan, "In the Valley of the Shadow of Death: The Photographs of Abu Ghraib," *Violence Performed: Local Roots and Global Routes of Conflict*, eds. Patrick Anderson and Jisha Menon (New York: Palgrave Macmillan, 2009), 379.
44. Phelan, "In the Valley of the Shadow of Death," 380.
45. Stuart Hall, "The Spectacle of the Other," *Representation: Cultural Representations and Signifying Practices*, ed. Stuart Hall (London: Sage Publications, 2003), 229.
46. Elaine Scarry, Tanner Lectures in Human Values, Stanford University, May 14, 2010.
47. Alan Dershowitz, "Tortured Reasoning," *Torture: A Collection*, ed. Sanford Levinson (New York: Oxford University Press, 2004). See also Jonathan Alter, "Time to Think about Torture?," *Newsweek* November 5, 2001.
48. Mark Danner, Tanner Lectures in Human Values, Stanford University, May 14, 2010.

49. Brothers, email correspondence.
50. Butler, *Precarious*, 20.
51. Scarry, *Body in Pain*, 9.
52. Lauren Berlant, "Introduction: Compassion and Withholding," *Compassion: The Culture and Politics of an Emotion* (New York: Routledge, 2004), 4.
53. Augusto Boal, *Theatre of the Oppressed*, trans. Charles A & Maria-Odilia Leal McBride (New York: Theatre Communications Group, 1979), 122.

CHAPTER 6

CHALLENGING THE "FETISH OF THE VERBATIM": NEW AESTHETICS AND FAMILIAR ABUSES IN CHRISTINE EVANS'S *SLOW FALLING BIRD*

Christina Wilson

Australian playwright Christine Evans aims to show her audience " 'a dream with a hard core of truth.' "[1] In her 2003 play, *Slow Falling Bird*, the hard truth emerges as the continuity of human rights abuse in Australia. Breaching several international laws, Australia currently confines undocumented asylum seekers to indefinite mandatory detention. *Slow Falling Bird* dramatizes the daily humiliation and terror of asylum seekers in Woomera, the nation's most infamous detention center.[2] Importantly, however, Evans divides her attention between Afghan and Iraqi detainees and their Australian guards, one of whom is an Indigenous Australian and victim of earlier crimes against the Stolen Generations. Evoking narrative conventions from Stolen Generations' texts, Evans connects Australia's treatment of refugees to earlier ideologies of discrimination. Thus, while the plights of

---

Slow Falling Bird was developed in 2003 at the Bay Area Playwrights Festival and was a finalist for the 2003 Patrick White Playwrights Award. Directed by Rebecca Novic, the play premiered at San Francisco's Crowded Fire Theatre Company in 2005. It has also been produced in Melbourne (2004) and Brisbane (2007), workshopped at London's Young Vic Director's Project (2007) and appeared as a reading at the Irish Repertory Theatre in New York City (2009). Evans received the Rella Lossy Playwriting Award (San Francisco, 2004) and the Monash Association National Playwriting Award (Australia, 2004) for *Slow Falling Bird*.

undocumented asylum seekers remain her focus, Evans maps these violations onto a trajectory of abuse.

If the situation at Woomera reveals a difficult truth, the "dream" appears in Evans's aesthetic. *Slow Falling Bird* presents meticulously researched events and conditions in a "hallucinatory" and "delirious" light.[3] As reports indicate severe psychological distress among detainees, Evans's aesthetic mirrors the actual trauma she depicts: her Woomera is "at once a real place; and a place inside a desert of the mind."[4] Evans's aesthetic is a sort of warped realism influenced by the stylings of physical theater. And although the term is most often associated with Latin American literature, *Slow Falling Bird* might usefully be understood in terms of magical realism because this style tends to use "fantastic/phantasmagoric characters ... to indict recent political and cultural perversions" and it also presents "historical narrative [not as] chronicle but clairvoyance."[5] Significantly, Evans is interested in "non-naturalistic and poetic approaches to writing politically engaged theater, especially in a time when the loudest drums we hear are those of testimony... I'm tired of the fetish of the verbatim."[6]

As Evans's remarks suggest, the dominant trend in literature purporting to bring visibility to human rights violations has been individual narratives of abuse. Joseph Slaughter has shown that human rights and storytelling are intimately aligned because "human rights abuse is characterized as an infringement on the modern subject's ability to narrate her story."[7] Kay Schaffer and Sidonie Smith further explain that, "life narratives have become one of the most potent vehicles for advancing human rights claims."[8] The power of legal testimony—the individual speech acts that help prosecute human rights crimes—certainly attracts frequent adaptation. However, questions have arisen about the limitations of testimony in the arts. Allen Feldman argues that the convergence of trauma-aesthetics and testimony "simulate[s] a cathartic affect that too easily transcends the violence described" because these narratives' "linearity ... establish[es] the pastness of prior violence."[9] If an audience can be lulled into displacing abuse temporally, then they may similarly distance themselves geographically. Rustom Bharucha contends that the unequal relationship between core and periphery may allow Western audiences to consume the Other non-critically;[10] in other words, dramatized testimony of suffering may provoke an unintended voyeurism that undermines the goals of the performance.

In *Slow Falling Bird*, Evans's nonrealistic aesthetic challenges audiences out of the comfort and "fetish of the verbatim." Rejecting what has become the hegemonic discourse of human rights, Evans instead connects and exposes abusive ideologies through an experimental aesthetic. As Evans evokes and then destabilizes the formal and thematic conventions from Stolen Generations texts, testimony and "home," respectively, the stories of both undocumented asylum seekers and the Stolen Generations take on new, forceful dimensions.

Slow Falling Bird opens with Woomera Immigration Detention Centre guards Rick and Micko scanning the desert horizon, on the lookout for human activity but spotting only rabbits on the run. Although the international community protects undocumented asylum, Australia's undocumented asylum seekers wait for their refugee applications to be processed while in detention, surrounded by barbwire fences; in effect, they are "'prisoners without having committed any offence.'"[11] Evans introduces three such detainees: Zahrah, a pregnant Iraqi widow, and the Afghan orphans Leyla and her brother Mahmoud, aged 15 and 12. Like their real-life counterparts, these asylum seekers "'[live] initially in the hope that soon their incarceration will come to an end but with the passage of time, the hope [gives] way to despair.'"[12]

Located in the South Australian desert, Woomera was once an army base for the United States.[13] Rick, the experienced guard and a white Australian from the area, tells Micko that after "the Yanks" left town, "the [detention] camp rescued this town from the morgue."[14] In her article "Asylum Seekers and 'Border Panic' in Australia," Evans explains

> With its status as a Defense Force town and history as missile testing range and joint U.S./Australia spy base, it's illegal to live at Woomera without a full time job.... It's no exaggeration then, to say that the incarceration of Middle Eastern asylum seekers has been keeping the town alive.[15]

In *Slow Falling Bird*, Evans primarily highlights the town's militaristic violence—an attitude that seeks to "protect" the nation but in doing so, harms others. However, Evans's Woomera also appears sleepily ominous: the isolation and quiet of this desert town keeps the realities of mandatory detention, the suffering and abuse, contained.

For Rick, the worst part of Woomera is not the riots or traumatized children "cutting themselves up," but rather, "the worst thing's the boredom."[16] Anxious for "something real" to happen, Rick is in luck for Evans's second scene reveals something both real and unreal through the figures of the Fish Child (the "hovering spirit" of Zahrah's baby) and a "spectral Chorus of Crows" named Mortein and Baygon ("the brand names of two leading Australian pest control products").[17] The Fish Child refuses to enter this world in the desert, insistent that she needs water to live. While the Fish Child hovers above the stage, Mortein and Baygon arrive ready for action. Mortein and Baygon, spiritual ferrymen, wait to collect those who will eventually "cross over."[18] As with Rick, Woomera bores Baygon early in the play; he is convinced that they have arrived in the wrong town but Mortein insists "misery leads to action."[19] Of course, Mortein is right and as he tutors Baygon, Mortein simultaneously leads the audience through the worsening conditions at the detention center. Mortein and Baygon engage with the living characters and help shape the action, keeping a particularly close eye on Micko.

Micko's navigation of Woomera largely informs *Slow Falling Bird*'s narrative arc. New to the area and the detention center, Micko displays palpable discomfort with his job. Ultimately, Mortein and Baygon prevent Micko from becoming another Rick, a hardened guard and damaged human being. One evening, after a particularly bad day at the detention center, Micko succumbs to Mortein and Baygon's provocations. As they interrogate him, Micko indicates that he is an Indigenous Australian and a member of the Stolen Generations—Aboriginal children who were forcibly removed from their families and placed in government custody.

With Micko's admission, *Slow Falling Bird* transitions from a play about one example of human rights violations to a play concerned with a trajectory of abuse. As the refugee scandal has taken place concurrently with reconciliation efforts toward the Stolen Generations, Evans suggests that nothing has materially changed in Australia. Indeed, the troubles of Australia's detainees become more obscene as Evans evokes the past treatment of Aboriginal and Torres Strait Islanders. Strikingly, the legal prejudices directed toward both Indigenous Australians and contemporary refugees intersect through the issues of citizenship and child abuse.

The early-nineteenth-century *terra nullius* ("no man's land") fiction exemplifies legal discrimination against Indigenous peoples. *Terra nullius*[20] established Australia as an uninhabited territory and effectively made Indigenous Australians legally invisible, enabling the British government to create a (white) Australia free of Indigenous complication. As noncitizens, Indigenous Australians were subject to abusive policies of exclusion late into the twentieth century. In fact, Indigenous peoples were not legally counted, and thus not legitimized as Australians, until the Constitutional Referendum of 1967.

Assimilation was a second tactic for eliminating Indigenous presence from Australia and was the primary motivation behind the forced removal of Indigenous children, the Stolen Generations. Between 1910 and 1970, an estimated 50,000–100,000 Indigenous children, usually of mixed race, were forcibly taken from their families and placed into white homes, mission centers, or orphanages where they were taught, among other things, the English language and Christian faith.[21] While the government outwardly aimed to "protect" these children, they also hoped to assimilate them into white Australia, breeding out the Aborigine. While children were placed in white families under the guise of adoption, they were most often treated as servants and suffered acute physical, psychological, and sexual trauma. Moreover, because of general mismanagement and falsification of documents, many stolen children were unable to reunite with their families as adults and thus suffered a lifetime of separation.

Following generations of suffering and decades of activism, Indigenous concerns finally caught the attention of the larger Australian populace and the international community by the 1990s. Prime Minister Paul Keating's 1992 Redfern Address stands out as one of the first official acknowledgements of Indigenous suffering: "We...smashed the traditional way of life....We took the children from their mothers. We practised discrimination and exclusion. It was our ignorance and our prejudice. And our failure to imagine these things being done to us."[22] Speaking on the eve of the United Nations Year of Indigenous Peoples, Keating famously accepted a degree of responsibility on behalf of wider Australia.[23]

Yet while Keating's Redfern Address highlights the beginnings of nationwide efforts toward reconciliation, his administration's immigration policy has an equally important legacy. Strikingly, the Redfern Address used Australia's history as a nation of immigrants to arouse empathy for Indigenous Australians:

> Australia once reached out for us. Didn't Australia provide opportunity and care for the dispossessed Irish? The poor of Britain? The refugees from war and famine and persecution in the countries of Europe and Asia? . . . if we can build a prosperous and remarkably harmonious multicultural society in Australia, surely we can find just solutions to the problems which beset the first Australians—the people to whom the most injustice has been done.[24]

As Keating promotes compassion and multiculturalism and recognizes injustice, it is bitterly ironic that this speech came within months of new immigration laws that laid the foundation for Australia's racist anti-asylum policies. Presumably, while "we" could not previously imagine having "our" children taken from "us," "we" remained stubbornly unimaginative—unwilling or unable to see the effects of indefinite imprisonment on refugee children and adults alike.

In August 1991, Minister for Immigration Gerry Hand began mandatory detention for asylum seekers who enter Australia without visas, individuals commonly referred to as "boat-people" due to their arrival by sea. Meant to deter unauthorized arrivals, mandatory detention reflects unreasonable expectations of orderly refugee migration.[25] James Jupp explains that "in the view of the [Australian] Immigration Department, there should be no undocumented arrivals," even though international law protects undocumented asylum seekers and allows for the necessity of unplanned refuge.[26] Initially, undocumented asylum seekers could be held for a maximum of 273 days; in 1994, the time limit was removed and indefinite detention began.[27]

The Keating administration also introduced the Migration Amendment Act of 1992, which established four-year temporary protection visas rather than permanent residency. Although the Amendment Act was abandoned in 1993, it resurfaced in 1999 under Keating's more conservative successor John Howard. The Howard administration's Temporary Protection Visas granted asylum for renewable periods of three years but did not extend asylum to a refugee's immediate family. In the foreword to *Human Rights Overboard*, Julian Burnside argues that this new restriction led to desperate behavior: in a single night, "353 people [mostly women and children] drowned as they tried to get to Australia to be reunited with their immediate family members who had already been accepted in Australia as refugees."[28]

By the late 1990s, the majority of undocumented asylum seekers came from Afghanistan and Iraq, fleeing either the Taliban or Saddam Hussein.[29] Conservative efforts to frame Middle Eastern asylum seekers as "terrorists" helped secure support for their detention. Labor Party leader Kim Beazley stated in 2001, " 'I don't think it's unhumanitarian to try and keep control of your refugee program. I don't think it's unhumanitarian to try to deter criminals.' "[30] Howard further insisted that without " 'a proper processing system' " the government would have no way of knowing whether the " 'people on these boats [were] terrorists.' "[31] (Mistakenly, Howard identifies mandatory detention as a "processing system" when it is, in fact, a punishment.)

The "Children Overboard" scandal best illustrates attempts to paint undocumented asylum seekers as criminals. Largely seen as political maneuvering on the heels of 9/11 and leading up to the November 2001 elections, Howard's government claimed that "boat people" had thrown their children into the sea to coerce the Australian Coastwatch into rescuing them. Later investigations found no evidence to support these claims, yet at the time, Howard remarked, "I certainly don't want to see people of that type in Australia, I really don't."[32] As Howard's response seems framed at keeping "that type" out of Australia, his view suggests that only the (white) Australian requires protection. Recalling earlier fears of racial and cultural mixing, the Middle Eastern refugee becomes Australia's new Other to exclude.

Rhetorical violence in vilifying asylum seekers as criminals works to justify their detention. And as they are first isolated in detention centers and then refused permanent asylum, refugees in Australia are segregated into what Suvendrini Perera calls "not-Australia." Linking asylum seekers to Australia's Stolen Generations, Perera argues that in this "ever expanding space of civil exclusion,"

> Australia's history reappears in unfamiliar yet still recognizable guises. Indigenous Australians remember other internment camps...The inmates of not-Australia are, in official phraseology, unlawful non-citizens. They are Not-Australians and unAustralian; the stuff of contraband...Non-people.[33]

For asylum seekers and Indigenous Australians alike, Perera's "not-Australia" recalls Hannah Arendt's assertion that "the loss of citizenship deprive[s] people not only of protection, but also of all clearly established, officially recognized identity."[34]

Exploited by a government that did not recognize them, the Stolen Generations suffered "the loss of their homes, and this meant the loss of the entire social texture into which they were born and in which they established themselves a distinct place in the world."[35] For asylum seekers, as Arendt argues, the trauma "is not [only] the loss of a home but the impossibility of finding a new one."[36] While Indigenous peoples became officially Australian in 1967, the combined effect of mandatory detention and temporary visas works to prevent undocumented asylum seekers from acquiring citizenship—and thus a home—completely. However, for both the Stolen Generations and the undocumented asylum seekers, citizenship is but one hurdle to a realized homecoming; the second difficulty lies in the disruption of normal familial relationships.

Forced into orphanages and mission centers, the Stolen Generations did not grow up surrounded by the relatives who loved and cared for them. And as Indigenous children were removed over the course of several generations, many individuals lost not only their parents but their own children as well. More recently, Australia's immigration policies have posed serious problems to asylum seekers and their families. Following the 1994 requirement for individual asylum applications, which provides no guarantee that members of a family would be granted refuge together, many undocumented asylum seekers are denied contact with their families outside the detention center, leaving their loved ones to wonder what has become of them. Most egregiously, mandatory detention includes children, a practice Chris Goddard and Linda Briskman describe as "organised and ritualised abuse."[37]

Between 1999 and 2003, Australia's detention centers held more than 2,000 children.[38] In detention, children are both victims of and witnesses to acts of violence and self-harm, including suicide. Though adult detainees are more often the targets of brute violence, children are affected as witnesses to their parents' abuse. Reports indicate that guards routinely, and indiscriminately, strike detainees with batons and use riot gear, including water cannons.[39] In addition to physical harm, detention severely undermines parents' ability to care for their children and, as a result, parents often suffer from "feelings of guilt, depression and a loss of self-esteem."[40] The authors of *Human Rights Overboard* argue that "both the deterioration in the mental health of their parents and the conditions of detention itself, [expose] the children held in detention to trauma."[41] In fact, nearly all detained children develop psychiatric disorders; a majority suffer from suicidal thoughts and "[a] quarter had self-harmed."[42] In an interview, one child described himself as a caged bird: "I am like a bird in a cage.... [One of his drawings was of an egg with a boot hovering above it ready to crush it. Pointing to the egg he said,] These are the babies in detention."[43] Although Australia signed the *Convention on the Rights of the Child* (CRC) in 1990, the Human Rights and Equal Opportunities Commission (HREOC) concluded in its 2004 report *A Last Resort?* that mandatory detention fundamentally violates article 37(b) of the CRC: "no child shall be deprived of his or her liberty unlawfully or arbitrarily. The arrest, detention or imprisonment of a child... shall be used only as a measure of last resort."[44]

While *A Last Resort?* details the devastating consequences of mandatory detention, it is another HREOC report, *Bringing Them Home* (1997), that plays a central role in the political and cultural landscape surrounding the Stolen Generations. Containing hundreds of testimonies, the report documents the terrible actualities of government policies. The rhetoric that once emphasized providing Aboriginal children with education was replaced in the popular imagination by stories of abuse and suffering. As the title suggests, recovery efforts for the Stolen Generations revolve around the metaphor of "home," finding a way back to the Indigenous family after decades of separation. The dominant trope of Stolen Generations' narratives involves the journey, actual or metaphorical, that a stolen child takes back to his or her mother and to his or her Aboriginal identity. For instance, one early best seller, Sally Morgan's *My Place* (1987), chronicles the author's discovery of her Indigenous ancestry as she investigates her mother and grandmother's pasts. More recently, Phillip Noyce's film *Rabbit-Proof Fence* (2002), based on actual events, depicts the story of three young stolen girls who escape from a mission center and, following a dangerous journey through the Australian outback, return home to their Aboriginal mother.[45]

Strikingly, in her article "Asylum Seekers and 'Border Panic' In Australia," Evans notes the story of Alamdar and Montazar Bhaktiari, detained asylum seekers who

> escaped from Woomera in 2002, making their way to Melbourne, where they walked into the British embassy and claimed asylum from persecution by the Australian government. Although their bid was quashed with cynical speed...[t]hey made visible to a general Australian public the faces, names and stories of some of those buried behind the wire and most shockingly, revealed themselves as preadolescent children.[46]

Echoing the desert voyage from *Rabbit-Proof Fence*, a film released the same year as the Bhaktiaris' flight, children become the faces of both forced removal and mandatory detention. The parallel between the Bhaktiaris' story and *Rabbit-Proof Fence* suggests that abuse in Australia continues under new guises, with new targets; importantly, it also indicates that while political and cultural sensitivity exists for one group of rights victims, such awareness has done little to prevent new violations. Indeed, while the young girls in *Rabbit-Proof Fence* return home, the Bhaktiaris—like all undocumented asylum seekers—remain homeless.

The Stolen Generations' thematic fixation with home resonates in Evans's contemporary concerns. Of course, Evans recognizes that undocumented asylum seekers have little chance of establishing a safe haven, let alone a home, in an atmosphere defined by mandatory detention. Consequently, Evans invokes and then subverts this trope in her play to express a bleaker truth. Though "home" is an achievable space in most Stolen Generations narratives, Evans's revision brings to light Australia's Stolen Generations who continue to suffer, as they are unable to find their families or otherwise complete the journey home.

Evans most clearly challenges Stolen Generations narratives through Micko. Deeply ambivalent, Micko represents both the adult child who travels to the desert to find answers about his past and the detention guard who keeps children locked away. Evans frames much of Micko's concern for the asylum seekers in terms of his own experiences. Still, Micko is uncomfortable voicing a strident defense of the detainees, seemingly afraid of being identified as an Other himself. When Micko tells Rick, "we'd better post [the paperwork for Leyla and Mahmoud], mate. It's the law," Rick responds with a stricter interpretation of the law: "They didn't ask for asylum at the initial interview. So immigration told us we can scrap it."[47] But Micko doesn't scrap their application; he secretly posts it through to lawyers.

Alone in an unfamiliar land, surrounded by authority figures whose language they do not speak, Leyla and Mahmoud must remind Micko of his own stolen childhood. Leyla and Mahmoud are "unaccompanied children" and represent approximately 14% of Australia's detained minors.[48] As Leyla struggles to maintain faith that someone will soon begin their processing, she insists that Mahmoud practice the only English they know: " 'Please sir, refugee from very bad fightings. Mother and father no. We ask please sir, an asylum.' "[49] With resignation, Mahmoud tells her, "No one's coming. No one ever comes."[50] Though they do not know it, Micko has ensured that help is on the way. However, Micko's sympathies lapse when Mahmoud insults him. Micko then begins "*roughing Mahmoud up*" until Rick takes over, beating Mahmoud so badly that the boy dies.[51]

Consistent with Evans's aesthetic, Rick's vicious attack in the detention center transforms into an obscene dance at the local bar later that evening. Here, Mortein and Baygon arrive to comment on the "good suntan" Micko has "for a long-sleeved job."[52] They then casually ask a drunken Micko if he is from the area:

Micko: Well, maybe. Might have used to be.
Mortein: "Might have used to be."
Micko: Yeah, well I sort of remember it but I dunno where from. I was born in the desert. Least I think I was. That's what they told me at the Mission, anyway.
. . . I was just another skinny outback kid. Could've come from anywhere and there's no-one to ask.[53]

Although Micko hints at his background earlier in the play, the above exchange solidifies Micko's identity as an Indigenous Australian and stolen child. Micko's revelation becomes more significant as it directly follows the assault on Mahmoud because Micko knows what it means to be alone and mistreated, a vulnerable child who has "no-one to ask" for anything.

While the detention center is primarily a locus of misery for asylum seekers, the abuse Micko experienced as a child echoes through Leyla and Mahmoud's anguish. Nonetheless, Micko retains hope that Woomera can alleviate his suffering. He explains

When I'm in the desert, I sort of recognize the light—So maybe I was born out here. I dunno. You know the way it shimmers so you can't see straight? . . . It's real beautiful, like a long drink of water when you don't know you're thirsty—and it reminds me.[54]

Micko's feelings toward the desert are saturated with his longing; and as Micko compares the light in the desert to "a long drink of water," the trick of the light stands in for the idea of home. Throughout *Slow Falling Bird*, water represents home as a necessity, restorative, and haven; indeed, water becomes a manifold metaphor for home. Most notably, water stands in for both a spiritual home and the very real and dangerous environment "boat people" must negotiate as they travel from one home in the hopes of finding another. Of course, as Woomera is located in the desert, *Slow Falling Bird* constantly reminds its audience that water—home—cannot be found here. Yet because undocumented asylum seekers are immediately sent to detention centers in Australia's deserts, the open waters become their last sanctuary.

The Fish Child, the spirit of Zahrah's baby, explains that not only does she "like the boat" Zahrah traveled in, but she views the sea as an extension of the womb.[55] When Zahrah goes into labor, Mortein and Baygon encourage the Fish Child to descend from her perch above the stage. As they tie a rope, her umbilical cord, connecting her to Zahrah, the Fish Child argues that she wants to "Go back in the water!"[56] Acting on her preference, the Fish Child unties her end of the rope and attaches it to a small plastic shark, her body. Though her body is delivered into the desert, the Fish Child's refusal traps her between worlds and separates her from her mother; as Zahrah and the plastic shark are taken off stage, the Fish Child panics, screaming "Mama? Mama!!!"[57] Later scenes reveal that Zahrah finds the separation equally distressing; she knows something is deeply wrong, for the child will not drink and has "cold fish eyes."[58]

In despair, Zahrah tries to coax the plastic shark with a lullaby. Recounting her husband's drowning in the offshore waters, Zahrah sings: "There's a cord from me to you/Made of dreams and seawater/And your daddy's open mouth/Singing shark lullabies."[59] The Fish Child listens from her perch and replies: "There's a cord from him to you/Tangled up in your daughter/As the sea rolls his bones/Through the green ocean dark."[60] While Zahrah cannot hear the Fish Child, the exchange indicates that there is indeed something that continues to bind this family together. According to the song, even as Australia's immigration policies tear families apart, the deep connections between mother and child, husband and wife, continue to exist. However, these connections can only be spiritual. And so, though it is a consuming and deadly sea, the water is also a place where members of a family can return to one another in a spiritual haven.

Zahrah's lullaby appears in various forms throughout the play to mark this alternative homecoming. After Mahmoud's death, Leyla sits alone in her cell where she simply "sucks her thumb and rocks";[61] traumatized, the only English she now knows was clearly learned from the guards: "Fucking animals. Refugee cunt."[62] Eventually, Leyla hangs herself. Yet her suicide is framed as if she is in a "*beautiful underwater cave*" and not a detention cell in the desert.[63] As she readies herself, laughing and smiling, "*transformed back into a hopeful young girl*," Mahmoud, Mortein, and Baygon gather to the side of the stage and sing: "There's a cord from me to you/Made of bones and seawater/And your brother's open mouth/Singing shark lullabies."[64] In this instance, the song marks Leyla's transition from Woomera to an oceanic spirit world where she reunites with her brother.

As the sea becomes the last available home for Australia's undocumented asylum seekers, Evans cohesively brings this thematic thread back to Micko with another song. After Micko discloses his Stolen Generations identity, Rick persuades him onto the karaoke stage where Micko sings along to Warumpi Band's "My Island Home." Often believed to celebrate Australia itself, "My Island Home" actually refers to lead singer (and Aboriginal Australian) George Rrurrambu's remote island homeland.[65] As Micko sings "six years I've been in the desert/And every night I dream of the sea," he sings about his own longings for a home as he simultaneously describes the undocumented asylum seekers he guards.[66] If the sea represents an idea of home, a place where families can reconnect, Micko is homeless in the desert. A stolen child still searching for his family, in the desert he thinks he might be from, Micko must wonder at the lyrics, "They say home is where you find it/Will this place ever satisfy me?"[67] Though his chances at homecoming appear slim, Micko wants to fulfill the promise of other Stolen Generations narratives and return home.

Centrally, the story of the Stolen Generations, including its thematic preoccupation with "home," is tied to the testimonial model. The HREOC's report, *Bringing Them Home*, identified human rights abuse through nearly 800 submissions, 535 of which were personal narratives. Since the rise of truth and reconciliation commissions, testimony or individual narration has been seen as a crucial step toward the end goals of justice, community reconciliation, and the furtherance of human rights. Public storytelling is often explained as a process of reinstating victims into the collective. If victimization is a condition of otherness, of isolation from the larger community, granting victims a space for their tale is seen as a means of augmenting official narratives to include those whose personal lives have been forever changed. The implied contract between narrator and addressee, victim and nation, embedded within most human rights narratives ensures that as the storyteller voices his or her experience, the audience must listen and acknowledge his pain; yet the addressee also expects that their attention will produce positive effects. Put another way, listening to testimony from human rights victims may be understood as the first step toward "bringing them home."

However, the model of storytelling as trauma alleviation is a thorny one. Recent trends in trauma studies suggest that storytelling may actually work to keep the past in the present; rather than healing, narration may instead oblige victims to carry their pasts into their futures. Feldman identifies an additional temporal problem with storytelling in that the linearity of first-person narrative enables audiences to "freeze the past" and thereby "situate the past as an object of spectatorship."[68] One consequence of Feldman's argument is that as abuse becomes localized as a problem of the past, audience responsibility in the present may be, at best, ambiguous.

Due to the overwhelming use of personal narrative in Stolen Generations texts, it is significant that *Slow Falling Bird* includes no personal stories of abuse. The absence of narration is most remarkable for Micko because, as a figure of the Stolen Generations, literary conventions demand Micko's narrative. By not telling his story, Evans's audience understands that Micko has yet to recover: he represents those Stolen Generations victims who have not been able to complete the journey home. Furthermore, Micko's silence puts the audience in the uncomfortable position of witnessing an untold story. If Micko does not narrate, they cannot listen and consequently, because narration has been understood as a means to both individual and community healing, Micko's silence denies both the audience and the character the possibility of catharsis.

Evans thus challenges her audience by highlighting Micko's past as a present absence, constructing a character whose pain is neither clearly understood nor easily reconciled. Fittingly, the undocumented asylum seekers do not narrate their unique pasts either. Putting aside Micko and the detainees' individual stories, Evans focuses attention on the larger history of abuse she illuminates through her experimental aesthetic. In this she suggests that storytelling cannot be enough because the story of the Stolen Generations is followed by the story of asylum seekers. Working to "un-freeze" the past, Evans interrogates the ways in which meaning has been made in Australia—how memory and representation have worked to redirect and sustain human rights abuse. In this, Evans allows her audience to see testimony as an aesthetical red herring: a form that capitalizes on the mesmerizing emotional appeal of the individual's path to healing rather than the causal forces of structural violence.

While testimonies have proven to be an effective strategy for both witnessing human rights abuse and facilitating empathy for victims, individual narratives may also obscure abusive ideological patterns as problems of the past. Of course, there are real-world consequences to this discursive problem insofar as the Australian government and public apologize to the Stolen Generations in one breath and condemn undocumented asylum seekers in the next. Thus, as Evans subverts the thematic convention of home, she must also subvert the dominant form in which that narrative appears: testimony.

Unable to reconstruct his narrative and recover home, Micko must leave Woomera. In the end, Leyla's suicide puts their mutual homelessness into stark relief. As Micko stands by the swaying dress that represents Leyla's body, he softly says, "I tried, all right?"[69] Seemingly understanding the consequences of the state's abuse and his own complicity, Micko then throws down his radio and leaves the stage. As the voice on the radio repeats "Over. Over," Mortein and Baygon appear and nod *"yes, it is over"*: the dream of home has ended for Mahmoud and Leyla, but it is also over for Micko.[70]

Micko's departure leaves Rick as the last guard standing. Although "home" is most explicitly denied to Australia's racial Others, Evans also shows that mandatory detention's exclusionary and xenophobic practices are not without consequences to white Australians. Throughout *Slow Falling Bird*, Mortein and Baygon explain that Rick is damaged: according to these guides, the "mad bastard thinks he's underwater."[71] Rick may delude himself into believing he has a fulfilling and sustainable home life, but his alcoholism and his interactions with his wife Joy strongly suggest otherwise. Joy suffers from severe depression and refuses to leave their tightly sealed house. Spending her days lamenting her infertility, longing for a baby who will have "eyes like a new suburb, empty of ghosts," Joy wants nothing more than to keep the realities of Woomera from contaminating her suburban fortress.[72]

Invoking another parallel from Stolen Generations narratives through the conflation of mother, child, and home, Evans shows the Fish Child wavering between Joy and Zahrah. The Fish Child sings to Joy: "There's a cord from me to Mama/Made of dreams and sea water...There's a cord from me to you/Made of longing for your daughter-/If you give me her name/Maybe I can come down-."[73] However, the Fish Child's future is tied to Zahrah's decisions, not Joy's. Seeing no alternative, Zahrah puts her baby down on the ground and, aided by Mortein and Baygon, climbs the detention center's fence and enters the Fish Child's spiritual realm. As Zahrah jumps from the fence, the Fish Child falls to the earth, fully arriving in the desert. Rick then takes the Fish Child home to Joy and destroys her file, obliterating her official presence.

Although the Fish Child enters Joy and Rick's family, finding a mother and consequentially a home, the play's closing scene posits this home as a sham. During a surreal family dinner, *Slow Falling Bird* comes to an abrupt ending after Rick passes the table salt to the Fish Child. The Fish Child and the spirits of the dead then pour salt and red dirt onto the stage. While salt typically evokes religious metaphors of permanence and purity, *Slow Falling Bird*'s usage more likely recalls the fact that salt is all that remains after water evaporates. Evans's last stage direction complicates the desert imagery: while the stage is lit with red lights and covered in salt and dirt, "*the sound of water falling builds until we are engulfed in the roaring of a flood.*"[74] As the characters on stage remain dry and homeless, the audience becomes enclosed by water, embraced (or consumed) by this primal home.

The play's final scene folds the audience into *Slow Falling Bird*'s narrative, shifting them from spectators to participants. In this, Evans requires that the audience consider their relationship to the characters on stage and the violations that have informed their individual and collective histories. Indeed, *Slow Falling Bird* ultimately positions the audience as the subject of its main interrogation, asking that they consider their role in how this story came to be. With her emphasis on the formation of reality, Evans recalls Feldman's argument that, "[i]f a society is to come to terms with a terror-ridden past, then it must be through a knowledge of how certain memory formations contributed to the creation of that violent past."[75] Because Rick is bored by the atrocities he witnesses daily and Evans has declared herself tired of testimony, *Slow Falling Bird* suggests that the usual ways of representing human rights abuse may be limited. Widening her scope to include not only the specific details of abuse against undocumented asylum seekers but also the ideological connections to the Stolen Generations, Evans focuses on this question of representation and understanding. Accordingly, then, *Slow Falling Bird* moves political theater in a new direction and expands the possibilities for representing human rights on the stage.

Notes

1. Qtd. in Scanlon, "Writ of Habeas Corpus," 26.
2. Burnside, "Foreword," 15, reports that in 2002, at Woomera alone, United Nations Justice Bhagwati observed violations of the International Covenant on Civil and Political Rights, the Convention against Torture, and the Convention on the Rights of the Child.
3. Evans, *Slow Falling Bird*, 4.
4. Ibid.
5. Zamora and Faris, *Magical Realism*, 6.
6. Evans, "Another Immigration Detention Center Play."
7. Slaughter, "A Question of Narration," 413.
8. Schaffer and Smith, *Human Rights and Narrated Lives*, 1.
9. Feldman, "Memory Theatres, Virtual Witnessing, and the Trauma-Aesthetic," 164, 170.
10. Bharucha, *The Politics of Cultural Practice*.
11. Qtd. Burnside, "Foreword," 14. To clarify: "asylum seekers" do not become "refugees" until that claim has been approved, as it eventually is for over 90% of Australia's detainees.
12. Ibid.
13. *Slow Falling Bird* was largely written and developed in the United States, where Evans now lives. It is beyond the scope of this essay to provide a detailed account of how the United States maps onto the play, but there are obvious connections to Guantánamo Bay. Moreover, while these detention centers are located in Australia, American-owned companies often employ the guards.
14. Evans, *Slow Falling Bird*, 7.
15. Evans, "Asylum Seekers and 'Border Panic' in Australia," 164.
16. Evans, *Slow Falling Bird*, 5, 8.
17. Ibid., 4, 9.
18. Ibid., 36.
19. Ibid., 35.
20. The Latin phrase *terra nullius* refers to unowned land. Originating in Roman law, *terra nullius* has been widely used internationally though the phrase is currently highly associated with Australia and its aboriginal peoples. In 1835, Governor Bourke invoked *terra nullius* as a means of asserting that no other group had prior claims on Australia before the British Crown, thereby stripping Indigenous Australians the right to sell or assign property. *Terra nullius* effectively remained Australia's official position until Mabo v. the State of Queensland (1992) in which the High Court of Australia rejected *terra nullius* and recognized that indigenous peoples had a pre-existing rights to Australia's land and waters.
21. Schaffer and Smith, *Human Rights and Narrated Lives*, 95.
22. Keating, "Redfern Address."
23. Accepting responsibility is not issuing an official apology, something Keating's successor John Howard infamously refused to do after HREOC recommendations in 1997. Prime Minister Kevin Rudd did issue an official apology in 2008.

24. Keating, "Redfern Address."
25. Burnside argues that mandatory detention was unsuccessful at deterrence for many asylum seekers did not know about the policy until they found themselves detained. Regardless of its expediency, deterrence uses "innocent people to achieve another objective." "Foreword," 12.
26. Jupp, *From White Australia to Woomera*, 190.
27. Briskman, Latham, and Goddard, *Human Rights Overboard*, 61–62.
28. Burnside, "Foreword," 11.
29. Jupp, *From White Australia to Woomera*, 52, 194.
30. Qtd. in Briskman, Latham, and Goddard, *Human Rights Overboard*, 49.
31. Ibid.
32. See Peter Mares, *Borderline*, 135.
33. Qtd. in Evans, "Asylum Seekers and 'Border Panic' in Australia," 166.
34. Arendt, *The Origins of Totalitarianism*, 287.
35. Ibid., 293.
36. Ibid.
37. Chris and Briskman, "By Any Measure It's Official Child Abuse," 17.
38. Human Rights and Equal Opportunities Commission, *A Last Resort?*, 66, cite the official number during this timeframe as 2,184; all these children were detained upon arrival and 92.8% were eventually found to be refugees. Briskman, Latham, and Goddard, *Human Rights Overboard*, 184, found that children were detained "for an average of one year and eight months including 'one child locked up for five years and five months.'"
39. Briskman, Latham, and Goddard, *Human Rights Overboard*, 177–180, report that "86 per cent of [detained] adults alleged they had been assaulted."
40. Ibid., 188.
41. Ibid., 189.
42. Ibid.
43. Human Rights and Equal Opportunities Commission, *A Last Resort?*, 81.
44. Office of the United Nations High Commissioner for Human Rights, *Convention on the Rights of the Child*.
45. The film is based on Doris Pilkington's memoir, *Follow the Rabbit-Proof Fence* (1996).
46. Evans, "Asylum Seekers and 'Border Panic' In Australia," 167.
47. Evans, *Slow Falling Bird*, 42.
48. Human Rights and Equal Opportunities Commission, *A Last Resort?*, 9.
49. Evans, *Slow Falling Bird*, 27.
50. Ibid.
51. Ibid., 61.
52. Ibid., 64.
53. Ibid., 65.
54. Ibid., 65–66 (original emphasis).
55. Ibid., 29.
56. Ibid., 19.
57. Ibid., 22.
58. Ibid., 43.
59. Ibid.
60. Ibid.
61. Ibid., 76.
62. Ibid.

63. Ibid., 88.
64. Ibid.
65. Neil Murray's website, "My Island Home."
66. Evans, *Slow Falling Bird*, 67.
67. Ibid., 67–68.
68. Feldman, "Memory Theatres, Virtual Witnessing, and the Trauma-Aesthetic," 165.
69. Evans, *Slow Falling Bird*, 89.
70. Ibid.
71. Ibid., 50.
72. Ibid., 80.
73. Ibid., 69–70.
74. Ibid., 93.
75. Feldman, "Memory Theatres, Virtual Witnessing, and the Trauma-Aesthetic," 182.

Chapter 7

Stages of Transit: Rascón Banda's *Hotel Juárez* and Peveroni's *Berlín*

Sarah M. Misemer

Víctor Hugo Rascón Banda, writing about theater and the border that separates the United States and Mexico, affirms that "[t]eatro es acción y conflicto. La frontera es conflicto en acción."([t]heater is action and conflict. The border is conflict in action)[1] I use Rascón Banda's quote as a springboard for my query as to how to conceive the experience of characters that constantly traverse borders not only in a neoliberal but also in a postliberal world, as is the case in Rascón Banda's *Hotel Juárez* (2008) and Gabriel Peveroni's *Berlín* (2007). Economics, media, and technological advances have made this new contact between nations possible. However, this same movement and access have also spawned inequities, violence, and terrorism. As a result, my project seeks to understand how economic neoliberal practices lead to porous borders through which goods, information, money, and services flow without restraint, while at the same time political practices of post-liberalism restrict the movement of people, aid, and, often times, dialogue among classes, cultures, and nations. This paradox arises out of a new reorganization among "the political, violence, and everyday life" that is a direct offspring neither of World War II nor of colonialism, but moves beyond these discourses.[2] As we shall see, a transformation of this sort results from the emergence and multiplication of new political subjects and the decentralization of sites of political antagonism in society, which in turn point to new targets of counterinsurgency, objects of repression, and new venues for intimidation and terror.[3]

Both plays exemplify this push and pull between shifting and variable extremes in physical and esoteric ways. As the title suggests, Rascón Banda's play takes place in a hotel in Ciudad Juárez, as a woman searches for her missing sister in the violent underworld of drugs, pornography, and corruption in this *maquiladora* (factory) border town. Peveroni's play occurs in an airport, when a tourist is detained because of terrorist activities as he tries to journey to Berlin: a trip that is real as much as metaphorical. He ultimately commits suicide by detonating a bomb. The plays situate their action in places of transit and integrate economic and political aspects of the contemporary world. Rascón Banda's play not only questions the internal terrorism of the drug culture, but also implicates the new economic order, as seen in the results of the 1994 NAFTA/TLCAN (North American Free Trade Agreement/Tratado de Libre Comercio de América del Norte), which created a culture and territory in which maquiladoras and violence became ubiquitous along the border. On the other hand, Peveroni's play insists we examine the trends taking place in security in democratic countries because of the fear of terrorism. As Peveroni's characters spar verbally, they expose the tensions between past and present economic policies (feudalism/capitalism/socialism/neoliberalism). In this context, Rascón Banda's concept of "conflict in action" reflects this dynamics of movement and resistance that characterizes the contemporary world of multiple and unpredictable centers of power and their agents, found also in the theatrical spaces of *Hotel Juárez* and *Berlín*.

Theatrical Trends

Mexico and the River Plate share similarities, not only in their prosperous and rich heritages as the two foundational centers for strong theatrical traditions in Latin America, but also in the kinds of theater they have been producing since the 1980s. Each of these countries has been marked by the transformation of their respective societies in response to neoliberal economic practices. In Mexico, these changes have been reflected in the theater by the so-called "novísimos" (newest of new) group, which began to take shape after 1982, when the state adopted new economic practices.[4] As Armando Partida Tayzán reminds us, this generation began to write in order to exorcise, "[l]os demonios que el neoliberalismo trajera consigo: nuevas circunstancias políticas, sociales, económicas, culturales y que, como generación, les tocaría vivir en el momento de su iniciación en la dramaturgia, o de sus primeras experiencias escénicas." ([t]he demons that neoliberalism would bring with it: new political, social, economic and cultural circumstances, and that, as a generation, would touch them right at the moment of their initiation into dramaturgy, or their first scenic experiences)[5] Fernando de Ita echoes this sentiment as he refers to Rascón Banda and his cohorts, who write with "el mismo aliento trágico y un parecido desencanto por la vida mexicana que les tocó dramatizar." (the same tragic breath or similar disenchantment with Mexican life is what they were left to dramatize)[6].

A similar phenomenon also occurred in the River Plate, as Osvaldo Pellettieri's "teatro de la desintegración" (theater of disintegration) suggests. Speaking specifically about Argentina, Pellettieri remarks: "[e]ste teatro mostrador de la desintegración, de la incomunicación familiar, del feroz consumismo, de la violencia gratuita, de la ausencia de amor de la 'convivencia posmoderna' es también intertextual con el contexto social, con el neoconservadorismo menemista que ha roto con las normas de la vida social." ([t]his theater, an example of disintegration, of familial incommunication, of fierce consumerism, of illicit violence, of the absence of love in "postmodern coexistence" is also an intertext of the social context, with the Menemist neoconservatism that has broken the norms of social life).[7] This disintegration spread throughout the Southern Cone in the postdictatorship period beginning in the mid-1980s, and most especially in response to the 2001–2002 crisis, which spilled over from Argentina's economic sector into its neighbor Uruguay's financial structures. Uruguayan theater critic Roger Mirza seconds this view of new trends in his country's theatrical production, suggesting that a "new scenic dramaturgy" has emerged to replace the old discursive tradition: "el encadenamiento causal y desarrollo lineal de la intriga, la reproducción mimética de ambientes han sido sustituídos por la fragmentación y la desintegración de los modelos interpretativos tradicionales." (the causal links and lineal development of plot, the mimetic representation of settings have been substituted by fragmentation and disintegration of traditional interpretative models).[8]

The aspects that define Mexican and River Plate stages from the mid-1980s onward respond to similar trends in neoliberalism in distinct ways. In the River Plate, inclusion of postmodern elements, reconsideration of the absurd, insistence on extreme pessimism, and unorthodox staging in nontraditional venues and with postdramatic sensibilities, among other elements, are of paramount importance. In the Mexican context, realism prevails as a way of denouncing abuses of power and social oppression.[9] This analysis of Rascón Banda's and Peveroni's works, however, seeks to go beyond the definitions of what Mexican and River Plate theater s mean within national contexts by exploring how movement across borders is encouraged as well as hampered by politics and economic policies. As these theatrical pieces traverse political and economic landscapes, they call into question both the scope and the efficacy of national and international human rights as they abut socioeconomic policies and terrorism.

Murder of the Real

In both Rascón Banda's and Peveroni's plays, the theme of murder is prevalent on a physical level. For example, as Angela searches for her missing sister, she encounters Lupe who tells her of the recent murders in Lomas de Poleo and the unscrupulous practices of the police, which often lead to the loss/corruption of evidence; Johny, who makes snuff films and tries to entice her into participating, the ghost of her sister who visits Angela in the night while she sleeps and tells her she lies bloody and rotting by the river, and the last scene's shootout in which Angela, her lover (a stripper named Ramsés) and the Comandante die, while Johny walks out unharmed. In Peveroni's play, Joy is detained by Anna and Valerie as they await news from the "atentados" (terrorist attacks) in various parts of the building.[10] In the end, Joy reveals: "SOY EL PANDA BOMBA. No se rían. ¿Quieren jugar con la verdad? No lo permitiré. No se los aconsejo. Voy a explotar en mil pedazos. Y esto es en serio. Yo no puedo salir. Pero ustedes tienen sus pasaportes. Ese papel que les dieron a la entrada. Sálvense." (I AM THE PANDA BOMB. Don't laugh. Do you want to play with the truth? I won't allow it. I wouldn't advise it. I'm going to explode in a thousand pieces. And this is for real. I can't leave. But you all have your passports. That paper that they gave you at the entrance. Save yourselves).[11] Joy breaks the fourth wall and includes the spectators in his plea to leave before he blows himself up. Murder, as these two plays suggest, is omnipresent on the stage and is a consequence of the increasing violence along the Mexico–United States border and internationally, as terrorism becomes widespread.

However, for those of us who live in the modern world, which turns upon the gears of globalization and the subsequent forces that these practices engender through increased contact between cultures via economic, political, and technological development, there is another level of murder which is, perhaps, more obscure yet prevalent. I argue that the experiences of the "novísimo" and "disintegración" trends rest on what Jean Baudrillard calls the "murder of the real." It is a death that occurs as we lose our sense of "patria," trading it for the indeterminate space of cybernetics, multinationals, and transit. As Baudrillard argues, the modern virtual world in which we live leaves us with no real referents. This situation, in turn, exterminates reality. Whereas traditionally knowledge has always moved in the same direction—from the subject to the object—today the opposite is true because it is marked by "processes of reversion."[12] The subject loses its hegemonic position and thus undoes the classical theory of knowledge.[13] In this context, "[r]eality becomes hyperreality—paroxysm and parody all at once. It supports all sorts of interpretations because it no longer makes sense."[14] Our excess of reality, security, and efficiency—bi-products of our technologies and modernity—has rendered us victims of an absence of destiny and illusion.[15] Simply put, a system that is pushed to the extremes of sophistication and totalization implodes "through ultra-realization and automatic reversal."[16]

Baudrillard is speaking specifically about the effects of the virtual world and technologies, but the theoretical implications of his argument apply to both *Hotel Juárez* and *Berlín* because they both show the extremes to which the systems have been pushed and the subsequent implosions these excesses cause. The technological advances and economic interconnectedness of the contemporary world should, theoretically, bring us together—and they do. However, these same efficient means of communication, contact, and interdependence also render us vulnerable and expendable in the face of shifting markets and alliances. Whereas the neoliberal discourse promised wealth, benefits, jobs, and more affluence for an even greater number of people, the transition also has had its failures, which included in the Mexican case: "devaluaciones, épocas de austeridad, y después de la famosa campaña de 'Solidaridad' de Carlos Salinas de Gortari, una serie de eventos reconocidos como los 'errores de diciembre' de 1994 y el 'crack' de 1995."(devaluations, austerity periods, and later the famous "Solidarity" campaign by Carlos Salinas de Gortari, a series of events recognized as the "errors of December" of 1994 and the crack in 1995).[17] The result of these debacles has been an increase in violence and the perception of political and economic instability.[18] In the River Plate, Paola S. Hernández writes in a similar vein that "el sistema neoliberal de mercado tanto como la globalización han traído una gama de problemas y condiciones sociales de pobreza, diferencia, escasez y pérdida de patrimonio cultural y nacional, además en algunos casos, un sentido de desorientación que lleva a una falta de memoria, historia y un centro familiar." (the market's neoliberal system just as much as globalization have brought the same range of problems and social conditions of poverty, difference, shortages and loss of cultural and national patrimony, along with in some cases, a sense of disorientation that carries with it a loss of memory, history, and familiar center).[19] As a result, when we trade "reality" for virtuality and the local for the global, citizenship and rights are tested.

At the heart of both Rascón Banda's and Peveroni's plays is a clash between universal human rights and those rights that are the domain of the nation-state. As Gershon Shafir and Alison Brysk note, citizenship may be becoming postnational thus invoking a renewed interest in human rights.[20] Whereas citizenship is a concept that is tied to a politically sovereign entity, human rights are coterminous with the individual because of his/her humanity and are not related to membership in any body politic.[21] The focus on human rights is a result of the growth of transnational and global economic, cultural, political, and legal frameworks.[22] These structures have begun to crop up as a result of the new frontiers and new agencies and actors that have become players in the international game. With the fall of the paternalistic state, violence is surging and citizenship and human rights are being tested as culture is destabilized.[23] Ignacio M. Sánchez Prado reminds us, "[v]iolence is a category that has become increasingly used in Latin American cultural analysis"; it is the "very centre of a newly emerging identity."[24] Rascón Banda's and Peveroni's plays show the uses and abuses of power as it is regulated, deregulated, and re-regulated within these power networks.

Connectivity

The full title for Peveroni's work is *Berlín: Un poema dramático para tres voces y una laptop* (*Berlín: A Dramatic Poem for Three Voices and One Laptop*). The subtitle reinforces the very themes that Baudrillard highlights through the transitory nature of the objects referenced (voices not characters/a portable laptop). As Peveroni notes, "*Berlín* es, ya no una frontera, sino directamente el teatro interpelado, puesto en tela de juicio desde su radical posdramaticidad." (*Berlín* is no longer a border, but directly questioned theater, which casts doubt from its position of radical postdramaticness).[25] It is postdramatic in several senses. In fact, the play grew out of a series of exercises created by Javier Daulte and implemented by Peveroni and his long-time collaborator, director María Dodera, making it a collective creation.[26] It was written between January and October of 2007, and premiered on October 26, 2007, at the Instituto Goethe in Montevideo, Uruguay. The actors, Álvaro Armand Ugón (Joy), Gabriela Iribarren (Anna), and Alejandra Cortazzo (Valerie), along with musicians Maximiliano Angelieri and Federico Deutsch and other technicians were all co-creators in this evolution of this dramatic piece.[27] It was conceived "desde el cero absoluto" (from absolute zero), as Peveroni explains.[28] Like many of Peveroni's previous dramatic works, *Berlín* is a fragmented and intertextual play with references not only to the music of the above-mentioned composers, but also to karaoke, as well as to novels by Amélie Nothomb and films by Jean Luc Goddard.[29] Finally, the theme of the play is born out not through the resolution of whether Joy is able to complete his trip to Berlin, but rather on the much larger philosophical question of whether he has come to the limit of borders, existing at once in flux and stagnation.

Bernardo Borkenztain's introduction "En tránsito" (In Transit) accompanies the text of the play (which, like all of Peveroni's plays, also serves as a handbill). This brief introduction references the lyrics from John Lennon's "Nowhere man in a Nowhere Land" in an epigraph.[30] Through this quote Borkenztain elaborates the themes of the play: "No linealidad, disrupciones temporales, fracturas, espacio que fluye mientras el tiempo se estanca. No son elementos oníricos, al menos para los desterrados es su cotidianeidad. Lo terrible es verse atrapado en el no-cambio, la estasis." (No linearity, temporal disruptions, fractures, space that flow while time stagnates).[31] Borkenztain identifies the characters as young people who have none of the traditional and sacred connections to people or places that have been characteristic of past generations.[32] Instead, cellular phones and laptops serve as the only cables that tie them—not to the ground—but to "connectivity."[33] These young professionals inhabit the world of luxury hotels, consume compulsively to compensate for the lack of affection in their lives, and view their passports not as their "patria," but rather as their "patria." (Fatherland).[34] Therefore, the crisis that serves as the nucleus of the play is stoked when Joy is denied access in the airport because of an expired passport. The rest of the crowd (spectators) has all been given proper documentation as their entrance into the spectacle.

Limits: *Berlín*

Violence permeates Peveroni's *Berlín*, most demonstrably through the explosion at the end of the work, but also through references to clashes throughout history. The first reference occurs in the second scene, "Check In," in which Joy recounts his father's history of escape during World War II. He remarks:

"Dicen que tengo que decir de dónde vengo. Aunque eso no debería importar. Lo que importa es adónde voy. El sentido. Berlín. Este. Oeste." (They say I have to say from where I'm coming. Although that really shouldn't matter. What's important is where I'm going. The direction. Berlin. East. West)[35] Joy tells Anna and Valerie that his father was German and tried to reach Berlin but was detained by the Gestapo. His birth city was transformed after the war into part of the Polish state. He spent two years in a concentration camp, where his mother (Joy's grandmother) died. Eventually he escaped to Yugoslavia, and although his family wanted him to journey on to Palestine with Jewish settlers, he chose to board a boat with Communist friends who had false Paraguayan passports. He arrived in Montevideo the first of January in 1939. Later in scene three, entitled "Tenis rojo," (Red Tennis) Joy explains that five months before the Berlin Wall fell in November 1989 his father traveled to Berlin, made a stopover in Frankfurt and was never heard from again.

Later in scene four, "Karaoke," Joy sings about injustices that have taken place around the world. He mixes politics, violence, and geography. His first example is Vietnam and the quagmire that lasted from 1959 to 1975; a war that also led to a division of the Vietnamese nation into North and South, much like the division of Germany into East and West after World War II. He rants:

¿Ves esa chica rubia en la ventana de cortinas lilas?/ Le han disparado en la cabeza/ fueron esos malditos vietnamitas./ Te pedí que cerraras la puerta de atrás, nena./ Y me sirvieras un trago, antes que te volaran la cabeza,/ esos gusanos vietnamitas./ Aunque quieras evitarlo, lo harán./ Son persistentes, insolentes, valientes, transparentes. (Do you see that blonde girl in the window with lilac curtains?/ They shot her in the head/ it was those damned Vientnamese./ I asked you to close the door behind, girl./ And, that you serve me a drink before they blew off your head,/ those Vietnamese worms./ Although you might try to avoid it, they will do it./ They're persistent, insolent, brave, and transparent)[36]

In the same song, Joy also implicates the more recent US-led wars in Iraq (the Persian Gulf War in 1991 and the Iraq War, which began in 2003). Joy's descriptions mix pornographic images and violence. He questions: "¿Te das cuenta que Bagdad está en tu propio ombligo?/ ¿Qué fue un maldito iraquí el que entró en tu trasero?" (Do you realize that Bagdad is in your own bellybutton?/ That it was a damned Iraqi that entered your ass?)[37] Here, the unresolved—and some might say, un-win-able—war is literally portrayed as a "pain in the ass" for the United States and its allies. It alludes to the politics of oil and terrorism that have taken center stage in recent decades as fossil fuel resources dwindle and the Western countries seek to influence the oil-producing governments in the Middle East that control production.[38]

The brief lyric ends with a commentary on immigration in the Latin American context. Joy exposes the anti-immigrant sentiment toward Central

America as he advocates for closing borders. He cautions: "Por eso, nena, siempre espero que no olvides cerrar la puerta/ porque van a entrar esos centroamericanos hambrientos./ Y van a romper las cortinas lilas./Y van a comer nuestra comida." (That's why, girl, I always hope you don't forget to shut the door/ because those hungry Central Americans are going to come in/ And, they're going to rip your lilac curtains./ And, they're going to eat our food).[39] Joy is most probably making reference to the iron wall separating the United States from its southern neighbors and the anti-immigration policies that have become more stringent after the 9/11 bombings. Anti-immigrant rhetoric often attributes the vulnerability of resources and services to the influx of people that often do not pay taxes to support the revenue structure of the United States; however, these same people do support the economy through labor and spending

Finally, in scene ten, "El número de Joy," (Joy's Number) Joy relives the painful history he witnessed as a youth during the military dictatorship from 1973 to 1985. The conservative dictatorship was part of a trend in Latin America that sought to stem the spread of Marxist "subversive" politics. A consequence of the Cold War, the conservative military dictatorship of Uruguay and those of its Southern Cone neighbors Argentina and Chile, resisted the influence of Communism through brutal force. Ironically, they touted the capitalist democratic military models of the United States and other Western countries, but maintained control through extreme conservative measures that included the torture and death of civilian and political opponents alike. Joy recounts his experience as a youth:

> Tenía catorce años cuando entraron los militares y se llevaron todas las cosas. Los libros, las cartas, el televisor blanco y negro. Rompieron la mesa cuando se subieron para buscar en el estante de arriba. [. . . .] Mamá miraba a la pared. Papá lo subieron al camión. (I was fourteen with the military men entered and took everything. The books, letters, the black and white television. They broke the table when they went to look on the top shelf. [. . .] Mom looked at the wall. They took Dad to the truck)[40]

In the wake of this traumatic experience, Joy stops reading and starts abusing alcohol while his mother shuts down emotionally. The wall they construct is an internal one that shuts out emotions.

These violent events from the past are interspersed with simultaneous terrorist attacks taking place in different parts of the airport and neoliberal practices in various regions of the world. Valerie comments on some of the violence in scene three: "En la T6. Acaban de informar. Acuchilló a 37 personas en 25 minutos." (In T6. They just made an announcement. He stabbed 37 people in 25 minutes).[41] In scene eleven "Último tenis," (Last Tennis) she complains that liberals, like ecologists, are hampering economic progress. She maintains: "No podemos detener el avance del pensamiento global. Nuestros enemigos son los idiotas comos ustedes, ecologistas de la televisión. Y todos aquellos que se dejen llevar por los viejos mitos." (We can't stop the advance of global thought. Our enemies are idiots like you guys, television ecologists. And all of those who let themselves get carried away by old myths).[42] In the final scene before Joy detonates his bomb, Anna muses on the difference between "implotar" (implode) and "explotar" (explode) noting that they both make noise.[43] Of course, the latter connotes a double meaning (explode/exploit) and the former echoes Baudrillard's collapse of systems.

These occurrences are symptoms of the contemporary violence that permeates society. Mirza envisions modern culture as one that is based on transitory and exploitative forces. His publication "Teatro y violencia en la escena contemporánea" (2009) emphasizes the fleeting nature of modern culture: "Ante esta cultura de lo efímero, lo polifacético y lo multicultural, que tiende a sustituir las experiencias vividas por excitaciones inmediatas, la sobreabundancia de estímulos impide toda forma de elaboración por la conciencia," (Setting before this culture of the ephemeral, the multifaceted and the multicultural, that tends to substitute immediate excitements for lived experiences, is the superabundance of stimuli that impedes all forms of elaboration by the conscience) and stresses that "[a]l mismo tiempo el nuevo 'orden' mundial excluye del banquete hedonista a la mitad de la población del planeta por el hambre, la miseria, la emigración y la catástrofe, en las fronteras de la pérdida de lo humano y la disolución social." ([a]t the same time the new world "order" excludes from the hedonistic banquet half the planet through hunger, misery, immigration, and catastrophe, on the borders of the loss of what is human and social dissolution)[44] According to Mirza, we experience something akin to Walter Benjamin's contemporary shock culture that developed at the turn of the last century.[45] This insecurity makes people vulnerable to lies and distortion—especially in the political arena. In fact, the logic of securitization rests, and indeed, requires the perpetuation of insecurity.[46] Returning to Baudrillard's thesis on the implosion of systems pushed to the extremes, we see that demands for security ultimately lead countries into highly undemocratic measures (Germany, Vietnam, the United States, Iraq, and Uruguay serve as examples in this play).

Peveroni and Dodera question the undeniable trends taking place in democratic countries because of the fear of terrorism; transformations that make these societies resemble their authoritarian enemies on many disturbing levels. They also probe the obstacles created by neoliberalism. As Damian Cox, Michael Levine, and Saul Newman point out in their study *Politics Most Unusual* (2009):

> While the discourse of security takes as its prerogative the protection of citizens from terrorist attacks, it provokes a permanent state of fear, vulnerability and insecurity; it is a (neo) liberal discourse, in the sense that it is driven, partly, by logic of capitalist globalization and the exigencies of liberal markets—and, at the same time, it is an authoritarian and highly regulatory post-liberal discourse which seriously violates the individual rights upon which any coherent understanding of liberalism is based.[47]

Ultimately, *Berlín* shows the disintegration of democratic practices, rights, and laws in favor of the naked grab for power in the name of security and prosperity. We are at once targets of terrorist attacks and potential terrorists, as Joy demonstrates.[48] The state, which operates under the doctrine of sovereignty, is always open to the possibility of exceptions (one in which normal legal protections are suspended), and when this happens it becomes what Cox, Levine, and Newman term a "no-man's-land," outside of the law.[49] Its security measures often become indistinguishable from those implemented in authoritarian states. This "no-man's-land" recalls Borkenztain's introduction and the lyrics from "Nowhere Man" in *Berlín*.

Invisible yet Infiltrating: Juárez

Michael Taussig writes in his study *The Nervous System* (1992) about his experiences with terror in Colombia and the "limpieza" (cleaning) of Cali, in which street people involved in petty crimes and drug dealing—beggars, prostitutes, homosexuals, transvestites, and others—were being wiped out by machine gun fires from pick-up trucks and motorbikes.[50] The effect was that the "limpiezas" and their uncertain violence were making the entire city fearful because anyone could become a target. Streets emptied and people stayed home. This underworld was seen as a threat because it exists as a "strategically borderless" being that is "invisible yet infiltrating" but always "Other."[51] Like Cox, Levine, and Newman, Taussig also sees terror as being characterized by oppositions. Such talk fluctuates between "dogmatic certainties" that a "reason and a center" exist and the opposite extreme of the "diffuse, decentered, randomness of the other."[52]

Taussig's context is outdated, but the relevance of his views on terror still apply to places like the border between Mexico and the United States—what he would call "An-Other" place—where indiscriminate violence is creating fear, but even more disturbingly a "politics as usual" approach.[53] He develops Walter Benjamin's theory of constancy of a state of emergency into his own terminology of *The Nervous System*: an optics that requires persistent movement between clarity and opacity.[54] One vacillates in a state of doubleness, wherein she or he accepts the situation as normal only to be thrown into panic by an event, rumor, or even that which is not said and which ultimately destabilizes the notion of "normal."[55]

Evidence of this kind of widespread fear and fluctuation between extremes is present from the moment that Angela arrives at Hotel Juárez. The hotel functions as a stratified society in which drug lords and powerful, corrupt members of the city's elite occupy the first two floors; on the other floors live immigrants and their smugglers, and on the sixth floor the prostitutes comingle with families searching for their lost daughters and parents who visit their children in jail. Victoria Martínez calls it a type of "infierno del cual no hay escape" (a hell from which there is no escape) in her introduction to the anthology of plays, which all deal with the Juárez murders, also named *Hotel Juárez* (subtitled *Dramaturgia de feminicidio*) published in 2008.[56]

This hellish scenario is a metaphor for the effects of the neoliberal project in Mexico. The hotel, like the Mexican state, is a place of transit for goods, services, and resources that are exported and consumed by others. It is also the site of a power vacuum in which re-regulation takes place. Neoliberal discourse may have promised free markets over government control, but as Richard Snyder argues "rather than ending government intervention in markets and narrowing the range of the political, neoliberal reforms result in a new politics of reregulation."[57] These reforms can either be oligarchic or be mass-based policy frameworks.[58] As Rascón Banda's play shows, the domination by a group of elites and their collusion of power have overtaken the border as a consequence of the NAFTA/TLCAN agreement and have resulted in the former policy framework—a clear contradiction of the neoliberal prosperity and freedom that were originally pledged to the masses.

In the hotel, Lupe advises Angela that she needs to proceed with extreme caution. She warns Angela: "te asaltan en el pasillo, se meten a tu cuarto cuando no estás o cuando estás dormida." (they'll jump you in the hallway, they go in your room when you're not there or when you're asleep).[59] Inviting Angela to a beer, which the latter tries to decline, Lupe insists "[v]amos, sirve que termino de darte las instrucciones de cómo sobrevivir en este hotel." (Let's go, it's about time I stop giving you instructions on how to survive in this hotel).[60] Ramsés also advises Angela that Juárez "es una ciudad flotante, una ciudad de paso" (it's a floating city, a city in passing) but notes that many stay: "los sin papeles, los fracasados, los débiles, los que dudan." (those without papers, the failures, the weak, those that doubt).[61] Life, according to Ramsés, exists only on the other side of the bridge (in El Paso). In these two passages, Lupe and Ramsés note the violent movement between floors and borders, which echoes the transitory flow of Taussig's Nervous System. They also highlight for Angela the perceived normality of the situation, which is only thrown into question when there is a disruption from the outside (such as a sister searching for her murdered sibling).

The very foundation upon which this violent infiltration is built has been the neoliberal economy of the border towns. In and of itself, the transition to a neoliberal market was perceived by many in Mexico as violent. It is a process that began well before 1994 and culminated in the NAFTA/TLCAN agreement. Claudio Lominitz uses the word "brutal" to describe the loss in wages suffered in Mexico City. Between 1982 and 1987, real working wages fell by 40–50% and layoffs were ubiquitous in state-run businesses beginning in 1983.[62] Mexico City declined precipitously; however, the border towns prospered in comparison.[63] The 1980s were marked by a schism between "free trade and national economy, between pro- and anti-globalization," which affected national identity.[64] However, despite the construction of *maquilas* (factories) as a result of the 1994 NAFTA/TLCAN economic trading bloc and the changing economic and social structure that these primarily female-staffed businesses brought to the region, the border retains its image as a deathscape. It is both a "dangerous and fertile margin."[65] Nowhere is this clearer than when Lupe reveals to Angela that there is a large room with shelves and boxes marked with labels for export from a US company. The room has only one bed, the windows are covered and blacked out, and wine bottles and trash litter the room. Lupe tells Angela that "se oyen gritos y quejidos. Como llantos de mujer." (they hear screams and moans. Like a woman crying).[66] The reference to pornographic/snuff films is clear, but there is also an implicit criticism of the "rape" of the female workers whose products are produced along the border and shipped elsewhere for international profit.

Another example of a curious crossing of borders takes place as Angela translates for the Licenciado. Whereas goods move freely across borders, scene twelve demonstrates how difficult migration of people is across national territories. When the Licenciado asks Angela if she can speak English, she assures him she is capable and reveals that she used to live in Kansas, but was thrown out ("Vivía en Kansas, pero me echaron" [I lived in Kansas, but they threw me out]).[67] The document she translates, however, is a legal one for the shipment of packages to El Paso, where they will be distributed via air to Rotterdam or "el destino que posteriormente podría ser comunicado a través del correo electrónico que las partes señalen." (the destination that later could be communicated through e-mail that the parts might show)[68] Pornographic films, packages for export, drugs, and electronic information flow freely across the border, but Angela's experience shows the "criminalization of international migration" when this scene is contrasted with the opening scene in which she is battered by a series of questions as she tries to check in to the hotel.[69] As she arrives at the hotel, the manager's barrage of questions and suspicion about her credit card that is not Mexican, the deposit he requires because she has no luggage, the questions about her occupations, her incomplete registration, and the fact that he will not accept her dollars because they might be false, demonstrate the selective porosity of the border when it comes to human beings.

Finally, Rascón Banda's play also illuminates the question of power and how it has been re-regulated as a consequence of neoliberal projects in Mexico. Two instances will highlight the ways in which the power vacuum has been filled by oligarchic policy frameworks. In scene nine, entitled "En el Bar," Ángela, Ramsés, Lupe, el gerente, Johny, and Rosalba watch a big screen. On it, a reporter is interviewing the Egyptian, a character based on the real-life Egyptian chemist Sharif Sharif, for his involvement in the Juárez murders.[70] The Egyptian maintains his innocence and instead points to Alejandro Maynez as the culprit for the *feminicidios* (murders of females). The Egyptian highlights the corruption inherent in Mexican politics when he reveals for the reporter that Maynez has been arrested numerous times for strangling and raping women, and has been a person of interest in the murder of a man, woman, and her three-month-old infant. When the reporter asks why he has not been detained, the Egyptian answers: "[s]alió libre porque su mejor amigo fue el jefe de homicidios en la judicial, era como su hermano. Alejandro Maynez es un hombre con mucho poder... él ayudó al jefe de homicidios a obtener su puesto... Está ligado al narcotráfico, es propietario de muchos bares." (he got off because his best friend was the Chief of Homicides at the justice administration, he was like a brother. Alejandro Maynez is a man with a lot of power... he helped the Chief of Homcides get his job... He's connected to narcotraffic, he's the owner of a lot of bars).[71] With his statement, the Egyptian suggests that the economic prosperity and the ties that Maynez has to the important economic underworld of drugs have made him untouchable. The cronyism among the elite reinforces the new power structures that have arisen in the border area in response to the neoliberal vacuum.

The second example of how power has been once more consolidated among a small group of elites in Mexico is the layout of the hotel, which functions, as we have seen, as a *mise-en-abyme*. The powerful all reside on the first few floors: the toreros (bullfighters), the narcotraficantes (drug traffickers), and a few municipales (municipal workers). The power structure that further reinforces this network can be seen in the conversation in scenesix, "El Licenciado en su cuarto" (The Graduate in His Room), that the Licenciado and the Gerente (the Manager) of the hotel have about Johny who works to collect girls for the snuff films. The girls are lured in at the hotel under the auspices of the manager (the public witnesses two examples with Johny's failed attempt to drug Ángela and use her in a pornographic film and his manipulation of Rosalba and her subsequent rape by the Comandante (Commander), as she waits to make what she thinks is an artistic film). Here, the film once more suggests the metaphoric consumption of docile female bodies as they are enticed into the exploitative *maquila* industry of the border. As Lupe explains to Ángela, "[n]o aceptan casadas, ni con hijos, ni mayores de treinta. Piden secundaria como base. No aceptan chavalas de prepa ni universitarias, porque dicen que esas chavas se vuelven subversivas y revoltosas." ([t]hey don't accept married women, women with children, or women older than thirty. They require highschool as a minimum. They don't accept girls from Prep. School or the University, because they say these girls turn subversive and rebellious).[72] The Licenciado is involved in the export of these films to El Paso, and as we have seen, used Ángela as his translator. The economic reforms that have made the international transport and sale of these films possible have opened up new possibilities for economic prosperity. However, as Rascón Banda's play makes clear, the abuses of power that have accompanied these opportunities have muddied the waters along the United States–Mexico border with corruption, violence, and the bodies of too many young women abused both physically and economically. Only a few it seems are enjoying the benefits, while the great majority live in a state of panic.

In sum, these two works, through their use of violence, demonstrate the conflict in action that Rascon Banda finds in both theater and borders. However, they also implicate the conflict among political, economic, and social tensions that permeates the hyperglobalized world of international travel, shipping, and multinationals. These works conform to the aesthetics of the "novísimos" (Mexico) and Teatro de la desintegración (River Plate), generations that are marked by and born out of neoliberal reforms and their subsequent traumas. In Peveroni's *Berlín* we see firsthand the "death of the real" through the traveler Joy and others in his generation who have lost all connections to their countries through their international business travels and can identify only with their passports. The limits of open transcontinental travel are reached when Joy is detained and terrorist activity ensues. The references to wars and terrorist activity test the notions of liberal and neoliberal economies, which rest on porous borders and a need for security in the face of violent cultural, political, economic, and religious clashes. In Rascón Banda's *Hotel Juárez*, the violence is contained within the transitory and metaphorical space of a hotel that stands for the border between the United States and Mexico. The increasingly criminal border is marred by dead female bodies, corrupt officials, drug lords, prostitutes, and *maquilas*. The relative ease with which services, products, and currency travel across the border is contrasted with a complete disregard for human life, the abuse of workers' and citizens' rights to safety, and a minimal guarantee for quality of life. The "conflict in action" that Rascón Banda identifies in the theater and along the border has been shown to be a constantly moving target both in *Hotel Juárez* and in *Berlín* because of the decentralization and multiplication of political, economic, and cultural sites of power in the contemporary world of globalization, neoliberal markets, and postliberal policies.

Notes

1. Rascón Banda, "El Teatro," 176.
2. Feldman, "Memory Theatres, Virtual Witnessing, and the Trauma-Aesthetic," 171.
3. Ibid., 171–172. Feldman explains the new social categories: "Previously inadmissible social categories—women, ethnic and racial minorities, peasants, the colonized, sexual minorities, fauna and flora, the disabled and the diseased, youth and children—emerged as political agents with their own political agendas and diverse sites of struggle" (170).
4. Others such as Guillermo Schmidhuber de la Mora offer another framework for defining the latest generation of Mexican playwrights, which he calls "Nueva Dramaturgia Mexicana" comprised of two groups: 1984–1998 and 1999–2013. Schmidhuber de la Mora, *Dramaturgia Mexicana*, 165.
5. Partida Tayzán, "La novísima dramaturgia mexicana," 18.
6. De Ita, "Las plumas del gallinero mexicano," 22. Fernando de Ita groups Rascón Banda with Sabina Berman, and Jesús González Dávila (21–22).
7. Pellettieri, "El teatro porteño del año 2000 y el teatro del futuro," 17.
8. Mirza, *Teatro rioplatense*, 10.
9. De Ita, "Las plumas del gallinero mexicano," 22.
10. I argue that the use of two females to detain Joy suggests an implicit relationship with the use of "torture chicks" in the Iraq War. In writing about the abuses of Abu Ghraib and Guatánamo, performance artist and critic Coco Fusco was shocked to find that "the Pentagon had approved sexual tactics in interrogation. Female interrogators were reported to be giving hand jobs and lap dances to prisoners at Guatánamo, and smearing them with fake menstrual blood. That made it clear [...] that while the Abu Ghraib prison abuse scandal was being treated as an anomaly, the use of women as sexual aggressors was planned as part of a program" (Fusco, *A Field Guide for Female Interrogators*,

26). She supports what Cox, Levine, and Newman sees as the erosion of agency in politics when the limits of force become unclear: "If we give up all efforts to identify and set limits to the uses of force that are excessive, unwanted, and unmerited, we [...] acquiesce to authoritarian control of our lives or those of others" (Fusco, *A Field Guide for Female Interrogators*, 25).
11. Peveroni, *Berlín*, 22.
12. Baudrillard, *The Vital Illusion*, 76.
13. Ibid., 76–77.
14. Ibid., 77.
15. Ibid., 81.
16. Ibid., 78.
17. Baudrillard, *The Vital Illusion*, 27. The error was a devaluation in the Mexican currency in December 1994, which stemmed from a need to stimulate the economy because of various factors, which included sluggish investment by foreigners as a result of the Chiapas uprising and the assassination of presidential candidate Luis Donaldo Colosio; hyperinflation and spending over the previous two decades; and a high debt load, insufficient cash reserves, and lower oil prices. By the first weeks of 1995, the peso had crashed causing what is known as the "Tequila effect," which impacted the Southern Cone's markets and caused a drop in currency. In literary and artistic terms, Ignacio M. Sánchez explains that "el *crack* concibió una estética que criticaba de manera simultánea a la modernidad nacionalista que ata a la literatura a un proyecto institucional de país, y a la modernidad neoliberal que considera a la cultura una función exclusive de mercado" (the crack was conceived as an aesthetic that simultaneously criticized nationalist modernity that tied literature to an institutional country project, and a neoliberal modernity that considers culture to be an exclusive function of the market) (Sánchez Prado, "La utopía," 11).
18. Anderson, "El futuro neoliberal y la utopía perdida en Lejos del paraíso de Sandra Cohen," 27.
19. Hernández, *El teatro de Argentina y Chile*, 19.
20. Shafir and Brysk, "The Globalization of Rights," 277.
21. Ibid.
22. Ibid., 279.
23. Sánchez Prado, "Amores perros," 39.
24. Ibid.
25. Peveroni, "Territorios posdramáticos," 12.
26. Ibid.
27. Ibid.
28. Ibid., 12, 15.
29. Ibid., 12.
30. The lyrics quoted are "He's a real nowhere Man/Sitting in his Nowhere Land/Making all his Nowhere Plans for nobody/Doesn't have a point of view/Knows not where he's going to/Isn't he a bit like you and me?" (Borkenztain, "En tránsito," 3). This song is from the album *Rubber Soul* released in 1965.
31. Borkenztain, "En tránsito," 3.
32. Ibid. He writes, "Son los desterrados, personas jóvenes, sin ataduras familiares que les impidan trasladarse, con una buena formación, profesional mayormente, que son reclutados de manera preferencial por las

multinacionales por su disponibilidad para viajar, que los convierte en engranajes más eficientes que los breeders, esos desagradables reproductores que anteponen valores tan arcaícos como establildad, familia y pareja a los sagrados intereses corporativos." (They are outcasts, young people, without family ties to keep them from moving, with good training, professional for the most part, that are preferentially recruited by multi-nationals because of their availability to travel, and which convert them into the most efficient cogs of breeders, unsavory reproducers, who put sacred corporate interests before those archaic values of stability, family and marriage).

33. Ibid.
34. Ibid.
35. Peveroni, *Berlín*, 6.
36. Ibid., 10.
37. Ibid.
38. Cox's (et al.) interpretation is helpful in this instance: "The invasion of Iraq, rather than having anything to do with combating terrorism or pre-empting supposed WMD threats, was more about violently integrating that country into the economic circuits of global 'free' trade" (*Politics Most Unusual*, 9).
39. Peveroni, *Berlín*, 10.
40. Peveroni, *Berlín*, 15.
41. Ibid., 7.
42. Ibid., 17.
43. Ibid., 22.
44. Mirza, *Teatro y violencia en la escena contemporánea*, 10.
45. Ibid.
46. Cox, et al., *Politics Most Unusual*, 7.
47. Cox, et al., *Politics Most Unusual*, 3.
48. Ibid., 5.
49. Ibid., xii.
50. Taussig, *The Nervous System*, 4.
51. Ibid.
52. Ibid., 18.
53. Ibid., 11.
54. Ibid., 17.
55. Ibid., 18.
56. Martínez, "La vida vale," 13.
57. Snyder, *Politics after Neoliberalism*, 4.
58. Oligarchic policy frameworks "generate monopoly rents for a narrow group of elites" whereas mass-based frameworks "distribute benefits widely to nonelite groups" (Snyder, *Politics after Neoliberalism*,11).
59. Rascón Banda, *Hotel Juárez*, 237.
60. Ibid.
61. Ibid., 255.
62. Lomnitz, *Death and the Idea of México*, 255.
63. Ibid., 449.
64. Ibid., 454.
65. Ibid., 475.
66. Rascón Banda, *Hotel Juárez*, 260.
67. Ibid., 257.
68. Ibid.

69. Lomnitz, *Death and the Idea of Mexico*, 476.
70. Sharif Sharif is the so-called "Jackal of Juárez" and was arrested in 1995 for the murders of countless women. However, the murders have continued after his arrest and subsequent sentence in jail.
71. Rascón Banda, *Hotel Juárez*, 253.
72. Ibid., 238.

Chapter 8

Migrant Melodrama, Human Rights, and Elvira Arellano

Ana Elena Puga

Elvira Arellano's decade-long struggle as an undocumented migrant combines the commonplace with the extraordinary in a manner that can easily be shaped into the sort of melodramatic narrative all-too-often required of performances intended to claim human rights. For some, Arellano embodies the heroic suffering-as-virtue and political-as-personal central to many such performances. What happens when the melodramatic imagination intersects with the human rights imagination in the realm of social protest? This chapter explores how these two imaginaries intersected on the figure of Arellano before, during, and after she and her son spent a year in sanctuary in a Chicago church.

Like hundreds of thousands of undocumented migrants arriving every year, Arellano was rounded up by immigration authorities and ordered to present herself for deportation. And like many of those deported, Arellano was a single Mexican mother with a US-born child who would either have to leave with his mother or remain in the United States away from her. Yet rather than accept deportation or risk time in prison by attempting to remain in the country as a "fugitive," Arellano openly defied what she and many others consider unjust immigration laws.[1] After her first deportation, in 1997, Arellano walked back over the border again. In 2002, when she was arrested in an

Immigration Control and Enforcement crackdown on O'Hare airport, she did not agree to the "expedited removal" offered by immigration authorities but instead appealed to an Illinois congressman, Rep. Luis V. Gutierrez, who introduced a private relief bill in the House that won her a stay of deportation based on her son's need for medical treatment.[2] She became a public figure in June of 2004, when she confronted then Mexican President Vicente Fox during a town-hall meeting with the Chicago-area Mexican community and urged him to reject George W. Bush's guest-worker plan. She had been an activist and a public figure for more than two years when on August 15, 2006, she sought sanctuary in Chicago's Adalberto United Methodist church, a small storefront in the Puerto Rican neighborhood of Humboldt Park. During the following year, as the first person granted sanctuary in what became the New Sanctuary Movement until her deportation, on August 20, 2007, she was the object of hundreds of news stories, television broadcasts, and internet discussions throughout the United States, Latin America, and Europe. After her deportation, media attention remained focused on her son Saul, by then eight years old, as he embarked on a 23-state speaking tour of the United States accompanied by New Sanctuary Movement activists Emma Lozano and the Rev. Walter Coleman.[3] In September, Saul rejoined his mother in Mexico.

To better understand how melodramatic imagination is used to represent, propel, but nevertheless constrain, the human rights of migrants, I focus a theater/performance studies lens on what I contend is melodrama(s) of social performance constructed by both Arellano supporters and detractors. Building on the work of literary critic Peter Brooks[4] and film scholar Linda Williams,[5] among others, I show how melodramatic imagination has real-world consequences, as the way we conceive of an undocumented migrant can determine whether we treat the person as a suffering mother or a criminal, a worthy victim or an unworthy victim, an "us" or a "them," a good citizen or a dangerous outsider.[6] Some tropes that can be traced back as far as nineteenth- and twentieth-century novels and plays are recirculated and redeployed today in the battle about whether and to what extent undocumented migrants deserve citizenship rights, or even human rights.

From political scientist Bonnie Honig's work on citizenship, I take the insight that the figure of the foreigner can quickly shift from the figure of the good citizen to the figure of the dangerous outsider—the hard worker becomes the person who might steal one's job.[7] Building on Honig, I seek to (1) account for how the figure of the foreigner, in this case an undocumented migrant, is embedded in a network of roles, or "cast" in the language of theater, and can be recast when roles are contested in what I call a "casting competition"; (2) better understand melodrama in social performance as a *dynamic* process, as a set of contradictory role assignments that jockey against each other, creating a chain of two or more competing melodramas in which different figures vie for the role of, say, virtuous victim or rescuing hero; and (3) delineate the potential and dangers of melodrama for migrants, how its characterizations, plot, spectacle, and Manichean worldview can sometimes win rights but sometimes lead to artificial resolutions about who belongs and who does not belong within the borders of the nation-state. My emphasis on the individual social performer as part of a cast of characters, along with the exploration of melodrama production as a social dynamic involving multiple recastings, is intended to reveal more about how longstanding melodramatic tropes are recirculated and deployed today by migrants, their advocates, and their opponents.

The social and cultural performances surrounding Arellano show how melodramatic imagination informs both attempts to negotiate experiences of racialized and gendered migration, and mechanisms of inclusion and exclusion into the nation-state. I analyze melodramatic imagination as applied specifically to undocumented migrants in order to help explain why and how many people, even sometimes migrants and migrant advocates, expect migrants to suffer and accept migrant suffering as natural and inevitable, if not entertaining. In short, I hope to help denaturalize migrant suffering.

MELODRAMA AS A DOUBLE-EDGED SWORD IN FILM AND THEATER

In film and theater studies, an immense body of work explores how melodrama reflects and shapes United States popular culture.[8] Here, I draw primarily from studies in sensation, domestic, and race melodrama. Nineteenth-century sensation melodrama, with its spectacular technological effects and the intense emotions triggered by those effects, had the potential to propel historical change through exchanges between staged social constructs and their audiences' evolving social identities.[9] Nicholas Daly explores sensation melodrama as an expression of anxieties about both technology and immigration.[10] Applying insights from Daly, as well as from Ben Singer's study of early twentieth-century sensation melodrama *Melodrama and Modernity*, to the very different context of contemporary migration journeys from Latin America, triggered the realization that the travels and travails of undocumented migrants—the journeys on trains and in buses, the border crossings, the pursuits, the arrests, the rescues, and the deportations—are often depicted in media and art alike with a similar, though of course not identical, anxiety about the chaos of contemporary life and the supposed contamination that "foreign bodies" can introduce into the nation.[11] Though extended meditation on contemporary sensation melodrama is beyond the scope of this chapter, I argue elsewhere that many recent documentary and fictional films, as well as journalistic accounts about undocumented migrants' journeys, include significant elements of sensation melodrama, most obviously anxiety about and fascination with the figure of the undocumented migrant on a dangerous train.[12] Within US melodrama scholarship, studies of immigrant melodrama have tended to focus on the role of film, theater, and fictional narrative as a purveyor of stereotypes, and also as a progressive force for collective identity formation and inclusion in the national imaginary.[13] My study of the female migrant today as mother and gendered worker however, builds on studies of domestic melodrama and literary sentimentality that stress that melodramatic theater and sentimental fiction cannot be reduced to either a force for liberation or a vehicle for domination.[14] Several studies of African American race melodrama have elucidated how attempts to use sentiment to win rights for the oppressed can in fact also perpetuate the marking of victim-as-victim and even fuel audience enjoyment of violence against the victim. Saidiya V. Hartman's pioneering work on this unintended consequence, Heather Nathans's study of early race melodrama, and Daphne A. Brooks's study of dissident African American performers in the late nineteenth and early twentieth century have shaped my understanding of melodrama as a double-edged political sword.[15]

In studies of Latin American and US Latina/o performance, study of melodrama's political effects has so far been extremely limited, though Jorge A. Huerta does briefly touch on the theme in his discussion of Luis Valdez's plays.[16] In a more extended discussion of Valdez, John D. Rossini succinctly expresses the negative side of melodrama's double-edged nature: "The deployment of melodrama to deconstruct or rewrite history thus runs the risk of creating new forms of stereotyped and conventional history in the process, not to mention reinforcing a reductive moral binary."[17]

Social Performance and Migrant Melodrama

Diana Taylor's important work on the political protests of the Mothers of the Plaza de Mayo in Argentina and her elucidation of what she calls "scenarios" are essential to an understanding of how performative patterns repeat, with variations, over different historical eras.[18] Scenarios include preset narrative plots and a range of corporeal behaviors that both reflect and structure our perception of a situation. Like scenarios, melodramas involve not only textual narrative but also embodied practice such as physical movement, gesture, and tone of voice. It is important, however, to distinguish melodrama from scenario. While one might imagine various types of melodramatic scenarios, or one might inject melodrama into a scenario that is not necessarily inherently melodramatic, melodrama cannot be reduced to a type of scenario. Melodrama has a specific history as a literary, theatrical, and film genre, with particular conventions that could be applied to almost any scenario, such as the "scenarios of discovery" or "scenarios of conquest" that Taylor describes. Thus, a single melodrama might involve one or more scenarios, say a "scenario of deportation" as well as a "scenario of family reunification." And such scenarios might or might not be performed in a fashion constitutive of melodrama, involving the conventions enumerated below.

Like scenarios, melodramas are more than a fictional genre; they are what Williams identified as a vital contemporary mode of imagination, a way of apprehending experience that orders our perceptions and helps us organize our world. I borrow from her work to define the conventions of the melodramatic mode as I use the term here:

1. a reformulation of collective political conflict as personal, individual experience; the individual protagonist embodies a just cause;
2. a confirmation of the justness of the protagonist's cause, and of his/her unblemished virtue, by how much undeserved violence he/she suffers;
3. a Manichean worldview that tends to divide the world into the virtuous victims who suffer and the evil villains who make them suffer;
4. a narrative structure built on suspense created by a complicated interplay between pathos and action (for example, scenes of attempted escape, chase scenes, rescues);
5. a culmination of the narrative in exposure and recognition of villainy and virtue, sometimes, though not always, accompanied by respective reward and punishment.

I use the term "migrant melodrama" to describe a contemporary mode of thought that includes the five elements listed above in both cultural production and everyday perception of migrants. Like melodrama in general, migrant melodrama is also both a genre and a habit of thought that may sometimes come to us through fiction, but also structures many of our ideas about nonfictional people and events, which in turn may fuel further cultural production. The recycling of melodramatic strategies of representation and performance about migrants can be seen both on television sitcoms and on the evening news, in courtroom dramas and in actual courtrooms, in Hollywood films and in nonfictional documentaries, in theaters and on sidewalks, on YouTube videos and in churches. Moreover, migrant melodrama is often transnational, taking place on both sides of and across many US-Latin American borders, and thus requires a cultural and historical situation on both sides of the borders. Here I offer a preliminary definition and description of the operations of migrant melodrama as a mode of imagination in social performance:

1. Migrant melodrama assumes virtuous suffering as the price of inclusion in the nation-state, or even to win rights within the state. When migrant melodrama is used to deny migrant rights, it often holds that migrants have not yet suffered enough, or have not suffered in the right way.
2. Migrant melodrama is often demanded or deployed to access rights that should be universal and in some cases have already been granted, at least on paper, by international and national law. I construe rights broadly here, as articulated by Article 25 in the United Nations' Universal Declaration of Human Rights: "Everyone has a right to a standard of well-being of himself and of his family, including food, clothing, housing and medical care and necessary social services, and the right to security in the event of unemployment, sickness, disability, widowhood, old age or other lack of livelihood in circumstances beyond his control."[19]

3. Migrant melodrama involves a power imbalance between performers and audience. In social performance, migrant melodrama can be crafted either by opponents of migration or by migrants themselves. It may constitute command performance(s) required by authorities, or persuasive performances crafted and performed by undocumented migrants and their advocates, or some complex combination of the two. When crafted by migrants themselves, the power imbalance structures performances intended to satisfy individuals or institutions that have the authority to grant basic residency, citizenship, or human rights. When crafted by opponents, the power imbalance may contribute to a successful "casting" of the migrant as villain.
4. Migrant melodrama is dynamic; the roles can shift. What I call "casting competitions" follow from attempts to peg individuals or institutions as certain character types. Thus, migrant melodrama can be deployed as a strategy to claim rights; or, it can be deployed as a strategy to deny rights. Its narrative and performance might for one period of time, or for one audience, involve a suffering mother, a wise child, and an evil state persecutor; at another moment, and/or for a different audience, the same figures might be represented as a criminal mother, an abused child, and a heroic state.

The theoretical stakes of migrant melodrama lead to some crucial questions: Is it possible or desirable to make claims to human rights without emphasizing suffering, without equating suffering with virtue, and without equating virtue with the unity of a family, often a heterosexual family? Would it then be possible to avoid the pitfall of dividing migrants into the good migrants who deserve rights and the bad migrants who do not? Would it be possible to make the claim that all migrants deserve human rights, deserve residency rights or even citizenship rights, regardless of whether or how much they have suffered, how good or evil they may be, whatever their family, or lack of family status? And how could such a claim be compelling? How can advocates for migrant rights best negotiate expectations, even demands, for moral clarity and spectacles of suffering as the price of inclusion in the national imagined community?

To explore migrant melodrama as performed in the context of Arellano's struggle to remain in the United States, I take an interdisciplinary Latina/o performance studies approach that draws on the work of social performance, media, literary, film, and theater scholars. While I borrow the term melodrama from theater studies, my actual examples of recycled melodramatic tropes, particularly in the twentieth century, often come from film, television, and narrative rather than theater proper. This is because mass media today, with its large audiences and relatively easy access, is more influential than theater in shaping the *zeitgeist* of social performers and their audiences. As Media and Latina/o Studies scholar Isabel Molina-Guzmán writes in *Dangerous Curves: Latina Bodies in the Media*: "To map out the Latina body in the U.S. media requires tracing it across the entire mediascape—fact and fiction, news and entertainment."[20] I aim to fulfill Molina-Guzmán's injunction by mapping out the bodies in performance of Arellano, her son, and to a more limited extent, the bodies of her advocates and opponents, across an eclectic range of primary sources that should provide a well-rounded delineation of migrant melodrama as social performance practice.

Plot, Setting, and Casting Dynamic

The domestic setting for the Arellano migrant melodrama was the apartment above the church where she lived with her son. Yet it unfolded on a world stage and became an allegory about transnational migration, the stuff of action-and-adventure, or contemporary sensation melodrama. The setting was both domestic and public, occupying both secular and sacred spaces. It took place not only in the apartment, but also in the church where she worshipped, and organized the congregation; on the streets where her supporters and detractors alike demonstrated; and on the Mexico–United States border, where her entrances and exits were recorded. Within this setting, the plot, as in a sensation melodrama, was full of suspense and intense emotion—in this case, created by the constant threat of deportation. And as in race melodrama, the protagonist's suffering was connected to her racialization, in this case her racialization as a brown-skinned working-class woman with limited education. The sentimental tropes of race melodrama, particularly the emphasis on the potential threat of family separation (remember the tragic mulatta Eliza and her son fleeing across the ice in the novel and stage adaptations of Harriet Beecher Stowe's *Uncle Tom's Cabin*?), were activated in attempts to win public sympathy that were not always successful. *Time Magazine*, for instance, opined: "Her case and her cause have also at times been handled inartfully—the aggressive use of her young son as a mascot for the movement at times bordered on being exploitative."[21]

As a dynamic, the Arellano melodrama evolved in at least three escalating, competing rounds of casting: (1) Arellano's performance of self as a virtuous, suffering mother and the casting of her son Saul as an innocent child-victim of unjust laws; (2) the response of Arellano's opponents: a competing assignment of roles that cast Arellano as a cruel, criminal mother who herself victimized her son; (3) the response of supporters to the attacks on Arellano: a postdeportation canonization of Arellano as a *madre dolorosa*, or sorrowing Virgin Mary figure; in other words, a martyr and a saint. In order to analyze the first two rounds, I reconstruct the first two competing melodramas primarily from news accounts and media photos. In considering round three, postdeportation representations, I look primarily at a contemporary painting by Javier Chavira. Whether in the media or in visual culture, I argue, the struggle around Arellano essentially centers on a metaphoric casting competition: We, the court of public opinion, are asked to determine which (social) actor deserves which role.

First Casting: Arellano as Suffering Mother, Saul as Innocent Child, ICE as Villain, and Church as Rescuer

I would argue that Arellano, her lawyers, her advocates in the Sanctuary Movement, and sympathetic news reporters and photographers collaborated on a representation, or "casting," of her as a suffering mother. It is impossible to determine exactly to what extent, if at all, this casting was conscious and whether Arellano exercised agency in her embodiment of the role. To some extent, her role was created for her, or at times even demanded of her, by her advocates, by the media, by legislators who accepted her petitions, and by the nation-state that had the power to deny her appeals and deport her. Arellano operated under severe historical, material, and ideological constraints; yet it would be condescending to assume that she had no conscious understanding of the power dynamics of her situation or of the importance of presenting herself in particular ways in public. Whether or to what extent she was conscious of her performance is less important than the fact that an interpretation of the performance can be constructed from the evidence of her public appearances.

In saying that Arellano played a role I do not mean to imply that Arellano's suffering, or that the suffering of Mexican migrant mothers, is not real. My point is that real suffering must be socially performed in order for it to be registered and responded to with empathy by audiences with the power to grant rights or to pressure for the granting of rights. As Rebecca Wanzo demonstrates in *The Suffering Will Not Be Televised* (2009), the suffering of white women has generally been held to count more than the suffering of women of color. And the suffering of the elite has often been more attended to than the suffering of the subaltern. But on the other hand, the suffering of women, both white and of color, both rich and poor, has also been glorified in popular culture, a glorification that perpetuates an ideology of sacrifice while holding out the hope that such sacrifice, if recognized as virtue, will yield acknowledgment and rewards in the form of more humane treatment. I offer a brief review of the tradition of the suffering mother figure in melodrama in order to point out some of the cultural tropes that may have shaped the ideology, not only of Arellano and her advisors, but also of her media audiences on both sides of the United States–Mexico border, predisposing both performers and audiences to encourage and even celebrate suffering. In my view, the problem is not only that the suffering of working-class women of color has not been sufficiently highlighted; it is that by highlighting suffering a demand can be created for further suffering.

The suffering mother is a cross-cultural melodramatic trope that literary critic E. Ann Kaplan traces back to Rousseau's eighteenth-century views about the centrality of the child to the life of the mother.[22] In both Mexican and US culture, we celebrate the pious mother who suffers, like Christ and like the Virgin Mary, so that her family can survive and thrive with its unity intact. In Mexico, the traditional mother was Catholic; in the United States she was Protestant. In both countries she was devout, slavishly devoted to her children, and willing to sacrifice everything for their sake. In Mexico, the melodrama mother comes down to us through the stereotype of the *"madrecita abnegada, la madrecita santa"* ["self-sacrificing mother, the saintly mother"] portrayed by Sara García in so many films between 1935 and 1971.[23]

Jorge Ayala Blanco notes the *madrecita*'s "glorious masochism" and suggests that suffering, along with a somewhat paradoxical combination of passivity and resourcefulness in the service of her family, is key to the composition of the character type.[24] Today, the melodrama mother lives on, not just in the old Sara García movies, but in many television shows, especially the television dramas known as *telenovelas*, in commercial and documentary films, and in nonfictional media narratives. In the immensely popular 1969–1971 telenovela *Simplemente María*, for instance, the protagonist is a rural–urban migrant seamstress and single mother who marries late in life, only after she has selflessly dedicated herself to raising her son.[25] In recent years, the increase in numbers of transnational women migrants who leave their children behind in order to provide financial support from abroad has provided a true-life melodramatic hook—family separation—for screenwriters and filmmakers crafting protagonists in the contemporary *madrecita* mode. Referring to the actual lives of women as a "melodramatic hook" might seem flippant or disregarding of actual suffering. Yet by using this phrase I seek to convey how actual suffering is absorbed and recirculated in a sometimes-trivialized fashion by mainstream popular culture.

Arellano's performance was consumed by audiences that have been primed to expect migrant mothers to suffer. To list just three saintly single migrant mothers in otherwise very different recent films from both sides of the border: the Mexican maid in the comedy *Spanglish* (dir. James L. Brooks, 2004), played by the Spanish actress Paz Vega, in yet another Hollywood elision of all Hispanics, as the savior of her Anglo employers who nevertheless fiercely protect her teenage daughter from supposedly corrupting US influences; the Mexican nanny in *Babel* (dir. Alejandro González Iñárritu, 2006), played by Adriana Barraza, torn between her responsibilities to her two young Anglo charges and her desire to attend her own son's wedding; and the migrant worker-mom in *La misma luna* (*Under the Same Moon*, dir. Patricia Riggen, 2007), played by Kate del Castillo.[26] The script of *La misma luna*, about the travails of a nine-year-old undocumented boy who travels alone to find his mother who has gone north to work and their eventual happy reunion, offers a comic version of the same basic plot as *Enrique's Journey* (2006), a nonfictional journalistic account by *Los Angeles Times* reporter Sonia Nazario. The latter work deploys melodramatic conventions to structure the more tragic story of a protagonist who is older, 16, but who suffers far more as he travels alone through dangerous territory to find his mother in the United States.[27]

In the United States, the melodrama mother dates back to nineteenth-century novels and plays that depicted middle-class women circumscribed by the expectation that they would be the "angel in the house," "expected to sacrifice all for the emotional, moral, and physical well-being of her husband and children."[28] Martha Vicinus argues that domestic melodrama between 1820 and 1870 responded to the growing dichotomy under capitalism between the pressures of production and an idealized private sphere that could serve as a refuge from the competition and exploitation of the public realm. Mothers in these works often combined self-sacrifice with rebellion, a rebellion that was usually paid for with punishment and additional sacrifice. White mothers in twentieth-century films such as *East Lynne, Stella Dallas* (dir. Henry King, 1925; dir. King Vidor, 1937) and African American mothers in films such as *Imitation of Life* (dir. John Stahl, 1934; dir. Douglas Sirk, 1959) continued the tradition of nobly absenting themselves so that their children might thrive.[29] Today, the narratives of transnational migrant mothers who leave their children behind in order to seek work and send back remittances in an attempt to improve the dire conditions of their children's lives—conditions exacerbated by neoliberal globalization—provide fodder for screenwriters once again inspired by the figure of the absent mother, now embodied by self-sacrificing Latinas.[30]

Unlike many migrant mothers, however, Arellano refused to separate from her son. She avoided the painful pattern of transnational motherhood described by Hondagneu-Sotelo and Avila,[31] instead seeking both improved economic circumstances and family unity. So, one might ask, where is the melodrama? It can be found, I would argue, in her attempt to base her claim to a right to remain in the United States in part on the figure of the suffering mother; the potential suffering that would result from the disruption of mother–child unity if she were deported while her son exercised his right as a citizen to remain in the United States, the suffering of a lower standard of living in Mexico, the suffering of spending all of one's time inside a church building. In addition to the lawsuit filed in federal court arguing that Saul Arellano's constitutional rights as a US citizen were being infringed, a lawsuit that was quickly dismissed, Arellano also staked a moral claim to residency rights, performing herself as a good mother, a desexualized, pious, Christian mother who cared deeply about her innocent, also suffering, child, a child who suffered at the hands of an unjust immigration regime.[32]

In all the photos I've found through internet searches, including some on Arellano's Facebook page and others published by mainstream newspapers such as *USA Today, The New York Times*, and the wire service the *Associated Press*, Arellano dresses modestly, often in pants and high-necked blouses, her long hair often pulled back into a low ponytail. (She never publicly mentioned current or former sexual partners and never identified Saul's father, referring to him only in the vaguest of terms and only when directly asked.) In photographs, while she sometimes looks directly at the camera, she also at times clutches Saul to her and keeps her head tilted and her eyes downcast in a typical Madonna gesture, thus adopting a posture associated with virginal mothers and facilitating the association of her son with the role of innocent victim.[33] Since many of these images were accessed online through Google image searches, and many of them were posted anonymously, it has not always been possible to ascertain their origin or to discern to what extent the photographers posed Arellano and her son. In one oft-posted photo that has no credit, Arellano appears seated next to a statuette of the Virgin of Guadalupe, a microphone in one hand and her other hand wrapped around Saul as he sits in her lap, dressed in a gray suit and a shiny red tie. Behind Arellano stands a life-sized placard with a dash-line outline of her body similar to those used in South America in the 1970s and 1980s to protest the disappeared. Above the outline, black letters read: "Don't let the migra take my mommy away." In the background, to the side of the placard, sits an unidentified man clothed in clerical garb. While the photo appears on at least one pro-Arellano blog,[34] it has also been posted on the website of an individual who posted the cutline under it: "Elvira Arellano & Anchor Baby Son Saul."[35] Thus an image that was most likely created in hopes of associating Arellano with the piety and goodness of the Virgin was "flipped" to assist in her demonization. In an antimigrant context, the use of the word "mommy," the language of a child, perhaps intended to evoke empathy or sympathy, instead taps into stereotypes of Latinas as hyperfertile threats to the nation.[36]

The day before she sought sanctuary in the Adalberto United Methodist Church, Arellano told *Chicago Sun-Times* reporter Esther J. Cepeda: "I can't go back, I have no job there, I have no savings, and what will I be able to take in one suitcase? What about my son? He is ready to go to second grade, and in Mexico I won't even be able to feed him" (August 14, 2006). Arellano's question, "What about my son?" foregrounds the potential suffering of an innocent child, not yet old enough to deserve punishment, and evokes the pitiful image of a boy, just out of first grade, starving to death in Mexico. Arellano herself, in this configuration, matters only in terms of her ability to provide for her son. And the boy matters both because of his status as an innocent child and because he is a US citizen.

Early news accounts in the *Chicago Sun-Times* and in the *Tribune*, just after Arellano sought shelter, tended to accept her self-presentation. McElmurry's thorough study of the Chicago newspaper coverage surrounding the Arellano case demonstrates that the Spanish-language press, far more than the English-language press, depicted Arellano as a "good mother."[37] Typical of the coverage is this quote from the Spanish-language newspaper *Hoy*:

> Al regresar a casa, su madre lo esperaba con comida recién preparada en el apartamento del segundo piso, justo arriba de la iglesia, donde ahora es su nuevo hogar. "Estaré con él siempre, para ayudarle con sus tareas y procurando que se gradúe y logre su sueño de ser bombero," comentó la madre mexicana (September 9, 2006, *Hoy*).[38]

> [Upon returning home, his mother awaited him with just-prepared food in the second-story apartment right above the church, which is now his new home. "I will be with him always, to help him with his homework and to make sure that he graduates and realizes his dream of becoming a fireman," said the Mexican mother.]

Emphasizing the "Mexican mother" designator, McElmurry credits *Hoy* with the construction of the good-mother identity. But I would argue that

Arellano and the *Hoy* journalist worked together to construct her identity. Arellano herself, if she is quoted correctly, vows to remain with Saul "forever" to help him realize his dreams, a vow that foregrounds her loyalty to his ambitions and makes no mention of any desires or dreams of her own apart from his. Arellano herself serves the meal in front of the journalist, performing motherhood through traditionally gendered domestic tasks. During her stay in sanctuary, because of her inability to leave the church property, Arellano was able to temporarily perform a culturally constructed ideal of intense middle-class mothering, which, as a single working-class Mexican woman employed in the low-status gendered and racialized job of cleaner, she perhaps perceived as a luxury.

Saul, or "Saulito" as he was sometimes called in the diminutive to extra sentimental effect, was often cast by the adults surrounding him as the melodrama child, the wise and innocent victim-as-savior who bravely faced the tragic threat of separation from his mother. I very briefly sketch out the history of the figure of the child in melodrama here in order to situate his casting and recasting in what I see as his command performances, demanded of him by a variety of adults with the power to affect the basic conditions of his life. Scholars have traced the figure of the melodrama child at least as far back as Charles Dickens and his boy-hero *Oliver Twist* (1837–1839). The figure of the abused child, often bereft of his/her parents, separated from them, or in danger of losing them, has long been used to condemn social ills, whether in narrative, on stage, on screen, or in photographic images circulated with the intention of promoting reform. Dion Boucicault's *The Poor of New York* (1857) and Augustin Daly's *Under the Gaslight* (1868) both featured impoverished-but-gutsy girls updated and refashioned for films much later in many Shirley Temple characters throughout the 1930s. Images of abused boys and girls were crucial to the struggle against child labor in Victorian England, in twentieth-century United States (most famously in the photographs of Lewis Hine), and today serve as mass media "poster children" for a variety of evils including, again, child labor, as well as world hunger, sexual trafficking, the havoc wrought by war, and a variety of diseases and disabilities.[39]

The bodies of Latino children were more recently pressed into service as evidence of supposed political evil during the 1960s Peter Pan airlifts from Cuba that have been thoroughly discredited by scholars and artists, including scholar María de los Angeles Torres[40] and playwright Sonia Lopez in *Sonia Flew*.[41] In an echo of the Peter Pan ideology, in 1999, when the six-year-old Cuban boy Elián González was found at sea off the coast of Miami he was hailed by opponents of Castro as a miraculous symbol of his deceased mother's sacrifice.[42] Given the proven track record of the immense symbolic power of children's vulnerable bodies and their ability to evoke sympathy, it is not surprising that migrant activists and their supporters have sometimes chosen to take children, including Saul Arellano, to Washington to lobby on their behalf and to highlight how much children suffer when families are separated through deportation.[43] I am not suggesting that the use of child performances in the migrant-rights movement is as exploitative or destructive as the Peter Pan program. Yet I do want to point out some potentially serious drawbacks, including a construction of "family" that focuses on the parent–child bond to the exclusion of childless migrants,[44] and a creation of such expectations, if not demands, for extraordinarily charismatic children that many minors will necessarily disappoint.

For example, columnist for the *Chicago Sun-Times* Sue Ontiveros highlighted Saul Arellano's small physical size and his US citizenship when she projected him as an emblem for the three million US-born children whose parents are undocumented. "Just as those children suffer, so does little Citizen Saul," she wrote on August 26, 2006. A week later, in response to emails she received from readers that rejected Saul's right to citizenship, she opened her column with a somewhat condescending bid to make Arellano herself seem child-like and vulnerable, while indirectly calling attention to some of her readers' racism, "My, my, one little brown woman sure has a lot of people very angry." Other journalists seemed disturbed by how Saul did not exude the air of wisdom and unusual compassion expected of melodrama child-heroes imbued with the power to redeem their parents or other wayward adults.[45] Some journalists noted with implied disapproval that Saul seemed shy, awkward, and at times downright resentful of his mother's activism.[46] At a rally in Tijuana shortly after her deportation, Arellano insisted that whatever distress the boy had experienced was the fault of the state. According to the Associated Press, Arellano narrated their saga in the third person as she told a small crowd of supporters: "He's a boy who has been suffering, because the US government told his mother she couldn't stay in their country anymore because she was undocumented."

In this round of casting, the melodrama villain, the personification of evil, is the arm of the state charged with deportations, Immigration Control and Enforcement, or "la migra" in colloquial Spanish. In the poster heading described above—"Don't let the migra take my mommy away"—that was recirculated in photos and on the Internet, "la migra" is vilified through its personification as a mother-snatcher.[47] The supposed voice of the child, (in fact, most likely created by adults) speaks as if to say, "Save me from the villain!" Some journalists even went so far as to indulge in the melodramatic tradition of depicting the villain as physically deficient and so unattractive. For example, Daniel Hernandez of *LA Weekly* described the Immigration Control and Enforcement (ICE) agent who spoke at the press conference after Arellano's deportation as "bald, stocky and arrogant." Arellano, in contrast, was described by Hernandez as "small-framed and soft-spoken" (Hernandez 2007). I agree with those who rightly point out that Immigration Control and Enforcement, taking its cue from the federal government, appears indifferent to the plight of mixed-status families and constructs working-class Latina migrants as illegal, thus providing a stream of cheap, disposable labor.[48] Yet to portray ICE agents as ugly thugs intent on separating children from their mothers overly personalizes the systemic violence of the nation-state.

The potential rescuers in the Arellano migrant melodrama are the Rev. Coleman and his wife Lozano, who housed Arellano in the apartment above their storefront church and used her embodied threat of mother–child separation to claim the moral high ground for the New Sanctuary Movement. To the New Sanctuary Movement churches around the country, which provide shelter to undocumented migrants, the defiance of nation-state laws constitutes civil disobedience of an immoral human law for the sake of adherence to a higher law. As the Rev. Coleman put it, "I care more about God's law than I do about Homeland Security."[49] It is difficult to ascertain whether, or to what extent, as part of their rescue mission, Coleman and Lozano may have helped "stage" Arellano in ways that unintentionally backfired, turning public opinion against her.

Recasting by Arellano's Opponents

I would argue that Saul was the pivot that opponents of undocumented migrants used to try to turn the melodrama around and recast the roles. Opponents kept the melodramatic structure intact, but implied that the character types had been incorrectly identified. Saulito, they claimed, was suffering alright, but not because an evil nation-state was persecuting his good mother. He was suffering because his mother was actually a cruel woman who was simply posing as a victim. And they undertook to expose her. The group Mothers Against Illegal Aliens staged several protests outside of the church to accuse Arellano of child abuse. They called Saul an "anchor baby" and said he had repeatedly been kept out of school to make public appearances. Moreover, they said, he was deprived of a normal social life with other children. Somewhat paradoxically, the proposed solution of the Mothers Against Illegal Aliens to the alleged child abuse was to pressure Immigration Control and Enforcement to do its job and deport Arellano, together with her son. They started an internet campaign to get people to telephone the agency to request that its agents arrest and deport her. Mary Romero has followed the activities of Mothers Against Illegal Aliens very closely and analyzed in detail how they constructed themselves as devotees of the cult of true, white middle-class motherhood, adopting the Madonna figure as their logo, though they were not a Catholic organization.[50]

After the protests by Mothers Against Illegal Aliens, the press coverage became more hostile. On the one-year anniversary of Arellano's entry into sanctuary, August 15, 2007, the *Sun-Times* ran an editorial headlined: "It's time to get out—Elvira Arellano has flouted the law long enough. She should leave the church and go back to Mexico."[51] (35). The editorial accused Arellano of exploiting her son for her own gain: "It's time Arellano stop using Saul as bait—like the shrewd panhandlers on the 'L' parading their young for change." This image of the evil mother using the innocent child as a tool for panhandling comes straight out of nineteenth-century melodrama. Vicinus, for example, describes a scene from the 1847 novel by G. W. M. Reynolds, *The Mysteries of London*, in which a mother suggests blinding her own children, because once blinded they will be less likely to escape her evil clutches:

> No one who has read G.W.M. Reynolds's *The Mysteries of London* (1847) will forget the mother who proposes blinding her children by placing a large insect between their lids and eyes; as blind children they will be more effective beggars and more dependent on her. Her motives are purely economic, but what we remember is the travesty of motherly feelings.[52]

The *Sun-Times* editorial appeals to readers' sense of outrage in its construction of Arellano as capable of such a travesty of the motherly love she had proclaimed and performed. Thus a derogatory trope—the unscrupulous beggar—dating back at least as far as Victorian London is redeployed against a contemporary Mexican woman, perhaps bringing to mind for some readers stereotypical racialized and gendered images of hyperfertile Mexican beggars whose poverty is their own fault, or whose poverty is merely an act devised to dupe the unsuspecting passerby into a foolish gesture of generosity. In the context of debate about which Latina/o migrants, if any, merit inclusion in the US nation-state, the migrant-as-beggar becomes an image that can trigger emotions, such as disgust or anger, likely to justify migrant exclusion.

Sun-Times reporter Esther Cepeda made a complete about-face in her coverage of Arellano. Toward the beginning of Arellano's sanctuary, Cepeda wrote fairly sympathetic articles and even called Saul a "little freedom fighter."[53] After Arellano's deportation, however, Cepeda wrote an opinion column condemning her for allegedly forcing her son to stand in the "hot sun" and hand out fliers about migrant rights.[54] Arellano's supposed offenses also included not allowing Saul to watch fireworks with his friends on the Fourth of July, an accusation that hinted at anti-American sentiment. Cepeda and other journalists thus transform Saul from potential melodrama rescuer, endowed with the redemptive power to save his mother, into the melodrama victim of an evil mother who is not worthy of rescue. In this casting, Rev. Coleman and Lozano are accomplices to the villain rather than rescuers; the real rescuer becomes ICE, for saving the new victim, the United States, from Arellano. Editorials in favor of Arellano's deportation often construed her removal as just retribution, or in other words, melodrama punishment, for her alleged misdeeds in defying immigration laws. Exultation over Arellano's deportation in several journalistic accounts takes on a nasty celebratory tone. Cepeda, for example, writes: "Adios and good riddance."

Arellano as Virgin and Saint

After Arellano's deportation, advocates of immigration reform tried to recast the melodrama yet again, as they began to depict both Arellano and Saul as martyrs, marking another significant shift in the melodrama dynamic. In the wake of Elvira's physical absence from the United States, references and images began to appear to fill in the gap. Large color photographs of Elvira's face now grace the walls of the Adalberto Methodist Church, flanking the image of the Virgin of Guadalupe. In October 2009, a group of about a dozen church members gathered to watch a preview of a new documentary film, *Immigrant Nation: The Battle for the Dream*, by independent filmmaker Esau Melendez.[55] In respectful detail, the documentary recounts Arellano's decision to seek sanctuary, her struggles as a political activist in Chicago, and her eventual return to her hometown in Michoacan, Mexico. Other activists and scholars began to refer to Arellano as the Rosa Parks of Latinas and Latinos, sparking a controversy that I have written about elsewhere.[56] But perhaps the most powerful contribution to the move to canonize Arellano came from the Mexican-American visual artist Javier Chavira. His 2008 painting, "Madre Dolorosa: Elvira Arellano" combines the European iconography of the "Mater Dolorosa," or "Sorrowing Mother," rooted in fifteenth-century Netherlands with contemporary Mexican iconography to depict Arellano as a Virginal figure defined by her strength, and also by her suffering, her pain, her resignation (see figure 8.1). Commissioned to create a piece for the National Museum of Mexican Art's 2008 "A Declaration of Immigration" exhibit, Chavira worked from an image of Arellano's mug shot that he found online to transform the criminal into the sacred.

Against a deep blue background evocative of both sky and of the Virgin of Guadalupe's cape, Arellano's mug-shot stare is now re-created in a 24-by-24 inch tempera painting finished with oil in a *technique mixte* used to render every shadow and line of her face in realistic detail. Her face and shoulder-length hair is framed by a halo fashioned from actual barbed wire, thorns, and rhinestones that stick out from the canvass to give the painting a sculptural dimension. The barbed wire recalls the fences intended to keep migrants out; the thorns recall Christ's crown of thorns; and the rhinestones, Chavira told me, symbolize the riches that migrants dream of accumulating in the United States. Monarch butterflies and white moths painted on the canvass appear to perch on the barbed-wire halo, making the process of human migration seem as natural and inevitable as that of the butterflies. Arellano's shoulders and upper chest are draped in a simple yellow mantle with a high square collar that serves as background for a nopal-heart carved out of wood, painted green, and spiked with the same thorns that grace her halo. In minimalist evocation of the seven spears, or "swords of compassion," that pierce the heart of the traditional Mater Dolorosa image and symbolize her empathy with Christ's suffering, a little jeweled dagger stabs the nopal-heart. The many actual thorns protruding from the heart, however, magnify the sensation and the threat of pain, both to Arellano and to us, were we to touch the heart. Unlike many traditional images that portray the sorrowing Madonna weeping, Arellano's eyes shed no tears and look directly out at the viewer; the mug shot convention dictating that she keep her gaze forward and her head straight, a posture that hints at defiance rather than submission or humility. Her mouth is set in a closed-lipped, slightly downturned angle

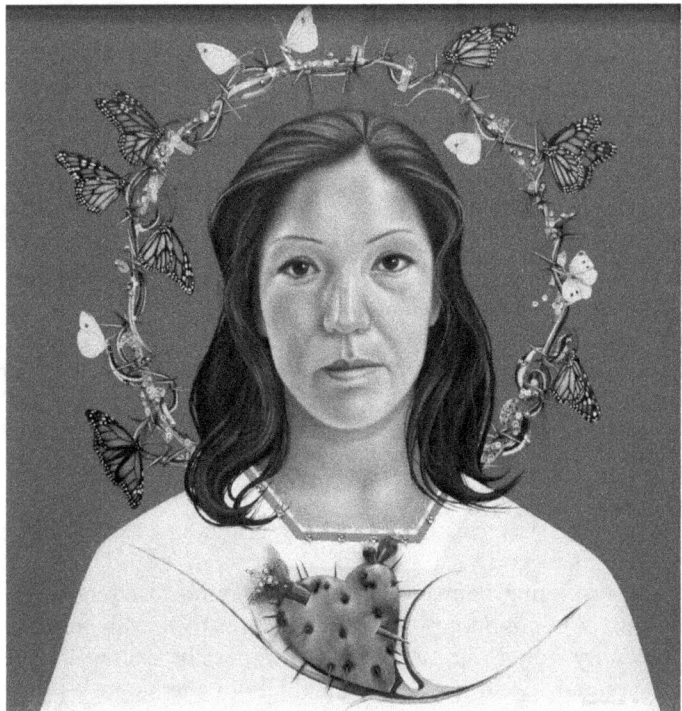

Figure 8.1 "Sorrowful Mother: Elvira Arellano." Artist Javier Chavira. Photo by Víctor M. Espinosa

that suggests resignation and endurance. While nothing about her expression is melodramatic—if anything it is restrained—I would argue that the painting simultaneously gives Arellano an eloquent voice of protest while limiting that protest to an expression of pain.

At the National Museum of Mexican Art in Chicago, *Madre Dolorosa: Elvira Arellano* was exhibited along with more than 60 other works within a context framed by an "official statement" that appropriated and revised the language of the Declaration of Independence to challenge equations of undocumented migrants with criminality. When commissioned to produce the work, Chavira said he immediately thought of the Arellano case, with which he was familiar only from news accounts. As he began to read about Arellano on the Internet, he said: "I found a lot of horrible racist websites out there about her. But I think she was very courageous and she is a role model, like the saints, following in the footsteps of Christ. And she is an icon of what's happening to countless women here in the United States."[57]

Despite the challenge to contemporary immigration policy posed by the exhibit concept, and despite the beauty and defiance of the Arellano portrait, the painting still unmistakably celebrates, within its lament, the suffering of mothers, specifically, in its allusion to the Virgin Mary, a mother who witnesses the death of her only child. But Saul Arellano is not dead. In fact, though he now lives in Mexico, he did not starve to death. Is the painting suggesting that living in Mexico is tantamount to crucifixion? And by positioning Arellano as a Virgin and a martyr, does the work make her vulnerable, upon the discovery of any human flaw, to the charge that she is an imposter, the bad witch posing as the good witch, the whore posing as the virgin? In the context of today's immigration debate, the painting continues a cycle of melodrama surrounding Arellano, pushing her image up to the next level of virtue—a response to those who criminalized her and celebrated her deportation that continues to depend on melodrama's Manichean worldview as well as on the "glorious masochism" of its mothers.

Beyond Melodrama?

The melodramatic strategies deployed by Arellano and her supporters constituted attempts to satisfy cultural, social, and even legal demands that her and her son's suffering be made legible. Immigration lawyers know all too well that it is not enough for potential immigrants to actually suffer. In order to win residency rights, the actual suffering must be crafted into convincing narratives and spectacles that highlight both the victim's pain and his or her "good moral character" for the benefit of immigration officials.[58] The specious distinction between political refugees and economic migrants in US immigration policy demands the creation of spectacles of suffering in its insistence that worthy asylum-seekers demonstrate a "well-founded fear of persecution."

The production and circulation of powerful emotions give melodrama its political impact: love, pity, hate, fear, outrage, and happiness, among others. These emotions are linked to moral and ethical judgments: We love and pity the heroine because she is good; we hate and fear the villain because he is evil. We are outraged that evil appears to be triumphing over good, or vice versa, delighted that good has won a victory over evil. Chronic cries for "civility" in political discourse, appeals to "tone down the rhetoric" can be viewed as efforts to escape emotional turmoil created by melodramatic imagination. I have begun to show here, however, with my account of the performances surrounding Arellano, that melodrama and its cyclical dynamic of casting and recasting in social performance is one of the longstanding mechanisms by which we invest emotionally in constructs such as "family" and "nation," in whatever way we conceive of them.[59] Thus it would be naïve and futile to end with a call for a moratorium on melodrama. I ask instead that we attend more to how it structures a wide variety of performances surrounding migration, including at times our own scholarship. Many works of recent scholarship have done an excellent job of deconstructing nativist ideology. As a heuristic device, migrant melodrama could prove useful both to further analysis of nativism and to self-reflection on our own work. Do scholars who support migrant rights (and I include myself in this group) sometimes cast migrants as innocent victims ennobled by undeserved suffering, worthy of rights *because* they have suffered? Do we ever cast nativists in cahoots with the state as their evil persecutors? And do we thus implicitly position ourselves as part of a valiant rescue effort? If so, we unintentionally naturalize the very suffering that we seek to denaturalize.

Acknowledgments

I wish to thank my fellow external faculty fellows at the Center for Comparative Studies in Race and Ethnicity at Stanford, Dolores Inés Casillas and Sergio de la Mora, for their careful reading and invaluable comments. An early version of this work benefitted enormously from the suggestions of the participants in the Newberry Library's Seminar in Borderlands and Latino Studies: Frances Aparicio, Geraldo Cadava, John Alba Cutler, Micaela Díaz-Sánchez, Gabriela Nuñez, and Ramón Rivera-Servera. Insightful responses from other friends and colleagues—María Eugenia de la Torre, Víctor M. Espinosa, Paola S. Hernández, Javier Villa-Flores, Patricia Ybarra, and Harvey Young—also helped me develop the notion of migrant melodrama.

Notes

1. Paulson, "For Mother and Son."
2. Ruethling, "Chicago Woman's Stand Stirs Immigration Debate."
3. Rev. Walter Coleman, 2009, personal interview.
4. Brooks, *The Melodramatic Imagination*.
5. Williams, *Playing the Race Card*.
6. The controversy surrounding the civil disobedience of undocumented migrant activist Elvira Arellano, has been scrutinized by Mary Romero from a sociological standpoint (2008), by Sara McElmurry (2009) from the vantage of media studies, and by Jane Juffer (2009) from a philosophical perspective.
7. Honig, *Immigrant America?*, 3.
8. For an extensive review of the literature on melodrama in theater, film, and narrative, see Buckley (2009, 176, note 1).
9. McConachie, *Melodramatic Formations*.
10. Daly, *Blood on the Tracks*.
11. Inda, "Foreign Bodies."
12. This chapter is excerpted from my book-in-progress, *Spectacles of Suffering and Migrant Melodramas: Undocumented Latin Americans*.
13. Wittke, "The Immigrant Theme"; Seller, *Ethnic Theater in the United States*; Haenni, *The Immigrant Scene*.
14. See Vicinus, *The Lost Apple*; Radway, *Reading the Romance*; and Howard, "What is Sentimentality?"
15. See Hartman, *Scenes of Subjection*; Nathans, *Slavery and Sentiment on the American Stage*; and Brooks, *Bodies in Dissent*.
16. Huerta, *Chicano Drama*, 30–32.
17. Rossini, *Contemporary Latino/a Theater*, 79.
18. Taylor, *Disappearing Acts*, 183–222; *The Archive and the Repertoire*, 54–78.

19. Weston et al., "Supplement of Basic Documents," 378. While I use the term "universal," I am aware that it has become problematic. For a critique of supposedly universal human rights as a Western construct, see Ignatieff, *Whose Universal Values?*.
20. Molina-Guzmán, *Dangerous Curves*, 17. Molina-Guzmán touches on Arellano's case in the course of her analysis of media representation of Elisabet Brotons, the deceased mother of Elían González, a Cuban boy who was rescued at sea in 1999 (*Dangerous Curves*, 31–33).
21. Thornburgh, "The Fallout from a Deportation."
22. Kaplan, *Motherhood and Representation*.
23. Bracho, "El cine mexicano."
24. Ayala, *La Aventura del cine mexicano*, 42–53.
25. Singhal, Obregon, and Rogers, "Reconstructing the Story of *Simplemente María*."
26. See also Molina-Guzmán on *Maid in Manhattan* (dir. Wayne Wang, 2002), in which Jennifer Lopez plays a Latina single mother (*Dangerous Curves*, 151–174).
27. Puga, "Poor Enrique and Poor María."
28. Vicinus, "Helpless and Unfriended," 133.
29. According to Kaplan, Ellen Wood's 1861 novel was adapted for the stage in nine different versions between 1866 and 1899 and was reincarnated several more times until 1965. It was adapted for the screen six different times between 1913 and 1931, when the version directed by Frank Lloyd was nominated for an Oscar. For an analysis of the theatrical and film versions of *East Lynne*, see Kaplan, *Motherhood and Representation*, 76–106. See Williams, *Playing the Race Card*, 307–330, on *Stella Dallas*. Also see Kaplan, *Motherhood and Representation*, for a comparison of *Stella Dallas* and *Imitation of Life*.
30. For an analysis of the Latina mother figure as an absence in contemporary theater and film, see Paredez, "All about My (Absent) Mother."
31. Hondagneu-Sotelo and Avila, " 'I'm Here but I'm There.' "
32. The language of the decision implies that Saul needed to make a stronger case for his potential future suffering: it finds that family separation would not inflict sufficient hardship to constitute his *de facto* deportation, in violation of his constitutional rights: "This is not to say that Saul will not suffer a hardship; undoubtedly he will. But the question before the Court is whether that hardship is of constitutional magnitude—under any construction of the alleged facts, it is not" (St. Eve, "Walter L. Coleman," 767). Along the same line of logic—the more you are likely to suffer the more you are entitled to exercise your rights—Saul Arellano, although a US citizen, was required to produce evidence of his hardship in the form of the medical condition Attention Deficit Hyperactivity Disorder, in order to win special permission from Congress for his mother to temporarily accompany him in his native country. See Bhabha (2009) for a persuasive argument that courts have relied on outmoded and discriminatory assumptions in refusing to recognize children's rights to family unity in their country of citizenship.
33. See, for instance, the photo posted on the "Elvira Arellano Friends" Facebook page (www.facebook.com, accessed January 30, 2010).

34. http://peruanista.blogspot.com/2011/10/dejando-wordpress-peruanista-regresa.html
35. www.debbieschlussel.com
36. Chavez, *The Latino Threat*; Gutiérrez, *Fertile Matters*, 2008.
37. McElmurry, "Elvira Arellano."
38. Cited in Ibid., 11.
39. For a performance studies analysis of Lewis Hines's photographs arguing that some of them were staged, see Pace, "Staging Childhood." For an anthropological perspective on the commodification of images of suffering children, see Kleinman and Kleinman, "The Appeal of Experience."
40. Torres, *The Lost Apple*.
41. González Mandri, "Operation Pedro Pan"; Lopez, *Sonia Flew*.
42. Molina-Guzmán, *Dangerous Curves*, 33.
43. Pallares, "Representing 'La Familia.'"
44. Ibid., 229.
45. See Decker, "'Unusually Compassionate,'" and Jackson, *Images of Children in American Film*, for analyses of the sentimental image of the child in American film melodrama.
46. Esposito, "Supporters Cheer Return of Saulito," *Chicago Sun-Times*, November 19, 2006; Mitchum, "Arellano's Son Back in City," *Chicago Tribune*, April 28, 2008; O'Donnell, "'Saulito' Delivers Message for Elvira,'" *Chicago Sun-Times*, April 8, 2008.
47. The role of the villain in melodrama has a history far too extensive and varied to detail here. But for a few succinct descriptions of the character type, see Grimsted, *Melodrama Unveiled*, 177–180; Singer, *Melodrama and Modernity*, 256–257; and Brooks, *The Melodramatic Imagination*, 17. For a post-9/11 study of the figure of the melodrama villain as a foreign invader who attacks a victim-United States, see Anker, "Villains, Victims, and Heroes."
48. De Genova, "The Legal Production of Mexican/Migrant."
49. Rev. Coleman, personal interview, 2009. For more on the New Sanctuary Movement, see Freeland, "Negotiating Place, Space, and Borders." In a fascinating, from the perspective of theater/performance studies, journalistic account of the New Sanctuary Movement, *The Nation's* Sasha Abramsky complains about "handlers" who stage a "scene" with a migrant sheltered in the Los Angeles area in a manner that does not seem sufficiently "authentic" ("Shelter: What the New Sanctuary Movement Offers," 27).
50. Romero, "'Go after the Women,'" 8.
51. *Chicago Sun-Times*, "It's Time to Get Out," August 15, 2007, 35.
52. Vicinus, "Helpless and Unfriended," 129.
53. Cepada, "Mexico Embraces Boy," *The Chicago Sun-Times*, November 16, 2006, 17.
54. Cepada, "Adios and Good Riddance," *The Chicago Sun-Times*, August 21, 2007, 14.
55. The film also includes close-ups of children sobbing as they recount their fears of family separation during a bus trip to Washington, DC to lobby for immigration reform.
56. See the article from which this chapter is excerpted in the journal *Latino Studies* (Fall 2012).
57. Javier Chavira, 2009, personal interview. Madre Dolorosa: Elvira Arellano was subsequently exhibited at the South Shore Arts Salon Show

(September 13–November 1, 2009), where it won a $250 merit award, and the Tall Grass Arts Association Gallery in Park Forest (December 4, 2009–January 31, 2010). It sells for $6,000.
58. Kanstroom, *Deportation Nation*, 228; Coutin, *Legalizing Moves*, 79–134.
59. My reading of Berlant, "The Subject of True Feeling," and Ahmed, *The Cultural Politics of Emotion*, inform this contention.

Section III

Transnational Publics

Chapter 9

"Get up, Stand up, Stand up for your Rights": Transnational Belonging and Rights of Citizenship in Dominican Theater

Camilla Stevens

Since the 1990s, Dominican theater artists have been countering homogeneous and territorially bounded visions of national identity by staging stories of transnational migration. The scenarios of Dominican transnationalism dramatized in their stories, and the creative practices of the artists themselves, are situated in social fields that straddle nation-states, making evident how in the age of globalization increasing numbers of people belong at varying degrees to more than one society.[1] Distinct from the one-way migration narrative of assimilation characteristic of the late nineteenth and early twentieth centuries, today's circular counterstreams of transnational migration exert pressure on both the sending and the receiving societies to extend frameworks of membership and to expand human rights. While the autonomy of the nation-state has been eroded by globalization, it continues to be the institution that guarantees rights of citizenship and the political framework in which immigrants form different senses of belonging such as rooted ethnic minority enclaves, transitory transnational circuits, and free-floating cosmopolitanisms. The stakes for developing new approaches to citizenship are high, for democracy cannot be maintained, let alone strengthened, in nations that have large populations of residents without citizenship. Any solution, suggest social scientists Stephen Castles and Alastair Davidson, "must lie in a mode of citizenship that reconciles the pressures of globalization with the reality that states will continue, for the foreseeable future, to exist as the most important political unit. One aim must be to dissolve the nation part of the nation-state and to replace it with a democratic state based on open and flexible belonging."[2] This essay argues that the collective endeavor of theater affords opportunities to think through what Castles and Davidson call "new rules for conviviality" that would foster equality, cross-cultural interaction, and the creation of new modes of collective belonging.[3] Works such as Claudio Mir's *Mondongo Scam* (1994) and María Isabel Bosch's *Las Viajeras* (The Women Travelers) (2003) give voice to undocumented Dominican immigrants and place audiences in the ethical position of having to assume a stance on the topic of human rights and citizenship.[4] Through their engagement with hybridity as a theme and an aesthetic strategy, Bosch and Mir's performances not only explore new understandings of political, personal, and artistic belonging, but they also join people in sites of conviviality that imagine a more open and flexible democratic body politic.

In his study on theater and human rights, Paul Rae frames his argument by noting that theater both treats the subject of human rights and is the object of those rights.[5] In addressing the subject of human rights, theater becomes a place in which "lives are given voice and experiences form, and where representatives of one group can make their address to others."[6] As we will see in *Mondongo Scam* and *Las Viajeras*, the voice and visibility granted to undocumented immigrants is central in confronting restrictive agendas of citizenship. Furthermore, as an object of human rights, the act of making theater is an exercise of assembly, free speech, and the sharing of cultural life.[7] While Bosch and Mir do not practice their art in places where these basic rights are threatened, as transnational artists their entry into the public sphere is complicated by the translocal US-Argentine-Dominican space from which their work is produced and received. Like their dramatic personae that struggle to be recognized as citizens, their work risks a lack of acknowledgement if nation-states focus on "national" artists and fail to recognize the work of artists who have a transnational conception of cultural identity and a creative *modus operandi* that spans more than one geopolitical space. Just as political theorists posit models for global citizenship, so, too, should arts organizations develop a global vision for supporting cultural production. Indeed, fomenting border-crossing cultural activity will encourage the intercultural and international communication necessary for imagining democratic global rights.

Theater constitutes a model for rehearsing (theorizing) and performing (putting into practice) new forms of conviviality because it is an inherently social activity. As Argentine theater theorist Jorge Dubatti states, "Sin convivio—reunión de dos o más hombres, encuentro de presencias en una encrucijada espacio-temporal cotidiana—no hay teatro" (without conviviality—the meeting between two or more people, the encounter of presences in an everyday crossroads of time and space—there is no theater).[8] Dubatti finds the essential qualities of theater in the symposium, *convivium*, and banquets of ancient Greek and Roman cultures, unrepeatable and finite communal encounters that implied orality, the distribution of roles, physical proximity, sensorial experience, and ritual transcendence.[9] Theater, like the rite of sociability of the banquet table, joins people together and assigns them different roles. In similar terms, political philosopher Hannah Arendt theorizes the public realm as individuals brought together at a dinner table: "To live together in the world means essentially that a world of things is between those who have it in common, as a table is located between those who sit around it."[10] For Arendt, the public realm is comprised of two related components, the *space of appearance* and the *common world*. Maurizio Passerin d'Entrèves writes that Arendt's public sphere "refers to that sphere of appearance where citizens interact through the medium of speech and persuasion, disclose their unique identities, and decide through collective deliberation about matters of common concern."[11] This space is only possible "if we share a common world of humanely created artifacts, institutions and settings, which separates us from nature and provides a relatively permanent or durable context for our activities."[12] In my view, theater is an exemplary context for enabling spaces of appearance in which people engage in speech and action, take on the roles of actors and observers, and disclose, in Arendt's terms, "who" they are, that is, their unique identity.[13] Theater, for Arendt, is by definition a political art because "only there is the political sphere of human life transposed into art. By the same token, it is the only art whose sole subject is man in relationship to others."[14] I would add, however, that it is not only the subject of theater that is about human relationships; it is the collective and participatory nature of its making and reception that makes it a microcosm of the public sphere.

Thus, in the chain of relations set in motion by the theater event—from the playwright, to the production (producers, directors, actors, and theater personnel), and to the audience (metaphorical political community)—performance offers an apt site to rehearse new rules of conviviality in an age of intense intercultural contact. And though theater is a part of the common world that facilitates the creation of the public realm, it often represents an alternative space in which groups made invisible in the public sphere of politics can be seen and heard and imagined as a collectivity. Theater, like the public realm, summons people to a temporary arena in which the dynamics of reciprocity, solidarity, and difference are constantly at play. As Arendt notes, the collective identity of the polis is not a fixed location, but rather an activity organized out of action and speech (in performative terms, polis is a "doing").[15] In the theatrical space of appearance created by Mir and Bosch's performances, a Dominican polis that embodies a transnational mode of collective belonging emerges.

Borrowed Identities: Performing the Dominican Diaspora

In spite of their contrasting tones, the intersecting thematic and formal components lend *Mondongo Scam* and *Las Viajeras* to a tandem reading. Both the performance pieces present the plight of undocumented Dominican immigrants through metatheatrical "monopolylogues" in which the actors play all the roles in dialogue with imaginary characters.[16] In Mir's comic play, the main character borrows the identities of dead people in order to access the citizenship that is denied to him by his undocumented status in the United States, but he is able to scam the legal system for only so long before he is caught and brought before a court of law. Achieving invisibility, that is, making his Dominican identity disappear into another is a Caribbean trickster survival strategy that ultimately fails because the increasingly hybrid cultural identity he performs never completely sheds his *dominicanidad*. Rather, borrowing identities constitutes a translation strategy that does not result in assimilation—replacing one nationalist attachment with another—but in hybrid identities that embody multiple identifications. Bosch also plays various roles, but the characters she embodies are based on real Dominican women she encountered in Buenos Aires. By borrowing their identities and performing their stories through narrative monologue and visual dramaturgy, she gives visibility to a growing global social problem of the illegal trafficking of women. As we will see, both the pieces employ strategies that place spectators in active interpretive roles and exemplify theater's ethical role in "managing the way people think about their relationships with one another and their potential for creating societies in which everyone can enjoy freedom as well as social solidarity."[17]

The unique interpretative positions in which *Mondongo Scam* and *Las Viajeras* place their spectators are generated by some of the aesthetic qualities Hans-Thies Lehmann identifies as "postdramatic."[18] In postdramatic theater, the narrative representation of action and speech of drama is no longer the privileged starting point. Rather than reading *Mondongo Scam* and *Las Viajeras* as pieces of dramatic literature, they are better understood as "theater works" that are only fully realized in performance, because although the artists work off written scripts, the text is only one element in the scenic creation that might be seen as a crossroads of visual arts, dance, and music.[19] Free from the teleological constraints of an Aristotelian-structured play, solo performance is a particularly effective theater form for exploring a single topic from various intellectual and affective vantage points. Monologues, moreover, create the illusion of privileging "reality" over "fiction" in that there often appears to be a direct connection between the actor and his/her character and the actor and the spectator. This impression is created by a shift from intra-scenic communication to stage–audience communication. Lehmann writes: "The actor's speaking is now accentuated above all as a 'speaking to' the audience; his/her speech is marked as the speech of a real speaking person, its expressiveness more as the 'emotive' dimension of the performer's language than as the emotional expression of the fictive character represented."[20] The monologue theatrical address in *Mondongo Scam* and *Las Viajeras* is strongly extra-scenic, which emphasizes "the communication taking place in the here and now of theatre."[21] As I have argued, the theater event is above all the relations established in the "here and now" of the *convivio*, the gathering to see and hear stories that encourage spectators to imagine themselves as a political community.

The solo performance in *Mondongo Scam* comprises a court defense in which the character Casiano Doroteo Antonio Tapia, who has been charged with impersonation and false identities, defends his case.[22] Throughout the piece, Mir plays a dizzying array of characters in dialogue with unseen interlocutors, and given that the audience implicitly serves as the jury (and at one point members of a Pentecostal church), Mir's address is equally extra-scenic as it is intra-scenic. During Casiano's defense a typical migration narrative emerges, in which transnational households and dreams of American material goods and an improved social status lure Dominicans to the United States at the same time as a stagnant economy pushes them to leave. Though not explicitly part of Casiano's defense, this story foregrounds the inevitability of border-crossing in a globalized world organized by economic and social transnational networks, thereby presenting to the judge and jury the factors that compel people to work and settle illegally in the United States.

Although Casiano went to New York knowing that he would overstay his visa and face the risks of becoming an undocumented worker, his hybrid cultural identifications and transnational sense of belonging make it difficult for him to accept that he is perceived as an illegal alien. When he was young, for example, the subject of Casiano's aunts in New York and Puerto Rico were so embedded in daily conversations that he thought they must be connected to the Dominican Republic by bridges. For Dominicans, New York (a synecdoche for the United States) represents a better life: money, education, and an elevated social status, even though obviously this does not turn out to be the case for all. Migration supposedly even "whitens," as an offhand compliment repeated by Casiano reveals: "Tu te has puesto más buen mozo y hasta más blanco desde que te fuiste pa Nueva York" [You have gotten better looking and even whiter since you went to New York].[23] Disappointed that his mother did not migrate, Casiano had to settle for used American goods sent by family members (such as prized athletic shoes he wore even though they were too small) and images of American culture transmitted on the television (the cop show *Kojak*) and in film (John Travolta and *Saturday Night Fever*). In a parodic moment of colonial mimicry, Casiano exuberantly imitates Dominicans disco dancing and phonetically singing songs from *Saturday Night Fever*.[24] But it is through repeating lines from English lessons that Mir most sharply articulates his critical point that the interpenetration of American and Dominican popular culture does not mean that Dominicans will be welcome in the United States: "America is a democratic country, isn't it? That is called the tag question, like, you aren't American, are you?"[25] By the late 1970s and 1980s, the cultural imperialism and the economic remittances from the United States had made the island a fundamentally transnational society. Before Casiano even fulfilled his destiny—"vamos a Nueva York, todos nacimos para venir a Nueva York" [we all go to New York, we're born to come to New York]—his sense of collective belonging spanned the two nation-states.[26] Dominicans like the fictitious Casiano have developed everyday-life practices that bridge the two spaces in ways that transgress the borders that nation-states continually try to erect.

Casiano's defense involves a different kind of border-crossing, a sort of metatheatrical migrancy in which he moves from one role to another in his survival strategy of using the documents of dead people to secure jobs and a driver's license. While it is clear that Casiano is a culturally dexterous pretender and that he has "scammed" the system, he presents part of his actions as out of his control and the result of supernatural forces. He explains to the judge and the jury that he is merely a *caballo*, or medium, in the spiritist tradition of Afro-Caribbean religions, possessed at will by spirits who live through him. Therefore, throughout the course of the monologue we witness Casiano suddenly become possessed by a force that transforms him from black to white, from evangelical to Jewish, from male to female, and briefly, in his sexual orientation. To some extent, impersonating others suggests the loss of his Dominican identity. He states that the day he became Ishmael Rosenthal, for example, "I knew I wasn't him, at the beginning, then after a week or two, I started to have problems recognizing myself, I didn't know who I was, but I knew that I wasn't Casiano anymore. I started eating Bagels with cream cheese."[27] But Casiano's Dominican identity, which is already seen as hybrid through his many references to the presence of American popular culture in his home country, is never entirely obliterated, and as Ishmael, he cannot resist attending a party hosted by Dominicans where the national specialty, *Jewish Manischewitz*, is to be served, and to which he brings both Caribbean rum and Jewish Manichewitz. On more than one occasion, Casiano's voice seeps through the language of his adopted character, revealing that his Dominican self is always present. In the raucous sermon he delivers as Pentecostal preacher Rev. George Aponte Solano, for example, his entreaties to pray and to rise up and sing turn into a politicized sermon that takes up the cause of immigrants:

> we need more people like you and you and you, people that believe in justice, we need more people, people willing to stand up against those whose actions have caused a lot of pain to our people, those who have pointed their fingers at us and accused us for all the sins and illness of society. God is showing us the way today, Jesus will demonstrate that we are humble, hardworking, tax paying, law obeying, family oriented and church going people.[28]

By this point in the sermon, the voice is predominantly that of Casiano in the role of self-appointed defense lawyer as he shifts into cross-examination mode. Likewise, the plural "you" of his flock/theater audience assumes the role of jury/theater audience and is asked not just to pray, but also to stand up for the rights of others.

All the characters Casiano plays perform an address that is extra-scenic, for they call upon the audience to perform the role of jury. Discussing the theatricality of court scenes, Rabih Mroué writes: "By definition, the trial gathers two opposing parties to confront one another verbally in front of a judge, each of them exposing their own point of view, defending it through various speeches and statements, presenting evidence and alibis, in the presence of a public intent on listening and witnessing, and awaiting the final decision of the judge who officiates in the name of law and justice."[29] On trial here is the criminalization of immigration in an epoch in which global world order has encouraged the mass movement of people across national borders. Like a trial, in theater there is a public "intent on listening and witnessing" and capable of discerning between the amusing stories of the personas who "occupy" Casiano and the voice of Mir (via Casiano) making a case for illegal immigrants. As a lawyer, Casiano again shows his trickster qualities and bicultural adroitness by letting the judge know he is confident in presenting his own case since he has watched many legal shows on television. He also tells the judge, "if you are a lawyer then I can be a lawyer too, this land is your land? This land is my land from California to the New York highland, therefore nadie nobody is a stranger, foreigner, an alien."[30] Not only does Casiano switch from English to Spanish words and pronunciation—"highland" for "island" and the redundant "nadie"/"nobody"—he also incorporates lyrics from one of the best known folk songs in the United States, Woody Guthrie's 1940 "This Land is Your Land." The song's theme of inclusivity and celebration of America's capacious geography has a truly ironic ring in the context of a trial against an "illegal alien," a term that puzzles a worldview like Casiano's, which understands the Americas as a fluid space of continuous cultural exchange.

Mondongo, the Dominican stew referred to in the play's title, like ethnologist Fernando Ortiz's description of the Cuban stew *ajiaco*, evokes a mixture of ingredients that compose a Dominican identity in a constant state of transculturation.[31] Using the bilingual neologism "mondongal," Casiano delivers an amusing closing statement that pleads for the jury to embrace the good and the bad that comes with the processes of transculturation:

> Ladies and Gentlemen of the Jury: by taking the stand I stand a chance, a chance to stand off instead of standing aside or what is worse stand back. I choose to stand by to protect the things that we stand for, and remember that to stand forth is to stand in, [it] is not standing in line or to stand in the way, it is to stand out, reach a conclusion by standing to reason and then and only then get up and stand up and stand up for your rights. It might sound confusing, but this is the way the world goes, the good mix in a big pot with the bad in an eternal mondongal relationship.[32]

In spite of his play with prepositional phrases, Casiano's circuitous call for social justice comes through clearly when spectators detect the rhythm and phrasing of Bob Marley's reggae classic "Get up, Stand up." Mroúe suggests that while the scenarios in theater and courts share many similarities, theater tends to put the burden of judgment on the audience rather than the judge. Theater presents the case in hand and leaves "enough breathing space for the audience to build their own opinions and decisions... It is the place where questions are asked, without reaching conclusions or judgments."[33] The question *Mondongo Scam* asks of its audience is whether it will stand up for immigrant rights and understand that multiple cultural and national affiliations do not constitute a crime.

Las Viajeras by María Isabel Bosch similarly places audiences in an ethical position of having to respond to a migration problem, but in this case, the crime is clear: trafficking of women for sexual exploitation.[34] While Bosch's piece also encourages audiences to "stand up" for the rights of undocumented immigrations, the tension between emotional identification and intellectual distancing at play in *Las Viajeras* produces a hybrid aesthetics that affords the spectator an ethical position that differs from traditional political theater. Unexpectedly, it was Bosch's tenure as a cultural attaché in the Dominican embassy in Buenos Aires that led to the conception of the piece, which was her first major solo project.[35] What began as a benign curiosity became an outrage when she learned that the clusters of cold, disoriented, and hungry Dominican women gathering at the embassy daily were the victims of sex trafficking. Bosch states that she was haunted by the stories and scenes she witnessed at the embassy long after her position there ended, and that her sense of helplessness turned into the first step in creating *Las Viajeras*.[36] She wrote letters from the points of view of composites of women she had met and had read about in the media, in legal documents, and in non-governmental reports on migration. As denunciatory as these means of communication may be, Bosch, in order to empathize with her compatriots' plight, shifted her position from witness to their suffering to adopting their voices and points of view. The text transformed into dramatic scenes when she began to improvise with the material with Argentine director Jorge Merzari. Choreographed dance-movement sequences, music, lighting, and minimalist props were added, transforming *Las Viajeras* into a theater work. The title was suggested by Bosch's mother, who told her that in the southern part of the island, *las viajeras* was the name used for women who migrated in search of a better life.[37] The term is a euphemism that belies the open secret that these "women travelers" are often recruited to become prostitutes.

The epistolary monologues have the extra-scenic effect of positioning spectators as the letter's addressees, which forces them to recognize their complicity in the silence surrounding the social problem. While the presence of Afro-Caribbean women is easily noticeable in the mainly white, European culture of Buenos Aires, the women are, in more than one sense, stripped of their rights and made legally invisible. Likewise, in the Dominican Republic these women are "forgotten" or made invisible through passive acceptance or denial of their experiences. The play thus critiques both the sending society for creating the conditions that force their departure and the receiving society that fails to help them. Fittingly, the play has reached audiences—that on some occasions included sex trafficking victims—in Latin America, the Caribbean, and Europe, having been performed more than 200 times. In addition to performing at international theater festivals to a wide cross-section of spectators, Bosch received funding from the Dominican government for a tour that performed at schools and community centers at ten towns on the island known as sources for women destined for commercial sexual exploitation. While the messages received by the transnational circuit of audiences obviously varied, as did the nuances of Bosch's performances in accordance with spectator response, there are formal elements that remain constant and structure the audience relationship with the performance.

Las Viajeras alternates between narrative monologue scenes in which Bosch performs four different characters and visual dramaturgy scenes in which she performs dance movements. The spoken narratives abide by the aesthetics of traditional realist theater in the sense that although the structure is one of episodic montage lacking causality, taken together the episodes tell a complete and chronological story of the circumstances leading a woman to migrate to Argentina; to the discovery that she has been duped and must work as a prostitute to repay the recruiter who lent her money for the journey and for documents (that turn out to be fake); to despair, and ultimately, to suicide. Although the play lacks the conventional three-dimensional setting of dramatic realism, the carefully drawn character psychology and wealth of details about the sex trafficking industry create a world on stage that gives rise to empathy and identification on the part of the spectator.

The narratives include the stories of women from different geographical points of the island. The performance begins with Bosch playing the role of Yurberkis, a naïve *campesina* from the interior of the island who is trapped in the patriarchal web of her husband, father-in-law, and the kindly don Tulio, who offers to help them get out of debt by paying for her trip abroad. In this scene, we witness Yurberkis's heart-wrenching departure—she leaves behind her small son—and rape by her soon-to-be *chulo* (pimp) once housed in a Buenos Aires *conventillo* (tenement). Reytania, by contrast, is a hairdresser and experienced prostitute from the south of the island. Her modest desire of having enough money to build a house of "blo' y cemento"[38] (blocks and cement) that might withstand hurricanes, and her more ambitious dream of owning a beauty salon are thwarted by the fear and hunger she suffers in Buenos Aires. Different from the violence of entrapment, coercion, and debt bondage, the third *viajera*, Inés, suffers the cruelty of being shunned. Her scene portrays her annual return visit to her middle-class home in Santo Domingo. Her family is aware that she never used her father's money to study computing as planned, but they never question how she manages to support herself, let alone send home monthly remittances. The hypocrisy of the family's repudiation of Inés is that of an entire society that passively accepts money from the illegal sex trafficking industry but fails to act to protect, locally and transnationally, both voluntary and involuntary sex worker's civil, labor, and human rights. The final story is Elsa's, a middle-aged laundress steeped in Afro-Caribbean spiritual practices from Punta Cana, the extreme southeast of the island. Elsa answered an ad offering domestic work in Argentina and soon found herself thrown out to sea once the traffickers realized they had netted a woman past her prime. Homeless and hungry, Elsa tells of absurd and poignant cultural misunderstandings that leave her with no chance of employment and therefore no possibility of returning home. For example, she is constantly insulted and fired for not understanding the usual domestic practices of an upper-class urban household, and when a man on the street yells "cuero barato,"[39] she takes offense, only to realize after smashing him on the head—and landing in jail for the attack—that in Argentinean Spanish he was hawking inexpensive leather, not identifying her in Dominican Spanish as a "cheap prostitute." When she ends her life by leaping in front of a train, her final wish is for her children not to learn of her fate, though she does hope that her story might serve as a warning for women back home about the dangers of the illegal movement across borders.

Though the character sketches performed by Bosch are intended to generate affective recognition and solidarity, the pull between psychological realism and stylized distancing techniques in her performance produces an ethical encounter rather than simply a didactic message. Ridout notes that "Increasingly, the relationship between theater and ethics comes to be a question of form rather than content. It is how you make it, and what relationships you establish in making it (between producers, consumers, actors, spectators, participants), that matters, not what message or ideology you are trying to communicate."[40] *Las Viajeras* places audiences in an ethical relationship with the performance through the fluctuation between aesthetics that seek different relationships between spectator and actor. In some regards, the performance answers Brecht's call for music, lighting, and choreography to stand as discrete elements alongside the drama as a means of creating alienation and intellectual empathy.[41] The play's visual and auditory dimension and the body in movement to music, undoubtedly breaks with the illusory dramatic world of the monologues. The lengthy interludes between each character's story and at the beginning of the piece are marked off by a change in lighting and an abrupt swelling of dramatic symphonic music. The audience no longer listens to a character but observes a nearly naked body execute slow dance movements while manipulating a number of lightweight white cuts of cloth; the play's only items for costuming and props. Dramatically speaking, we might read the body as stripped of character and as a result, focus on the social problem targeted by the play, the female body deprived of basic human rights and the circumstances that brought about this situation. However, for some viewers this sort of emotional distancing might be thwarted by the creators' musical selection, Henryk Górecki's Symphony No. 3 (*Symphony of Sorrowful Songs*).[42] The plaintive soprano voice and long, smooth *legato* string sounds create an atmosphere that emotionally draws in the spectator, likely causing him or her to lose sight of the play's moral argument.

Another tension between identification and distancing can be perceived in the construction of character. As I have noted, first writing letters and then embodying the voices of *Las Viajeras* is an act of actor–character empathy and identification, and there is no question that Bosch's performance also seeks audience identification with character. However, the play demands an alert spectator and denies the passive experience of being caught up vicariously in the drama because it constantly makes the spectator aware of the distinction between actor and character. This awareness is heightened primarily in the visual dramaturgy scenes in which the dancer's initially free form dance movements begin to approximate the distinct physicality of the different characters. As Bosch assumes the postures and expressions of each new character, she wraps and unwraps the gauzy cloths. At times she manipulates them in such a way that they suggest a form of protective covering or, conversely, an immobilizing restraint, and at others, they are shaped to form concrete costuming and props, such as a bundle that stands for Yuberkis's baby, Elsa's head wrap, and Reytania's dress. It is as though we are witnessing the Stanislavski system of an actor preparing her character. However, staging the normally off-stage imaginative work of building actor–character empathy paradoxically has the effect of blocking spectators from identifying with the characters and inviting them instead to observe an actor taking up a social problem through art.

In a similar way, a distancing effect is produced when the illusion of the fourth wall dividing the fictional world of the performance and the real world of the audience is broken through direct audience address. Each of the transitions between the dance interludes and the narrative monologues is marked by the actor, not the character, rehearsing in contrasting vocal styles, the recitation of verses from the social poem *La luna con gatillo* (1941) by Argentine poet Raúl González Tuñón. Each time the actor recites the poem she begins with its refrain "No quiero ser la mosca aplastada" (I do not want to be the squashed fly), and as she repeats the poem throughout the performance, she adds a series of verses that begin: "Tengo derecho al ... " (I have the right to ...) and end with a series of basic human rights such as the right to physical and intellectual sustenance and the right to free movement through and enjoyment of the amenities offered by an urban environment. As her repetition of the poem's refrain becomes increasingly sharp and accusatory, the audience becomes even more conscious of the performer's awareness of being observed and of the fact that she is returning the gaze to them. In short, the use of a variety of performance modes in narrating and embodying stories about *las viajeras* demands shifting interpretative strategies on the part of the audience, and it also suggests that no one representation can explain the social problem explored.

There is no doubt that the central objective of *Las Viajeras* is to raise consciousness about a global issue affecting women's rights, and that *Mondongo Scam* similarly advocates for the rights of undocumented immigrants. But in both pieces, the didacticism of the political message is less intriguing than the politics of the forms used in representing the stories. In the same vein as Ridout, Lehmann argues that it is not the direct political content that makes theater political; rather it is "through the implicit substance and critical value of its mode of representation."[43] Theater intervenes politically by offering a forum that links perception to experience. In the society of the spectacle, writes Lehmann, the bombardment of images of human suffering in the media "creates a radical distance for passive viewing" and dissolves "the bond between perception and action, receiving message and 'answerability.' "[44]

Theater works like *Las Viajeras* and *Mondongo Scam* confront spectators with the problem of having to react to what is being performed in their presence. The audience is engaged in the theatrical production of meaning, which for Lehmann is an experience that "would not only be aesthetic but therein at the same time ethico-political."[45] In theater, moreover, there is no comforting distance of "here" and "there" that one experiences in viewing global media; rather, there is a "mutual implication of actors and spectators," which offers an "aesthetic of responsibility (or response-ability)."[46] The ethical encounter in *Las Viajeras* is created through its epistolary framing and through a hybrid dramaturgy that mixes aesthetics of accessibility with aesthetics of estrangement, while in *Mondongo Scam*, the court scene framework and constant metatheatrical shift in roles place spectators in active interpretative roles. Moving between music, dance, and narrative, these theater works provoke both emotional empathy and intellectual distancing, allowing Mir and Bosch to resist settling for the shock tactics of "ripped from the headlines" sensationalism (the media) or the one-sided delivery of a didactic message (political propaganda).

On the contrary, the shifting modes of representation trigger the spectator's awareness of his or her capacity to respond, in Casiano's words—"to get up, stand up, stand up for your rights"—a responsibility and "response-ability" that, for Lehmann, is lacking in other contexts of image production.[47] Returning by way of conclusion to the public sphere imagined by Arendt as a dinner table that locates people in proximity with one another, both relating and separating them in such a way that they are able to engage in civil speech and action, so, too, does the theater event structure a forum of collective address in which people interact through speech and persuasion in the roles of actors and observers. In the *convivio* of the theater event, stories of Dominican migration are given form and witnessed, activating discussions, remembrances, and future imaginings crucial for claiming identity, space, and a political voice for communities that live across borders without the full rights of citizenship. Not only do the performances by Mir and Bosch evoke the "mutual implication" of the "here" and "there" of the stories represented on stage and the real-world space of the auditorium, their vision also speaks to both a local and a global audience and imagines a common, yet multisited Dominican polis inclusive of the constantly shifting "here" and "there" of transnationalism.

Notes

1. Significant numbers of Dominicans began migrating in the 1960s, when the 1965 United States Immigration and Nationality Act increased the number of Caribbean immigrants who could enter the United States each year. At the same time, the economic and political woes under the Balaguer regime (1966–1978) pushed Dominicans to leave the island. A Migration Policy Institute report estimates that nearly half of the over 1.1 Dominicans in the United

States arrived in the 1990s, and that in 2000, 13–15% of Dominican immigrants in the United States were undocumented. See Grieco, "The Dominican Population," 1, 10. According to José Itzigsohn et al., "the large size of the migration flows, and the relatively short period time in which they occurred caused a large transformation in Dominican society, making the Dominican case a paradigmatic one for the study of the rise of transnationalism." Itzigsohn et al., "Mapping Dominican Transnationalism," 318.
2. Castles and Davidson, *Citizenship and Migration*, viii.
3. Ibid., viii.
4. The cultural practices of María Isabel Bosch and Claudio Mir are transnational. Bosch resides in Argentina, but she divides her professional work in performance between Santo Domingo and Buenos Aires. Although she has made Argentina her home, she is lauded by a Dominican theater critic as "la mejor actriz dramática del país" (the country's best dramatic actress). See Juan Carlos Campos, "Las Viajeras," 6. Fellow Dominican performer Claudio Mir has been living in the United States since the 1990s. His artistic training has been transnational and transdisciplinary: in addition to participating in prestigious acting and directing workshops hosted by Eugenio Barba, Jerzy Grotowsky, Miguel Rubio, and Teresa Ralli in Italy and Spain, he holds a degree in acting from the School of Scenic Arts (Palacio de Bellas Artes, Santo Domingo), as well as degrees earned in the United States in photography and visual arts.
5. Paul Rae, *Theatre and Human Rights*, 6.
6. Ibid., 22.
7. Ibid., 24–29. These universal rights are noted in the United Nations Declaration of Human Rights in articles 19, 27, and 27(1).
8. Jorge Dubatti, *Filosofía del teatro I*, 43.
9. Ibid., 46–47.
10. Hannah Arendt, *The Human Condition*, 52.
11. Maurizio Passerin d'Entrèves, "Hannah Arendt," 146.
12. Ibid., 146.
13. Arendt, *The Human Condition*, 184–188. For Arendt, abilities and talents identify *what* a person is; while only through action and speech do people disclose *who* they are. Theater is a form of the storytelling or narrative-making that Arendt invokes as necessary for people to disclose to the world *who* they are.
14. Ibid., 148.
15. "In our simplest references, and in the blink of an eye, performance is always a doing and a thing done," Elin Diamond, *Performance*, 1996.
16. I borrow this term from Michael Peterson, *Straight White Male*, 14.
17. Ridout, *Theatre and Ethics*, 7–8.
18. For Lehmann, "postdramatic" describes a set of theater aesthetics, that do, in great part, coincide with many of the characteristics of postmodern cultural production, but he does not use the term as an epochal category or as synonymous with postmodernism.
19. Lehmann, *Postdramatic Theatre*, 31.
20. Ibid., 127.
21. Ibid., 128: "In postdramatic theatre, the theatre situation is not simply added to the autonomous reality of the dramatic fiction to animate it. Rather, the theatre situation as such becomes a matrix within whose energy lines the

elements of the scenic fictions inscribe themselves. Theatre is emphasized as a situation, not a fiction."
22. *Mondongo Scam* was written and first performed in 1994 as part of the Out of the Shadows Theatre Festival in New York City, a project directed by George Emilio Sanchez intended to support emerging minority artists. In addition to its premiere in New York City, *Mondongo Scam* has been presented at the Latin American Theatre Today Festival at the University of Connecticut in 2005 and at the Crossroads Theatre in New Brunswick, New Jersey (sponsored by Rutgers University) in 2008. My interpretation of the piece is based on the Connecticut and New Jersey performances, a video recording, and Mir's unpublished manuscript.
23. Claudio Mir, "Mondongo Scam," 2. All translations are my own.
24. While the hybridity of Casiano's cultural identifications is a comic moment that evokes the euphoria of the disco era, for Dominican nationalists, *Travoltismo*, the influence of the music, style, and rebellious attitude of Travolta's film characters on Dominican youth culture signaled cultural imperialism and the erosion of native customs and culture. For a discussion of *Travoltismo*, see Jesse Hoffnung-Garskof, *A Tale*, 231–235.
25. Mir, "Mondongo Scam," 5.
26. Ibid., 2.
27. Ibid., 2.
28. Ibid., 5.
29. Rabih Mroué, "Introduction," x.
30. Mir, "Mondongo Scam," 5.
31. See Ortiz, "Los factores," 1–21, for his description of Cuba as an *ajiaco*. See also Ortiz, "Del fenómeno," 129–135, for his definition of transculturation. In these essays, originally published in 1940, Ortiz's analysis of transculturation attempts to capture the complexity of the process of cultural synthesis. Transculturation includes deculturation, the destruction or loss of certain elements of a culture as it enters into contact with another, and acculturation, a period of readjustment and ultimately the creation of a new culture, a neoculturation. In my view, the metaphors of *mondongo* and *ajiaco* better describe the reality of the increasingly heterogeneous cultures of North America than the homogenizing metaphor of the melting pot, though they are not exempt from nuanced readings that examine just how the cultures are mixed or absorbed into the stew.
32. Mir, "Mondongo Scam," 8.
33. Mroué, "Introduction to," x.
34. New research is tracking the transnational lives of Dominicans in host countries other than the United States such as Spain, the Netherlands, and Argentina. The nearby Netherlands Antilles has been a longstanding destination for Dominican migrants, and it often serves as a stop point en route to Amsterdam. Dominicans rank as the largest group of foreign-born persons living in the Netherlands Antilles (topping the total of residents born in the Netherlands). See Migration Policy Institute, "Netherlands Antilles." Since the late 1980s, the Dominican population in Spain has grown to about 60,000. See Mar García and Denise Palewonsky, "Gender, Remittances," 25. Most recently, migrants from the Dominican Republic began arriving in Argentina in large numbers in the mid-1990s. The International Organization for Migration (IOM) estimates that 12,000 to 15,000 Dominicans migrated

to Argentina between 1995 and 2002. See IOM, "Migración, Prostitución," 19. Dominican migration to Argentina and Europe has captured the attention of researchers due to its disproportionate number of female migrants. Some of these women seek employment as domestic help and a good number end up working as prostitutes. According to IOM estimates, there are 50,000 women from the Dominican Republic working overseas in the sex industry, which ranks as the fourth highest number in the world after Thailand, Brazil, and the Philippines. See Donna M. Hughes, et al., "Dominican Republic."

35. Like many of her compatriots, Bosch left the island in the late 1990s, but the conditions under which she migrated were quite privileged, since she accompanied her parents on their diplomatic mission to the Dominican embassy in Buenos Aires. Having graduated with degrees in drama and dance from prestigious fine arts programs in the Dominican Republic and Spain, she was well prepared to develop her career in one of the top theater capitals of the world.

36. María Isabel Bosch, "Motivaciones para un espectáculo teatral," (unpublished manuscript). My analysis of the performance is based on Bosch's unpublished manuscript and a video recording.

37. Ibid.

38. María Isabel Bosch, "Las Viajeras."

39. Ibid.

40. Nicholas Ridout, *Theatre and Ethics*, 49.

41. Brecht writes: "So let us invite all the sister arts of drama, not in order to create an 'integrated work of art' in which they all offer themselves up and are lost, but so that together with the drama they may further the common task in their different ways; and their relations with one another consist in this: that they lead to mutual alienation" in *Brecht on Theatre*, 204.

42. This 1977 piece became popular in the 1990s after a 1992 recording conducted by David Zinman featuring soprano Dawn Upshaw was released in the memory of victims of the Holocaust. For a discussion of the image of the mother in Górecki's music, see Maja Trochimczyk, "*Mater Dolorosa*." Trochimczyk notes the "slow tempi and quietly sorrowful expression of the three movements." While it is most likely that Merzari and Bosch selected the music simply for the emotional effect that its slow, sorrowful sound would have on spectators, the symphony's theme of mother/child separation is relevant to the migration experiences of three of the *viajeras* who leave children at home in the Dominican Republic. In fact, the need to support their families is the main motivation for the women to take the risky trip abroad.

43. Lehmann, *Postdramatic Theatre*, 178.

44. Ibid., 184.

45. Ibid., 185.

46. Ibid.

47. Ibid.

CHAPTER 10

THEATERS OF VIGIL AND VIGILANCE: A PLAYWRIGHT'S NOTES ON THEATER AND HUMAN RIGHTS IN THE PHILIPPINES

Joi Barrios

Twenty-seven years ago, in 1984, I performed in the play *Oratoryo ng Bayan*[1] (People's Oratorio), staged by Peryante,[2] a street theater group. The play was based on the United Nations Universal Declaration of Human Rights, and I was both actor and production manager. I was 22 then, a young graduate instructor at the University of the Philippines in Diliman, and the Philippines was ruled by then President Ferdinand Marcos. Marcos had declared martial law on September 21, 1972; he "officially"[3] lifted it in 1981, but remained in power until his ouster in 1986 through what is now known as the "EDSA[4] people power revolt." My experience in this play, along with the other theater productions I performed in from 1979 to 1986, would later inform my work as a playwright.

In this essay, I chronicle my journey as a theater artist, a street theater scholar, and a human rights activist. I look back to the discourse on human rights in *Oratoryo ng Bayan* during the dictatorship era, and then discuss the following plays I have written in the last decade: *Gabriela: Isang Oratoryo* (Gabriela: An Oratorio) (Dulaang UP, 2006); *Mrs. B. Isang Monologo* (Mrs B: A Monologue) (Desaparecidos, 2009); and *Piketlayn Cantata* (Picketline Cantata).[5] These works, staged in the last decade, touch on the continuous violation of human rights even with the changing of presidents.

Performing the Universal Declaration of Human Rights: Humor at a Time of Repression

When I look back at *Oratoryo ng Bayan*, what I remember most was the humor of the play—a woman singing of the "true, the good, and the beautiful," while a group of male dancers dressed in tutus dance a mock ballet; actors wearing masks that eerily resemble the president and the first lady, students playing, and students singing and dancing. This in spite of the fact that we were talking about torture, corruption, poverty, and political struggle.

And why not? Philippine politics was a farce. We had a president who had reinvented himself as a war hero while battling rumors that he was sick through media releases showing him running and lifting weights. The first lady, who had a fondness for shoes, was also the governor of Metro Manila, and loved being requested to sing her favorite songs, never letting anyone forget that she was once a voice major. They had reimagined themselves as *Malakas* (the Strong) and *Maganda* (the Beautiful), the characters in the Filipino creation myth.[6]

The display of wealth and excesses of the regime were in sharp contrast to the economic and political crisis faced by the people. Inflation in 1984 was at an all-time high, at 63.8% in October, because of the continuing balance of payments difficulties, recent political developments, uncertainties concerning the exchange rate, and fluctuations in money supply.[7] From 1979 to 1984, the median growth rate of the GDP in developing countries in Asia was 5.5%, with China having the highest at 8.2%. The Philippines lagged behind, with a GDP growth rate of 1.9%, way below its rate of 4.5% from 1963 to 1972 and 6.4% from 1973 to 1979.[8]

Resistance to the Marcos regime was met by increasing political repression. Figures from Kessler, McCoy, the Task Force Detainees of the Philippines, and Amnesty International as cited by Nilan Yu show at least 70,000 arrests, 35,000 cases of torture, 3,275 extrajudicial killings and 737 cases of disappearances.[9] As I list these statistics, I remember: a fellow theater actor who disappeared and was later found floating in Pasig River; a beloved teacher and labor advocate shot; learning about fascism when we were beaten during a rally for education rights in 1980; a friend stopped at a checkpoint and detained for possessing a T-shirt that read "Boycott 1984 elections," and the sound of bullets as soldiers dispersed our rally in Welcome Rotonda in 1984.

Theater documented Philippine human rights violations during the Marcos years with plays performed both onstage and in the streets. Bonifacio Ilagan's *Pagsambang Bayan* (People's Worship), 1977, directed by Behn Cervantes and produced by UP Repertory Company used the form of the mass, and during the scene of the sermon, described acts of torture, killings, and massacres. Edgardo Maranan's *Panahon ni Cristy* (Cristy's Time), 1978, also produced by UP Repertory Company, narrated the plight of political prisoners. Al Santos's *Mene Mene Tekel Upharsim*, 1981, was an indictment of the torture of dissidents. Scenes from Chris Millado's *Buwan at Baril sa Eb Major* (Moon and Gun in Eb Major), 1985, showed an indigenous woman under militarized conditions, a socialite attending a rally that would be dispersed violently,[10] and a woman whose husband had been tortured and killed. Jose Ma. Sison's[11] poem "Fragments of a Nightmare" was transformed into a streetplay by director Chris Millado, using *noh*, a traditional Japanese theater form. These plays, performed during the 1970s and the 1980s, were significant in the following ways: first, the narratives were based on real-life experiences and research of the playwrights; second, they were staged at a time of print and film censorship, making theater an effective medium; and third, because studied alongside each other, these plays testify to the effective use of protest art and literature in the struggle against militarization.

And to this list of oppositional plays, we contributed *Oratoryo ng Bayan*—with hardly any resources, a minimal budget, and using as sets functional sculptures by Jerry Araos, himself a former political detainee. Directed by Chris Millado, Ces Mangay (now Ces Quesada), and Ching Arellano, the play was based on a script written by Rody Vera and Alan Glinoga and first mounted by the Philippine Educational Theater Association during the 1983 People's Theater Festival at Dulaang Rajah Sulayman, Fort Santiago, Manila. This musical play based on the UN Declaration of Human Rights, had ten scenes, among them scenes that focused on the right to education, free speech, assembly, peasant and labor rights, and the right to struggle. Millado's concept was to bring together street theater forms (the improvisational play, Augusto Boal's newspaper theater, songs with movement, vaudeville, mock ballet, choral recitations, poem-plays, effigy theater) we had used in our earlier performances outside traditional theater structures (lobbies, marketplaces, flowerpots on streets, rally stages). We staged the play at the lobby of the College of Arts and Sciences building (now renamed the College of Social Sciences building at the University of the Philippines), and then went on a school tour.

Of the scenes in the play, two stand out in my mind. One was the song alternately sung by Becky Demetillo Abraham, Malu de Guzman, and Bessie Lee, which started with the line "Sa kampo militar, saksihan..." (At the military camp, witness...), and then proceeded to enumerate forms of torture: "binunot ang aking kuko, habang buntis, pinahiga ako sa yelo..." (they took off my fingernails; while I was pregnant, they made me lie down on a block of ice).

Another was the last scene, in which I remember singing, as part of the chorus, the line "Karapatan ng bayang maghimagsik at lumaban..." (It is the people's right to revolt and fight). So as I write this essay, I read and reread the Universal Declaration of Human Rights. Where does it say, I ask myself, that the people have the right to revolt? I find it in the preamble, although phrased differently: "...Whereas it is essential, if man is not to be compelled to have recourse, as a last resort, to rebellion against tyranny and oppression, that human rights should be protected by the rule of law..."[12] The play, therefore, seems to have reinterpreted this statement into.. "it is the right of man to have recourse, as a last resort, to rebellion against tyranny and oppression." I believe that the play ended with a song that affirmed our right to rebellion because it was through the play that we "rebelled," and through it that we hoped to incite others to fight against the dictator.

The "right to rebellion" can also be found in Article II, Section 1 of the 1987 Constitution, a constitution drafted a year after the ouster of Marcos. This section affirms the sovereignty of the people: "Sovereignty resides in the people and all government authority resides in them."[13] The Constitutional Commission created by President Corazon Aquino in effect asserted the legitimacy of her revolutionary government. She came to power through a three-day revolt, and the constitution affirmed that the people had the right to revolt.

Why is this important? As I think back to the 1980s and my involvement in the national democratic movement that fought against the Marcos government, I realize now that the song in our play echoed our principles and the choice of several of us in that production to be organized toward the vision of national liberation. We believed then, as I believe now, that revolt was and is a basic human right for people living under tyrannical regimes.

It was also a decision that would ultimately shape my life and my work, long after 1986, and well into the first decade of the twenty-first-century, when, during the government of Gloria Macapagal Arroyo, the government launched an anti-insurgency campaign that sought to systematically annihilate all those associated with the political Left.

Death as Muse: 2001–2010

Human rights organization Karapatan[14] reports that "never, since the fourteen (14 years) of Marcos' outright fascist dictatorship (1972–1986) had human rights violations and suppression of civil and political rights been done with such extreme impunity as what the more than nine-year Arroyo regime did [sic]. It was state terror brought back."[15]

As documented by Karapatan, there had been 1,206 extrajudicial killings, 206 forced disappearances, 2,059 illegal arrests, 1,099 victims of torture, and 873,787 victims of forcible evacuation and displacement from 2001 to 2010.[16]

The killings rose to such proportions that even the United Nations sent a team, headed by Philip Alston, to the Philippines to investigate. The first paragraph of Mr. Alston's report to the United Nations, dated April 16, 2008, reads[17]:

> Over the past six years, there have been many extrajudicial executions of leftist-activists in the Philippines. These killings have eliminated civil society leaders, including human rights defenders, trade unionists and land reform advocates, intimidated a vast number of civil society actors, and narrowed the country's political discourse. Depending on who is counting and how, the total number of such executions ranges from 100 to over 800. Counter-insurgency strategy and recent changes in the priorities of the criminal justice system are of special importance to understanding why the killings continue...

One might ask, why did the killings continue? And why were there so many? This brings us to the counterinsurgency policy of the Arroyo government and its program called Oplan: Bantay Laya (literally, Operation: Freedom Watch; in short, OBL). The daily newspaper *Philippine Star* interviewed AFP (Armed Forces of the Philippines) spokesman Brigadier General Jose Mabanta Jr and reported:[18]

> ...Oplan Bantay Laya was launched in 2002 in a bid to end the decades-old communist rebellion in the country. The program, according to the government, would bring development to the countryside but militant groups said it has resulted in human rights abuses and extrajudicial killings. Despite the program, the Arroyo administration failed to achieve its goal to wipe out communist rebellion by June 30. The military, nevertheless, said Oplan Bantay Laya was a success, adding that the program was able to weaken the strength of the New People's Army by 50 percent to 4,642 from 9,260 in 2002...

Because the New People's Army[19] (NPA) of the Philippines has been waging a guerilla war from the countryside, OBL targeted instead, unarmed civilians, whom they had identified as members of Left-leaning organizations and political parties, alleging that these civilians were sympathetic to the NPA. They especially focused on members of party-list groups[20] Bayan Muna (literally, Country First)[21] and Anakpawis (literally, Children of Sweat), and the umbrella group Bagong Alyansang Makabayan (literally, New Patriotic Alliance), which counts among its members the labor center Kilusang Mayo Uno (May First Movement); the peasants' group Kilusang Magbubukid ng Pilipinas (Peasant Movement of the Philippines); the women's group Gabriela[22]; several youth organizations such as Anakbayan (literally Children of the People) and the League of Filipino Students, the Alliance of Concerned Teachers, and the Concerned Artists of the Philippines.

In the years of the Arroyo government, 222 members and staff of Bayan-affiliated organizations, 143 Bayan Muna members, and 50 Anakpawis members were summarily executed.

Why were these organizations targeted? In her article "Extrajudicial, Summary or Arbitrary Executions in the Philippines, 2001–2006," published in *Focus* June 2007, Maria Socorro Diokno explained the operational tactics of the Armed Forces of the Philippines. Diokno reports that in 2005, a Power Point presentation entitled "Knowing the Enemy" was produced by the General Headquarters of the Armed Forces of the Philippines. The presentation, which has 335 slides, names 54 organizations and groups as "legal front organizations" of the Communist Party of the Philippines and thus "enemies" of the state. According to Diokno:[23]

> These so-called "watch lists" contravene the 1987 Constitution, which mandates full respect for the political beliefs and aspirations of all Filipinos; the Constitution not only upholds the rights of Filipinos to form and join

organizations, but also encourages them to do so. The Constitution forbids the arrest and detention of persons "solely by reason of [their] political beliefs and aspirations."

Furthermore, the popularity of party-list groups resulted in three seats for Bayan Muna in every election it ran for—2001, 2004, 2007, and two in 2010. Similarly, Anakpawis has won one to two seats in the 2004, 2007, and 2010 elections. This in spite of the arrests of these representatives, incessant threats, and unrelenting black propaganda by the military.

Ironically, death has been the muse of artists and writers during the period of unprecedented state terrorism under Arroyo. It was thus the issue of human rights that informed the three plays (*Gabriela*, *Mrs. B*, and *Piketlayn Cantata*) I wrote between 2005 and 2011, two of which were performed in the Philippines, and one in the United States.

THE HUMAN RIGHTS "VICTIM" AS "INTERROGATIVE CHARACTER"

In two of the three plays I wrote, I did not start out writing with human rights being the issue I wanted to present. In *Gabriela, Isang Oratorio* (Gabriela: An Oratorio), 2005, I started with the idea of writing about the eighteenth-century heroine Gabriela Silang, for the twenty-fifth anniversary of the women's alliance named in her honor. For *Piketlayn Cantata*, I envisioned a play about caregivers in the Bay area and Dole plantation workers in Polomolok, Cotabato, in southern Philippines. However, because I wanted to talk about contemporary women in *Gabriela*, and because of recent events in the Dole plantation, human rights issues came to be foregrounded in these plays.

The second act of *Gabriela* focused on the present-day Philippines, and had for its lead characters, Gabby (performed by Lanie Sumalinog), a human rights advocate, and Gabby's boyfriend, a lawyer working with the peasants of a plantation. In the opening scene, activists sing the song "Ang Buhay Aktibista ay Buhay Langgam" (An Activist's Life is an Ant's Life) as they narrate the lives of activists in a militarized, politically charged Philippines. DJ then rehearses his rally speech with Gabby to introduce a "light" moment. However, in the next scene, the mood shifts—DJ is speaking at the rally, and he gets shot.

To portray grief, director Tony Mabesa[24] used images reminiscent of the *pieta* (the crucifixion of Christ, and the images of Christ with his mother Mary) while Gabby and the chorus chant their lines in the melody of the *pasyon* (literally, passion, or the Life and Passion of Jesus Christ). Why the "pasyon?" The *pasyon*, introduced during the Spanish colonial period, continues to be read during the celebration of Lent in the Philippines. By using this particular traditional cultural form, Mabesa likened the sacrifice of life of the character DJ to that of Jesus Christ. Mabesa's staging echoed Reynaldo Ileto's landmark *Pasyon and Revolution* where the historian argued that the revolutionaries saw parallels in their sacrifice for the revolution (leaving their homes, choosing the side of the less privileged, giving their lives) to that of the life and death of Jesus Christ.

The use of religious motifs in the script and the staging was not new. Playwright Bonifacio Ilagan and director Behn Cervantes utilized the form of the mass for *Pagsambang Bayan* (People's Worship) in 1977, 1979, and the subsequent stagings of the play. Al Santos's *Kalbaryo ng Maralitang Tagalungsod* (Calvary of the Urban Poor), 1991, staged in the streets of Metro Manila, draws from Lenten rites and plays in the Philippines. Aurelio Tolentino's *Bagong Cristo* (New Christ), a play on labor and capital written in the first decade of American colonial rule was staged in 1977 by Dulaang Babaylan, and again in 2008 by students and professors of the University of the Philippines in Los Baños.[25] In an interview with the *Philippine Daily Inquirer*, dramaturge Reagan Maiquez noted: "Similar with the play, we have seen laborers being killed like union leader (Diosdado) Ding Fortuna and other contemporary martyrs."[26]

If the play *Gabriela* can thus be likened to plays with similar themes of human rights and the "sacrifice" of activists, how did I endeavor to make the play different? I wanted to do three things: question the usual "activist role" attributed to women, interrogate the concept of a "well-made play," and portray activists less as the clenched–fist flag-waving stereotype and more as human beings with emotions and flaws. As I look back at this play five years after it was produced, I realize that I wrote it not only to draw attention to the problem of political killings and disappearances in the Philippines, but also for its audience of activists, many of whom openly wept during the performances. One of the most meaningful encounters I had was with the technical director, who approached me during the last day of the performance, and said that his mother had asked him to thank me. He then revealed that he was the son of Meliton Roxas, former Nestlé union president, assassinated in January 20, 1989. As he operated the lighting board every night, he remembered his father and cried, but never revealed to anyone else in the production why the play meant so much to him.

It is because of these interactions with the families of human rights victims that my next two plays would have the recurring theme of human rights. For the monologue *Mrs. B* (performed alternately by Gina Alajar and Bibeth Orteza), I focused on the life of Edith Burgos, mother of abducted peasant organizer Jonas Burgos. For *Piketlayn Cantata*, I centered most of the action on the militarization of Polomolok, where the Dole plantation and factory are located.

Mrs. B. was not originally my play. The production manager had sent me an email asking me to critique a monologue that had been written by two playwrights. Then, I was asked to revise the play, so the final product as staged by director Socrates Jose came from two scripts—my work and that of Grundy Constantino and Rowena Festin.

My input on the play was the setting and the action taking place. I did not want the character to just be telling the story of the abduction. Thus, I chose to portray Mrs. B as a mother preparing her house for the traditional Easter lunch. She is cooking in the kitchen (a device, I must admit, that had been used before), a rare occasion because, as she reveals, the family would usually eat out during Easter celebrations. She cooks a special dish for each child, while talking about the traditional Lenten rite of the "salubong" (literally, meeting)[27] in Angono Rizal, her life with her husband, the suspicious-looking car parked outside the house (perhaps a spy?), the woman following her around (another spy?). The phone rings and the caller informs her that the *lechon* (whole roasted pig) will not be delivered, and she gets upset because it is her son Jonas's favorite dish. It is here that she realizes that Jonas is not coming because Jonas has never been found.

Some facts about the Jonas Burgos case from my interview with Mrs. Burgos, her affidavit to the Department of Justice, and from newspaper articles and columns: According to witnesses Elsa Agasang, Jeffrey Cabintoy, and Larry Marquez, on April 28, 2007, Jonas was having lunch at the Hapag Kainan (literally, Dining Table) Restaurant at the Ever Gotesco Mall (along Commonwealth Avenue, Quezon City) when he was forcibly taken away by six men who identified themselves as "pulis" (police). When Cabintoy, a busboy trainee at the restaurant tried to intervene, a man identified as Harry Baliaga Jr. told him, "Wag ka nang makialam, kasi ang taong ito ay matagal na naming sinusubaybayan dahil sa droga," (Do not intervene because we have long been investigating this person because of drugs). As he was being dragged, Burgos kept shouting, "Aktibista lang po ako!" (I am just an activist!).

Mall security guard Larry Marquez then saw Burgos being forced into a vehicle with a license plate TAB194, a vehicle that was registered to a Mauro Mudong but had been confiscated for being in violation of Section 68 of Presidential Decree 75 "Transportation of Timber without a Permit," and brought to the headquarters of the 56th Infantry Battalion of the Philippine Army at Norzagaray, Bulacan. From the day Jonas was taken away until today, and in spite of witnesses who positively identified members of the armed forces as having abducted Jonas, the military continue to deny any knowledge of the abduction.

It was not the abduction but his mother's search, however, that the play focused on. I wrote the play as a comedy mainly because I felt that the topic was too "heavy," too depressing. The director, in the staging, wanted to insert more dramatic moments such as the confrontation between General Tolentino and Mrs. Burgos, which I subsequently wrote for the second draft, and Mrs. Burgos's recurring nightmare of Jonas's torture (from the original script)—which I consented to reluctantly. Plays, after all, are not just about the singular vision of the writer—I believe that playwrights should recognize that theater is a collective process and the director's concept is equally important.[28]

As in *Gabriela*, I wanted to portray Mrs. B. as a complex character—a woman whose heart had been set on being a lay Carmelite nun after her husband's death, and who had looked forward to a life of "silence," but then suddenly found herself being the spokesperson for the mothers and families of the abducted. Yet, even as I tried to look for punch lines and inserted comedic moments in the play, I wept continuously for the two months that I was writing. I watched Mrs. B. on a news video clip as she spoke at a rally in front of a military camp, unfazed that the soldiers were playing loud music as the families were praying. One soldier asked her: "Why do you keep looking for him?" And she replied, "I am his mother."

I also cried when, in an interview, she told me the story of a mother who had come up to her to ask, "Can I stand beside you when the media takes our picture?" She realized how privileged she was because her husband had been a well-known journalist and publisher. I wept as I wrote the last scene of the play. Mrs. B. had changed clothes because she was going to a meeting of Desaparecidos, the organization of the families of the disappeared. As she looked at herself in the mirror, she realized how much she had changed: She was wearing a T-shirt which had the words "Free Jonas Burgos!"; she was wearing jeans to go with the T-shirt, rubber shoes for comfort, and a backpack to carry all the meeting materials she needed. She now looked like an activist, very different from the lay Carmelite nun she was:

> ... Maiisip ba naman ni Mother Superior na mangyayari ito sa akin? Napaka-shy ko noon. Mother Superior, alam mo ba ang favorite picture ko ni Mama Mary, iyong tinatapakan niya ang mga ahas. Iyong matapang siya dahil isang ina siya, nanay siya.
>
> Kaninang umaga, nang bumababa ang anghel na nakaputi at kumakanta ng Regina Coeli Laetare, gusto kong kumaway, at sabihin: Dito hija, nandito ako, tanggalin mo rin ang belo ko, nanay rin ako. Gusto ko ring sumalubong ng anak...
>
> (Would Mother Superior have predicted for this to happen to me? I was so shy then. Mother Superior, do you know what my favorite picture of the Virgin Mary is, the one with the serpents beneath her feet. She was a mother, and she needed to be brave.
>
> This morning, when the angel was going down and singing Regina Coeli Laetare, I wanted to wave to her, tell her: Here! Here! I am here, remove my veil too, I am a mother too. I also want to meet my son...)

I wanted the play to end quietly, with a reference both to the Virgin Mary because of Mrs. B's own religiosity and unwavering faith, and to the Lenten rite called "salubong" or meeting.

New Administration, Same Policies, New Plays

By now, the second year of the Benigno Aquino administration, it has become clear that the all-out-war policy against activists remains. The most recent documentation provided by Karapatan show that from January to February 2011, there have been eight victims of extrajudicial killings, and 40 victims since the day President Aquino took office. This means that there is an average of one activist killed each week. The 2010 Karapatan report also shows that after only six months in office, the Aquino administration already has a long list of human rights violations in addition to the 40 extrajudicial killings: four enforced disappearances; 19 cases of torture; five frustrated extrajudicial killings, 36 cases of illegal arrest and detention; 34 illegal searches; 896 cases of forced evacuation; and 4,314 cases of threat, harassment, or intimidation. This, in spite of President Aquino's declaration in a meeting with European Union ambassadors at a time when he was still a presidential candidate: "Cases of extrajudicial killings need to be solved, [we must] not just identify the perpetrators but have them captured and sent to jail."

Thus, while Oplan Bantay-Laya (literally, Operation: Freedom Watch) has now been replaced by Oplan: Bayanihan,[29] the ultimate objective remains the same—"the reduction of the 'capabilities of internal armed threats'... to a level that they can no longer threaten the stability of the state and civil authorities can ensure the safety and well-being of the Filipino people."[30] And again, because members of leftist groups and organizations are seen to be sympathetic to the New People's Army, they become targets of the Armed Forces of the Philippines.

With Oplan: Bayanihan in place, it is therefore not surprising that even labor union elections have been militarized. Such was the case of the recent Dole union elections in the Dole pineapple plantation and factory site in Polomolok, Cotabato. According to a news article entitled "Martial Law-Type Repression by Dole Philippines vs. Union Alarms NGO," the Ecumenical Institute for Labor Education and Research had expressed concern over a militarized situation that was "reminiscent of the martial-law type repression which barred democratic activities of union then."[31] An independent monitoring team, the Center for Trade Union and Human Rights, reported the following: members of the Armed Forces of the Philippines 27th Infantry Battalion doing the rounds in polling places and visiting the homes of workers, buying votes, bribing workers not to show up in the elections, and even using a pre-school for their purposes.

What was even more surprising was the culture of militarism—the Armed Forces believed that they had the right to participate and were supported by the Department of Labor. On Facebook, the Philippine Army Public Affairs Office even posted an article entitled "Army Participates During the Certification Election at Dole Philippines."[32] This event led me to create two characters who sing parallel songs for *Piketlayn Cantata*—a blood-thirsty general called General P, and a nun, Sister Bonnie,[33] a human rights worker. Both refer to their pledge (*sinumpaan*), the former to defend peace and order; the latter to serve the poor and the oppressed. What I especially wanted to highlight in this scene was the power of words—how one can be branded as an activist or a communist and, when marked as such, how killing can then be justified. It is with an excerpt from this song, sung by Sister Bonnie and Biyang (played by Lourdes Oreo-Ramos and Cynthia Aban, respectively), that I wish to end this essay.

SISTER BONNIE AND BIYANG:
Ano ang halaga ng isang salita?
Sila nga ba'y inyong kilala
Sa isang bansag, sa isang tawag,
Walang pakumandang, lipulin kaming lahat.
(What is the power of a word?
Do you really know us?
By branding us, by calling us names,
Without any thought, annihilate us all.)

By demonizing activists, their lives are rendered less sacred. However, each play on human rights celebrates the persistent activist body—the dead speak again, families reenact their grief, the movement is challenged to carry on.

I was a student theater artist 30 years ago in 1980 when we set up our street theater group. I am a teacher now, writing plays for the human rights movement in Manila from wherever I am in the world. The call for action has not changed; but the national democratic movement to which I belong, now wages its struggles in multiple sites all over the world. And the theater of human rights remains our response to the culture of militarism.

Notes

1. The word "bayan" has flexible meanings: town, country, people. Historian Damon Woods discusses this in "The Evolution of Bayan" in *Diliman Review* 53, 2006, 1–4,
2. The word "peryante" comes from "perya" or fair, where vaudeville or "vaudeville-like" acts were performed during town fiestas or celebrations in the Philippines. These included songs and dances, magic acts, and the display of the "deformed" or unusual (little people, women who were like mermaids, huge people). Formed in 1983, the group was formed when former members of the student group UP (University of the Philippines) Tropang Bodabil (Vaudeville Troupe) left the company to form a new, more political street theater group.
3. No one really noticed the change with the "official" lifting of Martial Law.
4. EDSA stands for Epifanio de los Santos Avenue, a road that stretches from north to south in Metro Manila.
5. This was a staged reading by Balay Kultura, Committee for the Protection of Workers' Rights and Kul-Arts, 2011. A production workshop, as well as the premiere is scheduled for May 2013.
6. In the Filipino creation myth, a bird pecks on a bamboo pole, the bamboo splits open, and the first man (Malakas or the Strong) and woman (Maganda or the Beautiful) emerge.
7. Roberto Mariano, *Forecasting Monthly Inflation in the Philippines.* Quezon City: The Philippine Institute for Development Studies, 1985, 5, http://www3.pids.gov.ph/ris/ms/pidsms85-10.pdf
8. Alan Hughes and Ajit Singh, *The World Economic Slowdown and the Asian and Latin American Economies: A Comparative Analysis of Economic Structure Policies and Performance,* Wider Working Papers 42, April 1998. World

Institute for Development Economics Research of the United Nations University.
9. Nilan Yu. "Interrogating Social Work: Philippine Social Work and Human Rights under Martial Law." Paper presented. Global Social Work 2004: Reclaiming Civil Society, Adelaide, November 2–5, 2004, http://www.unisanet.unisa.edu.au/reclaimingcivilsociety/Papers/Interrogating.pdf
10. "Millado" refers to the same rally described in the preceding paragraph. Millado was the second chairperson of Peryante, succeeding founding chair Ralph Peña.
11. Sison is the alleged founding chair of the Communist Party of the Philippines.
12. The Universal Declaration of Human Rights, United Nations, 1948.
13. The 1987 Constitution of the Republic of the Philippines. http://www.chanrobles.com/article2.htm
14. The word "karapatan" literally means "rights."
15. Karapatan Alliance for the Advancement of Human Rights. "2010 Year-End Report on the Human Rights Situation in the Philippines." Quezon City: Karapatan, 2010, 17, http://www.karapatan.org/files/Karapatan%202010%20HR%20Report%20(updated).pdf
16. Ibid., Tables 8, 9, 16, pp. 16–25
17. Alston, Philip. "Report of the Special Rapporteur on Extrajudicial, Summary or Arbitrary Executions," United Nations General Assembly, April 16, 2008, http://www.karapatan.org/files/English_Alston_Report_Mission_to_the_Philippines_HRC8.pdf
18. Alexis Romero. "New AFP Tack vs Rebels to Uphold Human Rights." *The Philippine Star*. August 20, 2010
19. The New People's Army was formed in 1969. It is the army of the Communist Party of the Philippines.
20. Under the 1987 Philippine constitution, party-list organizations can run for seats in Congress. These gave under-represented sectors a voice in a congress that has traditionally been composed of the "privileged" in Philippine society. A vote of 2% is necessary to gain a seat, with a party-list group having a maximum of three seats.
21. In the Philippines, the terms "nationalism" and "patriotism" are rooted in the anticolonial and pro-sovereignty struggles of the country.
22. "Gabriela" stands for General Assembly Binding Women for Reforms, Integrity, Equality, Leadership, and Action. Formed in 1984, Gabriela also serves as a center for over a hundred women organizations, institutes, desks, and programs. It draws its name from Gabriela Silang (1731–1763), who led the revolt against the Spaniards in the Ilocos region after her husband Diego was killed.
23. Maria Socorro Diokno, "Extrajudicial, Summary, or Arbitrary Executions in the Philippines, 2001–2006," FOCUS, June 2007, Volume 48, Asia Pacific Human Rights Information Center, http://www.hurights.or.jp/archives/focus/section2/2007/06/extrajudicial-summary-or-arbitrary-executionsin-the-philippines-2001-2006.html
24. Tony Mabesa is the founding Artistic Director of Dulaang UP, the theater company of the University of the Philippines. I credit Mabesa with my development as a playwright because he directed my first play, "Saling-Pusa" for UP Playwrights' Theater in 1986. He is Professor Emeritus of Theater.

25. Although I performed in Pagsambang Bayan in 1980 and had personal knowledge of Al Santos's work, much of my knowledge of theater can be attributed to my teacher Nicanor Tiongson, author of *Dulaan: An Essay on Philippine Theater*, Cultural Center of the Philippines, 1989, and numerous other publications on Philippine theater.
26. Catherine Calleja, . "Fusion of Math, Theater, Brings New Twist to Tolentino Play." Inquirer Mobile. http://services.inquirer.net/mobile/08/03/21/html_output/xmlhtml/20080320-125782-xml.html
27. In the "salubong," the meeting of Jesus Christ and Mary are portrayed by two statues. An angel (played by a young girl) sings and lifts the Virgin's veil to signify the end of mourning.
28. Billing in the play reads: "Concept by Socrates Jose, Script by Joi Barrios, Rowena Festin and Grundy Constantino." Staged February 12–13, 2012. Bantayog ng mga Bayani Theater, Quezon City.
29. The term "bayanihan" refers to the traditional custom of community members helping each other out. This is exemplified by the iconic images of community members moving a "bahay kubo" (nipa hut) from one site to another.
30. Renato M. Reyes Jr, "Oplan Bayanihan: Grand Psywar Scheme and Continuing Violence against the People," Blog, January 18, 2011, http://natoreyes.wordpress.com/2011/01/18/part-2-oplan-bayanihan-grand-psywar-scheme-and-continuing-violence-against-the-people/
31. "Martial Law-Type Repression Alarms NGO." Bulatlat. Quezon City. February 2, 2011. http://bulatlat.com/main/2011/02/22/martial-law-type-repression-by-dole-philippines-vs-union-alarms-ngo/
32. Philippine Army Public Affairs Office. "Army Participates During the Certification Election at Dole Philippines." Facebook Page. February 28, 2011. http://www.facebook.com/note.php?note_id=202051273153628.
33. Sister Bonnie was the name of my high school teacher in Stella Maris College (Quezon City, 1978–1979) who greatly influenced my political consciousness. The role of Sister Bonnie was played by my former high school classmate, Marlo Oreo-Ramos for the San Francisco production.

CHAPTER 11

"THE SPECTACLE OF OUR SUFFERING": STAGING THE INTERNATIONAL HUMAN RIGHTS IMAGINARY IN TONY KUSHNER'S *HOMEBODY/KABUL*

Elizabeth S. Anker

Tony Kushner's *Homebody/Kabul* has received widespread attention for its foresight into the militarization of Afghanistan in the aftermath of 9/11. The play, however, was written before that cataclysmic event, with Kushner explicitly contextualizing its dramatic action with reference to "the American bombardment of the suspected terrorist training camps in Khost, Afghanistan, August 1998."[1] Yet at the same time as Kushner examines the global media's fixation on Afghanistan, *Homebody/Kabul* also mines the many tensions that afflict humanitarianism and liberal discourses of human rights—tensions only exacerbated in the wake of 9/11.

Akin to how proponents of the "War on Terror" make frequent recourse to the defense of women, human rights discourses commonly fetishize the iconic "Third World woman" as their paradigmatic subject-object, all the while fostering perceptions of cross-cultural solidarity. In doing so, however, these humanitarian campaigns marshal a number of enduring tropes of the rhetoric of empire.[2] Indeed, political speech, especially post-9/11, commonly enlists the rhetoric of human rights to justify policing the postcolonial world, sanctioning practices that are paternalistic and neoimperial.[3] *Homebody/Kabul* enacts these and other contradictions that trouble human rights discourses and norms, displaying how such appeals can discredit non-European cultural formations and operate as a bludgeon rather than a shield for the populations those standards ostensibly safeguard.

Homebody/Kabul's satirically allegorical portrait of current geopolitics acquires much of its force by probing the many expectations that underwrite dominant views about the globalization of human rights.[4] Its widely reproduced first scene contains an extended monologue by the "Homebody," a name that marks her as a figure for broader ideological currents that support European nationalism, in its domestic and international varieties. The Homebody meditates at length on the history and culture of Afghanistan while reading aloud from an outdated guidebook, and she interpolates herself within this imaginative odyssey as a savior of Afghan society and its many wounds. While conducting a type of travel, however, her reverie is delivered from the enclosed space of a London apartment, and with speech composed of esoteric, self-indulgent language that highlights both the solipsism of her humanitarian consciousness and the privileged nature of her guilt. Although replete with self-recrimination, the Homebody's regret is revealed to derive from narcissistic yearnings that index classically imperial anxieties. Her fantasies thus suggest that the humanitarian mandate is generated less by ethical responsibility than a self-interested quest for redemption, wherein suffering finds itself both commodified and exoticized.

Following its opening act, *Homebody/Kabul* abruptly shifts location to Afghanistan, after the Homebody has mysteriously vanished. The action in these ensuing scenes follows her husband Milton and daughter Priscilla as they journey to Kabul to obtain her allegedly dead body, although neither the Homebody's true fate nor her motives for fleeing are ever disclosed. Milton and Priscilla instead become caught up in a series of misadventures, many verging on the ridiculous, as they unsuccessfully navigate Afghan society. After much ado, they are unwittingly conscripted into smuggling military intelligence across the border and helping a female refugee, Mahala, escape to London. Overall, their exploits parody various dynamics of Western involvement in Afghanistan.

"IN THE SAFETY OF MY KITCHEN": NARCISSISM AND THE HUMANITARIAN IMAGINARY

The central conceit informing the Homebody's monologue is that she extrapolates from an "outdated guidebook" to Afghanistan.[5] This conjoined travelogue *cum* history of nearly 5,000 years both offers a panoptical view of the region and quotes a number of classically imperialist representational motifs. The Homebody reads—"[o]ur story begins at the very dawn of history"[6]—foregrounding her own inscription within empire's violent legacies. Nonetheless, the Homebody also imbibes and redeploys the intertwined prejudices and fantasies that she obtains from the guidebook. Catered to a European audience, its narrative is animated by the anxieties and desires that continue to regulate Western assumptions about the "exotic East." On the one hand, the guidebook romanticizes Afghan culture as a site of "remarkable cross-fertilization" between diverse religions and peoples.[7] On the other, Muslim influence is construed as an exogenous threat encroaching on that idyllic past of multicultural harmony; for example, the statement that "[s]everal hundred years were to pass before Kabul would fully surrender to Islam" configures Islam as a menace fated to overpower the region's passive population.[8] Here, precisely the Homebody's ready appropriation of the neoimperial gaze and provincialization of Afghan history enable her nostalgic idealization of Afghanistan, which is further implied to motivate her ambiguous suicide-defection.

Much as the truncation of this history renders it consumable, the guidebook's "outdated" status fails to trouble the Homebody. By relying on a 33-year-old rendition of Afghan culture, the Homebody not only neglects the fact that it contains outmoded information but also imaginatively relegates Afghanistan to a space outside modernity, or a condition of stasis and immaturity. As a prop, the guidebook thus anticipates the role of false "intelligence" within the second half of the play. If *Homebody/Kabul* prophesies post-9/11 geopolitics, then the Homebody's blinkered, self-absorbed appropriation of Afghan history subtly indicts the US bungling of intelligence in 9/11's aftermath.

At once, the guidebook masquerades as a travelogue, and the Homebody quotes multiple conventions of that genre. Ironically, the Homebody remains confined to "the safety of [her] kitchen," or firmly ensconced within the domestic.[9] This setting, combined with her self-referential reflections, enacts Western self-enclosure, rendering her myopia a case study in the limits of isolationism as a diplomatic strategy. That her character is a spokesperson for late imperial complacency is reinforced through her very name, which both celebrates the "homeland," or "mother country," and betokens a conservative fixation on security. Indeed, she informs the audience that her "borders have only ever been broached by books,"[10] casting her as little more than an armchair tourist—as well as, as I will discuss, an armchair humanitarian—who engages with Afghan culture through a strikingly unilateral, imbalanced circuit of exchange. As such, her physical and emotional isolation satirically mirrors the insularity and defensiveness of the European state. Moreover, her tangled fears and longings divulge the ambivalence of European nationalism, demonstrating why the specter of Otherness paradoxically consolidates its ethos. The Homebody's seclusion guarantees that her domain will be penetrated by no more than her own self-serving fantasies—even while those anxieties are indispensable to her basic self-image.

It is doubly significant that the Homebody obtains her knowledge of Afghanistan through the voracious consumption of books, as opposed to active experience. Here, she represents the quintessential reader, a position of luxury with which the audience-reader is complicit. Despite her peculiarities, her attitudes symptomatize broader mindsets that equally apply to the audience, both in her self-indulgence and in her enthrallment with exoticism, human rights abuse, Islam, and polarized East–West relations. Likewise, her rarefied, esoteric language identifies her as a specific kind of reader. While she insists mere lines into the script that "ours is a time of connection,"[11] her monologue stages her radical, incurable isolation, her abstruse vocabulary underscoring the futility of such a dream. Although her lengthy monologue enlists a superfluity of words, that outpouring fails to facilitate communication. Rather, her rhetorical excess—for instance, as she acknowledges that she speaks "Elliptically. Discursively"[12]—both signals the extravagance of her worldview and compounds her alienation. Kushner, as such, mines the paradox that the era celebrated for purveying truly global communication might have augured a breakdown in interpersonal understanding.

In these ways the Homebody's monologue opens up the psychic economy of late imperial decadence. Her reverie begins with the diagnosis that "we are, many of us, overwhelmed, and succumbing to luxury,"[13] an apparent assessment of global modernity at large. Her mood undergoes wild vicissitudes, fluctuating from despair to mania. These variations enact the sense of historical compression and amnesia endemic to, as well as the alarmism of, much contemporary political rhetoric. Here, the Homebody's relationship with her husband Milton similarly offers a metaphor for the malaise and attendant escapism in the late imperial center. Milton and the Homebody are dependent on antidepressants, the "portmanteau chemical cocktail word confected by punning psychopharmacologists," which even the erudite Homebody cannot recollect.[14] She recounts how they accidentally mix up and imbibe the other's specialized remedies. This need to self-anesthetize is both compulsive, given that the cycle of addiction rather than the particular tonic feeds their habits, and excessive—and glaringly so relative to the scenes of oppression that captivate the Homebody. In this respect, the Homebody's immersion in the guidebook produces a comparatively narcotic result, distracting her from her dissatisfaction while further elucidating the mutual imbrication of exoticism and capitalism, with the consumption of Otherness acting as a compensatory stave against suppressed truth.

The Homebody's addiction to antidepressants is accordingly framed as both a symptom of neoimperial guilt and a means to forestall self-knowledge. She recurrently describes her own geographical and historical positionality as an "awful place" that marks "the scene of our crime, the place of our shame,"[15] being haunted by "degrees of action" and corresponding "degrees of inertia."[16] This theme of what she calls "culpability" arises throughout her monologue.[17] Indeed, even her idiosyncrasies—her mania, her loquaciousness, her yearnings, her anxieties—attempt to neutralize her tangled feelings of complicity and remorse, while further displaying the circular logic that animates much present-day humanitarianism. In other words, it demonstrates how empire produces the basic conditions of suffering that warrant renewed cycles of neoimperial interventionism. As such, while the Homebody's monologue parodies European self-enclosure, it simultaneously interrogates the contradictions that subtend human rights activism, revealing its constitutive inscription within the *longue durée* of empire. Accordingly, the Homebody's anxiety-laden meditations converge on a double bind at the heart of the international human rights imaginary, revealing how the dual pretenses of humane concern and moral reckoning smuggle in a renewed guise of European paternalism—and one invariably colored by narcissistic self-interest.

Beyond her fascination with Afghanistan, the Homebody's monologue culminates with a protracted fantasy about a shopkeeper from whom she purchases imported hats for a "hat party" that she plans to host. Believing him to be an Afghan refugee, she notices "that three fingers on his right hand have been hacked off,"[18] which leads her to speculate over what caused that injury. Admitting that she "know[s] nothing of this hand, its history," she nevertheless tries to comprehend the wound's origins, constructing a number of elaborate and deeply exoticist scenarios. While wary of her own "morbid fascination," she is enthralled with what she interprets as a relic of atrocity, in a progression that demonstrates why a fetishization of Third World suffering and barbarity incurs legibility for humanitarian norms.[19] Notably, the Homebody's explanations for the wound are contradictory; she surmises that it was a punishment exacted by *both* the "Russians" *and* the "Mujahideen" in retaliation for *both* being an "informer" *and* for stealing bread.[20] These competing justifications only intensify her curiosity, much as they endow the hand with an almost phantasmagoric aura. Overall, her ruminations dramatize a central liability of popular human rights campaigns—namely, that they require compelling portraits of human suffering, causing persuasive advocacy to verge on sensationalism and exoticism. Ironically, human rights activism gains authority by relying on the abiding motifs of colonialist discourse, contaminating popular human rights discourses with the very legacies of injustice they aim to reverse.

The Homebody's conjectures about the wound morph into a related illusion of being "able to speak perfect Pashtu," which further enables the shopkeeper to conduct a plea for his and his country's salvation. That appeal, however, concludes with the remonstrance: *"you will never understand."*[21] Here, even within her self-serving fantasy, the Homebody confronts impediments to cross-cultural dialogue, as they directly imperil the humanitarian mandate. Her fixation on his injury is inextricable from an egoistic longing to heal it, exposing why humanitarian sympathy can serve to purge neoimperial guilt and ultimately provide a vehicle for European redemption. In effect, the Homebody not only capitalizes on but fully enlists distant atrocity to atone for her own shame, revealing that emotion to be deeply narcissistic—more a permutation of boredom than of principled outrage or concern. While the specter of victimization may trigger a moral reckoning, that relay relegates postcolonial suffering to a mere background to her own enlightenment; the shopkeeper's hardship neither impinges on her own well-being nor requires more than intellectual engagement.

The Homebody's monologue concludes with an explicitly eroticized desire that further interrogates the structure of humanitarian sentiment. She envisions herself transported to Kabul to be led on a "guided tour through his city,"[22] and this mystical journey climaxes as she imagines being penetrated by and physically engulfing the shopkeeper's wounded hand. While a figure for rebirth, the conspicuously sexualized fabric of her longings again highlights the narcissism fueling her guilt, or how humane beneficence masks a self-interested quest for fulfillment. We might, in turn, decipher this eroticization of abuse informing the Homebody's fantasy in terms of what Anne McClintock has called the "porno-tropics" of empire. While McClintock charts a long history in which narratives of conquest and discovery harness the dual mythologies of "travel as an erotics of ravishment" and a "gendered erotics of knowledge," the Homebody's humanitarianism is excited by a related "metaphysic of gender violence" and "erotics of engulfment."[23] Yet, as in historical apologias for empire, the Homebody's pornographic fetishization of violence ultimately denotes an ambivalence. That is, neoimperial desire is constitutively partner to an anxiety of exposure, disease, and contagion—or to the threat of being overwhelmed by the very objects arousing the appetite for conquest. Although the Homebody inverts this logic, her monologue demonstrates how a humanitarian intrigue with the suffering "Other" comes to exorcize imperial lassitude and paranoia. An antidote to fears of imperial decline, for the Homebody the humanitarian saga purveys the illusion that the shopkeeper both needs and desires her assistance, with a demand so intense as to be sexual. Thus compensating for Western insecurity, the alterity intrinsic to human rights abuse provides a screen onto which the tenuous European self-image projects its own internal misgivings, while simultaneously palliating self-doubt and resecuring the neoimperial mandate.

Furthermore, the Homebody's savior complex is cast as part and parcel of consumerism. Most immediately, she displays the widespread tendency to homogenize postcolonial cultures. The Homebody fails to name or specify the hat shop's location in her allusions to it, which the script denotes with a "_____" and the stage directions "(*Gesture*)."[24] These sweeping gestures preserve the shop's otherworldliness, figuring it as removed from ordinary time and space. This refusal to vest it with specificity further renders it interchangeable with countless other such repositories of immigrant culture. Indeed, this slippage between exotic alterity and substitutability illustrates how those dual biases reinforce one another. If the hat shop were singular or unique, the Homebody would be prevented from idealizing it. She would instead need to account for the shopkeeper's real-world entreaties. Paradoxically, then, at the same time as the shopkeeper iconically embodies Third World suffering, the conceit of his Otherness forestalls the Homebody's ability to grapple with his particularized traumas.[25]

Indeed, it is not accidental that the Homebody's humanitarian sentiment is instigated by her visit to the shop, which is to say that it is inseparable from the allure of the commodity—here, props that might cloak the ennui of her disappointing parties. Her initial description of the shop delineates this nexus between humanitarianism and the affective topography of late capitalism. The Homebody relates how she stumbles on

> ...a dusty shop crowded with artifacts, relics, remnants, little ... doodahs of a culture once aswarm with spirit matter, radiant with potent magic, the disenchanted dull detritus of which has washed up on our culpable shores, its magic

now shriveled into the safe contained of *aesthetic*, which is to say, *consumer* appeal. You know, Third World junk. As I remember, as my mind's eye saw, through its salt crust, Afghan junk. That which was once Afghan, which we, having waved our credit cards in its general direction, have made into junk.[26]

Superficially, the Homebody bemoans how the commercialization of culture divests its underlying objects of their emotional-ontological significance to become mere "junk." Yet, even that complaint embeds a classically Orientalist conceit that indigenous beliefs contain a storehouse of less alienated, more "enchanted" social relations. Her engrossment with Afghanistan arises from a fantasy of precapitalist harmony and, by extension, uncorrupted authenticity; she essentially embraces it as an antithesis to the spiritual impoverishment of the West. No doubt, a similar romance of purity and virtue underlies much human rights reportage. Much as imperial conquest was authorized by myths of virgin territory awaiting cultivation, humanitarianism gains international traction through the premise that military and other interventions will safeguard innocence. Makau Mutua has demonstrated how the human rights franchise relies on narratives of Western "saviors" who set out to deliver "victims" comprised almost entirely of women and children from male "savages."[27] Such a heuristic naturalizes humanitarianism not merely by deploying definitions of the inhumane but also through patronizing fictions of Third World purity, with its equally erotic and condescending undertones. The fact that the Homebody's fantasies assume a sexualized form, then, is far from surprising. That said, the Homebody's despair over the commodification of Afghan culture also productively underscores the imbalances of such transactions, leading the marketing of alterity to ultimately reinforce Northern hegemony. And it is precisely such a disparity that the remaining scenes of *Homebody/Kabul* invert when they move to war-torn Kabul after the Homebody's strange disappearance.

The Humanitarian Crusade

Following the opening Act, *Homebody/Kabul* abruptly shifts to Afghanistan with a sequence of events that become progressively more ludicrous. Milton and Priscilla travel to Kabul to retrieve the Homebody's body, only to be informed that she is alive and has married "a pious Muslim man of means."[28] While her family never discovers her real fate, they embark on one bizarre misadventure after another. As burqa-clad Priscilla traverses Kabul in search of her mother's body and memory, Milton ensconces himself in a hotel room, drugged, with Quango, an ex-NGO aid worker turned heroin addict who still wields control over various diplomatic measures. Along the way, Priscilla consents to prostitute herself to the corrupt Quango in exchange for transit papers to help Mahala, a former librarian who claims to be the ex-wife of her mother's new husband, escape from the country. However, they discover that they are inadvertently smuggling, in addition to Mahala, military secrets across the border. Adding to these surreal events, a significant portion of the dialogue is conducted in languages other than English, including Dari, Pashto, and French. While translated in the script, the audience in a performance would thus undergo a parallel cultural and epistemic disorientation as Kushner's characters, dramatizing both the importance of and linguistic impediments to cross-cultural understanding. Finally, the play's terminal scene—one even less conclusive than the incidents in Kabul—shifts back to the Homebody's living room as Mahala adopts the aspect of a "modern English woman."[29] Approximately a year after the exploits in Kabul, Priscilla returns home to encounter Mahala reading in the very chair from which the Homebody delivered her opening monologue, a substitution that enacts an uncanny doubling between the two women.

Beyond the plot's absurd twists, both its characters and its themes allegorically critique multiple dimensions of the ethics and politics of humanitarian aid and interventionism. In their mission to salvage the Homebody, Milton and Priscilla are cast as humanitarian crusaders—who, moreover, enter Afghanistan in pursuit of an object (her body) that is of doubtful existence. Scene Two's jarring removal to Kabul begins as an Afghan doctor, Doctor Quari Shah, catalogues the wounds inflicted on her body, although that account is later implied to be fictitious. As such, the insignia of atrocity are introduced as not only fabricated but also mythological in proportion, much as human rights reportage can endow events with a spectacular aura in excess of reality. The Homebody's dead body, with its questionable truth status, operates as something of a MacGuffin device; while she may or may not have been murdered, the characters go to exorbitant lengths to locate her. In effect, her body's authenticity becomes irrelevant, as Milton and Priscilla are increasingly motivated by goals unrelated to their original agenda. By extension, as effective humanitarians, their official warrant for intruding in Afghanistan is exposed as a ruse. Their mandate to remedy the human rights abuse inflicted on the Homebody is shown to be a cover—much as the war on terror legitimated the American bombardment in terms of which Kushner contextualizes the play.

It is further noteworthy that *Homebody/Kabul* refuses to resolve whether the Homebody has been murdered or willingly gone "AWOL." If the latter is the case, the Homebody implicitly resists the salvation that Milton and Priscilla aim to foist upon her, rendering their premise for invading Afghanistan illusory and misguided, in contradiction to her wishes. One suggestion is that the Homebody deliberately evades these paternalistic ends, which is all the more ironic due to the surmise that she trades Mahala for herself. *Homebody/Kabul*, as such, mines this disconnect between humanitarianism and the ideals of its objects-recipients. The Homebody's refusal to be saved queries whether Milton and Priscilla's designs are neoimperial ones, both oriented toward their own selfish desires and contrary to the Homebody's intent, ill-advised though it may be.

Akin to how Milton and Priscilla lose sight of their reasons for traveling to Afghanistan, the Homebody's intentions remain elusive. Much as the dialogue never divulges whether she has in fact converted to Islam, her original impetus for fleeing London is left unexplained. Nonetheless, the other European characters reductively deride her decision as equivalent to suicide, refusing to entertain the sorts of motive that might excuse her actions.[30] Through this ambiguity, *Homebody/Kabul* confronts a central impasse in debates about women's rights. Conversations about women's rights are commonly refracted through determinations of agentive choice, yet such a gauge is derived from as well as beholden to liberal norms regulating self-determination. Even as her family scoffs at her behavior, the liberal focus on autonomy would discount her actions as irrational, if not delusional. Either way, the Homebody's disappearance illustrates why liberal definitions of selfhood will misread her predicament. We must therefore ask whether calculations that treat self-determination as a proxy for human flourishing will depreciate registers of belonging and attachment that inform both many non-European epistemologies and many women's networks of belonging, even while the cultures that house them may contain oppressive elements. Although Milton and Priscilla proceed with the salutary aim of restoring the Homebody's human rights, the implication that she actively thwarts this policing of her decisions suggests why human rights standards might pose an inaccurate barometer for measuring certain experiences of meaning and fulfillment.[31]

Moreover, although Milton and Priscilla venture to Afghanistan with altruistic aims, it more accurately provides a theater for their own narcissistic dramas of self-redemption, much as the hat shop did for the Homebody. The humanitarian sentiment that inspires Milton and Priscilla is tainted by multiple kinds of self-interest, mirroring the compromises that often sully human rights activism.[32] While the objective of protecting innocent victims from savage perpetrators incurs popular support for the human rights franchise, the epic feats of their saviors procure deliverance not only for those victims but also for their activist-champions—which is to say that egoistic longings for atonement also consolidate humanitarianism as an ideology. Within Kushner's play, both Milton and Priscilla experience illusions of personal redemption. Although Milton is for much of the action in an opium-induced stupor, he nonetheless has a hallucinatory type of epiphany, which is humorously characterized as "an orgasm deep inside my head."[33] It is *Homebody/Kabul*'s three main female characters, however, who most visibly undergo forms of spiritual awakening tied to their roles in the humanitarian saga, although of varying degrees of ambivalence. We have already seen how the Homebody's fantasies assuage her solipsistic desires, and Priscilla's odyssey of self-discovery is, in many ways, counterpart to her mother's. Yet whereas the Homebody self-consciously pursues spiritual replenishment, Priscilla's insights emerge inadvertently and haphazardly. That said, even the stage directions associate her with illumination and renewal. In Afghanistan, she is repeatedly shown donning and removing her burqa, with the common motif of veiling emblematizing a dialectic of concealment and revelation.

While Priscilla's veiling thereby tracks her personal awakening, it also functions as a metaphor for women's oppression and liberation, and it is

Priscilla who most conspicuously negotiates the many tensions that haunt dominant, liberal expectations about women's rights. While I will conclude with such debates, on multiple occasions Priscilla willingly forfeits her dignity, self-possession, and rights, whether by wearing the burqa or sleeping with Quango to secure Mahala's passage. To such ends, her choices highlight the extent to which she perceives her rights as contingent on and relative to context—as opposed to being absolute, unyielding norms. For example, in the first Kabul street scene, Priscilla is encountered smoking a cigarette underneath her burqa, which compels her to frantically remove it to avoid burning herself, courting public censure. Beyond her vaudevillian antics, the hazards of smoking are juxtaposed with the restrictions of the Taliban. On the one hand, this contrast exposes the hypocrisy that can infect Western claims to the moral and cultural high ground, insofar as smoking represents a facile token of women's independence that is significantly more fraught with peril than the practice of veiling. Yet on the other hand, Priscilla's actions also beg the question of whether she can retain such behaviors while striving to inhabit the epistemological vantage point of an Afghan woman.

Of the European characters, Priscilla is most fully cognizant of her own complicities and their corresponding ethical dilemmas. While she meets with quasi-religious insight on numerous instances, she grapples with the pitfalls of those recognitions. In Kabul, Priscilla first experiences such an expanded consciousness in reaction to the sights she witnesses in a women's hospital while searching for her mother's corpse. Although she admits to "marvel[ing]" at her proximity to "suffering," she also underscores the "inappropriate" nature of such a response,[34] by extension indexing the prurient, voyeuristic sentiments that can animate the impulse to bear witness to atrocity. This double bind once again captures a central paradox of popular humanitarianism—namely, that it is energized by displays of egregious suffering that risk simultaneously galvanizing and traumatizing the observer. Much as classical formulations define the sublime in terms of an alchemy of awe and terror, imaginative encounters with human rights abuse can elicit their own kind of fascination, even while they induce a cathartic, or purgative, effect. Yet while Priscilla does not evade this particular Catch-22 of human-rights witnessing, her consciousness of her reactions' "inappropriateness" interrogates the psychic economy of the humanitarian gaze, displaying why even salutary impulses can be jeopardized by murkier appetites.

While laden with allegorical resonances, Priscilla and Milton's exploits offer an especially biting satire of the bungling, naiveté, and paranoia that has characterized European-American involvement in Afghanistan, especially post-9/11, and thus contribute to the play's prescience. As we have seen, their basic mission is fueled by egoistic goals: to return the Homebody—a placeholder for the "mother country"—after she has gone missing. They thus aim to salvage the tarnished national self-image after it has fallen prey to alien influences, making their incursions into Afghanistan first and foremost an exercise in restoring the inviolability of European domestic space. It is not incidental that one explanation for the Homebody's disappearance is that she has cuckolded Milton for an Afghan husband. As such, both of her alleged fates—whether her murder or consensual infidelity—constitute a violation of the body politic, and Milton and Priscilla are charged with repairing its integrity and safeguarding it against such penetration.[35] Milton and Priscilla's undertakings in Afghanistan thus ironically represent defensive measures geared to buttress European nationalism in the face of multiculturalism, even while their foibles reveal the nation's very fragility to extend from a xenophobic fear of contamination by Otherness—in other words, from the ongoing legacy of empire.

While Kushner satirizes the paranoid texture of European nationalism, Milton and Priscilla's mishaps indict the self-interest driving much humanitarian policy. If their recovery of the Homebody aims to restore the integrity of the body politic—or, less metaphorically, the integral family unit—then whatever altruism accompanies that mission disguises less valorous motives. On one level, their pretense of humane concern seems to exorcise their sense of irrelevance and abandonment at the Homebody's betrayal. Allegorically speaking, their endeavors can be seen to remedy parallel patterns of inaction and malfeasance in Afghanistan, here again adding to the play's uncanny insight into its post-9/11 militarization. To be sure, Milton and Priscilla's neglect of the Homebody's needs correlates with a long trajectory of diplomatic ineptitude (most notably the Cold War arming of the Taliban) that directly fostered the dire circumstances warranting Afghanistan's present-day occupation. On a separate level, successful recovery of the Homebody would symbolically verify the superiority of European culture and society, further illustrating why the humanitarian crusader inevitably peers into the mirror of his or her own tenuous self-image. Indeed, even their quest to liberate Mahala (arguably a representative of Afghani women as a whole) vindicates European preeminence. While a gesture of hospitality, it, too, confirms the European way of life, not only enabling Milton and Priscilla to play savior but also through Mahala's own wish to emigrate.

"Many Different Lanterns": The Promises of Multiculturalism

Astoundingly incompetent, Priscilla and Milton's search for the Homebody devolves into something of a wild goose chase that is undermined by subterfuge and double-dealing from the Afghans they petition for assistance. Here, too, their exploits mimic those of the United States and other European operatives, whose many errors precipitated the region's current volatility. Above all, Milton and Priscilla suffer from an inability to translate or otherwise interpret the diverse "intelligence" they accumulate. Without the capacity to navigate Afghanistan's confusing landscape or to decode the truth status of key facts pertaining to the Homebody, they are thrown into an informational vertigo analogous to the circumstances that confront all humanitarian missions, which are liable to being imperiled by the sheer challenge of verifying evidence on the ground. That said, the dramatic action of *Homebody/Kabul* gains its momentum, at times resembling a mystery, by staging the perplexity of its main characters. Milton and Priscilla project their disequilibrium onto their surroundings in a classically colonialist fashion, yet their confusion simultaneously inverts the power structures that ordinarily govern East–West relations. Here, too, eerily foretelling post-9/11 US involvement, Milton and Priscilla contend with not only a language barrier, as is highlighted throughout the script with its multiple languages, but also a dearth of sociocultural competence. Both such deficits are cast as conspicuous by-products of European self-enclosure.

Throughout, *Homebody/Kabul* dramatizes how language both facilitates and forecloses channels of communication. The play is preoccupied with languages and other systems for organizing and controlling information, as they work to both expedite and promote understanding. Milton is an expert in "network engineering." Mahala, a former librarian, is proficient in the Dewey Decimal System. And by no means last, Mahala nearly loses her life over Esperanto when Priscilla is duped into believing documents containing sensitive military intelligence to be poetry. In this case, Priscilla's credulity underscores the exorbitant stakes carried by language, while further creating a slippage between espionage and art. On one hand, the many languages that circulate throughout the play function as esoteric intelligence that erects impediments to cross-cultural dialogue. Much as language barriers frustrate Milton and Priscilla's pursuit of the Homebody, they allegorize comparable lapses that have foiled Western intervention in Afghanistan. At once, however, Kushner foregrounds the arbitrariness and ephemerality of the orders of knowledge and dominance that language administers. It is not accidental that both the Dewey Decimal System and Esperanto are basically obsolete. Beyond their constructed, non-organic statuses, they have each been superseded by newer regimes of communication—in which Milton, ironically, is fluent. That Priscilla is deceived by an artificial and passé idiom thereby captures the transience of the hierarchies legalized by any given language. And since it is the European characters who are hoodwinked due to their reliance on English, *Homebody/Kabul* might seem to forecast the waning of its hegemony.

On the other hand, the characters express high hopes for the capacity of language to usher in cosmopolitan ideals and solidarities. In turn, we might conclude that the play's meditations on language bear on the world's primary vocabulary for approaching social justice—namely, human rights. Milton, Mahala, and their Afghan guide Khwaja each gesture toward the universalizing designs inherent to the particular language they have mastered. Yet in doing so, they simultaneously acknowledge the colonizing logic of, as well as the disparities innate to, such ambitions. When Mahala characterizes the Dewey Decimal System as "one idea for the whole world," she aligns it with the goals of the "communists" and "Taliban."[36] As Mahala observes, even when supported by laudatory goals the pursuit of universal reference becomes totalitarian. Indeed, critics have censured human rights rhetoric in comparable terms, condemning humanitarian norms and practice alike for being merely the latest façade of imperialism, entrenching longstanding geopolitical exclusions. Along such lines, Khwaja acclaims the universalizing energies of Esperanto with a similarly utopian fervor. Describing it as "a mother tongue which draws from us our common humanity,"[37] he celebrates the ethical principles that language can harbor. For Khwaja, Esperanto is also distinctly itinerant—in his words, "homeless, stateless, a global refugee patois"[38]—and therefore cosmopolitan. Of course, the contradictions in Khwaja's romanticized vision of Esperanto emerge in the ends to which he conscripts it—that is, to smuggle military secrets that nearly bring about Mahala's death. Nonetheless, this outcome, too, captures why salutary principles will fail to prevent political discourse from serving inglorious causes. It is now a truism that precisely such tensions haunt human rights rhetoric; the enormous moral and political currency of rights talk is what leads to its enlistment in manifold kinds of wrong.

Last but by no means least, Milton's description of "network engineering" further indexes the many disparities authorized by language, even idioms that are ostensibly egalitarian. To explain his work to Mahala, he invokes an image of multicultural harmony, instructing her: "imagine a number of people in a darkened room—this is a metaphor, it's hard, very hard to find the right metaphor and I don't—at any rate, people in a darkened room, each has a torch, or a lantern, many different lanterns, each with a different colored flame."[39] Celebrating "many different lanterns," this vision valorizes both diversity and inclusiveness, explicitly attributing community to a multiplicity of "colored flames." For Milton, the constructed, artificial language of computing acquires universality precisely by exalting rather than erasing cultural and social variety. At the same time, however, Milton wrestles with the foreclosures inherent to his utopian longings. As he concedes: "It's an unforgiving place, science. If you don't speak its language it spits you out peremptorily."[40] Despite his optimism about the semiotics of computing, Milton acknowledges the privileges and exclusions that such a rarefied idiom will instate. Here again, if Milton's metaphor can be seen to pertain to the cosmopolitan underpinnings of human rights, Mahala's confusion points to the relative elitism of this expectation that their norms will transcend cultural particularities.

Much as Afghanistan has offered a theater for enforcing women's rights, women's freedoms have frequently provided a litmus test for evaluating the merit of multiculturalism as a political ideology. Multiculturalism is widely understood as a corollary to secular modernization, or as the only political framework that will allow diverse belief structures and worldviews to coexist, even while such inclusiveness may entail costs. Yet given that respect for cultural difference can indirectly work to apologize for a given group's mistreatment of women, critics have asked whether multiculturalism can be "bad for women."[41] For some, the fraught condition of women's rights within many societies exposes how as a normative principle it can sanction injustice. And since human rights statements in general protect cultural self-determination, their safeguards, too, become suspect, raising the question of whether certain human rights norms can paradoxically impinge on the freedoms of women. No doubt, while Milton applauds multiculturalism, he entertains that vision against the backdrop of the oppression of women under the Taliban, a contrast that in and of itself magnifies the limits of such an ethos.[42] The setting alone thus leads Kushner's characters' attraction to cosmopolitanism to appear blinkered and self-serving. We might therefore conceive of *Homebody/Kabul* as shedding light on the fault lines and contradictions within multiculturalism, which are brought into especially high relief when it comes to the protection of women.

Such quandaries about the relative meaning of women's agency and liberation are adjudicated over the course of *Homebody/Kabul*. With the Homebody, Priscilla, and Mahala, the play presents us with three models of female self-realization, as each character differently flouts liberal assumptions about women's emancipation. The dialogue amplifies the schisms between their competing perspectives by recurrently staging their incapacity to fully identify with one another's choices and values. Priscilla, most immediately, is an embodiment of what we might call "fourth-wave feminism," insofar as she disavows the label "feminism" while benefiting from advances in women's rights. Priscilla's conflicts with her mother enact such a generational divide, with Priscilla unable to comprehend her predecessors' struggles. Yet, liberal narratives of self-determination equally fail to resonate with her mother—meaning that the Homebody's crises also index the spent promises of the women's liberation movement. Visibly marked by her privilege, her possession of "too much liberty" is precisely what she experiences as oppressive. While we first encounter the Homebody symbolically and physically confined to the domestic, that condition is not socially enforced for her but instead a symptom of late imperial decadence. Ironically, a surfeit of freedom is what incites her reactionary decision to "go native," with all the problematic resonances of that term, rendering her an exemplar of a type of feminist backlash. The ambiguity of her fate queries whether the less equivocal norms of Afghan society offered a comforting alternative to the vagaries of her life in western Europe. And while such tensions may capture the inconsistent standards faced by her generation, the fact that Priscilla misreads her choices and condemns her for squandering those opportunities further elucidates the nature of their generational rift.

We might be tempted to read Priscilla's character, a woman in her early twenties, as a harbinger for the future of Western feminism; however, her conflicts, like her mother's, point to the deficiencies in the women's liberation movement. Priscilla, too, suffers the casualties of the ostensible freedoms claimed by her generation, as for instance exemplified in her choice to abort her child. Moreover, whereas her mother courts suicide by traveling alone to Kabul, Priscilla literally tried to kill herself, and multiple correspondences link these dual acts. While the Homebody self-medicates through antidepressants, Priscilla is nearly killed by an overdose of "many many many pills."[43] Similarly, much as the Homebody willingly secludes herself in her apartment, Priscilla is committed to an institution "with close solid walls" and a dearth of visitors, producing a loneliness that compels her to submit to "electroshock."[44] Insofar as these two characters embody broader social currents, their parallel fates register the ideological and political stalemate of women's liberation, interrogating the ideals that regulate liberal expectations about women's freedom. Both characters superficially possess freedom of choice and self-determination, yet their crises question whether those entitlements are burdensome and self-defeating, rather than cause for celebratory affirmation.

Furthermore, Priscilla is quick to compromise the tokens of her autonomy to fulfill wider goals, demonstrating the relativity of those standards. For example, when she prostitutes herself to Quango in exchange for Mahala's escape, she sacrifices her bodily integrity to achieve a larger good, although in a transaction that liberal definitions of selfhood would dismiss as exploitative and self-undermining. This tension highlights the circumstantial nature of corporeal self-possession as a measure for evaluating women's sociopolitical gains, seeing as, for Priscilla, it varies with context. Even if her bargain were purely consensual, it illustrates why calculations of self-determination will reductively neglect the complex ethical, emotional, and other factors that inform any given situation. In addition, the prioritization of autonomy within discussions of women's rights can serve to bolster the neoimperial myth of European cultural superiority, especially when it acts as a yardstick for proving the backwardness of certain cultures. As in post-9/11 interventions in Afghanistan, appeals to autonomy can levy that norm as a weapon rather than a shield, with the effect of legitimizing paternalistic structures of policing. Yet when autonomy is applied to scrutinize Western feminism's impossible demands, as for Priscilla, it looks increasingly like a double standard.

Thus representing a type of spokesperson for the many contradictions troubling Western feminism, Priscilla is constrained in her potential to understand the motives that guide not only her mother but also Mahala. Both Mahala and the Homebody adopt attitudes that liberal feminism would be quick to label either conservative or self-sabotaging, given that her mother converts and Mahala "becom[es] Muslim again" upon her arrival in London.[45] Priscilla struggles to comprehend these decisions, yet her incapacity to do so censures the ideological vantage that she inhabits for its impoverished explanatory arsenal. Priscilla lacks a nuanced analytic for deciphering and thereby authenticating such choices, and this failure of imagination registers a more totalizing descriptive paucity within Western feminism—a deficit that leads to the depreciation of cultural formations that do not verify a particular *Cosmopolitan*-style brand of women's liberation. Priscilla's inability to fathom the prospect that her mother might resist rescuing consequently marks a central lacuna within liberalism, showing how its focus on autonomy marshals a corresponding antipathy to social practices that derive from more complicated patterns of devotion and commitment. This privileging of notions of freedom over duty and obligation produces a unidimensional calculus that fails to comport with the social realities of many groups around the world, Northern and Southern.

The concluding scene of the play further probes such ambivalences through Mahala's character's espousal of the sort of belief structure that the logic of autonomous choice would write off as incoherent. Mahala welcomes her immigration to western Europe yet also holds that transition responsible for inciting her reconversion to Islam,[46] and she does not regard those two developments as incompatible. Instead, she configures religious devotion as a natural response to European society, a view that challenges the frequent equation of westernization and secularization. In turn, we must ask whether such a posture of commitment is held up within *Homebody/Kabul* as an antidote to the malaise rife within the late imperial center. Indeed, even Priscilla invokes the rhetoric of salvation and forgiveness in the play's concluding dialogue, seemingly also to compensate for the spiritual bankruptcy of her culture. As such, if both the fantasies attendant to armchair humanitarianism and a particular myth of liberal freedom represent dangerous decoys for Kushner's characters, it is not a stretch to decipher Mahala's rediscovered Islam as, albeit ironically, something of an ethical corrective.

Notes

1. Kushner, *Homebody/Kabul*, 5.
2. See Spurr, *The Rhetoric of Empire*.
3. See Anker, *Fictions of Dignity*, 35–46.
4. *Homebody/Kabul* was first staged and performed in New York City in December, 2001.
5. Kushner, *Homebody/Kabul*, 9.
6. Ibid.
7. Ibid., 16.
8. Ibid., 19.
9. Ibid., 26.
10. Ibid., 13.
11. Ibid., 11.
12. Ibid., 12.
13. Ibid., 10.
14. Ibid., 15.
15. Ibid., 11.
16. Ibid., 24.
17. Ibid.
18. Ibid., 21.
19. Ibid.
20. Ibid., 23.
21. Ibid., 23–24.
22. Ibid., 25.
23. McClintock, *Imperial Leather*, 22–24.
24. Kushner, *Homebody/Kabul*, 20.
25. Franco reads the play as staging a series of challenges for ethical recognition, which for Franco "recasts the question of responsibility." For instance, he argues that the "Homebody's journey points the way toward a different sort of

ethics, an acknowledgment of the precariousness of the other." *Race, Rights, and Recognition*, 159, 156.
26. Kushner, *Homebody/Kabul*, 17.
27. Matua, "Savages, Victims, and Saviors."
28. Kushner, *Homebody/Kabul*, 76.
29. Ibid., 136.
30. Ibid., 107.
31. For similar arguments about secularism, see Asad, *Formations of the Secular*; Hirschkind, *The Ethical Soundscape*; Mahmood, *The Politics of Piety*.
32. For such an argument about the nature of global capitalism broadly, see Cheah, *Inhuman Conditions*.
33. Kushner, *Homebody/Kabul*, 92.
34. Ibid., 65.
35. For such an argument about how idealized conceptions of corporeal dignity bolstered the national body politic in interwar France, see Dean, *The Frail Social Body*.
36. Kushner, *Homebody/Kabul*, 138.
37. Ibid., 58.
38. Ibid.
39. Ibid. 119.
40. Ibid., 120.
41. Susan Moller Okin's *Is Multiculturalism Bad for Women?* offers perhaps the best known statement of this debate surrounding cultural rights and women's freedoms.
42. We should further note that many histories of human rights plot their postwar ascendancy as something of a multicultural success story. See Glendon, "Propter Honoris Respectum."
43. Kushner, *Homebody/Kabul*, 63.
44. Ibid., 64.
45. Ibid., 137.
46. Ibid.

Chapter 12

Broadway without Borders: Eve Ensler, Lynn Nottage, and the Campaign to End Violence against Women in the Democratic Republic of Congo

Kerry Bystrom

On May 13, 2009, a select group of human rights activists spoke before the US Senate Foreign Relations Committee at a special hearing concerning violence against women in conflict zones, particularly in the Democratic Republic of Congo (DRC) and Sudan.[1] The guest speakers were Niemat Ahmadi, a women's rights activist and Save Darfur liaison from Sudan; Chouchou Namegabe Nabintu, a Congolese journalist who runs the South Kivu Women's Media Association; Robert Warwick, Executive Director of the Baltimore Office of the International Rescue Committee; John Prendergast, former member of Clinton's National Security Council and co-founder of the Enough Project; and feminist performance artist Eve Ensler. Ensler in fact set the stage for the other witnesses by opening the "outside expert" portion of the hearing with a graphic testimony of the atrocities inflicted on women in the DRC: "What I have witnessed in the DRC, frankly, has shattered and changed me forever. I will never be the same. I hope none of us will ever be the same. I think of Beatrice, who was shot in the vagina and now has tubes instead of organs; Honorata, who was raped by gangs as she was tied upside down on a wheel; Sowadi, who was raped and raped, and forced to eat dead babies."[2] The playwright here uses her voice to force participants and spectators to call to mind the absent bodies whose experiences are, presumably, the *raison d'être* of the hearing. This strategy was repeated at the close of the hearing, curiously by another performance artist, when attendees were invited to a special reception featuring African American playwright Lynn Nottage and actress Quincy Tyler Bernstine. At this reception, Bernstine performed a monologue about the experience of rape from Nottage's play *Ruined* (prem. 2008/ pub. 2009).[3]

There is much that could be said about the hearing as a whole, or even the small snippet of Ensler's testimony that I have reproduced here. As a site of convergence of aesthetics and activism, of testimony, spectatorship, and legislation, the hearing speaks to the inherently theatrical nature of human rights and humanitarian advocacy campaigns—even, and perhaps especially importantly, at the moment that advocacy is being translated into policy. This theatricality has recently become an object of sustained study in the work of performance scholars.[4] However, before reading this hearing as performance, a task I will return to briefly at the end of this chapter, it seems necessary to ask what these playwrights are doing at a Congressional hearing to begin with. Individuals such as Nabintu, a Congolese human rights activist and first-hand witness to the abuses, as well as representatives from established NGOs such as the International Rescue Committee, are expected in the cast of characters. But how did Ensler and Nottage become central figures in the campaign to stop sexual violence against women in the DRC? Since the answer to this question lies largely in the success of specific plays that these artists devised, it also raises the issue of the relation between more traditional theater, human rights, and humanitarianism.[5] This is the issue that I will focus on below.

In this chapter, I will examine how Ensler and Nottage use specific plays, and the publicity surrounding them, to intervene in and configure North American debates about the conflict in the DRC.[6] Both Ensler and Nottage aim to raise awareness about the situation of women in the war in particular and to inspire activism to stop gender-based violence. While they are not exactly representative of the Broadway invoked in my title, their work has achieved a popularity that allows them to reach wide and varied audiences. I am interested in tracing how Ensler and Nottage diverge in their approaches to these audiences, and what the effects of these divergences might be. I am also interested in interrogating the meaning of the sites of convergence of their work. As we will see, Ensler opts to foreground the spectacular physical suffering of the women of the DRC, in an effort to shame or shock Western spectators into action, while Nottage focuses on building affective and empathetic connections between audience members and rape survivors. Where they overlap is in structuring their performances around the specific medical condition of traumatic fistula—a condition that results when the wall between the vagina and the urinal or fecal tract is broken by mass rape or other forms of wounding (with sticks, broken bottles, guns, etc.). Why this would be the case, and what the implications of this choice might be, are among the puzzles that I hope to unravel.

Humanitarian Campaigns and Wounded Bodies

Life in the DRC has been marked by violence for well over a century. The atrocities perpetrated by King Leopold II of Belgium in his Congo Free State (1885–1908) are widely known.[7] After becoming a Belgian colony in 1908, the region was subjected to arguably more humane methods of economic and political exploitation that nonetheless took an enormous human toll. The relief promised by independence in 1960 was undercut by the assassination of Patrice Lumumba and the seizure of power by Joseph Mobutu, who installed himself as dictator, renamed the country Zaire, and relied on the repressive apparatus of the state to maintain power even as he siphoned enormous sums of state money into his own coffers. Mobutu ruled for decades, in part because his anti-Communist policy guaranteed Western backing; it was only in 1997 that post–Cold War geopolitics, combined with the influx of Rwandan refugees after the 1994 genocide and the ongoing struggle of internal resistance movements, prompted his fall from power. The next ruler, Laurent Kabila, then allowed the newly renamed Democratic Republic of Congo to explode into a conflict that has been termed "Africa's first world war," supported by Rwanda and Uganda on the one hand, and Angola, Namibia, and Zimbabwe on the other. This war lasted from 1998 to 2003. The 2003 peace agreement was followed in 2006 by the first democratic elections in over 40 years, won by Laurent Kabila's son Joseph. However, fighting has not ceased, especially in the eastern section of the country. Local and international actors keen on possessing the region's diamonds and minerals (such as niobium and coltan) support the continuation of armed conflict.[8]

Throughout this period, various humanitarian campaigns based in Europe and North America have arisen. First and foremost among them is the campaign mounted by E. D. Morel and the Congo Reform Association (CRA), an organization formed by Morel in 1904 to halt the abuse of workers and other civilians by Leopold and his concession companies.[9] The numerous reports published from the 1890s onward in Morel's newspaper *The West African Mail*, as well as widely circulated books such as his *Red Rubber* (1906), were instrumental in bringing the rubber-related atrocities to the attention of British and North American publics. Such activism intersected with the work of Morel's friend Roger Casement, author of an influential report about the Congo commissioned by the British Parliament in 1903.[10] Casement's report, published in 1904, traces his journey through the Upper Congo Basin and contains first-hand accounts of the cruelty of company officials and sentries as well as interviews with local missionaries and native Congolese people protesting mistreatment including forced labor, hostage-taking, and wounding in the form of the cutting off of hands.[11] His findings were corroborated by many others including Morel, who marshals stories by officers, merchants, and missionaries to define the situation in the Congo Free State as a "rubber slave trade."[12]

Along with narratives that describe the violence of Leopold's henchmen, both Morel and Casement relied upon what Nancy Rose Hunt, citing Roland

Barthes, calls "shock-images."[13] These were deployed to "produce revulsion and pity and to generate humanitarian funds."[14] One key example is that of Alice Harris's documentary photographs from the Congo Free State, which were used to illustrate Casement's report and *Red Rubber*. Missionaries and activists associated with the CRA also put on magic lantern shows with these images at sites across Europe and North America, with Harris and her husband themselves giving over 300 such lectures in the first year of the CRA's work.[15] The subject of the photographs varies, but—not surprisingly, as severed hands became "emblematic" of the horrors of the Congo Free State more generally—the most frequently reproduced were those of children with mutilated limbs, and particularly with missing hands.[16] As Sharon Sliwinski documents, these photographs played a critical role in creating an international outcry against Leopold's regime. In doing so, however, they also positioned the Congolese as brutalized and "undifferentiated" victims, dependent on the goodwill of more enlightened Europeans to protect them.[17] The images thus "raise awareness" of European savagery in a manner that resonates with imperial Western preconceptions, and feeds into the very structures of perception and representation that enabled the initial wounding of African bodies.[18]

The chopping off of hands has not been a common practice in the DRC since the time of Leopold, but its image seems to linger in local and global consciousness. Hunt recounts the reaction of one Congolese woman to the 2006 indictment of soldiers charged with war crimes; she proclaimed that, as punishment, government officials "should cut off their hands." This comment, according to Hunt, suggests that the Harris mutilation photographs remain as the "psychic and visual ruins" from the colonial period that mold the way information about more recent violence is understood.[19] Further, Hunt argues that these early and iconic depictions of mutilated limbs on the visual register historically displaced violence more easily described or accessed on other sensory registers, such as sexual abuse.[20] While sexual abuse was known to have occurred in the Congo during Leopold's reign, this crime was not addressed in the magic lantern shows that traveled through Europe and North America.[21] A similar displacement can be seen in the international media coverage of the war in the DRC. In the past decade much attention was paid to conflicts in Liberia and Sierra Leone, in part due to the gruesome yet historically familiar images of mutilation—the chopping off of hands, lips, and other body parts—that accompanied these conflicts. Yet despite its staggering casualty count of over five million victims, the war in the Congo remains largely absent from international public debates.[22] Such examples show how, as Ngwarsungi Chiwengo argues, certain "hegemonic narratives" of human rights abuses work to "silence counternarratives of violence such as those of rape of Congolese women."[23]

These dynamics of displacement have undergone complex transformation in the last few years, alongside the development of a new humanitarian campaign: the campaign to end sexual violence against women in the DRC. Miriam Ticktin[24] has traced the way gender-based violence emerged internationally as a central human rights issue in the 1990s. The work of international institutions and NGOs in the DRC falls in line with this general pattern; the early 2000s saw UN investigations into the situation of women in the Congo (2001), the release of the Human Rights Watch Reports *The War within The War: Sexual Violence against Women and Girls in the Eastern Congo* (2002) and *Seeking Justice: The Prosecution of Sexual Violence in the Congo War* (2005), and exposure of the mass rape of about 200 women and girls in the village of Nsongo Mboyo in December 2003. This latter incident resulted in the historic but ultimately largely ineffectual legal trials in 2006.[25] Building on this work, and since 2006 in particular, a larger if loose coalition of international activists have positioned rape as "the" symbol of the violence in the DRC, highlighting this crime to draw the attention of Europe as well as that of the North American public and the US government to the war in the Congo.[26]

As this campaign to end violence against women in the DRC develops, it has come to reflect the increasing "medicalization" of humanitarianism in general, and gender-based violence in particular, also charted by Ticktin.[27] As Ticktin points out, after "becoming consolidated as a legal category through the language of human rights," violence against women was transformed into "the poster-child for humanitarian aid" within the "medical humanitarian portfolio."[28] In the DRC, this medicalization centers on the condition of traumatic fistula.[29] The condition is foregrounded in documentary films such as the UNFPA's *Les âmes brisées* (2006); Lisa Jackson's *The Greatest Silence* (2007); Scott Blanding, Greg Heller, and Brad Labriola's *Women in War Zones* (2009); and Bent-Jurgen Perlmutt's *Lumo* (2009), as well as in the media blitz orchestrated by Ensler since 2007. The dissemination of what we might call "shock stories"—although rarely "shock photos"—of rape symbolized by vaginal wounding brings to mind the specter of the mutilation of hands, and suggests what Hunt refers to as "repetition and difference" in representational paradigms employed in the West for "helping" African "victims" of violence.[30] While on one level the focus on traumatic fistula may be read as an ingenious way to make rape "visible," to give it the weight and heft so often denied to it, it also may replicate the violence done to African subjects by earlier representations of their wounds.[31] As we will see, stories of traumatic fistula can be understood to circulate in ways similar to Harris's atrocity photographs, with all of the pitfalls they entail.

Baptized

Ensler's contributions to the campaign to end sexual violence in the DRC can only be understood in the context of her own performance history and her NGO V-Day. She became famous—or infamous, depending on one's feminist circles—for her one-woman show *The Vagina Monologues* (prem. 1996/ pub. 2001). This play stitches together commentary by Ensler about the continuing oppression of women with facts about the vagina and the violence to which it is subjected, as well as a series of short monologues based on or inspired by interviews that Ensler completed with over 200 women. In its published form, her Obie Award-winning script begins with a monologue that lays out the many reasons why Ensler is "worried about vaginas" and ends with a monologue about her experience witnessing the birth of her grandchild, which unfolds the similarities between the vagina and the heart. The pieces in-between range from the narrative of an American woman who locates her clitoris for the first time during a group workshop to the story of a female sex worker and a fragmented testimonial based on the story of a female Bosnian rape camp survivor and dedicated to the women of Bosnia and Kosovo.[32]

While always intended to raise consciousness about gender-based oppression, the show was not initially conceived of as the central node in a global web of activism that it would later become; Ensler reports that it was the surprising response of spectators to *The Vagina Monologues*, which included many women spontaneously sharing their personal stories of sexual abuse, that prompted her to create an organization that would work in tandem with *The Vagina Monologues* to "end violence against women."[33] The result was "V-Day," an NGO founded in 1998. As Nicole Lewis explains, V-Day raises money from individual donors and from performances of the play—there are specific benefit events, 5% of the royalties from *The Vagina Monologues* go to V-Day, and a surcharge is levied on tickets for general commercial performances. This money is then awarded to groups doing grassroots work preventing rape and other forms of physical violence against women.[34]

Beginning in 2002, V-Day decided to "spotlight" one particular group of women per year, making them the central issue for both awareness and fund raising. The V-Day spotlight settled in 2009 on "Women and Girls of the Democratic Republic of Congo."[35] The campaign, built around the focus "Stop Raping Our Greatest Resource: Power to the Women and Girls of the Democratic Republic of Congo," continues through 2010 and may continue until 2013.[36] Ensler's interest in this particular topic began with an interview that she had with Dr. Dénis Mukwege, a Congolese surgeon who has dedicated his career to repairing traumatic fistulas, in New York in December 2006. After visiting Mukwege at Panzi Hospital in Bukavu in 2007, she started working with UNICEF to develop a public campaign that is multifaceted and transnational in scope, and includes tactics that range from publishing articles in *Glamour* magazine to organizing "Breaking the Silence" events in the DRC in which Congolese women publicly narrate their stories and building a community for rape survivors called (infelicitously, perhaps) the "City of Joy."[37] Within the United States, "Stop Raping Our Greatest Resource" has at its core the yearly commercial, college, and community performances of *The Vagina Monologues*. It is this element that I will examine here, not only because it is the symbolic center of the campaign, but also because it reveals the outlines and closures of Ensler's particular configuration of the conflict in the Congo.

Generally speaking, the 2009 performances of *The Vagina Monologues* spotlighting the DRC follow a script nearly identical to the 2001 published version described above, but end with either an additional "Spotlight Monologue" or an additional "Spotlight Video."[38] In the first case, after the monologue that depicts Ensler's experience watching her daughter-in-law give birth, and seeing her vagina become a "wide pulsing heart...capable of sacrifice...able to forgive and repair...to bleed and bleed us into this difficult, wondrous world," the monologue "Baptized" is performed.[39] "Baptized" is also written from what is ostensibly Ensler's point of view, and depicts an encounter she had with a rape victim in the DRC. With a reminder that, coming after a long series of graphic testimonials, the monologue may seem less stark than it does on its own, I quote it in its entirety:

> Look out your window/ The dead lie everywhere/ Think of your luxuries as corpses/ Count the bodies/ 30 hacked children for Jed's new playstation/ 20 tortured women so you can SMS photos from a party/ 50 amputated men, waving their missing hands as your sweet Andrew/ mindlessly bounces his rubber ball/ I held an eight year old girl in my lap/ Who had been raped by so many men/ She had an extra hole inside her/ When she accidentally peed on me/ I was baptized/ It isn't over there/ The Congo/ It's inside everything you touch and do/ Or do not do.[40]

At the risk of stating the obvious, in this dramatic rendering of Ensler's visit to a Congolese girl suffering from traumatic fistula, a few things stand out. The first is the assertion of Western complicity in violence, a complicity mediated through consumption. "Think of your luxuries as corpses": because their circuit boards and chips rely on coltan and cassiterite, minerals that are heavily mined in the DRC, our cell phones and our Sony Play-Stations are connected to the ongoing conflict. They are made of the bodies, in the same sense in which "red" rubber was said to contain the blood of Congolese workers in Morel's time. The second is the way in which a specific wound mediates the relationship between Westerner and Congolese native; the mutilated hands so often reproduced since the time of Leopold are here juxtaposed with and replaced by the "extra hole" in the eight-year-old girl's vagina, the sign of traumatic fistula. It is by and through this wound that Ensler, and the audience, by extension, can be "baptized." This term "baptized" is a third element to pause on. It evokes a second life, a rebirth into a community of faith—a community of feminist activists rather than the community of the Church. While the idea of fervent converts to human rights has a certain resonance, the Christian allusion here is disturbing, since it begs the question of what specifically we are to have faith in. Has the eight-year-old girl here become a sacrificial lamb cleansing the world of our sins of consumption? What are the ethics—and the effects—of turning her pain into a spectacle in this fashion?

Such questions also emerge from the Spotlight Video, which ends with a version of this monologue. The roughly six-minute video consists of three different "poems" written by Ensler that appear as white text on a black screen, interspersed with video footage shot by Ensler and still photographs of a trip to the Congo in 2008. The first poem, "Beneath Her Pange," focuses on a town hall meeting of 250 female rape survivors. The silent footage that illustrates this poem was taken during the meeting and—as in the rest of the video—has a soundtrack of local music. The second poem, "Fistula," is about Ensler's experience watching a fistula operation and speculating on what prompts men to cause such injury. Much of the accompanying imagery depicts row after row of Congolese women in hospital beds. The third poem is the text of the monologue "Baptized." In between lines, images of women's faces and video footage of women giving testimony appears on the screen, but they remain silent behind the music. This silence is ambiguous. It may be a cue to recall the untranslatability of the traumatic event, reminding the viewer to avoid an easy identification with the suffering of the Congolese women. Yet the poetry can also be seen as a kind of "subtitling" that stands in for the original stories of pain, making the victim's own words unnecessary since Ensler's words subsume them.[41] A similar erasure happens as the aspects of the film meant to celebrate the power of activism are subverted by its focus on what James Dawes calls "document[ing] harm."[42] If the first piece depicts women transcending pain, the wound—the fistula—ultimately becomes the central bridge between the three poems and between the poems and the spectator. Particularly in the movement from "Fistula" to "Baptized," the wound becomes the "shock-story" through which any response—from pity to rebirth into a community of feminist activists—must be channeled.

The effects of this performance can be difficult to parse. Speaking of *The Vagina Monologues* in general, the play's capacity to raise money is not in dispute; and this is no small matter. However, its capacity to facilitate collective action to stop violence against women rather than to "merely" inspire donations may be subject to question. Shelly Scott applauds Ensler's success at creating a community of spectators within the audience, and generating an outflow of emotion and energy that makes spectators feel like they are at a party rather than a political performance. She queries, though, how this sense of celebration leads to political action.[43] Indeed, she suggests that the play is more about providing "catharsis" than leading to a "next step" of activism.[44] Christine M. Cooper takes up Scott's critique and develops it further. She describes the play's intended "political message" as follows: "we must hear each other's voices to understand each other, that understanding thus fueling anger, compassion, and a sense of shared mission to foster change."[45] As Cooper sees it, however, the play stops audience members from really hearing each other or generating an actually useful shared mission by promoting a falsely universal vision of womanhood, by privileging personal disclosure as the means to liberation, and by focusing attention entirely on sexualized violence. While activism beyond merely staging the play is unlikely to result, any "next-step" collective action that does emerge would be pointed in the wrong direction.[46]

These concerns become even more pressing when we move the frame from stopping violence against women in general to the specific context of the "Stop Raping Our Greatest Resource" campaign. Ensler certainly attempts to force spectators in the United States to confront the situation in the DRC. She does this through shock stories—monologues or poems that create a verbal snapshot of extreme violence—that make the suffering of these women visible. In order to counter the distancing effect that might result from the graphic nature of these "snapshots," she places the story of women of the DRC in the context of other stories of women that would be more familiar, and constructs a continuum or web of social and physical violence against women that begins at home and stretches around the globe. Further, in the short space of time dedicated to the DRC through the Spotlight Monologue or the Spotlight Video, the performance helps the audience access the issue by narrating the plight of these women through the perspective of Ensler, whose "ethnographic voice" (to borrow a term used by Scott[47]) signals her self-consciousness as an observer and consolidates her status as a focalizer. This positioning seems designed to inculcate a sense of engagement in the spectator. If, as Kay Schaffer and Sidonie Smith[48] and Meg McLagan[49] have argued, personal testimony has become the key narrative and visual genre for making rights claims, then Ensler here serves as a proxy for the women of the DRC and offers her testimony as a way to precipitate what Schaffer and Smith term the "ethics of recognition."[50] Once they have recognized Ensler's witness, spectators may be motivated to go to the V-Day website to learn, and do, more.

There are, though, limitations to this strategy. It seems important (if not surprising from the creator of *The Vagina Monologues*) that women are called upon to relate to other women through their vaginas, and the actual or potential harm done to their vaginas; men are asked to connect through their concern for the vagina. In each case, women are reduced to their vaginas. As an older American character announces at the end of one of the monologues: "my vagina, my vagina, me."[51] This clearly repeats the historical reduction of women to their sexual organs at the heart of Western patriarchal institutions.[52] Further, in the Spotlight Monologue or Video, what is reinscribed is not only sexism but also the racism that underlies Western imperialism. Here, we have a white woman usurping the voice of black African women and turning them into vaginas, and damaged vaginas at that. Whether these vaginas are objects of repression or salvage, they remain objects.[53] It is this kind of rhetorical strategy that leads Wendy Hesford to label Ensler as a "feminist cosmopolitan" rather than a "transnational feminist"—the former means an activist who spectacularizes and sentimentalizes the suffering of marginalized women in such a way that their stories merely facilitate the "personal liberation" of Western audiences, and the latter means someone who creates real links by drawing attention to unequal conditions structuring the relationship between various female populations.[54] Such a strategy not only re-entrenches racial and gender stereotypes, but also eclipses other possible forms of representing the conflict in the DRC.[55]

This reduction of African women to damaged vaginas may have further practical negative consequences. It takes the focus away from the kinds of violence against women that are not sexualized, drawing attention away from a whole range of other hardships created by the war.[56] It also feeds into the medical humanitarian narrative in problematic ways. As referred to above, Ticktin[57] argues that the dominant imaginary of humanitarian action has become linked to disease or injury and its treatment. In the specific case of the DRC, the injury seems to be the traumatic fistula. The treatment is corrective surgery. This formulation of the "problem" and its "solution" implies that what is needed is more doctors and delivery of healthcare. Without downplaying the obvious fact that doctors would be very helpful for the affected women, one might note that this medical narrative of the conflict in the DRC may eclipse the larger, and deep-seated, political and economic conditions that allow rape to happen in the first place. At the same time, it may convert women into subjects that, even when their vaginas are surgically "rescued," are incapacitated as citizens and circumscribed to a limited definition of the human.[58]

In an important move, the monologue "Baptized" balances this powerful medical narrative by explicitly calling for a reformation of consumer practices rather than importing doctors to the DRC. For those familiar with the geopolitics of the Great Lakes region and its connections to Western economies, the links between Congolese minerals and American cell phones are quite clear, and create a different activist schema. The "problem" in this version is conflict minerals, and the "solution" is to stop buying goods made with such minerals. The figure of the commodity made of dead bodies fuses the suffering of Congolese people with North American daily habits. Yet—while acknowledging Ensler's step beyond the "suffering victim" paradigm associated with "shock stories" traumatic fistula—we might still want to ask to what extent the average Western spectator is in the position to unpack this figure. The monologue after all does not explain how these things are connected. Will spectators process it as just another attempt to cultivate white liberal guilt for having things while African people do not, in an echo of the childhood admonition to clean our plates because people in Ethiopia are starving?[59] Further, even if the links between people, minerals, and commodities are made, will consumption patterns actually change as a result?[60] Finally, if so—and this is a serious question—is altering consumer demand an adequate response to the underlying structural conditions causing the crisis in the DRC? Is a community of "compassionate shoppers" the community of activists we want to be "baptized" into?

An African Mother Courage?

If Ensler's recent attention to the women of the DRC is one aspect of her larger mission to end violence against women globally, it can only be understood in the context of her long-running piece *The Vagina Monologues* and its companion NGO V-Day. However, Nottage "spotlights" the women of the DRC in a more traditional way. That is, she writes a contextually specific and largely self-contained piece of dramatic literature. Nottage, a former employee of Amnesty International, is a widely respected feminist playwright whose plays—including *Intimate Appeal* (2003) and *Fabulations, or The Re-education of Undine* (2006)—are focused on the themes of recovering silenced voices and representing the processes of black women's self-definition.[61] She became interested in the issue of sexual violence in the DRC in 2004. The playwright originally planned to draw international attention to this problem, which was still largely absent at that time from media debates, by staging a production of Brecht's *Mother Courage and her Children* set in the DRC.[62] After Nottage and director Kate Whoriskey went in 2004 and 2005 to visit refugee camps in Uganda that shelter a number of Congolese survivors of sexual violence, however, she decided to do a looser riff on Brecht's classic play.[63] The resulting piece, entitled *Ruined*, swept major drama awards in 2009—winning the Drama Desk Award, the Obie Award, and the Pulitzer Prize, among others. It played to sold-out theaters in Chicago and New York, and has generated continuing attention from diplomats and politicians.[64]

Nottage's play is set in the middle of the war in the Ituri forest of the Northeastern DRC, a tropical mining region near the Ugandan border. The region is the object of dispute between Government and Rebel soldiers, each claiming to be on the side of "the people" and forced into brutality only by the horrific actions of the other side. The audience learns about the war from exchanges that take place within a bar and brothel owned by Mama Nadi, the protagonist of the drama and Nottage's Mother Courage. Mama Nadi is a consummate businesswoman. Having witnessed her family lose their farm to white Europeans, she does everything she can to make money to buy herself a piece of land. This commercial endeavor requires an attitude of cynical self-protection. As she tells Christian, the poet-professor-traveling-salesman who asks her to take in two young women: "I open my doors, and tomorrow I'm a refugee camp overrun by suffering. Everyone has their hand open since this damned war began. I can't do it."[65] When she is finally convinced to give the two women, Salima and Sophie, a job, she sets out a few ground rules: "If things are good, everyone gets a little. If things are bad, Mama eats first."[66]

Despite her attempts to remain closed-fisted and closed-hearted, however, Mama Nadi eventually finds herself torn between her lust for profit and her maternal affection for the "girls" she employs. These women are the other central characters in the play. One is Josephine, the daughter of a chief who was abandoned by her people, and who has been with Mama Nadi for some length of time. The other two are Sophie and Salima, brought to Mama Nadi by Christian. Salima was captured and made into a sexual slave to a local Mayi-Mayi rebel group. After she escapes and returns to her village, she is rejected by her husband and the rest of her family because she was "made poison by their fingers."[67] Sophie, who is Christian's niece, has also been gang-raped and, as a result, is "ruined"[68]—a term that, along with serving as the densely metaphoric title of the play, is a euphemism for suffering from traumatic fistula.

Ruined follows the characters through various stages of the war, as first one side and then the other appears to be winning. Mama Nadi steadfastly refuses to take sides, claiming: "My doors are open to everybody."[69] Her refusal to take a political side or a moral stance in the conflict in order to guarantee a steady income finally backfires when Colonel Osembengo, the leader of the Government troops, is informed that she has been providing services to Jerome Kisembe, his counterpart among the Rebels. Osembengo's destruction of the bar and the murder of everyone within its walls is halted only by the dramatic suicide of Salima, who kills herself in order to avoid further violation. Death is the only way that she, as a woman, can imagine finding freedom; as she exclaims to everyone in the bar in one of the play's few overtly moralistic moments, "You will not fight your battles on my body any more."[70] This suicide is followed by an equally melodramatic *denouement*. Christian returns to profess his love for Mama Nadi and to give her a chance to begin a new life with him. Mama Nadi eventually reveals why it is that she has rejected him all along. She, like Sophie, is "ruined."[71] After confessing this secret, Mama Nadi gathers the courage to join Christian in the dance that he has asked her for since the first scene. The curtain falls on Josephine and Sophie watching and cheering.

Ruined, as summarized here, makes some clear interventions into hegemonic representations of rape in the DRC. Most importantly, it diverges from the reliance on the disruptive "shock stories" seen in Ensler's work. While some of the descriptions of violence, such as Christian's reports of the massacre of civilians by child soldiers, are overwhelming both to the characters on stage and to the audience, they do often balance graphic physical imagery with attention to other details. Salima's testimonial monologue can be read in this light. The character takes great pain to set the scene in which she is first violated and her small baby Beatrice was murdered:

> I was working in our garden picking the last of the sweet tomatoes... The sun was about to crest, but I had another hour before it got too hot. It was such a clear and open sky. This splendid bird, a peacock, had come into the garden to taunt me, and was showing off its feathers. I stooped down and called to the bird, "Wssht, Wssht." And I felt a shadow cut across my back.[72]

The shadow is that of her assailants, whose actions she describes simply as the feeling of one heavy boot on her chest as "the others... 'took' [her]."[73] The death of her child under the same soldier's boot is described with equal economy of words. While Salima's testimony reveals the horror of the acts she experiences and witnesses, it does so without arresting attention on the fact of exceptional physical violence, by gesturing to the network of everyday relationships and practices that this violence ripped her from and by revealing the psychological afterlife of this experience. Further, and even more importantly, this testimony forms a small part of a hundred-page script or three-hour performance. Over the course of the play, women are presented not only as victims but also as nurturers, as devoted lovers and the object of devotion, and as strong leaders able to hold together a community. *Ruined*'s portrayal of women as survivors rather than victims is further enhanced by the comedic elements of the play, which balance out the pathos of moments like Salima's testimony.

The overall result is that Congolese women are portrayed not as brutalized or wounded objects reducible to traumatic fistula, but as individuals that witness and experience violence and are finding ways to fold this fact into rich lives that extend beyond the moment of victimization and to support each other in this process. They become three-dimensional subjects that spectators can feel for and identify with. Nottage describes her own feeling of connection to the women about whom she wrote the play when she points to a photograph of her and the women that she interviewed in Uganda, and claims: "I can't pick myself out in the picture."[74] While this is a strange authorial fantasy, given the asymmetry of experience between African Americans and Central African women who have lived through years of armed conflict, US audiences not able to travel to Uganda or the Congo are offered the possibility to have similar moments of intense identification with Congolese women through the medium of actors who are speaking what is at least in part the original testimony of people interviewed by Nottage in Uganda. As it offers this experience, the play opens space for reshaping conceptions of the crisis beyond representations of women as suffering victims. This makes it fall much further toward a productive "transnational feminism" than a reductive "feminist cosmopolitanism" on the "continuum" set out by Hesford.[75] Returning to Schaffer and Smith's concept of the ethics of recognition, one might say that the play's portrayal of the lives of Mama Nadi, Josephine, Salima, and Sophie, which represents as well as repeats in part the testimony given by the victims themselves, creates the ground for an affective connection that is the precondition of a substantive and ethical response from viewers.[76]

Nottage's call for emotional engagement is nowhere more evident than in the final scene of the play, in which Mama Nadi admits to her own "ruination" before accepting the love of Christian. Yet the very success of the ending in terms of triggering an affective response calls forth a new set of problems relating to the question of theater and activism, particularly when we read this scene in counterpoint with the ending of *Ruined*'s Brechtian original—a play designed to expose the entanglement of capitalism and war.[77] In *Mother Courage and Her Children*, the sacrifice of Kattrin, which Salima's suicide evokes, provides a dramatic climax that is undercut by the final scene, in which Mother Courage goes right back to her old ways. Contemplating life after the death of her daughter, the woman comforts herself by getting back into the harness of her cart. "Be all right," she tells herself: "Got to get back in business again."[78] Ronald Woodland argues that this ending is intended to alienate spectators from empathy, producing a distance between them and the characters that they witness on stage that allows for rational, critical reflection on the social and historical causes of the situation represented in the play.[79] This mirrors Brecht's own view that the provocation of emotion through thoroughgoing identification short-circuits critical engagement; the audience's absorption with the success or failure of the protagonist blinds it to ongoing structural problems and to its own participation in or complicity with these problems. Such concerns have been echoed by a newer generation of critical human rights scholars. Joseph R. Slaughter[80] and James Dawes[81] both suggest that the empathetic and cathartic narratives constructed by people purporting to "help" in the full implementation of human rights may actually have the opposite effect.

As a playwright contemplating adaptations of Brecht, Nottage is surely aware of the concerns raised by this theorist, and specifically rejects them. Her project is to elicit emotional connection rather than rational reflection.[82] In choosing to end with identification rather than estrangement, Nottage rightly calls for a reassessment of older visions of the relation between critique, emotion, and political action. At the same time, this choice means forgoing the possibility for deconstructive, gender-conscious, and materialist critique that scholars have located in Brecht's theatrical paradigm. Elin Diamond points to the ability of "estrangement effects" to destabilize hegemonic gazes and to dramatize the process of watching people and events as they are constructed through ideology.[83] Building on Diamond, Kim Solga suggests that *Mother Courage* allows this work of unmasking gendered ideology to be performed.[84] These openings are not taken by Nottage; the construction of the category of "African women" who play certain social roles within the global regime of free trade capitalism that enables and indeed promotes war in the Congo is not revealed but rather naturalized in the ending of *Ruined*. The channeling of sympathy to Mama Nadi in the final scene seems to shut down the kind of alienation that a radical project of exposure would depend on. It further undercuts the more general critique of capitalism and its relation to war that are mounted, at earlier moments in the play (such as when, unlike in Ensler's monologue, a character explains how coltan is related to cell phones[85]). One reading of *Ruined*'s melodramatic finale is that it transforms a complex story of violence perpetrated by multiple and interwoven local and global forces into the background for one woman's tale of redemption. The result for North American audiences, as Laura Edmondson argues, is that of "discourag[ing] activism."[86]

This de-historicizing and disabling ending is foreshadowed earlier in the piece by its depiction of the different forces fighting for control of Ituri. The play gestures toward the colonial history of the Congo as well as the more recent transnational economic and political context of the war. However, the way in which it represents the leaders of the conflict as interchangeable brutes—particularly as the play was staged at the Manhattan Theatre Club, when the same actors play soldiers on each side—suggests that the overarching narrative best suited for understanding the violence in the DRC is that of inexplicable "chaos." This "chaos narrative" is familiar to global readers and spectators of Africa; the only answer to it, suggests Michael Ignatieff in a critique of contemporary understandings of global obligation, is humanitarian rescue.[87] By reiterating it, purposefully or not, *Ruined* may obscure a deeper understanding of the lines of accountability and responsibility that tie together Congolese women in a brothel in Ituri, soldiers on both sides of the war from the Congo and other countries in Africa, UN workers, Sony, GATT, the US government, and, indeed, American citizens watching *Ruined*. Without making these connections clearer, and especially given its title, the play risks becoming—if one may say this—just another exposé of mass rape in the DRC seen through the lens of traumatic fistula.

From Broadway to Capitol Hill

Ensler and Nottage's pieces are not performances that exist in a vacuum, but are inspired by earlier humanitarian campaigns and interconnect with other contemporary efforts to end sexual violence in the DRC. In some sense, it is the publicity created by their performances, rather than the performances themselves, that allows the two playwrights to have a strong voice in relation to this issue. The critical and media attention surrounding the V-Day Spotlight performances of *The Vagina Monologues* as well as *Ruined* give their creators authority and legitimacy to appear in front of very different audiences or publics in very different spaces, from local communities in the DRC to members of Congress on Capitol Hill. This circulation in turn opens up opportunities for these artists to strategically craft their message and performance strategies for different audiences.[88] Their various theatrical and more directly political performances then link up with a broad range of documentary films, news reports, protests, and other modes of drawing attention to the war in the DRC, forming what Schaffer and Smith call a "meshwork" of advocacy.[89]

For all the actual and potential diversity of forms of advocacy, however, certain strategies seem to repeat in, and thread together, different kinds of performances within the meshwork created by activists around the DRC. This can be understood if we turn again to the Senate Foreign Relations Committee hearing with which I opened this chapter. The hearing, co-chaired by Senators Russell Feingold and Barbara Boxer, proceeded in two parts. The first was moderated by Feingold and featured a technical report by US diplomats and officials from the State Department. The second—which clearly stole the show—was moderated by Boxer and presented the nongovernmental expert witnesses. As noted above, Ensler was the first to speak in this second panel, and her testimony strikes a very similar tone to "Baptized." She includes a number of policy suggestions that do not appear in her theatrical performances, including training female police officers, pushing for a firmer stance on Rwanda and Uganda's involvement in the war, and involving local Congolese women in all negotiations. But she designs her speech to provoke horror at the physical violence done to women, by telling the stories described earlier along with that of the traumatic fistula suffered by eight-year-old Noella, a girl "so young, she didn't even know what a penis was" who now "urinates and defecates on herself and lives a life of humiliation."[90] This strategy is echoed again and again throughout the hearing. Nabintu tells the story of a mother forced to eat the flesh of her own children, and women raped by soldiers who then poured gasoline in their vaginas and set them on fire—a story which led to audible gasps from the audience and Nabintu herself to break down in tears.[91] Boxer herself recounts Associated Press reports of the rape of an 11-month-old baby and the destruction of the vagina of a 12-year-old girl, in order to convince her spectators of the "urgency" of the situation in the DRC.[92]

Indeed, that Ensler followed the strategy of telling shock stories to evoke an urgent response of the audience is an apt description of the way the session as a whole was designed. As a politician keenly aware of the "short attention span" of her multiple audiences, Boxer relies upon narratives of wounding to keep the attention of spectators of the hearing, even as she reminds them all of the necessity to make the US public "focus, focus, focus" on this issue.[93] Paired with these shock stories are assertions of emotive response, such as the example of Ensler's "passionate" advocacy for the women of the DRC and Boxer's own sense of "shame" that leads her to pledge that "just me, just this voice, is going to be heard."[94] This framing sets up the problem in the DRC as a lack of horror and a related deficit of caring. The message to the various publics addressed seems to be that if we felt bad enough, if we cared enough, we would solve the problem. This imperative to care for wounded bodies, built as it is around the performance of shock stories of traumatic fistula and forced cannibalism, may not only be seen to participate inadvertently in the ongoing victimization of Congolese women, but also to prioritize short-term solutions. In this case, these solutions may not ultimately solve the problem Boxer, Ensler, and others so passionately want us to address, although they come to overshadow other options articulated in the hearing.

The following exchange, between John Prendergast and Boxer, illustrates this dynamic. Prendergrast is the last expert witness to speak, coming after Ensler, Ahmadi, Nabintu, and Warwick, and he tries to move beyond a consideration of the symptoms of the wars in the DRC and Sudan to action that will end the wars themselves. He argues that: "When we refocus our policy on dealing with the root causes of these wars, we will save literally—it's no exaggeration—literally billions of dollars and hundreds of thousands of lives. That, Senators, is the best way to protect women and girls in the Congo and Sudan in the long run, by ending the world's two deadliest wars."[95] Boxer responds by acknowledging the value of what Prendergast has said, but nevertheless reiterating her focus on immediate response to wounded women. "You've really taken our breath away with your explanation of the problem, and what is happening on the ground is just too hard to listen to," she notes, adding: "What I'm going to do myself, because I've got other incredible people [Senators Feingold, Durbin and Brownback] to lead in these other areas [minerals and boycotting], supporting them, I want to focus on making things better for women now, so I'm going to focus on that."⁹⁶ She continues:

> And John, you're totally right. That is an outflow of these wars, but until you guys have figured it out, we women, I think, are going to start stepping up to call attention to this... So the things I am trying to get at is what we can do right now...
>
> Now, the first thing we can do is shine the light, and so what we are going to do now is send a follow up letter to our great new President and our great new Secretary of State... What are the things I should put in the letter? Here are the things I am planning on putting in the letter. First, we need to get more doctors out there... We want to get more doctors out there. These are things I picked up. We want a special person... who focuses on violence against women and publishes what is going on, and kind of outs these countries for what's going on there to put the shame of public opinion on them... [we] need to get more women involved in the security, in the police force, in the UN peacekeepers... [and] more aid to organizations.⁹⁷

It would be too easy to fault Boxer for wanting to ignore—though agreeing with, "a thousand percent"—Prendergast's assessment, and reiterating as policy initiatives to move forward to President Obama and Secretary Clinton what she "picked up" about the need for doctors, policewomen, a UN Special Rapporteur, and more aid to humanitarian NGOs. As the many emotional speeches suggest, what has happened to victims of rape in the DRC is an atrocity that demands an immediate response, and space must be carved out and protected for dealing with the needs of these victims. Increased medical capacity, whether this comes through importing or training doctors in traumatic fistula operations and other forms of surgery, can help victims in a way that lengthy deliberations over trade regimes, debt relief, and institutional reforms cannot. At the same time, this singular focus on the urgent situation of women, and women suffering from traumatic fistula specifically, has its dangers—it might be read as a publicity strategy designed as much to draw attention to Boxer herself as to the women of the DRC, and one that may in the end lead to increased rather than decreased suffering. For, if activists and lawmakers singularly focus on the narrow issue of traumatic fistula, or even on the larger issue of wartime violence against women, the armed conflict is left on its own to produce ever more victims.

With this last point, we arrive at the central dilemma of humanitarian work vis-à-vis human rights activism: the trade-off between immediate relief and long-term transformation. It seems to me that the challenge is not to resolve this dilemma—surely it is unresolvable, surely both are needed—but to recognize the way certain kinds of activist performances shape the horizon of possibilities for responding to the needs of others. While I have focused on Ensler's shock strategy in these last few paragraphs, Nottage in this case may not provide a better alternative. At the special reception following the hearing, she opens her comments by reiterating the equation between passion and shame set up earlier in the afternoon: "Thank you to all the panelists for speaking so passionately and directly to this issue. It's like 'shame on us' if we don't keep our eyes open to this issue."[98] Further, the scene of *Ruined* that she presents is Salima's testimonial monologue of rape. I suggested earlier that this monologue could be read to challenge the suffering victim paradigm; by foregrounding the destruction of Salima's marriage in particular, it gestures to the destruction of social relations as well as to the physical body that results from rape. Nevertheless, it remains the one piece of the script that comes closest to the typical shock stories employed by Ensler. This affinity is heightened when the monologue is separated from the contextualization of the rest of the play; all of which leads to the question of what a better alternative might be, and how to stage structural and material connections in the theater or the halls of Congress.

Acknowledgements

This work was presented in different forms in a working group for the 2009 ASTR convention in Puerto Rico and in a smaller faculty workshop at the University of Connecticut, Storrs in May 2010. I would like to thank the members of these workshops for their comments. Particular thanks are due to Florian Becker, Eleni Coundouriotis, Laura Edmondson, Allen Feldman, Paola Hernández, Wendy Hesford, Tom Keenan, Miriam Ticktin, and Brenda Werth.

Notes

1. The full transcript of the hearing, "Confronting Rape and Other Forms of Violence against Women in Conflict Zones; Spotlight: The Democratic Republic of Congo and Sudan" is available online at: http://foreign.senate.gov/hearings/2009/hrg090513p.html. The hearing was also recorded and is available at: http://foreign.senate.gov/hearings/hearing/20090513_3/
2. Ibid., 31.
3. On Nottage and Bernstine at the hearing, see Whoriskey, "Introduction," xiii and Healey, "Women of 'Ruined,'" *New York Times*, May 12, 2009. Footage of this presentation is available online at: http://www.youtube.com/watch?v=SsqyhiaacO8&feature=channel
4. Richard Schechner's classic *Essays on Performance Theory* lays the groundwork for this approach, which has been taken up for instance by Diana Taylor (*Disappearing Acts; The Archive and the Repertoire*) and the work done by her Hemispheric Institute for Performance and Politics as well as by Catherine Cole ("Performance, Transitional Justice and the Law")
5. While human rights and humanitarianism are often conflated in academic discussion, I follow Wilson and Brown ("Introduction," 209) in making the distinction between human rights as a political project based in legal empowerment and humanitarianism as relief work aimed at alleviating the suffering of others and reliant on emotional connection and senses of moral obligation.
6. Because my focus in this chapter is on the impact of humanitarian campaigns on Western audiences, I am not able to fully address the impact of the

activism of Ensler, Nottage, and others on local Congolese and wider African populations. This would be an important area for future research; see Edmondson ("Transnational narratives") for an example of this approach to Nottage's play *Ruined*.
7. See, for instance, Joseph Conrad's canonical *Heart of Darkness* and Adam Hochschild's popular history *King Leopold's Ghost*.
8. This short summary provides only the barest outline of this history; for more information, see Hochschild, *King Leopold's Ghost*, Nzongola-Ntalaja, *The Congo from Leopold to Kabila*, and Prunier, *Africa's World War*. For an accessible timeline of the DRC from Independence onward, see the BBC "Country Profile: The Democratic Republic of Congo," available on-line at: http://news.bbc.co.uk/2/hi/africa/country_profiles/1076399.stm
9. O'Siochain and O'Sullivan, *The Eyes of Another Race*, 26.
10. See Hochschild, *King Leopold's Ghost*, for a detailed account of Morel, Casement, and the CRA.
11. O'Siochain and O'Sullivan, *The Eyes of Another Race*.
12. Morel, *Red Rubber*, 39.
13. Hunt, "An Acoustic Register," 222.
14. Ibid., 238.
15. Sliwkinski, "The Childhood of Human Rights," 347.
16. O'Siochain and O'Sullivan argue that "[o]ne of the most notorious aspects of the Congo was the cutting off and smoking of hands, and stories, photographs and slides of such horrors gained almost mythic proportions in Britain... The mutilated arms, and the baskets of smoked hands became emblematic of all that was wrong with the Congo State, and continued to represent the worst symbol of the system which Casement and others hoped to replace" (*The Eyes of Another Race*, 37–38).
17. Sliwkinski, "The Childhood of Human Rights," 352–353; see also Hunt, "An Acoustic Register," 223.
18. As Allen Feldman ("Strange Fruit") argues in the context of colonialism, segregation and apartheid in South Africa, strategies of dehumanization including mutilation were used to transform black Africans into a "useful" labor force for the emerging capitalist regime. The strategies used to "authenticate" the suffering of black bodies for white publics—the public exposure of physical wounds—in order to inspire humanitarian action thus replicate the very strategies used to turn indigenous people into docile working bodies (Feldman, personal communication, May 2010).
19. Hunt, "An Acoustic Register," 221.
20. Ibid., 223.
21. Hunt finds evidence of sexual abuse both in pictures from the Morel collections that did not circulate with the lantern show, and in testimonies given at King Leopold's 1905–1906 Commission of Inquiry or collected in 1953 by Flemish missionary Edmond Boelaert ("Acoustic Register," 223–225 and 230). The forms of this abuse, including cutting open pregnant women's wombs, filling vaginas with clay and pushing sticks into vaginas, eerily prefigures the more grotesque forms of gender-based violence occurring in the DRC today ("Acoustic Register," 235–237). On a separate note, see Azoulay ("Has anyone ever seen a photograph of rape?") for a discussion of why rape seems to be so difficult to photograph, and what the implications of this constructed difficulty might be.

22. Chiwengo, "When Wounds and Corpses Fail to Speak"; Wilson and Brown, "Introduction," 19.
23. Chiwengo, "When Wounds and Corpses Fail to Speak," 80. While I have located this displacement in the imaging of violence and compared it to Liberia and Sierra Leon, Chiwengo ("When Wounds and Corpses Fail to Speak") points to the experience of the Tutsi genocide in Rwanda as the key "hegemonic narrative" blocking identification with suffering in the DRC.
24. Ticktin, "The Gendered Human of Humanitarianism," 251–252.
25. Puechguirbal documents her work with the UN to increase attention to the situation of women in "Women and War"; Hunt ("An Acoustic Register," 220) discusses the Nsongo Mboyo case. Chiwengo ("When Wounds and Corpses Fail to Speak," 88–91) discusses the Human Rights Watch Reports to argue that the representation of Congolese suffering in them is insufficient, because they place the blame for the violation of women on "backwards" Congolese law and traditions rather than identifying Rwanda as a main culprit, and, in doing so, "denies them subjectivity, for the cultural differences invoked maintain their difference and barbaric alterity" (at 89).
26. Some of the organizations that have been jointly active on this topic include V-Day, Enough Project, Friends of the Congo, Heal Africa, Associacion des Femmes des Médias, Amnesty International, Georges Malaika Foundation, and the International Rescue Committee. Here though it seems important to remember Wilson and Brown's point that the field of humanitarian action cannot be treated as monolithic, but—even within one campaign—humanitarianism is a series of sometimes contradictory yet interwoven strands (Wilson and Brown, "Introduction").
27. Ticktin, "The Gendered Human of Humanitarianism," 254–256.
28. Ibid., 250–251.
29. Hunt, "An Acoustic Register," 238.
30. Ibid., 237.
31. Ticktin goes further to suggest that the medicalization of rape is a way of making rape and other forms of gender-based violence "visible" that "has the strange effect of erasing gender—that is the power relations that produce gender" ("The Gendered Human of Humanitarianism," 251). In other words, it erases the social, psychological, political, and economic aspects of the crime, leaving behind only disempowered and de-historicized "universal" suffering bodies.
32. Ensler has also written a full-length play about the mass rapes in the former Yugoslavia, *Necessary Targets* (prem. 1996/ pub. 2001). The case of Bosnia and Kosovo is only one example of Ensler's interest in global women's issues, as we will see.
33. Ensler, *The Vagina Monologues*, xxxi–xxxii; Shalit, "Join the V-Day Movement," 173.
34. Lewis, "Staging an End to Abuse."
35. The first spotlight was on Afghan women. Others include "Missing and Murdered Women in Juarez, Mexico" to "Women of Iraq, Under Siege" and "The Women of New Orleans." A history of the spotlights is available on the V-Day website. See http://www.vday.org/spotlight+history
36. An overview of the "Stop Raping Our Greatest Resource" campaign is available on the organization's website. See http://drc.vday.org/spotlight2009
37. Information drawn from the V-Day website. Ensler's article in *Glamour* (August 1, 2007) is entitled "Women left for dead—and the man who's

saving them." Available on-line at: http://www.glamour.com/magazine/2007/08/rape-in-the-congo

38. The published script contains sections that are not included in the performance scripts, which change slightly from year to year and are not available to the general public. I am grateful to Laura Waleryszak from V-Day, who provided me with the most recent performance script and graciously answered my questions about it.
39. Ensler, *The Vagina Monologues*, 124–125.
40. The text of this monologue is available on the V-Day website as part of the "Spotlight Video," as described below. See http://drc.vday.org/spotlight2009.
41. Wendy Hesford points to the "voice over" as a rhetorical strategy that allows white Western feminists to control stories of women from the global South ("Cosmopolitanism and the Geopolitics of Feminist Rhetoric," 65.)
42. Dawes, *That the World May Know*, 78.
43. Scott, "Been There, Done That," 411.
44. Ibid., 415–416.
45. Cooper, "Worrying about Vaginas," 728.
46. Ibid., 729–730, 753–754.
47. Scott, "Been There, Done That," 413.
48. Schaffer and Smith, *Human Rights and Narrated Lives*.
49. McLagan, "Human Rights, Testimony and Transnational Publicity."
50. Schaffer and Smith, *Human Rights and Narrated Lives*, 12.
51. Ensler, *The Vagina Monologues*, 50. This line is also cited in Cooper, "Worrying about Vaginas," 738. For a more extended discussion of the way in which *The Vagina Monologues* confines women to their vaginas, see Scott, "Been There, Done That," 417–418 and Cooper, "Worrying about Vaginas," 732.
52. Cooper, "Worrying about Vaginas," 733–734.
53. This argument can be backed up by Cooper's point that Ensler depicts white vaginas as achieving liberation whereas black and foreign vaginas are seen to be under threat (Cooper, "Worrying about Vaginas," 749). This is part of a larger argument Cooper makes about Ensler's "missionary feminism" and her "colonization" of the experience of Bosnian rape survivors (Ibid., 745–749).
54. Hesford, "Cosmopolitanism and the Geopolitics of Feminist Rhetoric," 55 and 58–59. Hesford's piece, which I encountered late in the process of writing this chapter, resonates with and amplifies the critiques of Scott and Cooper cited above.
55. Chiwengo, "When Wounds and Corpses Fail to Speak," 90–91. Chiwengo cites the example of Baenga Boyla's *La profanation des vagins* (2005), which takes as a main intertext Ensler's *Vagina Monologues*.
56. Cooper, "Worrying about Vaginas," 739–740.
57. Ticktin, "Where Ethics and Politics Meet"; Ticktin, "The Gendered Human of Humanitarianism."
58. Ticktin, "Where Ethics and Politics Meet," 36, 46.
59. Thanks to Florian Becker for formulating this question.
60. Thomas Keenan ("Publicity and Indifference"; "Mobilizing Shame") reminds us that the activist axioms that knowledge leads to action, and that shaming decreases the incidence of human rights abuses, must be reconsidered.
61. Shannon, "An Intimate Look at the Plays of Lynn Nottage," 187.
62. Whoriskey, "Introduction," ix–x.
63. Ibid., xi.

64. Ibid., xiii. I recently had lunch with a program director at UNDP who recommended *Ruined* as the best thing to see to understand sexual violence in the Congo, because it allowed audiences to identify with the women there.
65. Nottage, *Ruined*, 14.
66. Ibid., 17.
67. Ibid., 67.
68. Ibid., 12.
69. Ibid., 76.
70. Ibid., 94.
71. Ibid., 100.
72. Ibid., 68.
73. Ibid.
74. McGee, "Approaching Brecht, By Way of Africa."
75. Hesford, "Cosmopolitanism and the Geopolitics of Feminine Rhetoric," 55.
76. Schaffer and Smith, *Human Rights and Narrated Lives*, 4–5.
77. Thanks are due to Florian Becker for helping me work through the significance of Brecht in the following paragraphs.
78. Brecht, "Mother Courage and Her Children," 181.
79. Woodland, "The Danger of Empathy," 126.
80. Slaughter, *Human Rights, Inc.*
81. Dawes, *That the World May Know*.
82. McGee, "Approaching Brecht, By Way of Africa."
83. Diamond, "Brechtian Theory/Feminist Theory," 85, 89.
84. Solga, "Mother Courage and Its Abject," 339–340.
85. Nottage, *Ruined*, 25.
86. Edmondson, "Transnational narratives," 3. Interestingly, Edmondson argues that the very problematic aspects of the ending with regard to Western spectators may allow it serve as a source of inspiration for African audiences.
87. Ignatieff, "The Stories We Tell," 2.
88. McLagan, "Human Rights, Testimony and Transnational Publicity," 315.
89. Schaffer and Smith, *Human Rights and Narrated Lives*, 8.
90. "Confronting Rape and Other Forms of Violence," 31.
91. Ibid., 38.
92. Ibid., 17–19.
93. Ibid., 65.
94. Ibid., 30, 41.
95. Ibid., 57–58
96. Ibid., 57–58
97. Ibid., 57–58.
98. See again the video from the Congressional hearing reception, available online at http://www.youtube.com/watch?v=SsqyhiaacO8&feature=channel

Bibliography

A Comuna. Colectivo de Trabalho Trabalhadores dos Caminhos de Ferro de Moçambique e Estudantes da Universidade Eduardo Mondlane. Maputo: Instituto Nacional do Livro e do Disco, 1979.

Abramsky, Sasha. "Gimme Shelter: What the New Sanctuary Movement Offers, Beyond a Safe Space, for the Undocumented." *The Nation* 286 no. 7. February 7, 2008, 24–28.

Abrevaya, Sebastián. "Para que los argentinos podamos volver a mirarnos la cara" *Página 12* November 21, 2007.

Acree, William. "The Trial of Theatre: Fiat iusitia, et pereat mundus" *LATR* 40 no. 1 (Fall 2006): 39–59.

Actis, Munú et al. *Ese infierno: conversaciones de cinco mujeres sobrevivientes de la ESMA*. Buenos Aires: Editorial Sudamericana, 2001.

Agamben, Giorgio. *Homo sacer: Sovereign Power and Bare Life*. Trans. Daniel Heller Roazen. Stanford: Stanford University Press, 1998.

———. *State of Exception*. Trans. Kevin Attell. Chicago: University of Chicago Press, 2005.

Ahmed, Sara. *The Cultural Politics of Emotion*. Edinburgh: Edinburgh University Press, 2004.

Aizpeolea, Horacio. "Las Madres de Plaza de Mayo tomaron posesión de un predio de la ESMA." *Clarín*. February 1, 2008. Web September 9, 2010. http://edant.clarin.com/diario/2008/02/01/elpais/p-00801.htm

Alston, Philip. "Report of the Special Rapporteur on Exrajudicial, Summary or Arbitrary Executions." New York: United Nations General Assembly 2008. http://www.karapatan.org/files/English_Alston_Report_Mission_to_the_Philippines_HRC8.pdf

Alter, Jonathan "Time to Think about Torture?" *Newsweek* November 5, 2001: 45.

Anderson, Danny J. "El futuro neoliberal y la utopia perdida en *Lejos del paraíso* de Sandra Cohen." *Symposium* 61 no. 1 (2007): 27–42.

Anderson, Patrick and Jisha Menon. *Violence Performed. Local Roots and Global Routes of Conflict*. Afterword by Peggy Phelan. Basingstoke: Palgrave Macmillan, 2009.

A'Ness, Francine. "Resisting Amnesia: Yuyachkani, Performance, and the Post-War Reconstruction of Peru." *Theater Journal* 56 (2004): 395–414.

Anker, Elizabeth. *Fictions of Dignity: Embodying Human Rights in World Literature*. Ithaca, NY: Cornell University Press, 2012.

———. "Villains, Victims and Heroes: Melodrama, Media, and September 11." *Journal of Communication* 55 no. 1 (2005): 22–37.

Antze, P. and M. Lambek, eds. *Tense Past: Cultural Essays in Trauma and Memory*. New York: Routledge, 1996.

Archard, David. *Children: Rights and Childhood*. London: Routledge, 1993.

Arditi, Benjamin. "Insurgencies don't have a plan—they are the plan. The politics of vanishing mediators of the indignados in 2011." Unpublished ms., forthcoming from JOMEC, *Journal of Journalism, Media, and Cultural Studies* no. 1 (2012), http://www.cardiff.ac.uk/jomec/jomecjournal/1-june2012/arditi_insurgencies.pdf.

Arendt, Hannah. *Eichmann in Jerusalem: A Report on the Banality of Evil*. New York: Penguin Books, 2006.

———. *The Human Condition*. Chicago: University of Chicago Press, 1998.

———. *The Origins of Totalitarianism*. New York: Harcourt, Inc., 1968.

———. *The Origins of Totalitarianism*. New York: Meridian Books, 1962.

Asad, Talal. *Formations of the Secular: Christianity, Islam, Modernity*. Stanford: Stanford University Press, 2003.

The Associated Press. "Deported Immigration Activist Says Son to Move to Mexico." September 13, 2005. International News.

Austin, John L. *How to Do Things with Words*. Cambridge, MA: Harvard University Press, 1962.

———. "Performative Utterances." In *Philosophical Papers*, edited by J. O. Urmson and G. J. Warnock, 233–252. Warnock Oxford: Oxford University Press, 1970.

Avery, Gordon. *Ghostly Matters: Haunting and the Sociological Imagination*. Minneapolis: University of Minnesota Press, 1997.

Ayala Blanco, Jorge. *La aventura del cine mexicano*. Mexico, DF: Grijalbo, 1993.

Azoulay, Ariella. "Has Anyone Ever Seen a Photograph of Rape?" In *The Civil Contract of Photography*, edited by A. Azoulay. New York: Zone Books, 2008.

Bal, Mieke, et al., eds. *Acts of Memory: Cultural Recall in the Present*. Hanover and London: Dartmouth College, University Press of New England, 1999.

Balandier, Georges. *Le pouvoir sur scènes*. Librairie Arthème Fayard, 2006.

Barrios, Ana Laura. "Entrevista a María Dodera: Las múltiples caras de la dramaturgia." May 25, 2011. Web July 4, 2009. http://entretablas.blogspot.com/2009/07/entrevista-los-macbeths-las-multiples.html

Barrios, Joi. "Gabriela: Isang Oratoryo (Gabriela: An Oratoryo)." Musical play. Unpublished manuscript. Presented by by Dulaang University Press. Directed by Tony Mabesa. Quezon City, January-February 2006.

———. "Mrs. B." Play. Presented by Desaparecidos. Directed by Socrates Jose. Quezon City, February 2010.

———. "Piketlayn Cantata." Musical play. Staged reading presented by the Committee for the Protection of Workers's Rights, Balay-Kultura and Kul-arts. Directed by John Caldon. San Francisco, April 30–May 1, 2011.

Barros, António Augusto. "Editorial." *Setepalcos: Revista do Programa Cena Lusófona* 0 (November 1995): 2–3.

Baudrillard, Jean. *The Vital Illusion*, edited by Julia Witwer. New York: Columbia University Press, 2000.

Benamou, Catherine L. "Televisual Melodrama in an Era of Migration." In *Latin American Melodrama: Passion, Pathos, and Entertainment*, edited by Darlene J. Sadler, 139–171. Urbana: University of Illinois Press, 2009.

Benhabib, Seyla. *The Claims of Culture: Equality and Diversity in the Global Era*. Princeton: Princeton University Press, 2002.

Benjamin, Walter. "The Work of Art in the Age of Its Mechanical Reproducibility." In *The Work of Art in the Age of Its Mechanical Reproducibility*, edited by

Michael W. Jennings, Brigid Doherty and Thomas Y. Levin, 19–55. Cambridge, MA: Belknap, 2008.

Bennett, Tony. *The Birth of the Museum: History, Theory, Politics*. New York: Routledge, 1995.

Berlant, Lauren. "Introduction: Compassion and Withholding." In *Compassion: The Culture and Politics of an Emotion*, edited by Lauren Berlant, 1–14. New York: Routledge, 2004.

———. "The Subject of True Feeling: Pain, Privacy, and Politics." In *Left Legalism/Left Critique*, edited by Brown W. and Halley J., 105–133. Durham: Duke University Press, 2002.

Bey, Hakim. *T.A.Z: The Temporary Autonomous Zone, Ontological Anarchy, Poetic Terrorism*. Brooklyn, NY: Autonomedia, 1991.

Bhabha, Jacqueline. "The "Mere Fortuity of Birth"?: Children, Mothers, Borders and the Meaning of Citizenship." In *Migrations and Mobilities: Citizenship, Borders, and Gender*, edited by Benhabib S. and Resnik J., 187–227. New York: New York University Press, 2009.

Bharucha, Rustom. *The Politics of Cultural Practice: Thinking through Theatre in an Age of Globalization*. Hanover, NH: Wesleyan University Press, 2000.

The Bill of Rights Defense Committee. "Guantánamo Reading Project." http://www.bordc.org/grp/readings/hostcities.php.

Boal, Augusto. *Theatre of the Oppressed*. Trans. Charles A and Maria-Odilia Leal McBride. New York: Theatre Communications Group, 1979.

———. *Theatre of the Oppressed*. Trans. Charles A. and Maria-Odilia Leal. McBride. New York: Theatre Communications Group, 1985.

———. *Legislative Theatre. Using Performance to Make Politics*. Trans. Adrian Jackson. London: Routledge, 1998.

Borkenztain, Bernardo. "En tránsito." *Berlín. Poema dramático para tres voces y una laptop*. Gabriel Peveroni, 3–4. Montevideo: Mado Ediciones, 2007.

Bosch, María Isabel. "Las Viajeras." Unpublished manuscript, 2003.

———. "'Las Viajeras,' motivaciones para un espectáculo teatral." Unpublished manuscript, 2003.

Boucicault, Dion. "The Poor of New York." In *American Melodrama*, edited by Daniel C. Gerould, 31–74. New York: Performing Arts Journal Publications, 1983.

Bracho, Diana. "El cine mexicano: ¿y en el papel de la mujer... Quien?" *Estudios Mexicanos*. 1 no. 2 (1985): 413.

Braslvasky, Guido. "Kirchner y Cristina oficializaron la creación del Museo de la ESMA. *Diario Clarín*. November 21, 2007. Web September 20, 2008. http://www.clarin.com/diario/2007/11/21/elpais/p-00801.htm

Bratman, Michael. "Shared Cooperative Activity." *Philosophical Review* 101 (1992): 327–341.

Brecht, Bertolt. *Brecht on Theatre*. Trans. John Willett. Great Britain: Methuen and Co., 1964.

———. *Brecht on Theatre: The Development of an Aesthetic*. Edited and translated by John Willet. London: Methuen, 1974.

———. "Der Messingkauf." *Werke: Große kommentierte Berliner und Frankfurter Ausgabe*, edited by Werner Hecht, Jan Knopf, Werner Mittenzwei, Klaus-Detlef Müller, Volume 22.2. Berlin and Weimar: Aufbau-Verlag/ Frankfurt am Main: Suhrkamp, 1988–1998.

———. "Mother Courage and Her Children." In *The Good Person of Szechwan*.Trans. John Willet. New York: Arcade, 1993.

———. *Os Dias da Comuna*. Vol 10: Teatro Completo em 12 volumes. Trans. Fernando Peixoto. São Paulo e Rio de Janeiro: Paz e Terra, 1993: 11–106.

Briskman, Linda, Susie Latham, and Chris Goddard. *Human Rights Overboard: Seeking Asylum in Australia*. Victoria, Australia: Scribe Publications, 2008.

Brison, Susan. *Aftermath: Violence and the Remaking of a Self*. Princeton: Princeton University Press, 2002.

———. "Trauma Narratives and the Remaking of the Self." In *Acts of Memory: Cultural Recall in the Present*, edited by Mieke Bal, Jonathan Crewe, and Leo Spitzer, 39–54, Hanover and London: Dartmouth College, 1999.

Brittain, Victoria and Gillian Slovo. *Guantánamo: Honor Bound to Defend Freedom*. London: Oberon Books, 2008.

Brodsky, Marcelo. *Memoria en construcción: el debate sobre la ESMA*. Buenos Aires: La marca editora, 2005.

Brook, Peter. *The Empty Space*. New York: Atheneum, 1969.

Brooks, Peter. *The Melodramatic Imagination*. New Haven, CT: Yale University Press, 1976.

Brooks, Daphne A. *Bodies in Dissent Spectacular Performances of Race and Freedom, 1850–1910*. Durham, NC: Duke University Press, 2006.

Brothers, Julia. Email correspondence. 17 June 2010.

Buckley, M. S. "Refugee Theatre: Melodrama and Modernity's Loss." *Theatre Journal* 61 no. 2 (2009): 175–190.

Burgos, Edita. Affidavit Complaint to the Department of Justice. June 9, 2011. http://freejonasburgosmovement.blogspot.com/

Burnside, Julian. "Foreword." In *Human Rights Overboard: Seeking Asylum in Australia*, edited by Briskman, Latham, 11–16. Goddard. Victoria, Australia: Scribe Publications, 2008.

Butler, Judith. *Precarious Life: The Power of Mourning and Violence*. New York: New Left Books, 2004.

Bystrom, Kerry. "Human Rights and the Novel." *Journal of Human Rights* 7 no. 4 (2008): 388–396.

Cabral, Amílcar. *Return to the Source: Selected Speeches of Amílcar Cabral*. Edited by Africa Information Service. New York: Monthly Review Press, 1973.

Calleja, Nina Catherine. "Fusion of Math, Theatre Brings New Twist to Tolentino Play." *Philippine Daily Inquirer*, March 20, 2008. Web. June 12, 2011. http://newsinfo.inquirer.net/inquirerheadlines/regions/view/20080320-125782/Fusion-of-math-theater-brings-new-twist-to-Tolentino-play.

Campbell, Neil. *The Rhizomatic West: Representing the American West in a Transnational, Global, Media Age*. Lincoln, University of Nebraska Press, 2008.

Campos, Juan Carlos [Koldo. pseud.], "Las Viajeras y María Isabel Bosch." Cronopiando, *El Nacional* (Santo Domingo), March 12, 2002, 6.

Canning, Charlotte. "Feminist Performance as Feminist Historiography." *Theatre Survey* 45 (2004): 227–233.

Carlson, Marvin A. *Places of Performance: The Semiotics of Theatre Architecture*. Ithaca, NY: Cornell University Press, 1989.

Casey, Valerie. "Staging Meaning: Performance in the Modern Museum." *The Drama Review* 49 no. 3 (Fall 2005): 78–95.

Castaneda, Dabet. "For Land and Wages: Half a Century of Peasant Struggle in Hacienda Luisita." *Bulatlat*, December 19, 2004. Web June 12, 2011. http://

bulatlat.com/main/2004/12/19/for-land-and-wages-half-a-century-of-peasant-struggle-in-hacienda-luisita-2/.
Castel-Branco, Carlos Nuno. "Economia extractiva e desafios da industrialização em Moçambique." In *Economia extractiva e desafios da industrialização em Moçambique*, edited by Luís de Brito, Carlos Nuno Castel-Branco, Sérgio Chichava, António Francisco, 19–109. Maputo: Instituto de Estudos Sociais e Económicos, 2010.
Castles, Stephen and Alastair Davidson. *Citizenship and Migration: Globalization and the Politics of Belonging*. New York: Routledge, 2000.
Cepeda, Esther. J. "Adios and Good Riddance, Elvira Arellano—Felon with Huge Sense of Entitlement Mocked Law, Gave Immigrants Stigma." *The Chicago Sun-Times*. August 21, 2007, final ed., news: 14.
———. "Mexico Embraces Boy Pleading Mom's Case." *The Chicago Sun-Times*. November 16, 2006. final ed, news: 17.
———. "Vigil Set to Halt Migrant's Deportation." *The Chicago Sun-Times*. August 14, 2006, final ed, news: 11.
Chavez, Leo R. *The Latino Threat: Constructing Immigrants, Citizens, and the Nation*. Stanford, CA: Stanford University Press, 2008.
Chavira, Javier, interviewed by Ana Elena Puga, November 30, 2009.
Cheah, Pheng. *Inhuman Conditions: On Cosmopolitanism and Human Rights*. Cambridge, MA: Harvard University Press, 2006.
Chicago Sun-Times. "Immigrant Mother Hurts Her Cause with Standoff." December 21, 2006: ed final, editorials, 33.
———. "It's Time to Get Out—Elvira Arellano Has Flouted the Law Long Enough. She Should Leave the Church and Go Back to Mexico." August 15, 2007: ed final, editorials, 35.
Chiwengo, Ngwarsungu. "When Wounds and Corpses Fail to Speak: Narratives of Violence and Rape in Congo (DRC)," *Comparative Studies of South Asia, Africa and the Middle East* 28 no. 1 (2008): 78–92.
Chouliaraki, Lilie. *The Spectatorship of Suffering*. London: SAGE Publications, 2006.
Cohen, Stanley. *States of Denial: Knowing about Atrocities and Suffering*. Cambridge: Polity, 2001.
Cole, Catherine M. "Performance, Transitional Justice and the Law: South Africa's Truth and Reconciliation Commission." *Theatre Journal* 59 (2007): 167–187.
Comisión de la Verdad y Reconciliación, "Informe Final." May 26, 2007. http://www.cverdad.org.pe/ifinal/index.php
"Confronting Rape and Other Forms of Violence against Women in Conflict Zones. Spotlight: DRC and Sudan." Committee on Foreign Relations of the United States Senate. May 13, 2009. Available on-line at: http//www.access.gpo.gov/congress/senate
Conquergood, Dwight. "Lethal Theatre: Performance, Punishment, and the Death Penalty." *Theatre Journal* 54 no. 3 (2002): 339–367.
Conrad, Joseph. *Heart of Darkness*. New York: Oxford University Press, 2008.
Cooper, Christine M. "Worrying about Vaginas: Feminism and Eve Ensler's *The Vagina Monologues*," *Signs* 32 no. 3 (2007): 727–758.
Cosentino, Olga. Interview with Griselda Gambaro. "Desconfío de tanta aprobación," June 4, 2011. Web June 28, 2008. http://edant.revistaenie.clarin.com/notas/2008/06/28/01703461.html

Coutin, Susan B. *Legalizing Moves: Salvadoran Immigrants' Struggle for U.S. Residency Rights.* Ann Arbor: University of Michigan Press, 2000.
Couto, Mia. "As outras nações de Moçambique." *O País.* September 18, 2010: 4.
———. *Pensatempos: Textos de opinião.* Lisboa: Caminho, 2005.
———. *Setepalcos: Revista do Programa Cena Lusófona* 0 (November 1995): 30–31.
Cox, Damien, Michael Levine and Saul Newman. *Politics Most Unusual: Violence, Sovereignty, and Democracy in the "War on Terror."* New York: Palgrave Macmillan. 2009.
Crane, Susan, ed. *Museums and Memory.* Stanford: Stanford University Press, 2000.
Cristóvão, Fernando, et al., eds. *Dicionário temático da lusofonia.* Lisboa [Lisbon]: Texto Editores, 2005.
Cruz, Duarte Ivo. "O Teatro em português: Da expansão às independências." *Camões: Revista de Letras e Culturas Lusófonas* 19 (December, 2006): 14–61.
Cvetkovich, Ann. *An Archive of Feelings: Trauma, Sexuality and Lesbian Public Cultures.* Durham: Duke University Press 2003.
Daly, Augustin. "Under the Gaslight." In *American Melodrama*, edited by Daniel C. Gerould, 135–181. New York: Performing Arts Journal Publications, 1983.
Daly, Nicholas. "Blood on the Tracks: Sensation Drama, the Railway, and the Dark Face of Modernity." *Victorian Studies* 42 no. 1 (1998): 47–76.
Danner, Mark. Tanner Lectures in Human Values. Stanford University, May 14, 2010.
Dawes, James. *That the World May Know: Bearing Witness to Atrocity.* Cambridge, MA: Harvard University Press, 2007.
Dean, Carolyn J. *The Frail Social Body: Pornography, Homosexuality, and Other Fantasies in Interwar France.* Berkeley and Los Angeles, CA: California University Press, 2000.
de Certeau, Michel. *The Writing of History.* New York: Columbia University Press, 1988.
Decker, Christopher. "'Unusually Compassionate': Melodrama, Film, and the Figure of the Child." In *Melodrama! The Mode of Excess from Early America to Hollywood*, edited by Kelleter F., Krah B., and Mayer R. Heidelberg, 305–328. Germany: Universitätsverlag Winter, 2007.
De Genova, Nicholas. "The Legal Production of Mexican/Migrant 'Illegality.'" *Latino Studies* 2 no. 2 (2004): 160–185.
De Ita, Fernando. "Las plumas del gallinero mexicano." *Un viaje sin fin: Teatro mexicano de hoy*, edited by Heidrun Adler and Jaime Chabaud, 13–28. Frankfurt: Vervuert, 2004.
Delegates of the International Committee of the Red Cross. *ICRC Report on the Treatment of Fourteen "High Value Detainees" in CIA Custody.* February 2007. http://www.derhuman.jus.gov.ar/espacioparalamemoria/
Derrida, Jacques. *Specters of Marx: The State of the Debt, the Work of Mourning, and the New International.* Trans. Peggy Kamuf. London: Routledge, 1994.
Dershowitz, Alan. "Tortured Reasoning." In *Torture: A Collection*, edited by Sanford Levinson, 257–280. New York: Oxford University Press, 2004.
Diamond, Elin. "Brechtian Theory/Feminist Theory: Toward a Gestic Feminist Criticism," *TDR: The Drama Review: A Journal of Performance Studies* 32 no. 1 (1988): 82–94.

———, ed. and intro. *Performance and Cultural Politics*. New York and London: Routledge, 1996.

Diéguez, Ileana. "Escenarios Liminales: donde se cruzan el arte y la vida (Yuyachkani...más allá del teatro)." *Teatro al Sur* 27 (November 2004): 11–15.

Diokno, Maria Socorro. "Extrajudicial, Summary or Arbitrary Executions in the Philippines, 2001–2006." In *Focus* 48 (2007). Web June 12, 2011. http://www.hurights.or.jp/archives/focus/section2/2007/06/extrajudicial-summary-or-arbitrary-executionsin-the-philippines-2001–2006.html.

Dodera, María. Interview. *Entretablas*, January 10, 2011. Web. July 9, 2009. http://entretablas.blogspot.com/2009/07/entrevista-los-macbeths-las multiples.html.

———. "Introduction." *Sarajevo esquina Montevideo*. Montevideo: Ediciones Trenes y Lunas, 2003: 4.

Dolan, Jill. *Utopia in Performance: Finding Hope at the Theater*. Ann Arbor: University of Michigan Press, 2005.

Douzinas, Costas. "Human Rights and Postmodern Utopia." *Law and Critique* 11 (2000): 219–240.

Draper, Susana. "The Business of Memory: Reconstructing Torture Centers as Shopping Malls and Tourist Sites." In *Accounting for Violence: Marketing Memory in Latin America*, edited by Ksenija Bilbija and Leigh Payne, 127–150. Durham and London: Duke University Press, 2011.

Dubatti, Jorge. *Filosofía del teatro I (convivio, experiencia, subjetivdad)*. Buenos Aires: Autel, 2007.

Duncan, Carol. *Civilizing Rituals: Inside Public Art Museums*. New York: Routledge, 1995.

Edmondson, Laura. "Transnational Narratives of violence in Lynn Nottage's *Ruined*," lecture at the American Society for Theatre Research convention, San Juan, Puerto Rico, 2009.

Ensler, Eve. *The Vagina Monologues. V-Day Edition*. New York: Villard, 2001.

Esposito, Stefano. "Supporters Cheer Return of 'Saulito': Boy, 7, back from Mexican tour for immigrant mom." *Chicago Sun-Times*. November 19, 2006, final ed, news: A9.

Evangelista, Patricia. "Jonas Burgos, 41." Column. In *Philippine Daily Inquirer*, June 11, 2011. Web June 12, 2011. http://opinion.inquirer.net/6141/jonas-burgos-41

Evans, Christine. "Another Immigration Detention Center Play," *Writing Performance* (blog), March 5, 2008, http://xtine3.wordpress.com/2008/03/05/another-immigration-detention-center-play/ (accessed April 29, 2012).

———. "Asylum Seekers and 'Border Panic' in Australia." *Peace Review* 15 no. 2 (2003): 163–170.

———. *Slow Falling Bird*. 2008. Unpublished ms.

Fanon, Frantz. *The Wretched of the Earth*. Trans. Richard Philcox. Foreword by Homi K. Bhabha. New York: Grove Press, 2004.

Feitlowitz, Marguerite. *A Lexicon of Terror: Argentina and the Legacies of Torture*. Oxford: Oxford University Press, 1998.

Feldman, Allen. "Memory Theatres, Virtual Witnessing, and the Trauma-Aesthetic." *Biography* 27 no. 1 (2004): 163–202.

———. "Strange Fruit: The South African Truth Commission and Demonic Economies of Violence," *Social Analysis* 46 no. 3 (Fall 2002): 234–265.

Felman, Shoshana. *The Juridical Unconscious: Trials and Traumas in the Twentieth Century*. Cambridge, MA: Harvard University Press, 2002.

Felman, Shoshana and Dori Laub, M. D. *Testimony: Crises of Witnessing in Literature, Psychoanalysis, and History.* New York and London: Routledge, 1992.

Fernandez, Doreen G. *Palabas: Essays on Philippine Theatre.* Quezon City: Ateneo de Manila University, 1996.

Fiebach, Joachim. "Dimensions of Theatricality in Africa." In *African Drama and Performance*, edited by John Conteh-Morgan and Tejumola Olaniyan, 24–38. Bloomington: Indiana University Press, 2004.

Fletcher, Laurel E, and Eric Stover. *The Guantánamo Effect: Exposing the Consequences of U.S. Detention and Interrogation Practices.* Berkeley: University of California Press, 2009.

Forsyth, Alison, and Christopher Megson, eds. *Get Real: Documentary Theatre Past and Present.* Houndmills, Basingstoke, Hampshire [England]: Palgrave Macmillan, 2009.

Franco, Dean J. *Race, Rights, and Recognition: Jewish American Literature since 1969.* Ithaca, NY: Cornell University Press, 2012.

Fraser, Nancy. "Reframing Justice in a Globalizing World." *New Left Review* 36 (November/December 2005): 1–19.

———. "Rethinking the Public Sphere: A Contribution to the Critique of Actually Existing Democracy." In *Habermas and the Public Sphere*, edited by Craig Calhoun, 109–143. Cambridge, MA: The MIT Press, 1992.

———. "Transnationalizing the Public Sphere: On the Legitimacy and Efficacy of Public Opinion in a Post-Westphalian World." *Theory, Culture & Society* 24 no. 4 (2007): 7–30.

———. *Unruly Practices: Power, Discourse, and Gender in Contemporary Social Theory.* Minneapolis: University of Minnesota Press, 1989.

Freeland, Gregory. "Negotiating Place, Space, and Borders: The New Sanctuary Movement." *Latino Studies* 8 no. 4 (2010): 485–508.

Fresu, Anna and Mendes de Oliveira. *Pesquisas para um teatro popular em Moçambique.* Maputo: Cadernos Tempo, 1982.

Fried, Michael. *Absorption and Theatricality: Painting and Beholder in the Age of Diderot.* Chicago: University of Chicago Press, 1988.

Fuchs, Elinor, and Una Chaudhuri. *Land/Scape/Theater.* Ann Arbor: University of Michigan Press, 2002.

Fusco, Coco. *A Field Guide for Female Interrogators.* New York: Seven Stories, 2008.

Gambaro, Griselda. *La persistencia.* Buenos Aires: Norma, 2007.

García, Mar and Denise Palewonsky. "Gender, Remittances and Development: The Case of Women Immigrants from Vicente Noble, Dominican Republic." Santo Domingo: United Nations International Research and Training Institute for the Advancement of Women (UN-INSTRAW), 2006.

Garcilaso de la Vega, el Inca. *Comentarios reales de los incas.* Reprint. Madrid: Castalia, 2000.

Glendon, Mary Ann. "Propter Honoris Respectum: Knowing the Universal Declaration of Human Rights." *Notre Dame Law Review* 73 (1997): 1153–1176.

Goddard, Chris and Linda Briskman. "By Any Measure It's Official Child Abuse." *Herald Sun* (Melbourne, Australia), February 19, 2004.

González Mandri, Flora M. "Operation Pedro Pan: A Tale of Trauma and Remembrance." *Latino Studies* no. 6 (2008): 252–268.

Górecki, Henryk. Symphony No. 3, Op. 36 ("Symphony of Sorrowful Songs"). London Sinfonietta. David Zinman. With Dawn Upshaw. Nonesuch B000005J1C, 1992, compact disc.
Graham-Jones, Jean. *Exorcising History: Argentine Theatre under Dictatorship.* Lewisburg, PA: Bucknell University Press, 2000.
Grieco, Elizabeth M. "The Dominican Population in the United States: Growth and Distribution," Migration Policy Institute Report (Washington, DC: Migration Policy Institute, 2004). http://www.migrationpolicy.org/pubs/MPIReportDominicanPOPUS.pdf.
Grimsted, David. *Melodrama Unveiled: American Theater and Culture, 1800–1850.* Chicago: University of Chicago Press, 1968.
Grupo Cultural Yuyachkani. "Adios Ayacucho." Video and unpublished script. No Dates.
———. "Alma Viva." DVD. Directed by Miguel Rubio. Yuyachkani, 2002.
———. "Rosa Cuchillo." Performance, Trinity College, Hartford, CT, USA, April 15, 2005.
Guerrero, Victoria. "El cuerpo muerto y el fetiche en Sendero Luminoso: el caso de Edith Lagos." *Ciberayllu* [on line], March 30, 2006. Web August 30, 2008. http://www.andes.missouri.edu/Andes/especiales/VG_CuerpoMuerto.html.
Guglielmucci, Ana. "La objetivación de las memoias públicas sobre la última dictadura militar argentina (1976–1983): El 24 de marzo en el ex centro clandestino de detención ESMA." *Antípoda* 4 (Enero-junio 2007): 244–265.
Gupta, Akhil and James Ferguson. "Beyond 'Culture' ": Space, Identity and the Politics of Difference." In *Culture, Power, Place: Explorations in Critical Anthropology,* edited by Gupta and Ferguson, 33–51. Durham: Duke University Press, 1991.
Gusmão, Fernando. *A Fala da memória: Factos e notas de um homem de teatro, 1947–1984.* Lisboa: Editorial Escritor, 1993.
Gutiérrez, Elena R. *Fertile Matters: The Politics of Mexican-Origin Women's Reproduction.* Austin: University of Texas Press, 2008.
Gutiérrez, Laura G. *Performing Mexicanidad: Vendidas y Cabareteras on the Transnational Stage.* Austin: University of Texas Press, 2010.
Habermas, Jürgen. *The Structural Transformation of the Public Sphere: An Inquiry into a Category of Bourgeois Society.* Cambridge, MA: MIT Press, 1991.
Haenni, Sabine. *The Immigrant Scene: Ethnic Amusements in New York, 1880–1920.* Minneapolis, MN: University of Minnesota Press, 2008.
Halbwachs, Maurice. *The Collective Memory.* Trans. Francis J. Ditter and Vida Yazdi Ditter. New York: Harper & Row, 1980.
Hall, Stuart. "The Spectacle of the Other." In *Representation: Cultural Representations and Signifying Practices,* edited by Stuart Hall, 223–290. London: Sage Publications, 2003.
Hamilton, Russell G. "Portuguese-Language Literature," In *A History of Twentieth-Century African Literatures,* edited by Oyekan Owomoyela, 240–283. Lincoln: University of Nebraska Press, 1993.
———. *Voices from an Empire: A History of Afro-Portuguese Literature.* Minneapolis: University of Minnesota Press, 1975.
Hanlon, Joseph and Teresa Smart. *Do Bicycles Equal Development in Mozambique?* Oxford: James Currey, 2008.
Hart, H. L. A. *The Concept of Law.* Oxford: Clarendon Press, 1961.

Hartman, Saidiya. *Scenes of Subjection: Terror, Slavery, and Self-Making in Nineteenth-Century America*. New York, NY: Oxford University Press, 1997.
Healey, Patrick. "Women of 'Ruined' to speak in Washington about Rape," *New York Times*, May 12, 2009. Web June 6, 2009. http://artsbeat.blogs.nytimes.com/2009/05/12/women-of-ruined-to-speak-in-washington-about-rape/
Herman, Judith Lewis. *Trauma and Recovery*. USA: Basic Books, 1992.
Hernandez, Daniel. "Broken Sanctuary: Did Elvira Arellano Need to Martyr Herself?" *LA Weekly*. August 23, 2007.
Hernández, Paola S. *El teatro de Argentina y Chile: Globalización, resistencia y desencanto*. Buenos Aires: Corregidor, 2009.
Hesford, Wendy. "Cosmopolitanism and the Geopolitics of Feminist Rhetoric." In *Rhetorica in Motion: Feminist Rhetorical Methods and Methodologies*, edited by Schell and Rawson, 53–70. Pittsburgh: University of Pittsburgh Press, 2010.
———. "Staging Terror." *The Drama Review* 50 (2006): 29–41.
Hirsch, Marianne. *Family Frames: Photography, Narrative, and Postmemory*. Cambridge, MA: Harvard University Press, 1997.
Hirschkind, Charles. *The Ethical Soundscape: Cassette Sermons and Islamic Counterpublics*. New York: Columbia University Press, 2006.
Hochschild, Adam. *King Leopold's Ghost: A Story of Greed, Terror and Heroism in Colonial Africa*. New York: Mariner Books, 1998.
Hoffnung-Garskof, Jesse. *A Tale of Two Cities: Santo Domingo and New York After 1950*. Princeton: Princeton University Press, 2008.
Hohendahl, Peter Uwe. "The Public Sphere: Models and Boundaries." In *Habermas and the Public Sphere*, edited by Craig Calhoun, 99–107. Cambridge, MA: The MIT Press, 1992.
Hondagneu-Sotelo, Pierette and Ernestine Avila. "'I'm Here but I'm There': The Meanings of Latina Transnational Motherhood." *Gender & Society* 11 no. 5 (1997): 548–571.
Honig, Bonnie. "Immigrant America? How Foreignness "Solves" Democracy's Problems." *Social Text* 56 (1998): 1–27.
Horton, Murray. "The Second Front in the War on Terror: Us Military Back in the Philippines with a Vengeance." Essay. Peace Researcher: Journal of the Anti-Bases Campaign. Christchurch, New Zealand. Number 26, October 2002. Web June 12, 2011. http://www.converge.org.nz/abc/pr26–64.htm.
Howard, June. "What Is Sentimentality?" *American Literary History* 11 no. 1 (1999): 63–81.
Hoyland, William. Class discussion. University of Texas at Austin. October 2, 2008.
Huerta, Jorge. A. *Chicano Drama: Performance, Society, and Myth*. Cambridge, UK: Cambridge University Press, 2000.
Hughes, Donna M., Laura Joy Sporcic, Nadine Z. Mendelsohn, and Vanessa Chirgwin. Coalition against Trafficking in Women. "Dominican Republic." The Factbook on Global Sexual Exploitation, 1999. http://www.uri.edu/artsci/wms/hughes/domrep.htm.
Human Rights and Equal Opportunities Commission. *A Last Resort? National Inquiry into Children in Immigration Detention*. Sydney: Human Rights and Equal Opportunities Commission 2004. http://www.unhcr.org/refworld/pdfid/49997af31c.pdf (accessed April 29, 2012).
Hunt, Lynn. *Inventing Human Rights: A History*. New York: Norton, 2008.

Hunt, Nancy Rose. "An Acoustic Register, Tenacious Images and Congolese Scenes of Rape and Repetition." *Cultural Anthropology* 23 no. 2 (May 2008): 220–253.
Huyssen, Andreas. *Present Pasts: Urban Palimpsests and the Politics of Memory*. Stanford: Stanford University Press, 2003.
———. "Human Rights and Globalising Memory Culture," In *The Essentials of Human Rights*, edited by Rhona K. M. Smith and Christien van den Anker, 162–175. London: Hodder Arnold, 2002.
Ignatieff, Michael. "The Stories We Tell: Television and Humanitarian Aid." *The Social Contract* 10 no. 1 (1999): 1–8.
———. *Whose Universal Values?: The Crisis in Human Rights*. Amsterdam: Stichting Praemium Erasmianum, 1999.
Ileto, Reynaldo Clemena. *Pasyon and Revolution*. Quezon City: Ateneo de Manila University Press, 1979.
Inda, Jonathan Xavier. "Foreign Bodies: Migrants, Parasites, and the Pathological Nation." *Discourse* 22 no. 3 (2000): 46–62.
International Organization for Migration (IOM), "Migración, Prostitución y trata de mujeres dominicanas en la Argentina." Buenos Aires: IOM, 2003.
Itzigsohn, José, Carlos Dore Cabral, Esther Hernández Medina, and Obed Vázquez. "Mapping Dominican Transnationalism: Narrow and Broad Transnational Practices." *Ethnic and Racial Studies* 22 no. 2 (1999): 316–339.
Jackson, Kathy Merlock. *Images of Children in American Film: A Sociocultural Analysis*. Metuchen, NJ: The Scarecrow Press, 1986.
Jackson, Naomi M, and Toni S. Phim. *Dance, Human Rights, and Social Justice: Dignity in Motion*. Lanham, MD: Scarecrow Press, 2008.
Jelin, Elizabeth. *Los trabajos de la memoria*. Buenos Aires: Siglo Veintiuno, 2002.
———. "The minefields of memory" *NACLA Report on the Americas* 32 no. 2 (September/October 1998): 23–29.
Johnson, Kevin R. *The "Huddled Massses" Myth: Immigration and Civil Rights*. Philadelphia, PA: Temple University Press, 2004.
Johnson, Lyman, ed. *Death, Dismemberment, and Memory in Latin America*. Albuquerque: University of New Mexico Press, 2004.
———. "Why Dead Bodies Talk: An Introduction." In *Death, Dismemberment, and Memory in Latin America*, edited by Lyman Johnson, 1–26. Albuquerque: University of New Mexico Press, 2004.
Joseph, May. *Nomadic Identities: The Performance of Citizenship*. Minneapolis: University of Minnesota Press, 1999.
Juffer, Jane. "Compassion and Rage: The Face of the Migrant." *South Atlantic Quarterly* 108 no. 1 (2009): 219–235.
Júnior, Rodrigues. *Para uma cultura moçambicana. (Ensaio)*. Lisboa: Actividades Gráficas, 1951.
Jupp, James. *From White Australia to Woomera: The Story of Australian Immigration*. New York: Cambridge University Press, 2002.
Kanstroom, Daniel. *Deportation Nation: Outsiders in American History*. Cambridge, MA: Harvard University Press, 2007.
Kaplan, E. Ann. *Motherhood and Representation: The Mother in Popular Culture and Melodrama*. London: Routledge, 1992.
Karapatan Alliance for the Advancement of Human Rights. "2010 Year-End Report on the Human Rights Situation in the Philippines." Quezon City, 2010. Web June 12, 2012 http://www.karapatan.org/files/Karapatan%202010%20HR%20Report%20(updated).pdf

Keating, Paul. "Redfern Speech (Year for the world's Indigenous People)." Redfern Park, Redfern, New South Wales, Australia, December 10, 1992. Web. April 29, 2012. http://aso.gov.au/titles/spoken-word/keating-speech-redfern-address/extras/

Keenan, Thomas. "Mobilizing Shame." *The South Atlantic Quarterly* 103 no. 2–3 (2004): 435–449.

———. "Publicity and Indifference (Sarajevo on Television)," *PMLA* 117 no. 1 (2002): 104–116.

Kenny, M. G. "Trauma, Time, Illness and Culture. An Anthropological Approach to Traumatic Memory." In *Tense Past: Cultural Essays in Trauma and Memory*, edited by Paul Antze and Michael Lambek, 151–172. New York: Routledge, 1996.

Kleinman Arthur and Joan Kleinman. "The Appeal of Experience; The Dismay of Images: Cultural Appropriations of Suffering in Our Times." *Daedalus* 125 no. 1 (1996): 1–23.

Kluge, Alexander and Oskar Negt. *Public Sphere and Experience: Toward an Analysis of the Bourgeois and Proletarian Public Sphere*. Minneapolis: University of Minnesota Press, 1993.

Kruger, Loren. *Post-Imperial Brecht. Politics and Performance, East and South*. Cambridge: Cambridge University Press, 2004.

Kushner, Tony. *Homebody/Kabul*. Revised Version. New York: Theater Communications Group, 2004.

LaCapra, Dominick. "Absence, Trauma, Loss." *Critical Inquiry* 25 no. 4 (Summer 1999): 696–727.

Lamarque, Peter and Stein Haugom Olson. *Truth, Fiction, and Literature*. Oxford: Clarendon Press, 1994.

Lambright, Anne. "A Nation Embodied: Woman in the Work of Yuyachkani." *Letras Femeninas* 35 no. 2 (Winter 2009): 133–152.

Landsberg, Alison. *Prosthetic Memory: The Transformation of American Remembrance in the Age of Mass Culture*. New York: Columbia University Press, 2004.

Lehmann, Hans-Thies. *Postdramatic Theatre*. Translated and introduction by Karen Jürs Munby. London and New York: Routledge, 2006.

Lewis, Nicole. "Staging an end to abuse." *The Chronicle of Philanthropy* 13 no. 13 (April 19, 2001): 7–9.

Lima, Fernando. "Até à próxima crise em Moçambique." *Visão* September 9–15, 2010, 72.

Lionnet, Françoise, and Shumei Shi. *Minor Transnationalism*. Durham: Duke University Press, 2005.

Lobato, Alexandre. *Sobre 'Cultura Moçambicana': Reposição de um problema e resposta a um crítico*. Lisboa: n.p., 1952.

Lomnitz, Claudio. *Death and the Idea of Mexico*. New York: Zone, 2005.

Lopez, Melina. *Sonia Flew*. New York: Dramatists Play Service, 2009.

Lucas, Carlos Brandão. "Painel de Opinião." *Setepalcos: Revista do Programa Cena Lusófona* 0 (November 1995): 22.

Machado da Graça, João and António Sopa. "Teatro em Moçambique." In *Dicionário temático da lusofonia*, edited by Cristóvão, Fernando, et al., 911–914. Lisboa [Lisbon]: Texto Editores, 2005.

MacIntyre, Alisdair. *A Short History of Ethics: A History of Moral Philosophy from the Homeric Age to the Twentieth Century*. New York, NY: Macmillan, 1966.

Madureira, Luís. "Nation, Identity and Loss of Footing: Mia Couto's *O Outro Pé da Sereia* and the Question of Lusophone Postcolonialism." *Novel: A Forum on Fiction* (Spring/Summer 2008): 200–229.

Mahmood, Saba. *Politics of Piety: The Islamic Revival and the Feminist Subject.* Princeton: Princeton University Press, 2005.

Majul, Luis. "¿Son los Kirchner los dueños de los derechos humanos?" lanacion.com, March 25, 2010. Web April 2, 2011. http://www.lanacion.com.ar/nota.asp?nota_id=1247001.html.

Mamdani, Mahmood. *Citizens and Subjects.* Princeton: Princeton University Press, 1996.

Mares, Peter. *Borderline: Australia's Response to Refugees and Asylum Seekers.* 2nd ed. Sydney: University of New South Wales Press, 2002.

Mariano, Roberto. "Forecasting Monthly Inflation in the Philippines." Quezon City: The Philippine Institute for Development Studies, 1985. Web June 12, 2011. http://www3.pids.gov.ph/ris/ms/pidsms85-10.pdf.

"Martial Law-Type Repression Alarms NGO." News Release. In *Bulatlat*, February 22, 2011. Web. February 22, 2011. http://bulatlat.com/main/2011/02/22/martial-law-type-repression-by-dole-philippines-vs-union-alarms-ngo/

Martin, Carol. "Bodies in Evidence." *The Drama Review* 50 no. 2 (Fall 2006): 8–15.

———. *Dramaturgy of the Real on the World Stage.* Basingstoke [England]: Palgrave Macmillan, 2010.

Martínez, Victoria. "La vida vale: Once obras acerca de los asesinatos de mujeres." *Hotel Juárez: Dramaturgia de feminicidio.* Durango, Mexico: Siglo XXI, 2008, 5–18.

Massey, Doreen B., et al. *City Worlds.* London; New York: Routledge in association with the Open University, 1999.

Mbembe, Achille. "La 'chose' et ses doubles dans la caricature camerounaise. *Cahiers d'études africaines.* 36 no. 141–142 (1996): 143–170.

McClintock, Anne. *Imperial Leather: Race, Gender, and Sexuality in the Colonial Contest.* New York: Routledge, 1995.

McConachie, Bruce. *Melodramatic Formations: American Theatre and Society, 1820–1870.* Iowa City, IA: University of Iowa Press, 1992.

McElmurry, Sara E. "Elvira Arellano: No Rosa Parks, Creation of 'Us' Versus 'Them' in an Opinion Column." *Hispanic Journal of Behavioral Sciences* 31 no. 2 (2009): 182–203.

———. "Mother, Immigrant, Criminal: Newspaper Coverage and the Construction of Identity in the Elvira Arellano Controversy." Unpublished paper delivered at the Centro de Idiomas, Universidad Tecnológica de la Mixteca. Available online at http://www.utm.mx/~mtello/Extensos/extenso190209.pdf Accessed December 19, 2009.

McGee, Celia. "Approaching Brecht, by way of Africa." *New York Times* January 25, 2009. Web 1 June, 2009. http://www.nytimes.com/2009/01/25/theater/25McGee.html

McLagan, Meg. "Human Rights, Testimony and Transnational Publicity." In *Nongovernmental Politics,* edited by Michel Fehrer, 304–317. New York: Zone Books, 2007.

Mendoza, Zoila S. *Shaping Society through Dance: Mestizo Ritual Performance in the Peruvian Andes.* Chicago Studies in Ethnomusicology. Chicago and London: The University of Chicago Press, 2000.

Metz, Thaddeus. "Toward an African Moral Theory." *Journal of Political Philosophy* 15 no. 3 (2007): 321–341.

Mignolo, Walter D. *Local Histories/Global Designs: Coloniality, Subaltern Knowledges, and Border Thinking.* Princeton and Oxford: Princeton University Press, 2000.

Migration Policy Institute. "Netherlands Antilles." Migration Information Source, October 16, 2006. http://www.migrationinformation.org/datahub/countrydata.cfm?ID=464.

Miguel, João Dias. "A guerra do pão." *Visão* September 9–15, 2010: 60–71.

Mir, Claudio. "Mondongo Scam." Unpublished manuscript, 1994.

Mirza, Roger. *Teatro rioplatense. Cuerpo, palabra, imagen: La escena contemporánea: una reflexión impostergable.* Montevideo: Facultad de Humanidades y Ciencias de la Educación Universidad de la República, 2007.

———. *Teatro y violencia en la escena contemporánea.* Montevideo: Ministerio de Educación y Cultura, 2009.

Misemer, Sarah M. "Juegos de apertura y contención: las relaciones fractales en Groenlandia." In *Groenlandia,* 5–10. Montevideo: Estuario, 2008.

Mitchum, Robert. Arellano's Son Back in City—Saul, 9, Returns to U.S. for Immigration Events. *Chicago Tribune.* April 28, 2008, final ed, metro: 3.

Molina-Guzman, Isabel. *Dangerous Curves: Latina Bodies in the Media.* New York: New York University Press, 2010.

Morel, E. D. *Red Rubber: The Story of the Rubber Slave Trade Flourishing on the Congo in the Year of Grace 1906.* New York: Negro Universities Press, 1969.

Muguercia, Magaly. "Perú. Cuerpo y política en la dramaturgia de Yuyachkani." *Teatro Celcit* 9 no. 11–12 (1999): 48–57.

Murray, Neil. "My Island Home," *Neil Murray.* http://www.neilmurray.com.au/pages/song_islandhome.html (accessed April 29, 2012).

Mutua, Makua. "Savages, Victims, and Saviors: The Metaphor of Human Rights." *Harvard International Law Journal* 42 no. 1 (2001): 201–245.

———. "Human Rights and the African Fingerprint." In *Human Rights: A Political and Cultural Critique,* edited by Mutua Makau, 71–93. Philadelphia: University of Pennsylvania Press, 2002.

Nathans, Heather S. *Slavery and Sentiment on the American Stage, 1787–1861 Lifting the Veil of Black.* Cambridge, UK: Cambridge University Press, 2009.

Nazario, Sonia. *Enrique's Journey.* New York: Random House, 2007.

Nhlongo, Lindo. *Duas Peças de Teatro: Os Noivos ou Conferência Dramática sobre o Lobolo e As Trinta Mulheres de Muzeleni.* Maputo: Associação dos Escritores Moçambicanos, 1990.

Nickel, James. *Making Sense of Human Rights.* 2nd ed. Malden, MA: Blackwell, 2007.

Nkashama, Pius Ngandu. *Théâtres et scènes de spectacle (Études sur les dramaturgies et les arts gestuels).* Paris: Éditions L'Harmattan, 1993.

———. "Theatricality and Social Mimodrama." In *African Drama and Performance,* edited by John Conteh-Morgan and Tejumola Olaniyan, 238–247. Bloomington: Indiana University Press, 2004.

Nora, Pierre. *Realms of Memory: Rethinking the French Past.* Vol 1. Trans. Arthur Goldhammer. New York: Columbia University Press, 1996.

Norris, Andrew. "Giorgio Agamben and the Politics of the Living Dead." *Diacritics* 30 no. 4 (Winter 2000): 38–58.

Nottage, Lynn. *Ruined.* New York: Theatre Communications Group, 2009.

Nzongola-Ntalaja, Georges. *The Congo from Leopold to Kabila: A People's History.* London: Zed Books, 2002.
"O Projecto e a sua Concretização." *Setepalcos: Revista do Programa Cena Lusófona* 0 (November 1995): 4–13.
Obama, Barack. "Presidential Memorandum—Closure of Detention Facilities at Guantánamo Naval Base." *Office of the Press Secretary.* December 15, 2009. http://www.whitehouse.gov/the-press-office/presidential-memorandum-closure-dentention-facilities-guantanamo-bay-naval-base.
———. "Statement by the President on H.R. 1540." *Office of the Press Secretary.* December 31, 2011. http://www.whitehouse.gov/the-press-office/2011/12/31/statement-president-hr-1540.
O'Donnell, Maureen. " 'Saulito' Delivers Message for Elvira—Boy at Church Where He, Mom Spent Year." *Chicago Sun-Times,* April 8, 2008: final, news, 15.
Office of the United Nations High Commissioner for Human Rights. "Convention on the Rights of the Child." November 20, 1989. http://www2.ohchr.org/english/law/crc.htm (accessed April 29, 2012).
Okin, Susan Moller. *Is Multiculturalism Bad for Women?* edited by Joshua Cohen, Matthew Howard, and Martha C. Nussbaum. Princeton: Princeton University Press, 1999.
Ontiveros, Sue. "Vote If You Support Elvira Arellano: Voting Is the Only Way to Make Those in Power Sit Up and Pay Attention." August 26, 2006: final, news, 12. *Chicago Sun-Times.*
Ortiz, Fernando. "Del fenómeno social de la 'transculturación' y de su importancia en Cuba." In *Contrapunteo cubano del tabaco y el azúcar,* 129–135. Barcelona: Ariel, 1973.
———."Los factores humanos de la cubanidad." In *Etnia y sociedad,* 1–20. Havana: Editorial de Ciencias Sociales, 1993.
Osiel, Mark. "The Mental State of Torturers: Argentina's Dirty War." In *Torture: A Collection,* edited by Sanford Levinson, 129–141. Oxford: Oxford University Press, 2004.
O'Siochain, Seamus and Michael O'Sullivan. *The Eyes of Another Race: Roger Casement's Congo Report and 1903 Diary.* Dublin: University College Dublin Press, 2003.
Owen, Hilary. *Mother Africa, Father Marx: Women's Writing in Mozambique (1948–2002).* Lewisburg, Maine: Bucknell University Press, 2007.
Pace, Patricia. "Staging Childhood: Lewis Hine's Photographs of Child Labor." *The Lion and the Unicorn* 26 no. 3 (2002): 324–352.
Páges, Verónica. "El horror detrás del horror." *La Nación,* May 25, 2011. Web. June 17, 2007. http://www.lanacion.com.ar/918078-el-horror-detras-del-horror.
Pallares, Amalia. "Representing 'La Familia': Family Separation and Immigrant Activism." In *¡Marcha! Latino Chicago and the Immigrant Rights Movement,* edited by Pallares, Amalia and Flores-González Nilda, 215–236. Urbana, IL: University of Illinois Press, 2010.
Partida Tayzán, Armando. "La novísima dramaturgia mexicana." In *Teatro mexicano reciente: Aproximaciones críticas,* 15–54. Mexico, DF: Ediciones y Gráficos Eon and University of Texas at El Paso, 2005.
Passerin d'Entrèves Maurizio. "Hannah Arendt and the idea of citizenship." In *Dimensions of Radical Democracy,* edited by C. Mouffe, 145–168. London: Routledge, 1996.
Patraka, Vivian. *Spectacular Suffering: Theatre, Fascism, and the Holocaust.* Bloomington, IN: Indiana University Press, 1999.

Paulson, Amanda. "For Mother and Son, an Immigration Predicament." *The Christian Science Monitor.* August 28, 2006. Electronic document available at http://www.csmonitor.com/2006/0828/p01s03, accessed December 21, 2009.

Pellettieri, Osvaldo. "El teatro porteño del año 2000 y el teatro del futuro." *Latin American Theatre Review* 34 no. 1 (Fall 2000): 5–24.

Persino, María Silvina. "Cuerpo y memoria en el Teatro de los Andes y Yuyachkani." *Gestos* 43 (April 2007): 87–103.

Peter, Jeremy W. "In Two Guantánamo Tours, Many Questions, Few Answers." *The New York Times.* August 11, 2010. Web. August 12, 2010. http://www.nytimes.com/2010/08/12/us/12gitmo.html?pagewanted=all.

Peterson, Michael. *Straight White Male: Performance Art Monologues.* Jackson: University Press of Mississippi, 1997.

Peveroni, Gabriel. *Berlín.* Montevideo: Mado, 2007.

———. "Territorios posdramáticos." *Lo nuevo*, 9–17. Ministerio de la Cultura, 2009.

———. *Sarajevo esquina Montevideo.* Montevideo: Ediciones Trenes y Lunas, 2003.

———. "Interview with Gabriel Peveroni. De los Balcanes a la Villa del Cerro." *El país.* May 25, 2011. Web. April 25, 2003. http://www.elpais.com.uy/03/04/25/pespec_38508.asp

Phelan, Peggy. "In the Valley of the Shadow of Death: The Photographs of Abu Ghraib." In *Violence Performed: Local Roots and Global Routes of Conflict*, edited by Patrick Anderson and Jisha Menon, 372–384. New York: Palgrave Macmillan, 2009.

———. "Marina Abramovic: Witnessing Shadows." *Theatre Journal* 56 no. 4 (2004): 569–577.

———. *Unmarked: The Politics of Performance.* New York: Routledge, 1993.

Philippine Army Public Affairs Office. "Army Participates During the Certification Election at Dole Philippines." Facebook Page. Manila, 2011. http://www.facebook.com/note.php?note_id=202051273153628

Prunier, Gérard. *Africa's World War: Congo, the Rwandan Genocide and the Making of a Continental Catastrophe.* New York: Oxford University Press, 2009.

Puechguirbal, Nadine. "Women and War in the Democratic Republic of Congo," *Signs* 28 no. 4 (2003): 1271–1281.

Puga, Ana Elena. *Memory, Allegory, and Testimony in South American Theater: Upstaging Dictatorship.* New York: Routledge, 2008.

———. "Poor Enrique and Poor María, or the Political Economy of Suffering in Two Migrant Melodramas." In *Performance in the Borderlands,* edited by Ramón H. Rivera-Servera and Harvey Young, 225–247. New York: Palgrave Macmillan, 2011.

Rabih, Mroué, Introduction to *Theatre and Human Rights* by Paul Rae, ix-xii. Houndsmills, England: Palgrave Macmillan, 2009.

Radway, Janice. *Reading the Romance: Women, Patriarchy, and Popular Literature.* Chapel Hill, NC: University of North Carolina Press, 1991.

Rae, Paul. *Theatre and Human Rights.* Houndsmills, England: Palgrave Macmillan, 2009.

Rancière, Jacques. *The Emancipated Spectator.* Trans. Gregory Elliott. London and New York: Verso, 2009.

Rascón Banda, Víctor Hugo. "El teatro que vino del norte." In *Teatro mexicano reciente: Aproximaciones críticas*, 175–183. Mexico, D. F.: Ediciones y Gráficos Eon and University of Texas at El Paso, 2005.

———. *Hotel Juárez. Hotel Juárez: Dramaturgia de feminicidio*. Durango, Mexico: Siglo XXI, 2008, 233–288.
Rawls, John. "Two Concepts of Rules." *Philosophical Review* 64 (1955): 3–32.
Rebello, Luiz Francisco. *História do Teatro de Revista em Portugal*. Vol. 1: *Da Regeneração à República*. Lisboa: Publicações Dom Quixote, 1984.
Reis, António. "Panel de Opinião." *Setepalcos: Revista do Programa Cena Lusófona* 0 (November 1995): 20–21.
Rev. Walter Coleman, interviewed by Ana Elena Puga, October 25, 2009.
Reyes, Renato M. Jr. "10 Years of VFA: The Return of US Bases and Combat Involvement of US Troops." *Paninindigan*, 2009. Also found in "Like a Rolling Stone" Blogsite. Web June 12, 2011. http://natoreyes.wordpress.com/2009/09/17/10-years-of-vfa-the-return-of-us-bases-and-the-combat-involvement-of-us-troops-in-the-philippines/.
———. "Oplan Bayanihan: Grand Psywar Scheme and Continuing Violence against the People." Blog. Quezon City, January 18, 2011. Web June 12, 2011. http://natoreyes.wordpress.com/2011/01/17/oplan-bayanihan-grand-psywar-scheme-and-continuing-violence-against-the-people/.
Ricardo, Celso. "Manifestações para além do custo do pão" *O País*. July 9, 2011. Web. July 10, 2011. http://www.opais.co.mz/index.php/entrevistas/76-entrevistas/15079-manifestacoes-para-alem-do-custo-do-pao.html
Richey, Lisa Ann and Stefano Ponte. "Better Red Than Dead? Celebrities, Consumption and International Aid." *Third World Quarterly* 29 no. 4 (2008): 711–729.
Ricoeur, Paul. *Memory, History, Forgetting*. Trans. By Kathleen Blamey and David Pellauer. Chicago and London: The University of Chicago Press, 2004.
Ridout, Nicholas. *Theatre and Ethics*. Houndsmills, England: Palgrave Macmillan, 2009.
Rizal, Jose. *Noli Me Tangere* [Noli me tangere]. Trans. Maria Soledad Lacson-Locsin. Honolulu: University of Hawaii, 1997.
Rokem, Freddie. *Performing History: Theatrical Representations of the Past in Contemporary Theatre*. Iowa City: University of Iowa Press, 2000.
Romero, Alexis. "New AFP Tack Vs Rebels to Uphold Human Rights." News Article. In *Philippine Star*, August 16, 2010. Web June 12, 2011. http://new.philstar.com/nation/top-stories/603077/new-afp-tack-vs-rebels-to-uphold-human-rights.
Romero, Mary. " 'Go After the Women': Mothers Against Illegal Aliens' Campaign Against Mexican Immigrant Women and their Children." *Indiana Law Journal* 83 (2008): 1355–1390.
Rosenberg, Carol. "Reporting Guantánamo: America's Experiment in Extraterritorial Detention." Lecture, *Ethics and War Series*. Stanford University. November 16, 2011.
Rosencof, Mauricio. *Las cartas que no llegaron*. Montevideo [Uruguay]: Alfaguara, 2000.
Rossini, Jon D. *Contemporary Latina/o Theater: Wrighting Ethnicity*. Carbondale, IL: Southern Illinois University Press, 2008.
Rothberg, Michael. *Multidirectional Memory: Remembering the Holocaust in the Age of Decolonization*. Stanford, CA: Stanford University Press, 2009.
———. *Traumatic Realism. The Demands of Holocaust Representation*. Minneapolis: University of Minnesota Press, 2000.
Rubio, Miguel. *El cuerpo ausente (performance política)*. Lima: Yuyachkani, 2006.

———. *Notas sobre Teatro.* edited by Luis A. Ramos-García Lima-Minnesota: Yuyachkani, 2001.

———. "Persistencia de la memoria." June 12, 2007. http://hemi.nyu.edu/esp/newsletter/issue8/pages/rubio.shtml

Rubio, Miguel and Teresa Ralli. "Notas sobre 'nuestra' Antígona." June 8, 2007. http://www.geocities.com/antigona_yuyachkani/Nuestra.html

Ruethling, Gretchen. "Chicago Woman's Stand Stirs Immigration Debate." *The New York Times.* August 19, 2006. A1:10.

Sagrada Família. Grupo Cénico das F.P.L.M. Maputo: Imprensa Nacional, 1980.

Said, Edward. *Culture and Imperialism.* New York: Vintage Books, 1994.

———. *From Oslo to Iraq and the Road Map.* New York: Pantheon Books, 2004.

Salazar de Alcazar, Hugo. *Teatro y Violencia: Una aproximación al teatro peruano de los 80.* Lima: Centro de Documentación y Video teatral, 1990.

Sánchez Prado, Ignacio M. "Amores perros: Exotic Violence and Neoliberal Fear." *Journal of Latin American Cultural Studies.* 15 no. 1 (2006): 39–57.

———. "La utopía apocalíptica del México neoliberal." *AlterTexto* 10 no. 5 (2007): 9–15.

Santos, Boaventura de Sousa. "Between Prospero and Caliban: Colonialism, Postcolonialism and Inter-Identity." *Luso-Brazilian Review* 39 no. 2 (2002 Winter): 9–43.

Santos, Vítor Pavão dos. *A revista à portuguesa.* Lisboa: O Jornal, 1978.

Sarlo, Beatriz. "La pesadilla circular." Lanacion.com. March 21, 2010. Web April 21, 2011. http://www.lanacion.com.ar/nota.asp?nota_id=1249125.html

Sassen, Saskia. *Territory, Authority, Rights: From Medieval to Global Assemblages.* Princeton, NJ: Princeton University Press, 2006.

Savage, Charlie. "Two Guantánamo Detainees Freed, the First in Fifteen Months." *New York Times.* April 19, 2012. Web. April 19, 2012. http://www.nytimes.com/2012/04/20/world/americas/2-guantanamo-bay-detainees-freed-in-el-salvador.html?_r=1.

Scanlon, Robert. "Writ of Habeas Corpus: Christine Evans's *Trojan Barbie.*" *Theatre Forum* 35 (2009): 26–27.

Scarry, Elaine. *The Body in Pain: The Making and Unmaking of the World.* New York: Oxford University Press, 1985.

———. Tanner Lectures in Human Values. Stanford University. May 14, 2010.

Schaffer, Kay and Sidonie Smith. *Human Rights and Narrated Lives: The Ethics of Recognition.* New York: Palgrave, 2004.

Schechner, Richard. *Essays on Performance Theory.* New York: Routledge, 1988.

———. *Performance Studies: An Introduction.* London and New York: Routeledge, 2002.

Schmidhuber de la Mora, Guillermo. *Dramaturgia mexicana: Fundación y herencia.* Guadalajara: Universidad de Guadalajara, 2006.

Schmidt, Camacho A. R. "Ciudadana X: Gender Violence and the Denationalization of Women's Rights in Ciudad Juarez, Mexico." *Cr: the New Centennial Review* 5 no. 1 (2005): 255–292.

Scott, Shelly. "Been There, Done That: Paving the Way for the Vagina Monologues," *Modern Drama* 46 no. 3 (2003): 404–423.

Searle, John R. *Speech Acts.* Cambridge: Cambridge University Press, 1969.

Seller, Maxine S. *Ethnic Theater in the United States.* Westport, CT: Greenwood Press, 1983.
Serra, Carlos. *Em cima duma lâmina: Um estudo sobre a precariedade social em três cidades de Moçambique.* Maputo: Imprensa Universitária, UEM, 2003.
Shafir, Gershon and Alison Brysk. "The Globalization of Rights: From Citizenship to Human Rights." *Citizenship Studies* 10 no. 3 (July 2006): 275–287.
Shahani, Aarti. "Sanctuary's Human Face. ColorLines." January/February 2008. Web. May 9, 2010. http://www.colorlines.com/article.php?ID=263, accessed May 9, 2010.
Shalit, Donna. "Join the V-Day Movement." In *The Vagina Monologues.* V-Day Edition, edited by E. Ensler. New York: Villard, 2001.
Shannon, Sandra G. "An Intimate Look at the Plays of Lynn Nottage." In *Contemporary African American Women Playwrights: A Casebook,* edited by Philip C. Kolin, 185–193. London: Routledge, 2007.
Simbulan, Roland. "Exposing the VFA Balikatan War Machine in the Philippines." In *Paninindigan.* University of the Philippines Law Center, Quezon City: BAYAN, 2009. Web June 12, 2011. http://www.yonip.com/archives/editorial/ed-000062.html.
Singer, Ben. *Melodrama and Modernity Early Sensational Cinema and Its Contexts.* New York, NY: Columbia University Press, 2001.
Singhal, Arval, Rafael Obregon, and Everett M. Rogers. "Reconstructing the Story of *Simplemente María,* the Most Popular Telenovela in Latin America of all Time." *Gazette* 54 (1994): 1–15.
Skloot, Robert. ed. *The Theatre of Genocide. Four Plays about Mass Murder in Rwanda, Bosnia, Cambodia, and Armenia.* Madison: University of Wisconsin Press, 2008.
Slaughter, Joseph R. "A Question of Narration: The Voice in International Human Rights Law." *Human Rights Quarterly* 19 no. 2 (1997): 406–430.
———. *Human Rights, Inc.: The World Novel, Narrative Form and International Law.* Fordham, NY: Fordham University Press, 2007.
Sliwkinski, Sharon. "The Childhood of Human Rights: The Kodak in the Congo." *Journal of Visual Culture* (2006): 333–363.
Snyder, Richard. *Politics after Neoliberalism: Reregulation in Mexico.* Port Chester, NY: Cambridge University Press, 2001.
Soeiro, Manuela. *Setepalcos: Revista do Programa Cena Lusófona* 0 (November 1995): 28–29.
Solga, Kim. "Mother Courage and Its Abject: Reading the Violence of Identification." *Modern Drama* 46 no. 3 (2003): 339–357.
Sontag, Susan. *Regarding the Pain of Others.* New York: Farrar, Straus and Giroux, 2003.
Sousa, Pedro Rebelo de. *Setepalcos: Revista do Programa Cena Lusófona* 0 (November 1995): 31.
Soysal, Yasemin N. *Limits of Citizenship: Migrants and Postnational Membership in Europe.* Chicago: University of Chicago, 1994.
Spurr, David. *The Rhetoric of Empire: Colonial Discourse in Journalism, Travel Writing, and Imperial Administration.* Durham, NC: Duke University Press, 1993.
Stavig, Ward. "Túpac Amaru, the Body Politic, and the Embodiment of Hope: Inca Heritage and Social Justice in the Andes." In *Death, Dismemberment, and Memory in Latin America,* edited by Lyman Johnson, 27–62. Albuquerque: University of New Mexico Press, 2004.

St. Eve, A. J. Walter L. Coleman, as next friend of the minor child, Saul Arellano v. the United States. 454 F. Supp. 2nd 757, 2006.

Steyn, Johan. "Guantánamo: A Monstrous Failure of Justice." *Common Dreams*. November 27, 2003. Web April 19, 2012 http://www.commondreams.org/views03/1127-08.htm.

Stiglitz, Joseph. "On Liberty, the Right to Know, and Public Discourse: The Role of Transparency in Public Life." In *Globalizing Rights*, edited by Matthew J. Gibney, 115–156. Oxford: Oxford University Press, 2003.

Taussig, Michael. *The Nervous System*. New York and London: Routledge, 1992.

Taylor, Diana. *The Archive and the Repertoire: Performing Cultural Memory in the Americas*. Durham, NC: Duke University Press, 2003.

———. *Disappearing Acts*. Durham, NC: Duke University Press, 1997.

———. "Rewriting the Classics: *Antígona furiosa* and the Madres the la Plaza de Mayo." In *Perspectives on Contemporary Latin American Theater*, edited by Frank N. Dauster, 77–93. Bucknell Review. Dover: University of Delaware Press, 1996.

———. "Staging Social Memory: Yuyachkani." *Performance and Psychoanalysis*, edited by Adrian Kerr and Patrick Campbell, 218–236. London: Routledge, 2001.

Teitel, Ruti. "For Humanity." *Journal of Human Rights* 3 no. 2 (2004): 225–237.

"Tenso inicio del juicio por la ESMA" lanacion.com. December 11, 2009. Web April 21, 2011. http://www.lanacion.com/ar/nota.asp?nota_id=1210835.html.

Thomasson, Amie L. "Fictional Characters and Literary Practices." *British Journal of Aesthetics* 43 no. 2 (April 2003): 138–156.

Thornburgh, Nathan. "The Fallout from a Deportation." *Time Magazine* August 21, 2007.

Ticktin, Miriam. "The Gendered Human of Humanitarianism: Medicalizing Sexual Violence," *Gender & Society* 23 no. 2. (August 2011): 250–265.

———. "Where Ethics and Politics Meet: The Violence of Humanitarianism in France," *American Ethnologist* 33 no. 1 (February 2006): 33–49.

Tiongson, Nicanor G., ed. *The Politics of Culture: The Philippine Experience: Proceedings and Anthology of Essays, Poems, Songs, Skits and Plays of the Makiisi 1, People's Culture Festival*, December 28–30, 1983, Dulaang Raha Sulayman, Fort Santiago, Intramuros Manila. Manila: Philippine Educational Theatre Association with People's Resource Collection, Philippine Assistance for Rural and Urban Development, 1984.

———. "Dulaan: An Essay on Philippine Theatre." Monograph. Manila: Cultural Center of the Philippines, 1989.

Torres, Maria de los Angeles. *The Lost Apple: Operation Pedro Pan, Cuban Children in the U.S., and the Promise of a Better Future*. Boston, MA: Beacon Press, 2003.

Trastoy, Beatriz. *Teatro autobiográfico: los unipersonales de los 80 y 90 en la escena argentina*. Buenos Aires: Editorial Nueva Generación, 2002.

Trilogía del nazismo. Aut. Patricia Suárez and Leonel Giacometto. Dir. Alejando Ullua. Teatro del Artefacto. Buenos Aires. July 2007.

Trochimczyk, Maja. "*Mater Dolorosa* and Maternal Love in the Music of Henryk Górecki." *Polish Music Journal* 6, no. 2, 2003. http://www.usc.edu/dept/polish_music/PMJ/issue/6.2.03/Trochimczykmater.html.

"Um teatro nosso crescendo ao nosso ritmo e medida." *Savana* February 5, 1999.

"Un espacio que conmociona." Lanacion.com, November 4, 2009. Web April 21, 2011. http://www.lanacion.com.ar/nota.asp?nota_id=1193995.html.

United Nations. "The Universal Declaration of Human Rights." 1948. Web. July 7, 2011. http://www.un.org/en/documents/udhr/index.shtml

Van Alphen, Ernst. "Symptoms of Discursivity: Experience, Memory, and Trauma." In *Acts of Memory: Cultural Recall in the Present*, edited by Meike Bal, et al., 24–38. Hanover and London: Dartmouth College, University Press of New England, 1999.

Verdery, Katherine. *The Political Lives of Dead Bodies*. New York: Columbia University Press, 1999.

Vicinus, Martha. "Helpless and Unfriended: Nineteenth-Century Domestic Melodrama." *New Literary History* 13 no. 1 (1981): 127–143.

Walas, Guillermina. "Alternativas testimoniales: gestión cultural y memoria en Argentina." *Revista Iberoamericana* LXXVII no. 236–237 (Jul-dic 2011): 885–917.

Walton, Kendall L. *Mimesis as Make-Belief*. Cambridge, MA: Harvard University Press, 1990.

Wanzo, Rebecca. *The Suffering Will Not Be Televised: African American Women and Sentimental Political Storytelling*. Albany, NY: State University of New York, 2009.

Watanabe, José. *Antígona: Versión libre de la tragedia de Sófocles*. Lima: Yuyachkani/Comisión de Derechos Humanos, 2000.

Werth, Brenda G. *Theatre, Performance, and Memory Politics in Argentina*. New York: Palgrave Macmillan, 2010.

Weston, Burns J., Richard A. Falk, and Hilary Charlesworth. *Supplement of Basic Documents to International Law and World Order*. 3d ed. St. Paul, MN: West Publishing, 1997.

Whoriskey, Kate. "Introduction." In *Ruined*, edited by L. Nottage. iii-ix. New York: Theatre Communications Group, 2009.

Williams, Linda. *Playing the Race Card: Melodramas of Black and White from Uncle Tom to O. J. Simpson*. Princeton, NJ: Princeton University Press, 2001.

Wilson, Richard, ed. *Human Rights, Culture, and Context. Anthropological Perspectives*. London: Pluto Press, 1997.

Wilson, Richard A. and Richard D. Brown. "Introduction." In *Humanitarianism and Suffering: The Mobilization of Empathy*, edited by Richard A Wilson and Richard D. Brown, 1–30. Cambridge: Cambridge University Press, 2009.

Wiredu, Kwasi. *Cultural Universals and Particulars: An African Perspective*. Indianapolis: Indiana University Press, 1996.

Wittgenstein, Ludwig. *Philosophical Investigations*, edited and translated by Elizabeth Anscombe. Oxford: Blackwell, 2001.

Wittke, Carl. "The Immigrant Theme on the American Stage." *The Mississippi Valley Historical Review* 39 no. 2 (1952): 211–232.

Woods, Damon. "The Evolution of Bayan." *Diliman Review*, 53 (2006): 1–4.

Woodland, Ronald S. "The Danger of Empathy in Mother Courage." *Modern Drama* 15 (1973): 125–129.

Yu, Nilan. "Interrogating Social Work: Philippine Social Work and Human Rights under Martial Law." *International Journal of Social Welfare* 15 no. 3, 257–263.

Zamora, Lois Parkinson and Wendy B. Faris, eds. *Magical Realism: Theory, History, Community*. Durham: Duke University Press, 1995.

Notes on Contributors

Elizabeth S. Anker teaches in the Department of English at Cornell University, and her research and teaching focus on contemporary world literature, law and literature, and the relationship between aesthetics and politics. Her first book, *Fictions of Dignity: Embodying Human Rights in World Literature* (Cornell University Press 2012), draws on phenomenology to develop an embodied politics of reading and account of human rights. In addition, she has recently published on animal rights in *New Literary History* and the 9/11 novel in *American Literary History*. She is currently working on a book project provisionally entitled "Constitutional Failure and the Aesthetic Formations of Sovereignties in Crisis," as well as two edited collections.

Joi Barrios teaches Filipino and Philippine Literature at the University of California at Berkeley and serves as Literary Manager of Ma-yi Theater Company in New York. She is the author of the book *From the Theater Wings: Grounding and Flight of Women Playwrights in the Philippines* (University of the Philippine Press 2008) as well as several poetry collections and Tagalog textbooks. She has received numerous literary and achievement awards, among them the Weaver of History Award from the Philippine Centennial Commission (Women's Sector) in 1998, the TOWNS (The Outstanding Women in the Nation's Service) in 2004, and the Palanca National Literary Awards in Manila for her play "Gabriela" in 2006. She is also a member of BAYAN Philippines Women's Desk.

Florian N. Becker is an associate professor of German and comparative literature at Bard College and Director of Bard Programs at ECLA of Bard in Berlin. He studied philosophy, politics, and economics at Magdalen College, Oxford, before earning his PhD in German literature at Princeton. Recent articles have appeared in *Modern Drama*, the *Brecht Yearbook*, and the *Routledge Handbook of Human Rights*. He has completed a monograph on Bertolt Brecht, Peter Weiss, and Heiner Müller, *Theater and Praxis: Realism as Critique in Twentieth-Century German Drama*, and is currently co-editing a companion to the works of Heiner Müller.

Kerry Bystrom is an associate professor of English and human rights at Bard College and Bard faculty representative to ECLA of Bard. She was formerly an assistant professor of English and Director of the Research Program in Humanitarianism at the University of Connecticut, Storrs. She has published numerous book chapters and articles on topics relating to literature and human rights and is co-editor of a special issue of *Journal of Human Rights* (forthcoming 2012) on the theme "Humanitarianism and Responsibility." She is also a specialist in Southern African literature and culture.

Notes on Contributors

Paola S. Hernández is an associate professor of Spanish at the University of Wisconsin-Madison. Her book, *El teatro de Argentina y Chile: Globalización, resistencia y desencanto* (Corregidor, 2009) studies how theater explores and reacts to the effects propagated by economic and cultural globalization through texts, aesthetics, characters, production, and theater practitioners. Her current research focuses on contemporary documentary theater in Peru, Argentina, Mexico, and Colombia.

Anne Lambright is an associate professor of language and culture studies at Trinity College in Hartford, CT. Author of *Creating the Hybrid Intellectual: Subject, Space, and the Feminine in the Narrative of José María Arguedas* (Bucknell, 2007) and co-editor of *Unfolding the City: Women Write the City in Latin America* (with Elisabeth Guerrero, Minnesota, 2007), she is writing a book on ethnicity and cultural production in the Peruvian transitional justice process.

Jill Lane is an associate professor of Spanish and Portuguese and Director of the Center for Latin American and Caribbean Studies at New York University. She is the author of *Blackface Cuba 1840–1895*, and is co-editor with Marcial Godoy-Anativia of e-msiférica, the journal of the Hemispheric Institute of Performance and Politics.

Luís Madureira earned his PhD in comparative literature from the University of California at San Diego. His major areas of specialization include Luso-Brazilian colonial and postcolonial studies, as well as modernism and modernity in Latin America, Africa, and the Caribbean. He has written two books, *Imaginary Geographies in Portuguese and Lusophone-African Literature: Narratives of Discovery and Empire* (2007), which studies figurations of empire, nation, and revolution in Portuguese and Lusophone African literatures; and *Cannibal Modernities* (2005), a reexamination of the Brazilian and Caribbean avant-gardes from a postcolonial perspective. He has published several articles on topics ranging from Luso-Brazilian literature and cinema to early modern travel narratives and postcolonial theory. His current research focuses on Mozambican theater and the politics of time in contemporary Lusophone fiction.

Lindsey Mantoan is a PhD candidate in drama at Stanford University. Her research interests include representation and mediatization of the Iraq War, documentary theater, and performative responses to the same-sex marriage debate. She teaches in the English Department of the Prison University Project at San Quentin Prison and serves on the board of Performance Studies International.

Sarah M. Misemer is an associate professor of Hispanic Theatre at Texas A&M University and associate director of the Melbern G. Glasscock Center for Humanities Research at Texas A&M University. Dr. Misemer is the author of *Secular Saints: Performing Frida Kahlo, Carlos Gardel, Eva Perón, and Selena* (Tamesis, 2008) and *Moving Forward, Looking Back: Trains, Literature, and the Arts in the River Plate* (Bucknell UP, 2010). She has published numerous articles on contemporary River Plate, Mexican, Spanish, and Latino theater in journals such as *Latin American Theatre Review, Gestos, Revista Canadiense de Estudios Hispánicos, Symposium: A Quarterly Journal in Modern Languages, Letras Peninsulares, Revista Hispánica Moderna*, and *Hispanic Poetry Review*. Dr. Misemer is also the Editor for the Latin American Theatre Review Book series and serves on the Editorial Board for the journal *Latin American Theatre Review*. Her main areas of research include contemporary Argentine and Uruguayan theater, performance, and literature.

Notes on Contributors

Ana Elena Puga is an assistant professor in the Departments of Theatre and Spanish & Portuguese at The Ohio State University. She is at work on a book that questions why migrants are often expected to perform suffering in return for human or citizenship rights: *Spectacles of Suffering and Migrant Melodramas*. Puga is also the author of *Allegory, Memory, and Testimony: Upstaging Dictatorship*. A dramaturge and translator, she has edited two anthologies that include her own work as a translator: *Finished from the Start and Other Plays*, six plays by the Chilean playwright *Juan Radrigán*, and *Spectacular Bodies, Dangerous Borders: Three New Latin American Plays*, featuring contemporary theater from Argentina, Mexico, and Venezuela. Her translations have appeared in anthologies including *Stages of Conflict*, eds. Diana Taylor and Sarah J. Townsend, and *Theater of the Avant-Garde, 1950–2000*, eds. Robert Knopf and Julia Listengarten. Her essays and criticism have also appeared in *Theatre Journal*, *The Latin American Theatre Review*, *Theatre Survey*, *Latino Studies*, and *Symposium: A Quarterly Journal in Modern Literatures*.

Camilla Stevens is an associate professor at Rutgers University, where she holds a joint appointment in the Department of Spanish and Portuguese and the Department of Latino and Hispanic Caribbean Studies. Her book, *Family and Identity in Contemporary Cuban and Puerto Rican Drama* (University Press of Florida, 2004), offers a comparative analysis of how Cuban and Puerto Rican domestic dramas allegorize divergent views of national identity from the second half the twentieth century. She has published articles on cultural identity and racial politics in Caribbean theater in journals such as *Gestos*, *Hispania*, *Latin American Theatre Review*, *Modern Drama*, and *Revista Canadiense de Estudios Hispánicos*. Her current research focuses on Dominican playwrights and performance artists whose works challenge traditional notions of citizenship and national belonging.

Brenda Werth is an associate professor in the Department of World Languages and Cultures at American University in Washington, DC. Her research focuses on Latin American theater, performance, memory studies, and human rights. She is the author of the book *Theatre, Performance, and Memory Politics in Argentina* (Palgrave 2010). Her current project explores urban imaginaries in twenty-first-century theater and performance in the Americas.

Christina Wilson is a PhD candidate in the English Department at the University of Connecticut. She studies modern drama and performance and is writing a dissertation on contemporary performances of Scots-Irish identity.

Index

9/11, 16, 102–5, 114, 126, 209, 218–23

Abu Ghraib, 115, 150
Acree, William, 72
Adiós Ayacucho, 28–32, 35–9
Adorno, Theodor, 11
Agamben, Giorgio, 11, 34, 102
Agasang, Elsa, 202
Ahmadi, Niemat, 227
Ahmed, Ruhel, 104, 115
AIDS, 15
Alfonsín, Raúl, 72
Al-Harith, Jamal, 104–5
Alliance of Concerned Teachers, 199
Al-Rawi, Bisher, 104–5
Al-Rawi, Wahab, 104–5
Alston, Philip, 198
Amaru, Túpac, 31
American Declaration of Independence, 7
Anakbayan (Children of the People), 199
Anakpawis (Children of Sweat), 199–200
Anderson, Patrick, 11
Andric, Ivo, 88
Angeles Torres, María de los, 166
Angelieri, Maximiliano, 142
Antígona furiosa (Furious Antigone), Griselda Gambaro, 91–2
Antígona, Yuyachkani, 28–34
Antigone, Sophocles, 41
Antze, Paul, 73
Aqui é Portugal, 50–1
Aquino, Benigno, 203
Araos, Jerry, 197
Arditi, Benjamin, x
Arellano, Ching, 197

Arellano, Elvira, 18, 107, 165–73
Arellano, Saul, 156, 161–89
Arendt, Hannah, 13, 16, 126–81
Arguedas, José María, 38
Aristotle, 9, 60
Armand Ugón, Álvaro, 142
Artaud, Antonin, 11
Asociación Pro Derechos Humanos (APRODEH), 29
Associação Africana, 50–2
"Asylum Seekers and 'Border Panic' in Australia," 123–8
Atando cabos (Tying Loose Ends), 92
Avery, Gordon, 27
Ayala Blanco, Jorge, 163
Ayarachi (Peru), 38–9

Babaylan, Dulaang, 201
Babel, 163
Bagong Alyansang Makabayan (New Patriotic Alliance), 199
Bagong Cristo, 201
Bagram Airforce Base, 104–6
Balandier, Georges, 48
Bal, Mieke, 68
"bare life," 11, 34–5
  see also Agamben, Giorgio
Barraza, Adriana, 163
Barroca, Norberto, 53–5
Barthes, Roland, 230
Baudrillard, Jean, 140–1, 145
Bayan Muna (Country First), 199–200
Beazley, Kim, 126
Beckett, Samuel, 11
Beecher Stowe, Harriet, 161
Begg, Moazzam, 104
Berlant, Lauren, 117
Berlín, 18, 85–90, 137–50

Beslan Schoolhouse Massacre, 15, 83, 91–5
Bey, Hakim, x
Bhaktiari, Alamdar and Montazar, 128
Bharucha, Rustom, 8, 122
Bignone, Reynaldo, 72
"black sites," 16, 116
Blanding, Scott, 231
Boal, Augusto, 197
Boltanski, Luc, 84, 93
"Book of John [*João*], The," 56
Borkenztain, Bernardo, 142, 146
Bosch, María Isabel, 19, 180–90
Bosnian War, 15, 83, 232
Boucicault, Dion, 166
bourgeois public sphere, 3–6
  construction of, 3–5
  public sphere, in relation to, 3–6
  rights, in relation to, 6
  state, in relation to, 5
  universalism, in relation to, 6
Boxer, Barbara; Senator, 241
Brado Africano, 50–2
Brecht, Bertolt, 10–12, 59–61, 112, 188, 193, 237–40
Bridge on the Drina, The, 88
Bringing Them Home (HREQC), 131
Briskman, Linda, 127
Brison, Susan, 73, 110
Brittain, Victoria, 17, 103
Brook, Peter, 67, 73
Brooks, Daphne A., 158
Brooks, Peter, 156
Brothers, Julia, 112, 116
Brysk, Alison, 141
Burgos, Edith, 201
Burgos, Jonas, 201–3
Burnside, Julian; *Human Rights Overboard*, 125
Bush, George W., 16, 156
Butler, Judith, 11, 106, 117
Buwan at Baril sa Eb Major (Moon and Gun in Eb Major), 196

Cabintoy, Jeffrey, 202
Cabo Delgado, Mozambique, 53
Cabral, Amílcar, 53
campesinos (Peru), 32, 39
Canning, Charlotte, 101, 110
Capitol Hill, 103, 241

Capucha, 72
Capuchita, 72
Carlson, Marvin, 87, 94
Casafranco, Augusto, 35
Casement, Roger, 229
Casino de oficiales, 71
Castel-Branco, Carlos Nuno, 60
Castillo, Kate del, 163
Castles, Stephen, 179–80
catharsis, 14, 112, 132
Center for Constitutional Rights, 16
Center for Trade Union and Human Rights (Philippines), 204
Centro Associativo dos Negros de Moçambique, 51
Cepeda, Esther J., 165, 169
Certeau, Michel de, 109
Cervantes, Behn, 196, 201
Chaudhuri, Una, 94
Chavira, Javier, 161, 170–1
Cheney, Dick, 16
Chicago Adalberto United Methodist Church, 156, 165, 170
Chigubo, 51
"Children Overboard" scandal, 126
Chiwengo, Ngwarsungi, 230
Chouliaraki, Lilie, 84
citizenship
  and asylum, 126
  forms of, 12
  and Guantánamo, 102–7
  and human rights, 116, 160, 180
  and indigenous Australians, 124
  and migration, 186
  in Mozambique, 14–15, 46–8
  and place, 104–7
  postnational, *xi*, 141
  transnational, 19
  within US borders, 18, 167, 182, 190
  and "War on Terror," 21
Ciudad Juárez, 38, 147
Clarke, Tom, 114
Cohen, Stanley, 70, 78
Colchado Lucío, Oscar, 37
Cold War
  dissolution of, 8
  and liberalism, 21
  and Mobutu, 229
  and Southern Cone dictatorships, 144
  and Taliban, 219

Cole, Catherine, 14
Colegio Militar, 72
Coleman, Rev. Walter, 156
Comisión de Verdad y Reconciliación (CVR) (Peru), 14, 27–37, 40
A comuna, 59–61
Concerned Artists of the Philippines, 199
Congro Reform Association, 229
Conquergood, Dwight, 13
Constantino, Grundy, 201
Constitutional Referendum of 1967 (Australia), 124
Contraelviento, 29
Convention on the Rights of the Child (CRC), 127
Conversaciones con chicos (Conversations with Children), 92
Cooper, Christine M., 234
Correa, Ana, 37–8
Cortazzo, Alejandra, 142
Cosentino, Olga, 92
Couto, Mia, 46–7, 56–7
Cox, Damian, 145
Crane, Susan, 70
Craveirinha, José, 50
Cuatro columnas, 71
Cuauhtémoc, 31
Cultural Center Haroldo Conti, 74–5, 79
Cvetkovich, Ann, 101, 109

Daly, Agustin, 166
Daly, Nicholas, 157
Dangerous Curves: Latina Bodies in the Media, 160
Davidson, Alastair, 179
Dawes, James, 11, 234, 240
Days of the Commune, The, 59
decolonization (Mozambique), 56
Del sol naciente (From the Rising Sun), 91
Demetillo Abraham, Becky, 197
Derrida, Jacques, 38–9
desaparecidos
 in Argentina, 70
 in Peru, 35, 43
 in The Philippines, 203
Desaparecidos, 195
"Descrobrimento" (Discovery), 56

detainees
 in Argentina, 71
 in Australia, 121–32
 in Guantánamo, 102–16
 in The Philippines, 196–7
Deutsch, Federico, 142
Diamond, Elin, 240
"diasporic public spheres," 19
 see also Fraser, Nancy
Dickens, Charles, 166
Diderot, Denis, 9
Diéguez, Ileana, 37
Diokno, María Socorro, 199
Dios no nos quiere contentos (God Does Not Want Us Content), 92
"Dirty War," 15, 69
Disla, Frank, 19
Distant Suffering, 93
 see also Boltanski, Luc
Dodera, María, 86, 142
Dolan, Jill, 113
dominicanidad, 182
Donne, John, 107
Draper, Susana, 68
Drina River, 88–9
Dubatti, Jorge, 180
Duncan, Carol, 68

East Lynne, 164
"EDSA people power revolt," 195
El Cerro, 86–9
El hueco (una tribu urbana) [The Gap (An Urban Tribe)], 85–6
El mar que nos trajo (The Sea that Brought Us Here), 92
embodiment
 and agency, 162
 of the dead, 14, 35, 38, 40
 and memory, 47
 and theater, 11
 and witnessing, 112
empathy
 and agency, 95
 emotional, 190
 "empathic unsettlement," 43, *see also* LaCapra, Dominick
 and history, 125
 and identification, 9, 187
 intellectual, 188
 and melodrama, 165

empathy—*continued*
  and suffering, 170
  and testimony, 132
  and theater, 10, 19, 162, 239
enemy combatants, 17–18, 101, 114
Enough Project, The, 227
Enrique's Journey, 163
Ensler, Eve, 20, 227–44
escraches, 69
Escuela de Mecánica de la Armada (ESMA), 15, 67–79
  see also Navy School of Mechanics, The (ESMA)
Espacio Cultural "Nuestros Hijos" (EcuNHi) (Cultural Space "Our Children"), 71
Eu quero ser swingista (I want to be a swing dancer), 51
Evans, Christine, 17, 121–33
"Extrajudicial, Summary or Arbitrary Executions in the Philippines, 2001–2006," 199

Fabulations, or The Re-education of Undine, 237
Fanon, Frantz, 49, 53
Feingold, Russell; Senator, 241–3
Feldman, Allen, 122, 131–3, 244
Felman, Shoshana, 14, 108
Ferguson, James, 105
Festin, Rowena, 201
fistula, 228, 231–43
flo6x8, x–xii
Forsyth, Alison, 87
Fortuna, Ding, 201
Fox, Vicente, 156
Fraser, Nancy, 6, 19, 96
Frelimo, 45, 52–3, 58
French Declaration of the Rights of Man and the Citizen, 7
Fresu, Anna, 53
Fried, Michael, 9
Fuchs, Elinor, 94
Fujimori regime, 28

Gabriela: Isang Oratoryo (Gabriela: An Oratorio), 20, 195, 200–3
Gabriela (Women's Group), 199
Gambaro, Griselda, 15, 42, 83–5, 90–6
García, Sara, 163

General José Mabanta Jr, 199
Geneva Convention, The, 16, 102
genocide
  in Argentina, 75
  in Rwanda, 229
Giacometto, Leonel, 84
Glinoga, Alan, 197
globalization, *xi*, 17, 90, 140, 141, 145, 147, 150, 164, 179, 180, 210
  and economic order, 13, 16–17, 99
  and the "global public sphere," 19, *see also* Fraser, Nancy
  and neoliberalism, 18, 240
Goddard, Chris, 127
Goddard, Jean Luc, 142
González, Elián, 166
González Iñárritu, Alejandro, 163
González, Raúl, 189
Górecki, Henryk, 188
Graham-Jones, Jean, 84
Grandmothers of Plaza de Mayo, 72
Greatest Silence, The, 231
Grémio Africano, 50
Grupo Cénico das Forças Populares de Libertação Nacional, 58
Grupo de Arte Callejero (GAC), 69
Guantánamo, 1, 16, 101–17, 134
Guantánamo: Honor Bound to Defend Freedom, 17, 101–17
Guebuza, Armando, 45
guest-worker plan, 156
Guevara, Ernesto "Che," 30
"Guinea Portuguese," 50
Gungu (Mozambique), 52
Gupta, Akhil, 105
Gusmão, Fernando, 58
Guthrie, Woody, 185
Gutierrez, Rep. Luis V., 156
Guzman, Malu de, 197

habeas corpus, 101–2
Habermas, Jürgen, 5–8
Halbwachs, Maurice, 70
Hall, Stuart, 115
hamartia, 60
Hamilton, Russell G., 55–8
Hand, Gerry; Minister of Immigration, 125
Hapag Kainan (Dining Table), 202
Harris, Alice, 230–1

Hartman, Saidiya V., 158
Hegel, Georg Wilhelm Friedrich, 46
Heller, Greg, 231
Herman, Judith Lewis, 111
Hernández, Daniel, 167
Hernández, Paola S., 141
Hesford, Wendy S., 114, 235, 244
Hijos por la Identidad y la Justicia contra el Olvido y el Silencio (H.I.J.O.S.) (Children for Identity and Justice against Forgetting and Silence), 68
Hine, Lewis, 166
Hirsch, Marianne, 74
Holocaust Museum, Washington DC, 75
Holocaust, representation of, 11, 84, 193
Homebody/Kabul, 20, 209–24
Homeland Security, 168
Honig, Bonnie, 156
Hotel Juárez, 18, 137–50
Howard, John, 125
H.R. 1540 (The National defense Authorization Act for Fiscal Year 2012), 103
Huamanga (Peru), 28, 39
Huanta (Peru), 28, 36–9
Huerta, Jorge A., 158
Human Rights and Equal Opportunities Commission (HREQC), 127
human rights imaginary, 3, 20, 209, 212
Humboldt Park, Chicago, 156
Hunt, Lynn, 8
Hunt, Nancy Rose, 229
Hussein, Saddam, 106, 125
Huyssen, Andreas, 69, 73, 94

Ignatieff, Michael, 240
Ilagan, Bonifacio, 196, 201
Ileto, Reynaldo, 200
Imitation of Life, 164
Immigrant Nation: The Battle for the Dream, 170
immigration
  in Australia, 125
  and gender, 163
  and Guantánamo, 104
  and human rights, 156, 179
  and melodrama, 159–73
  in Montevideo, 86

undocumented, 157, 168, 170, 171, 185, 189, 190, 192
  to the US, 146, 169, 180, 184
Immigration Control and Enforcement (ICE), 156, 167–8
indignados, x
Instituto Goethe, Montevideo, 142
International Rescue Committee, 227–8
interpretive community, 4, 13
Intimate Appeal, 237
intromissão, 49
Iraq War, The, 17, 121, 125
Iribarren, Gabriela, 142
Ita, Fernando de, 138
Ituri Forest (DRC), 237, 240–1
Ivo Cruz, Duarte, 50

Jackson, Lisa, 231
James L. Brooks, 163
Javali-Javalismo (Wild Boar-Wild Boarism), 58
Jelin, Elizabeth, 69, 73
Johnson, Lyman, 30
Joseph, May, xi
Jose, Socrates, 21
Juárez: Dramaturgia de feminicidio, 146
Júnior, Rodrigues, 50, 55
Jupp, James, 125

Kalbaryo ng Maralitang Tagalungsod (Calvary of the Urban Poor), 201
Kandahar, 104
Kaplan, Ann E., 162
Karapatan Report, 197–8, 203–4
Keating, Paul; Prime Minister, 124
Kilusang Magbubukid ng Pilipiinas (Peasant Movement of the Philippines), 199
Kilusang Mayo Uno (May First Movement), 199
King, Henry, 164, 188
King Leopold II, 229, 233
Kirchner, Néstor, 72
Kruger, Loren, 14
Kushner, Tony, 20, 209–24

Labriola, Brad, 231
LaCapra, Dominick, 31, 40
Lagos, Edith, 31
La luna con gatillo, 189

Lambek, Michael, 73
La misma luna, 163
"Land is Your Land, This," 185
Landsberg, Alison, 85, 94–5
La persistencia, 15, 83–4, 90–3
Las cartas que no llegaron (The Letters that Never Came), 84
A Last Resort? (HREQC), 127
Las Viajeras, 180–90
late capitalism, 214
La trilogía del nazismo (The Nazi Trilogy), 84
Laub, Dori, 73
League of Filipino Students, 199
Lee, Bessie, 197
Lehmann, Hans, 85, 90, 95, 182
Les âmes brisées, UNFPA, 231
Lessing, Gotthold Ephraim, 9
Levine, Michael, 145–6
lieux de mémoire, 67–8
Lionnet, Françoise, 90
Lobato, Alexandro, 50
Lominitz, Claudio, 147
Lopez, Sonia, 166
Lourenço Marques Guardian, 51
Lourenço Marques, 49, 54
  see also Maputo, Mozambique
Lozano, Emma, 156
Lumo, 231
Lumumba, Patrice, 229
Luna roja (Red Moon), 85
Lusófona, Cena; The Portuguese Association for Theater Exchange, 57
lusofonia, 57

Mabesa, Tony, 200
Macapagal Arroyo, Gloria, 198
"Madre Dolorosa: Elvira Arellano," 161, 170–1
Magaiça, 51, 54
Maganda (the Beautiful), 196
magical realism, 122
Maiquez, Reagan, 201
Malakas (the Strong), 196
Mangay, Ces (Ces Quesada), 197
Mankell, Henning, 57
Mapiko dance (Mozambique), 53
Maputo, Mozambique, 45–57
maquiladora, 138

Marcos, Ferdinand, 195
Marley, Bob, 185
Marquez, Larry, 202
martial law (The Philippines), 20, 195, 204
Martin, Carol, 86
Matola, Mozambique, 45
Maynez, Alejandro, 148–9
Mbembe, Achille, 45
Mboyo, Nsongo, 231
McClintock, Anne, 214
McLagan, Meg, 235
Megson, Chris, 87
Melendez, Esau, 170
melodrama, 18, 156–73, 238–40
Melquiades, Fidel, 38–9
Mendes, de Oliveira, 53
Mendes, João, 56
Mene Mene Tekel Upharsim, 196
Menon, Jisha, 11, 101
Mercier, Louis-Sébastian, 9
mestiços (Mozambique), 50–1, 56
Migration Amendment Act of 1992, 125
mileux de mémoire, 67–8
Millado, Chris, 196–7
Mir, Claudio, 19, 180
Mirza, Roger, 139
Misemer, Sarah, 85
Mobutu, Joseph, 229
Moleque (Houseboy), 51
Molina Guzmán, Isabel, 160–1
Mondlane, Eduardo, 52
Mondongo Sam, 183, 189–90
Monomopata, 58
Morel, E.D., 229, 233
Morgan, Sally, 128
Mother Courage and her Children, 239
Mothers Against Illegal Aliens, 168
Mothers of Plaza de Mayo, 68–72, 79–80
Moyano, María Elena, 31
Mroué, Rabih, 184
Mrs. B. Isang Monologo (Mrs. B: A Monologue), 20, 195, 200–3
"Mujahideen," 213
Mukwege, Dénis, 232
multiculturalism, 125, 219, 221–2
multidirectional memory, 85
  see also Rothberg, Michael
Mutua, Makau, 215

Mutumbela Gogo, 57
My Place, 128
Mysteries of London, The, 168–9

National Memory Archives, 74
National San Martín Theater, 91, 94
Navy School of Mechanics, The (ESMA), 15, 68–70, 76–8
Nazario, Sonia, 163
neoliberalism, 17, 59, 138–9, 145
Nervous System, The, 146–7
A'Ness, Francine, 35
Newman, Saul, 145
New People's Army of the Philippines (NPA), 199, 204
New Sanctuary Movement, 156, 162, 168
Ngandu Nkashama, Pius, 48
Ngwenha, Malangatana, 54
Nhlongo, Lindo, 53
Nogar, Rui, 50
noh, 197
No me toquen ese valse, 29
Nora, Pierre, 67–8
North American Free Trade Agreement (NAFTA), 138, 147
Nottage, Lynn, 20, 227–40
"novísimos," 138, 149
Noyce, Phillip, 128
Núcleo de Estudantes Secundários Africanos de Moçambique (NESAM) (The Nucleus of African Secondary School Students), 52
Nuhoğlu Soysal, Yasemin, *xi*
Nyau dance (Mozambique), 53

Obama, Barack, 16, 102–3, 243
Occupy, ix, x
Oliver Twist, 166
Ontiveros, Sue, 167
Oplan: Bantay Laya (OBL) (Operation: Freedom Watch), 199, 204
Oratoryo ng Bayan (People's Oratorio), 195–7
Ortega, Julio, 35
Ortiz, Fernando, 185
Os bêbados (The Drunkards), 51
Os engraxadores (The Shoeshine Boys), 51
Os Noivos ou Confêrencia Dramática sobre o Lobolo (The Betrothed, Or, A Dramatic Conference on the Lobolo), 53
Owen, Hilary, 56

Pachacutic, 37, 40
Pagsambang Bayan (People's Worship), 201
Parodi, Guillermo, 79
Parodi, Teresa, 71
Partida Tayzán, Armando, 138
Passerin d'Entrèves, 181
Pasyon and Revolution, 200
Patraka, Vivian, 75
Pellettieri, Osvaldo, 139
People's Theater Festival at Dulaang Rajh Sulayman, 157
Perera, Suvendrini, 126
Perlmutt, Bent-Jurgen, 231
Perón, Eva, 30–1
Persian Gulf War, The, 143
Peryante, 195
Peter Pan Airlifts, 166–7
Peveroni, Gabriel, 15, 18, 83, 96, 137
Phelan, Peggy, 109, 115
Philippine Educational Theater Association, 197
Pierce, Gareth, 106
Piketlayn Cantata (Picketline Cantata), 195, 200, 201, 204
Pizarro, Francisco, 36–7, 42–3
Poetics, 9
"political performatives," x, xi
see also Arditi, Benjamin
Politics Most Unusual, 145
Polomolok, Cotabato, 200–4
Poor of New York, The, 166
Postdramatic Theatre, 95, 182
postnational, ix, xi, 141
"precarious life," 11
see also Butler, Judith
Prendergast, John, 227, 242–3
privatization, *xi*
prosthetic memory, 85, 94–5
see also Landsberg, Alison

Quechua, 29, 35, 38–9
Quijano, Aníbal, 58

Rabbit-Proof-Fence, 128
Rae, Paul, 14, 180
Ralli, Teresa, 32, 34, 38, 191
Rancière, Jacques, 60
Rascón Banda, Víctor Hugo, 18, 137–50
Rebello, Luiz Francisco, 51–2
reconciliation, 14
  in Argentina, 74
  in Australia, 125
  in Peru, 27–8, 31–2
Redfern Address, 124–5
Red Rubber, 229–31
refugees
  Afghan, 17, 210, 213, 221
  children, 125
  Congolese, 237
  crisis, 15
  Iraqi, 17
  political, 172
  rights of, 16
  Rwandan, 229
  treatment of, in Australia, 121, 123–9
  in the US, 172
Reis, António, 57
Resistência e Vitória Popular, 58
"response-ability," 85, 95, 190
  see also Lehmann, Hans
Retorno, 29
revistas, (Mozambique), 49, 51
Reynolds, G.W.M, 168–9
Ricoeur, Paul, 73
Ridout, Nicholas, 188–9
Riggen, Patricia, 163
Rokem, Freddie, 87
Rosa Cuchillo, 28–9, 32, 38–9
Rosenberg, Carol, 109
Rosencof, Mauricio, 84
Rossini, John D., 158
Rothberg, Michael, 11, 85, 94
Roxas, Meliton, 201
"rubber slave trade" (Democratic Republic of Congo), 229
Rubio, Miguel, 31, 191
Ruined, 20, 228–44
Rumsfeld, Donald, 113

A Sagrada Família, 58
Said, Edward, 50
Salazar, António de Oliveira Salazar, 51
Salinas de Gortari, Carlos, 141
Sánchez Prado, Ignacio M., 141, 151
San Francisco Brava Theatre Center Production, 112
Santiago, 29
Santos, Al, 196, 201
Sarajevo esquina Montevideo (Sarajevo, at the Corner of Montevideo), 15, 83–93
Sassen, Saskia, *xi*
Saturday Night Fever, 183
Save Darfur, 227
Scarry, Elaine, 113, 116–17
Schaffer, Kay, 122, 235
Schechner, Richard, 74, 244
Scilingo, Adolfo, 69
Scott, Shelly, 234
Sebastião, come tudo (Sebastian Eats it All), 51
Seeking Justice: The Prosecution of Sexual Violence in the Congo War, 231
September riots (Mozambique), 46–7, 61, 123
Serra, Carlos, 46, 48
Setepalcos, 57
Shafir, Gershon, 141
Sharif Sharif, 148
Shih, Shu-mei, 90
Shining Path, The, 14, 27–34, 37
"shock images," 230
  see also Barthes, Roland
Silang, Gabriela, 200
Simplemente María, 163
Sion, Brigitte, 74
Sirk, Douglas, 164
"situated freedom," *ix*
Slaughter, Joseph, 122, 240
Slovo, Gillian, 17, 103
Slow Falling Bird, 17, 122–33
Smith, Sidonie, 122, 235
Snyder, Richard, 147
Soeiro, Manuela, 57
Solarich, Iván, 86–7
Solga, Kim, 240
Sonia Flew, 166
Sontag, Susan, 11, 89, 115
Sophocles, 32
Sousa, Noémia de, 50, 54, 56
Sousa Santos, Boaventura de, 56
Spanglish, 163

"Spectacle of the Other, The," 115
Spectatorship of Suffering, The, 84
specters, 38, 43
   see also Derrida, Jacques
Stafford Smith, Clive, 106
Stahl, John, 164
Stanislavski, Constantin, 189
"state of exception," 102–3, 117, 146
   see also Agamben, Giorgio
"stateless zones," 16, 18
Stella Dallas, 164
Steyn, Johan, 101, 106–7
"Stolen Generations" (Australia), 17, 121–8, 131–3
"Stop Raping Our Greatest Resource," 232, 235
Suárez, Patricia, 84
Sudan, 227, 242
Suffering Will Not Be Televised, The, 162
Sumalinog, Lanie, 200
Symphony No. 3 (*Symphony of Sorrowful Songs*), 188, 193

Tabligh, 104
Taliban, 125, 218–22
Tambobambino, 38–9
Taussig, Michael, 146–7
Taylor, Diana, 3, 42, 47, 74, 80, 158, 244
Teatro Alegre Company, 49
Teatro Puerto Luna, 86, 94
"temporary autonomous zones" (TAZ), x
   see also Bey, Hakim
Tense Past: Cultural Essays in Trauma and Memory, 73
terra nullius, 124
terrorism
   under Arroyo, 200
   fear of, 145
   and Fujimori Regime, 28–9
   international, 138–40, 144
   state-sponsored, 29–30, 200
   in wake of 9/11, 105–6, 116
   war against, 19
Tete Province (Mozambique), 53
"Third World Woman," 209
Ticktin, Miriam, 230–1, 236, 244
TLCAN (Tratado Libre de Comercio de América del Norte) (North American Free Trade Agreement), 138, 147
Toledo, Alejandro, 27–8
Tolentino, Aurelio, 201
transculturation, 185
transitional justice, 12–13, 20–1, 28
"traumatic realism," 11
   see also Rothberg, Michael
Travolta, John, 183
Tribunal Plays, 103
Tricycle Theatre Company, 101–3
Truth and Reconciliation Commission (TRC), 14, 27, 31–2, 131
Tyler Bernstine, Quincy, 228

Uncle Tom's Cabin, 161
Under the Gaslight, 166
UNESCO, 74
United Nations' Universal Declaration of Human Rights, 20, 159, 196–7
United Nations Year of Indigenous Peoples, 124–5
University of Philippines, 20, 195, 197, 201, 205
unlawful enemy combatant, 101, 144
USS Cole, 102
US Senate Foreign Relations Committee, 227, 241

Vagina Monologues, 20, 231–6, 241
Valdez, Luis, 158
vaudeville, 49, 52–3, 197, 205
V-Day, 20, 230–6, 241
Vega, Garcilaso de la, 37
Vera, Rody, 197
verbatim, 17, 103, 121–2
Verdery, Katherine, 30
Vicente, Gil, 50, 57
Vicinus, Martha, 164
Videla, Jorge Rafael, 72
Vidor, King, 164
Violence Performed, 11
Virgin of Guadalupe, 165, 170

Walas, Guillermina, 68
Wanzo, Rebecca, 162
"War on Terror, The," 16–18, 21, 101–10, 209, 216

The War within the War: Sexual Violence against Women and Girls in the Eastern Congo, 231
Warwick, Robert, 227, 242
Watanabe, José, 32
Whoriskey, Kate, 237
Williams, Linda, 156
Wilson, Richard, 8
Women in the War Zones, 231

Woomera, 17, 121–33
World War II, 16, 17, 84, 137, 142–3

Xilinguine, 48
Xipamanine, 51, 55

Yuyachkani, 14, 28–40

Zapata, Emiliano, 30

GPSR Compliance
The European Union's (EU) General Product Safety Regulation (GPSR) is a set of rules that requires consumer products to be safe and our obligations to ensure this.

If you have any concerns about our products, you can contact us on

ProductSafety@springernature.com

In case Publisher is established outside the EU, the EU authorized representative is:

Springer Nature Customer Service Center GmbH
Europaplatz 3
69115 Heidelberg, Germany

www.ingramcontent.com/pod-product-compliance
Lightning Source LLC
LaVergne TN
LVHW012059070526
838200LV00074BA/3668